The Collected Stories

The Collected Stories

CLARE BOYLAN

COUNTERPOINT
WASHINGTON, D.C.
NEW YORK, N.Y.

Selected stories from: *A Nail on the Head* first published by Hamish Hamilton Ltd. 1983, *Concerning Virgins* first published by Hamish Hamilton Ltd. 1989, *That Bad Woman* first published by Little, Brown 1995.

"Edna, Back from America" was broadcast on Radio 4's *Short Story* and appeared in *Telling Stories III*. "My Son the Hero" first appeared in the *Mail on Sunday*. "You Don't Know You're Alive" first appeared in *Living*. "The Picture House" first appeared in the *Irish Times* and *Cosmopolitan*. "Affairs in Order" first appeared in *Good Housekeeping*. "Technical Difficulties and the Plague" first appeared in *Perspective*. "L'Amour" first appeared in *Foreign Affairs* (anthology) and *Woman's Journal*. "The Stolen Child" first appeared in *Writing on the Wall* (anthology), *Present Laughter* (anthology), and *Living*. "Poor Old Sod" was broadcast on Radio 4's *Short Story* and appeared in *Telling Stories IV*. "Villa Marta" first appeared in the *Irish Times*. "Concerning Virgins" first appeared in *Image* magazine and was read in the BBC's *Morning Story* series. "A Model Daughter" first appeared in *Woman's Journal*.

Library of Congress Cataloging-in-Publication Data
Boylan, Clare.
    [Short Stories]
    The collected stories / Clare Boylan.
        p.   cm.
    ISBN 1-58243-261-9
    1. Ireland—Social life and customs—Fiction. I. Title.
PR6052.O9193 A6 2002
823'.914—dc21   2002022752

COUNTERPOINT
387 Park Avenue South
New York, NY 10016-8810

Counterpoint is a member of the Perseus Books Group

10 9 8 7 6 5 4 3 2 1

To the memory of my mother,
who started the stories

Contents

Introduction

by Clare Boylan

The stories in this collection include my earliest and most recent tales. They were begun in my late twenties and completed when I was midway through my forties. They cover that substantial chunk when a woman experiences the best and worst in life. Re-reading them makes me think of looking in the wardrobe and re-discovering strange and exotic, eccentric and uncomfortable clothes I once wore. The stories are not about my life, yet are inhabited by all my past selves. The early ones now seem enviably energetic and arrogant and brave. I am surprised by how much I knew about things I had not yet experienced. I notice that as I get older I get kinder to my characters and that they grow more vulnerable.

I have been told my stories can be disconcerting. It seems strange to me as nothing in my life has made me so happy as writing short stories. The happiness is akin to that feeling, as a small child, of capturing the light of the sun in a magnifying glass and watching the earth catch fire. I love the feeling, with the short story, that the world is in the detail and that small random acts can set ordinary lives alight or consume them to ash.

I am often asked if my own life has been as peculiar as that of my characters. To me my characters seem quite normal and like most short story writers I come from a very conventional background. This ought not to be a surprise. The short story is orderly in shape (although frequently unruly in content). And the "ordinary" family is no more than the compression of its abnormalities.

I grew up in a red-brick suburb of Dublin. George Bernard Shaw, who spent his unhappy early years in a similar Dublin house, said that families stay together in order to protect the skeletons in their cupboards. A suffocating respectability combined with a feeling of being center-stage (for God and the neighbours saw all things) meant that we lived in a constant state of fear and stasis. Behind lace curtains, eccentricities, failures, petty scandals loomed like monsters. But the real terror was of being seen for what we really were. Children must be seen and not heard. Adults invented more ideal selves. All of life was a kind of fiction.

The biggest influence of my childhood was my mother, an early feminist who wrote a very powerful little novel about a witch-girl called Edith who used her spells to make bullies look absurd. From the start, my mother decided that I would be the writer of the family. I was to be her replacement self. I became a writer, but the complexity of mother-daughter relationships is one of my dominant themes. In "A Model Daughter" a woman invents a child for financial gain, but the fantasy overtakes the material objective. In "The Stolen Child" a maternal fantasy turns to nightmare when the angelic pink-clad infant taken by a childless woman turns out to be a screaming boy.

My sisters and I led a dismally quiet life but like a trio of inept Brontes, wrought a ferment of creativity in our dark, suburban house. Mother painted one kitchen wall black and left a large box of chalks beside it so that we could draw to life size. Before I could write I drew stories as cartoon strips. At the age of ten I won a prize for a story about a reformed drunkard. At fourteen I was hard at work (under the desk) on an oeuvre entitled "The Hard Young Men."

I went into journalism, but shortly discovered that the factual truth has little bearing on the emotional one. Although literally, there are thieves, murderers, adulterers, arsonists, drug addicts, embezzlers, the reality is a band of radical dreamers resorting to desperate measures. I found myself turning over each story to see what was on the other side and soon I was writing fiction.

I have always loved the economy and deftness of the short story. Unlike the novel, whose length and cumulative structure makes me think of Saint-Beuve's character of Madame d'Albany in "Lundis," whose figure "had somewhat collapsed under her weight," a good short story has a perfect shape and seems to me like a portable life coach. The late Irish-American writer Mary Lavin (a regular contributor to *The New Yorker*), enchantingly described the short story as "an arrow in flight": No beginning and an unseen destination, it is an incident crystallized in time yet it is also a pathfinder.

Perhaps because of my journalistic background, a lot of my stories have an entry point of reality–an anecdote, a scrap of conversation, a line in a newspaper. The stories "To Tempt a Woman" and "Concerning Virgins" were based on wonderful real-life stories recounted by other people–the first by a farmer's wife who told me of a bright young girl in 1960's rural Ireland, who wanted to go to university but was married off to a bachelor farmer whom she would only meet at the altar; the second by the late Anglo-Irish novelist Molly Keane who delighted me with the story of a landed gent so unpleasant that he could not get a replacement for his dead wife. When he advertised anonymously the only replies were from his two spinster daughters, desperate for escape. Molly read the collection in which it featured and said how much she liked it. I reminded her that she had told me the story in the first place. She had no recollection of it. Was this merely old age or had she made it up? No matter! Story-telling is circular and the stories are not about these things, but about innocence, guile, illusion, disillusion. Besides, the function of the story is not to tell the truth but to discover the truth.

My first published short story, "Appearances," came about when my mother told me about her infatuation with a tram driver. She was twelve. She walked one way to school so as to purchase a love offering (a little currant cake) to present to him on the tram journey home. After months of her silent worship he asked her to meet him in secret as he wanted to show her something private. Alone with him, in a remote and forbidden wood, she began to be afraid. The man started to undress and told her to close her eyes and not to open them until instructed. When the moment came she was almost blinded by the flash of sunlight on a spectacular array of holy medals pinned to his undershirt.

I loved the idea of the transposed roles; the child's sexuality and the adult's innocence. I also found in that anecdote my fictional métier – the rich and hazardous world of misunderstandings.

Many of my stories are about love – not so much about the pursuit of love, as the pursuit of a lovable self in a perfect other. Lacking self-knowledge love becomes a series of wrong turnings in a hall of mirrors leading ultimately to a harsh reflection of self. This isn't due to a pessimistic outlook, but a belief that ultimately all journeys must lead to oneself.

In my short stories, dreams are fragile gladiators in an arena of hoary old lions of reality. The downtrodden married woman who finally escapes her dreary domesticity for an idyll with her bachelor lover, discovers that his yearning is not for a love affair, but for a bout of housewifely care. A middle-aged man, bitterly resentful of the financial demands of his cast-off family, finds that his release from them erases the best part of himself. But dreams don't quite get vanquished. What emerges is a mating of dream and reality, which pretty much defines the human condition.

Although my tales mostly have a psychological rather than a geographical landscape, my characters are a consummately Irish collection of anarchists, dreamers and outsiders. My stories have been described by reviewers as "savage comedy." Comic, I hope they are, but I prefer Carol Shields's definition of "serious comedy." "Painful tales of love's humiliation," one critic deemed them, but to me they are tales of life's infinite possibility and the comic grandeur of impossible dreams.

Housekeeper's Cut

❧*ᔐᔐᔐ*❧

Edward kept looking into the refrigerator. It gave him a sense of faith. This peculiar sensation billowed inside his chest in the manner competently wrought by carol singers and card senders at Christmas. It was not the same as religious faith. Edward was too modest for that. He was experiencing another sensation never before aspired to in his life, a faith in ordinary things.

There was butter and bacon, eggs, milk, ice-cream; a clutter of untidy vegetables – carrots, cabbage, onions, mushrooms. He had purchased them recklessly from a stall in a food market, cramming his string bag with scabby-looking roots with the air of a man who knows exactly what he is doing. He had no notion of any practical application for such primitive nutrients. They might have been employed by men who lived in caves to club their enemies. He was familiar with food that came in plastic bags and could be persuaded, with boiling water, to imitate a meal.

He knew, all the same, in the way a blind man knows that the world over his head is blue and grey and the world under his feet is green and grey and the top part is safer, that these items belonged at the very heart of things and that this was where he was going.

The thing that pleased him most was his roast. It held the centre of the refrigerator, lightly covered in butcher's paper. He had watched it in the meaty window for several minutes before striding in and claiming it. He did this by pointing because he had no idea what it was. He was appalled at the price. It cost over four pounds. He was neither poor nor mean, merely accustomed to buying a slice or two of roast beef from the delicatessen or a couple of spiced sausages, and there was always plenty of change left over from a pound. Now that it was his he could see that it was worth the money, swirling fat and flesh tied with a string in the middle; already he could hear the clash of knives being sharpened, the rattle and scrape of plates, like sounds of battle imagined by a child in a history class.

He used to meet Susan between meals. She was worn out from making excuses and he had to give her glasses of wine to make her look the way he imagined her when she was not there. She grumbled about the needs of her children, the demands of her husband, his capacity for chops and potatoes and apple tarts. It appeared that her whole life was dragged down by the weight of her husband's appetite; she was up at dawn wringing the vitamins from oranges, out hampered by enormous sacks of groceries during the day. Afternoons were taken up with peeling and grating, marinating, sieving. After a time her abused features would soften and she would say: 'It would be different if it was for you. I always think of that when I'm cooking. I always pretend it's for you.' She would come to him then, dipping her face to his lips. She sat across his legs as if he was a see-saw. 'If you were with me, ' he would say, 'I would give you six months of tremendous spoiling. Then I'd put you to work.'

Sometimes he did, just to watch her, just for fun. He put her beside the cooker with mushrooms and cream, small morsels of fish, tasty things.

She was too tired. The food got burnt, the mushrooms went rubbery. Or they became distracted. He would come up behind her and put his arms around her and she would swivel round and burrow to him. When they were in bed smells of burning food and sounds of music drifted up from rooms below.

Inside her, he found a love that wanted to be taken advantage of and although he did not wish to hurt her, he found himself complaining about the comfortlessness of his life; the meals taken in restaurants with people who meant nothing, just to fill an evening. He dined out most evenings because he was lonely in the house without her. She never asked about his companions, but about the interior features of the restaurants, the designs on menus and then in detail, the meal. 'It's a waste,' he said, 'to be anywhere without you.

When he went back to the city he forgot about her. There were moments when he felt a hollowness which he recognised as the place in him where she had been, but he had always known it would come to an end. He looked on love as a seasonal pleasure, like sunshine. Only a savage expected the sun to shine all year round.

She telephoned from public call boxes. Her voice was the ocean in a seashell. He remembered that they had made together a splash of happiness on a pale canvas but he knew that she did not carry this glow alone, without him. When they said goodbye for the last time, he had watched her running away, a drooping figure, disarrayed, a spirit fleeing an exorcism. He listened to the cascade of coins following the operator's instructions and then after a pause, her weary voice. 'I miss you.' He saw her in a headscarf with a bag of groceries at her side and small children clawing on the outside of the glass, trying to get at her.

He was at home now, busy, surrounded by people who were skilled in the pleasures of living – conversation and lovemaking – as people in the country had never been.

Even she, to whom he had leapt as determinedly as a salmon, held within her a soft hopelessness which begged, come in to me, fill me up, I have nothing else.

One day on the phone her voice sounded different: 'I'm coming up,' she said. He frowned into the machine receiving the bubbles of her tone. This possibility had not occurred to him. She was too firmly anchored with groceries. 'Two whole days,' she was telling him through her laughter, gasping about excuses and arrangements so complicated that he knew she would tunnel under the earth with her hands to reach him if necessary. 'That will be very nice, ' he said inadequately. 'I'll look forward to that.' It was when he had replaced the receiver and was still washed by echoes of her foolish joy that he understood properly what she was saying. She had disposed, for a time, of all the open mouths that gaped at her for sustenance. She had put them aside. She was coming to do her proper task. He was tenderly agitated by the thought of her frail figure scurrying from one area of usefulness to another. This was blotted out by the shouts of his own areas of deprivation, crying out to be seen to. He wanted her to look after him.

When he met her at the station she was tremulously dressed up, a country woman on an outing. She threw him a reckless smile from under a hat. Alarming blue carnations sprang up around her skull. She dropped her cases and raced into his arms. Her feet flailed heedlessly and the flowers on her hat dipped like the neck of a heron. She thudded into him and he felt the needy probing of her tongue. He held her patiently, employing his training as a man to grind down the stone in his chest, of disappointment, that she had not kept a part of herself solid and available to his needs.

'Look at that!' She kept stabbing at the window of the car with her gloved finger, demonstrating pigeons and churches and department stores. 'Look!' 'You sound like a tourist,' he said. She kept quiet after that. She hadn't ever been to the city before.

Inside his flat she walked around all the rooms, inspecting his clothes on their hangers, patting the bed, trying out chairs. He was surprised when she sat down without giving a glance to the refrigerator. 'What shall we do?' she said.

She was slouched in a red leather armchair, her white skirt bunched under her thighs. He imagined that she ought to be in the kitchen doing something with the roast. He could picture it bulging in a tin, strung about with peeled potatoes and onions. He wanted to watch her bending at the oven, her frowning face pink, her straight hair shrivelling into tiny curls around her face. He had bought an apron for her. It was white with a black and red frill at the bottom. It hung on a nail by the sink. He had no clear idea of what they would do with all the time they now had to spend together. She was the one who was married, who was skilled in the sectioning of time. He had vaguely imagined that women liked to be busy in a house, arranging flowers, punching pastry, stirring at saucepans on the stove, and that it was a man's role to encircle this ritual with refinement, music and drinks and occasional kisses, creating a territory for their contentment, a privacy for their love.

He had not set his heart on this course of events. He did not mind if she preferred to take a nap or read a book or sit on his knee. The thing that was foremost in his mind was that their pursuits of the afternoon would be overlaid by ovenly aromas, snaps and splutterings and the delicious sting on their senses of roasting meat.

He asked if she was hungry and she said that she was, standing up instantly, brushing down her skirt. She took a mirror from her bag and gazed at her face, pressing her lips together, peering into her eyes for flaws. He took her hand and led her through to the kitchen. He pulled open the door of the refrigerator as if he was drawing back a stage curtain and she peered, awed, at the overcrowding of nourishment. 'What are you going to do with all this?' she said, and he laughed. 'There's cold meat and cheese,' he said. 'We could have that for lunch.' She stood gazing into the fridge with a melancholy expression while he removed the slices of ham and the tubs of potato salad and the oozing triangle of Brie.

When he had set the table and opened a bottle of wine he came back to find her still transfixed in front of the open cabinet with that expression housewives have, and he thought she was sizing up the contents, planning menus. 'That,' he said, pointing in at his slab of meat on the shelf as if it was a lovely trinket in a jeweller's window, 'is for dinner.' She sat down at the table without a word. He sensed, as she ate her ham and potatoes and swirled her wine around in the glass, that she was disappointed. This feeling communicated to himself and he poured wine into his leaden chest, blaming himself. He had probably pre-empted her plans for lunch. She might have been planning to surprise him with a home-made soup. She raised bleak eyes to him over her glass. She was not her normal self, full of cheerful complaint and breathless love. She was ill at ease and sad. 'Aren't we going out?' she said. The thought to him was preposterous. Now that they finally had a stretch of privacy, she wanted to race out into the cold where they would be divided by elements and the curious looks of strangers.

He drove her to a park and they huddled under some trees against the cold, watching cricket players and a family of deer in the distance like an arrangement of dead branches. He had brought a box of sweets that she had sent him. It had seemed a sentimental gesture, saving them to share with her. Now that he was pulling off the wrapper he could see it was tactless, taking them out so much later. She would think he had not wanted them. He laid the open box in the grass. After a moment or two, the arrangement of confectionery was swarming with ants.

He was tired when he got home and beginning to get hungry. Susan wanted a bath. He took the meat from the fridge and laid it on a plate on the counter. He hazarded the skinning of several potatoes. He carried a clutch of jaundiced-looking parsnips and placed them in a bowl, close to the liquidiser. This tableau was completed with a blue tin of curry powder. Once, in a restaurant, he had been given a curried parsnip soup and it was delicious.

When she joined him in the kitchen she was wearing a black dress down to her feet. Her mouth was obscured in magenta. He put his arms around her and kissed her laundered neck but she struggled from his grasp and pointed to the ranked ingredients. 'What are you doing?' she said. 'Just hamming.' He smiled guiltily.

She looked from him to the food, back again. Her hands, he noticed, wrestled with the string of a tiny evening bag. 'I thought,' she said, 'that we'd be going out.' 'Going where?' he said, exasperated. 'I don't know.' Her shoulders drooped. 'The theatre, a restaurant.' He could not keep her still, draw her back to the things that mattered. 'Do you really want to go out?' She nodded her head. He sighed and went to telephone a theatre. When he came back the counter had been cleared of his work and offered instead a meagre plate of toast and a pot of tea.

In the city she was happy. She sipped cocktails and laughed, showing all her teeth, raising her eyebrows larkily. Although her clothes were not suited to the theatre, not suited to anything really, she carried her happiness with dignity. Men looked at her, old ones, young ones, brown, grey. She was aware of this but her eyes were for him. He thought he understood now. She was sure of herself on this neutral territory. She did not wish to be plucked by him from their complicated past. Here, she was a woman alone. She wanted him to court her. He took her hand and kissed her cheek, catching scents of gin and perfume. He felt desire. This seizure of lust was new. It had not touched him when they were in the park or shut up in his living quarters. He had felt love and compassion but no selfish stirrings.

During the play he watched her, writing his own theme, making her free and carefree as his needs required, as her loud laughter would lead anyone to believe.

Afterwards he turned the car quickly homeward. She kept looking out the window, like a child. When they were home she said fretfully: 'We haven't had anything to eat, not really.' He was no longer concerned about food. There was plenty, in any case, in the fridge. She cooked some eggs and a packet of little onions, frozen in sauce. It was a strange combination but he drove the food into his mouth and pronounced it delicious.

They went to bed. Their sex was full of need and passion. They came with angry shouts. They could not find their love. 'I love you,' she said. 'Yes,' he said. 'Yes.' And then they were silent, each saying to themselves: 'Tomorrow will be different.'

In the morning she was up early to make his breakfast, her toes crackling with joy as she reached up to shelves for coffee and marmalade. She felt wrapped around him as a cardigan. As she waited for the coffee to boil she sensed a warm splash on her feet and it was his seed, langorously detaching itself from her. She felt a minute sense of loss, wanting to let nothing go, wanting to be pregnant.

Edward had to work after breakfast. He did not mind leaving her on her own. She seemed happy as she punished pillows and washed out the breakfast things. He found himself whistling as he bent over his set square. After a time she came and sat beside him. She had been washing her hair. She combed it over her face in long strokes that emanated a faint creak. Inky streamers swam through the air and clung to his clothing. He could not work. He gave her an irritated glance and she went away. She came back dressed in high shoes and a blue suit – a costume, rather, he thought – her face matt and piqued with make-up. She was carrying cups of coffee. When she put his coffee down she quickly sought his hand with hers, and although their grasp was warm and steady there was some central part of them that was trembling and they could feel it through their palms. 'Now,' he thought, 'we could go to bed. We could love each other.' It made sense. They had always done their loving in the day. Her bright armour kept him distant.

'I'd like,' she said, 'to see the sights.'

He took his hand away and wrapped it around the cup of coffee, needing warmth. He did not look at her. 'There's nothing to see out there, ' he said. 'Believe me. We could have a quiet lunch and listen to some music. We could read to each other.' 'But it's London!' she protested.

He said, thinking to stop her: 'You go if you want. I must work for a little while. I couldn't bear to see the sights.' He did look up then and saw her soft round face boxing up a huge hurt in an even larger resolve. She kissed the side of his face and he wanted the salt of her mouth but she was so different, so devoid of humour and generosity, that he believed even her taste might have changed. She clopped off on her high heels and he heard the sorrowful bang of the door.

He could not work. He was exasperated to distraction. There crept in on him thoughts, malice-filled whispers. He shook them off as if they were wasps at his ears.

He had established in his mind, long months before, that she was the one in his life who truly loved him, wanting nothing, knowing that nothing was possible. When they parted he had savoured the sorrow of it, knowing that this was real. They had been severed by fate, an outsider, a true professional. There would be no festering, only a clean grief gleaming like stainless steel around the core of a perfect happiness, safely invested in his centre. He had been content to leave it at that. He would have loved her, at the back of his head, until his death.

It was she who had come back like a vengeful spirit to incorporate him in her discontent, to mock his faith, to demonstrate to him, in her ghostly unreachableness, the great stretch of his own isolation.

He went to look for some lunch. There was nothing in the refrigerator that he could understand. He was exploring parcels of foil, hoping for some forgotten cheese, when he heard a commotion coming from the garden.

Susan was in a restaurant. She had a chocolate éclair that she was breaking with the side of her fork. She had taken a taxi to Madame Tussaud's and the Planetarium. Outside each was a long queue of foreigners and a man selling balloons on a stick for fifty pence. There was no glamour, no sense of discovery. They were like people queueing for food in the war. She had wanted him to take her to a gallery of famous paintings and show her the pictures he liked. No point in going on her own; she could never understand pictures, always wanted to see the scene as it really was.

She left the stoic queue and went back to the taxi rank. She could not think where to go. 'Bond Street,' she said to the driver, liking its sound. She did not know where it was but it seemed to her, as the streets unravelled like red and grey bandages, she was being taken further and further away from Edward. When they got to Bond Street, she was ordered out of the dark enclosure. She tried to thrust a fan of notes at the back of the driver's neck, through the sliding glass door, but he was suspicious and made her go out on the street and put them through a side window.

She stumbled along in front of the smart shops. She ached to be with Edward, to feel his hand or even the cloth of his jacket; and then, perversely, she felt lonely for home, wanting to butter toast for the children or to fluff the top of a shepherd's pie for her husband. She understood their needs. She knew how to respond. When she had exhausted several streets she found a café and she went in and ordered herself a cake. A tear dropped into it and she did not want to eat it. She would go back, she promised herself. She would talk to him.

He was standing at the window, shoulders bent, head at a quizzical angle and sunlight teasing his hair into infantile transparency. She had let herself in with the key he had given her and he did not notice her. Watching his back, she felt as if all the ordinary things had been vacuumed out of her body and replaced by love, lead-heavy, a burden. 'I want to talk to you,' she said. 'Shhh,' he said, not turning around. 'Edward?' she begged. He turned to her. His face was white, filled with horror. 'It's a bird,' he said.

'What are you talking about?' She went to the window and looked out. She could see a ragged tomcat standing at a tree, his back arched. She ran to the back door and out into the garden, down the length of the path.

The tree was root deep in rattling leaves and when she got to it she could see that the leaves were in permanent motion as if agitated by a slow motor under the earth. She saw then that it was a dowdy grey bird, lopsided, helplessly urging an injured wing to flight. The cat held its victim with a gooseberry gaze. She picked up the cat and put it on the wall, slapping its behind to make it jump into the next garden. 'Bring me a box,' she shouted out to Edward's white face at the window. He advanced with a shoe box. She snatched it from him, piling it with leaves, roughly cramming in the damaged bird. She slammed the lid on the bird's head and carried it indoors. She looked, Edward thought, like a housewife who has just come upon some unpleasant item of refuse and means to deal with it; but when she got indoors she sat in a chair and emptied bird and leaves into her blue linen lap. She held the bird in cupped hands and crooned gently into its dank feathers.

He brought her tea and fed it to her, holding the cup to her mouth. She minded the bird like a baby, making noises with her lips, rocking back and forth as once she had minded him. He was unnerved by a pang of jealousy. 'Did you have a nice morning?' he said. 'Oh, yes,' she said, distantly, rocking. He could see that she was in her element. He was excluded. He crumbled bread into a bowl of milk and pushed little spoons of it at the dry nib of the bird's beak. The bird seemed to be asleep. She pushed his hand aside and swept the bird, leaves and all, back into the box. 'Open the bedroom window,' she said. She followed him upstairs and put the box on the ledge without its lid. 'If his wing isn't broken he'll fly away,' she said. 'But if it is broken?' he said helplessly. 'He'll die,' she said.

In the course of the morning he had taken the meat and vegetables from the fridge once more. There had been nothing readily edible and he was hungry. When they came downstairs again she saw them and said: 'I have to phone my husband,' as if they had reminded her of him, which they had.

He heard her on the phone. She sounded as if she was defending herself. She said then: 'I miss you.' It was an echo from his distant past. He went in and found her sitting on the sofa, her fist to her mouth, crying. He touched her hair lightly with his fingers, afraid to do more. 'I'll just put the meat in the oven,' he said hopefully. 'What?' She glared at him. Her tearful face was full of scorn. 'Have you still got your heart set on that?' 'I bought it for you,' he said. 'You bought that for me? I have tasted prawns and sole in my life, you know. I have had fried steak.' She was attacking him. He didn't know what was the matter. He assumed her husband had said something to upset her. 'It's all right,' he soothed. He tiptoed out as if she were sleeping.

The potatoes, peeled from yesterday, had blackened. He flung them hopefully into the tin. He peeled four onions and tucked them into the corners; in the centre, as he had imagined it, the round of juicy meat.

It looked perfectly fine. He put a pat of butter on the top and a sprinkling of salt and pepper. He cut up a clove of garlic and scattered it over the food. He thought he had seen other women doing something like this. He turned the oven up to a rousing temperature and pushed the tin inside. It was done. There was nothing to it.

He blamed himself for Susan's outburst. He should not have left her to wander around the city on her own. She was used to a more protected way of life. He must make it up to her.

He took champagne from a cool cupboard and dug it into a

bowl with ice. He found music on the radio. He brought the
wine with glasses to the bedroom. Music drifted up from
downstairs. He drew the curtains and switched on a little lamp.
'Susan,' he called.

He heard her dragging steps on the stairs. A face loomed
round the door, self-piteous. Her sharp eyes flashed about suspiciously, took in the details – and were radiant. She was a
child; all troubles erased in a momentary delight. She ran to
him and was caught in his arms. They stroked hair, pulled
buttons, tasted flesh. She laughed greedily. At last they had
met.

They made love boastfully, tenderly, certain of their territory.
He held her feet in his hands. She took his fingers in her
mouth. They embroidered one another's limbs with their atten-
tions. He felt with his lips for the edges of her smile and could
find no end. They were separated only by the selfishness of
their happiness. Afterwards, she gave a deep unlikely chortle
from her satisfied depths and he laughed at her.

They drank the champagne crouching at opposite ends of
the bed in the intimate gloom, striking up flinty tales of childhood for sympathy.

When they crawled towards each other, he with bottle and
she with empty glass, only their mouths met and he took the
breakable things and put them on the floor because they had to
make love again.

They emptied the bottle of champagne. They lay beside
each other, gazing. 'I must look awful,' she said. He surveyed
her snarled black hair and the matching dark scribble under a
carelessly disposed arm; the smear of make-up under her eyes,
her sated face scrubbed pink. 'You look fine to me,' he said. He
felt exuberant, relieved, re-born, at ease. 'You look,' he teased,
but truthfully, 'like my mistress.'

She swung away from him, rolled over and clung to her
pillow, a mollusc on a rock. He could not tell what was in her
head. He patted her back but she shook him off and murmured sadly through the pillow: 'I smell something.' She
looked up at him, one moist eye rising above its ruined decor.
He had offended her. But when the rest of her face rose above

the sheets he could see that her eyes were watering with laughter.

'What is it?' he smiled tenderly. 'It's perfect,' she said. 'It's exactly as it used to be – us, together, the music and the smell of burning food.' She laughed.

He jumped out of bed and ran to the kitchen. Smoke gusted out around the oven door. The air was cruel with the taint of burning beast. He pulled open the oven door and his naked body was assaulted by the heat of hell. He dragged the roasting tin clear of the smoke with a cloth. The cloves of garlic rattled like blackened nails on the tarry ruin.

He was worn out. He felt betrayed. He could not believe that it had happened so quickly, so catastrophically. He felt his faith sliding away. 'Edward?' Susan called out from the bedroom. 'It's all right!' he shouted; and after he had said it he felt that it had to be. He opened the window to let out the smoke and went to the bathroom for a dressing-gown.

Bolstered by champagne and the satisfactoriness of the afternoon's loving he made himself believe that the meat could be repaired. He forked the meat on to a scallopped plate and began to hack away with a sharp knife at the charred edges of the tormented flesh.

He was agreeably surprised to find that the meat was still quite rare on the inside – almost raw, in fact. He found it hard to make an impression with the knife but he put this down to lack of practice and the fact that the carving implements were not much in use. He sawed, glad of the little box of cress in the fridge which would decorate its wounds and the rest of the vegetables which Susan would cook and toss in butter while he put on his clothes.

Susan came up behind him. She had been standing in the doorway in a nightdress like a flourbag, frilled on cuff and sleeve. She tiptoed on bare feet, so that he sensed her at the last moment, tangled wraith blanched and billowing.

'It's no use,' she whispered. 'It's fine,' he said. 'It's not bad at all.' 'It's no use,' she cried brokenly. 'There's no Bisto, no stock cubes. There's nothing in your cupboards, nothing ordinary – no flour or custard, there isn't a packet of salt. It's all a pretence.'

She put out a hand, and he reached for it, needing something to hold. Her hand shot past him. She struck at the meat. It sailed off the plate and landed on the floor, blood gathering at its edges. 'That's all you think of me,' she said violently, through trembling jaws. 'You think that's good enough for me! Housekeeper's Cut! I wouldn't have that on my own table at home. I wouldn't give that to my children if they were hungry. That's all I'm worth.'

They ate in an Italian restaurant close to where he lived. It was not a place he had been before. The tables were bright red and the menu leaned heavily to starch but there was no time to book a proper restaurant. He had to have something to eat.

'Have some veal,' he said. 'That should be good.' He poured wine from a carafe into their glasses. She ordered a pizza. Her hair fell over her face. He could see her knuckles sawing over the fizzing red disc but none of it seemed to go to her mouth. The waiter said that the lady should have an ice-cream. She shook her head. 'Cassatta!' he proclaimed. 'It means,' he wheedled, '*married.*'

Edward laughed encouragement but she did not see. Her head was turned to the waiter, nodding, he could not tell whether in request or resignation.

In the morning she was gone. The sheets still burned with the heat of her body. She had been up at six, packing, making coffee, telephoning for a taxi. Her feet on the floor made a rousing slap like the sound of clapping hands. At one point he heard her whistling. He knew that he should drive her to the station but he would not hasten her back to the disposal of her lawful dependants. He would not.

'Edward!' Her hands clung to the end of his bed and she cried out in distress, her face and her night-dress trailing white in the grey morning light. 'Yes, love,' he said inside, but he only opened a cautious eye and uttered a sleepy 'Mmm?' 'I bought nothing for the children,' she said. 'They'll be expecting presents. I always buy them something.'

She stood at the window, dressed in hat and coat, in the last moments, waiting for her taxi. 'Edward!' she cried. He sat up this time, ready to take her in his arms. 'The bird!' she said. 'He flew away.'

When she was gone he traced with his fingers her body in the warm sheets, bones and hair and pillows of maternal flesh. He kept his eyes closed, kept her clenched in his heart. The day bore in on him, sunshine and telephone bells and the cold knowledge that she did not love him. All the time she pretended to care for him, she had been jealous of his wealth, greedy for glamour. She was a pilgrim, stealing relics of the saints.

It was not him she desired. She wanted to snatch for herself some part of a glittering life she imagined he was hoarding. He tried to bring her face to mind but all he could see was a glass box, clawed by children and inside, a housewife in a headscarf, bags of groceries at her side.

Susan did not cry until she was on the train. The tears fell, then, big as melted ice cubes. There was a man sitting opposite with a little boy. The child had been given a magic drawing pad to occupy his hands and he made sketches of her melting face, squinting for perspective.

As the tears dashed from her eyes she felt that she was flying to pieces. Soon there would be nothing left of her; at any rate, nothing solid enough to contain the knowledge that he did not love her.

She had expected so little. She only wanted to fill up the gaps in their past. Often, when they were together, he had spoken of the hurt of being anywhere without her; the wasted nights with strangers; the meals in restaurants, not tasted. It was terrible to her that she had only given him her leftover time. She had to make it up to him. She wanted him to know that she would risk anything for him. She would shine beside him in the harsh glare of public envy. For a very little time she would be his for all the world to see, whatever the world might say.

Now she did not know what she would do except, in time, face up to her foolishness. He had not been proud of her. He wanted to hide her away. Established in his own smart and secret life, he had been ashamed of her.

The man on the seat opposite was embarrassed. It was her

huge tears, her lack of discretion, the critical attention of his little boy. He felt threatened by their indifference to proper codes of behaviour. He snatched the magic pad and threw it roughly to the far end of the seat. The boy gazed idly out the window.

Accustomed to inspecting the creative efforts of the children, Susan reached for the sketch pad. The boy was not as clever as her own. His portrait was a clown's mask, upside down. She rubbed out his imprint and sat with the pad on her knee, acquainting herself with the raw, hurting feeling of her mind and her skin, settling into the pain. She had to stop crying. The children would notice. Tomorrow she would buy them presents. Tonight, they would have to content themselves with ice-cream. 'Ice-cream' she scratched absently on the magic pad. Her tired mind grizzled over the necessities of tea and she wrote, without thinking, 'eggs, bacon, cheese'; and then, since days did not exist on their own but merely as transport to other days, and since she on this vehicle of time, was a stoker, she continued writing: 'carrots, cabbage, onions, mushrooms.'

The Wronged Wife

✦✦✦

'My wife would like to meet you,' Matthew said one day when she was gazing out the window at a stubble of bluebells wobbling in the breeze.

'I am your wife,' Vanessa said. 'I've met myself.' She turned to look into eyes that were blue and wobbled with the same charming uncertainty as the flowers. 'Margaret,' he specified. 'Oh, that wife,' she smiled, coming over to rub his hair in the hope that he would clasp his hands around her bottom, and he did.

She was disturbed. Getting Matthew through his divorce had been like setting a person's house on fire and then rescuing them from the blaze. She woke each morning like a child at Christmas, afraid to open her eyes in case the gift was not there. She still held her breath in awe at the precious bulk in the blankets and felt faint with pride when he called her name in the evenings as he stepped into the hall.

She had not unpacked all her clothes for fear of intruding too massively on his wardrobe.

When she first came to the house there were traces of Margaret. It was a perfume, an atmosphere. The place was meticulously clean, cleaner than any place she had ever been in. So remorselessly had it been polished that it was weeks before she had anything to do. She passed her days in opening spotless cupboards searching for Margaret. And there she was; in the lists that had been pasted up on the insides of the doors, specifying the correct contents of each cupboard so that replacements could be made before they became necessary; in the curious military ranking of drinking glasses and bottles which suggested she was not aware they had any pleasure to offer other than the arranging of them; in the set of silver cutlery which she disturbed from its gleaming repose on a bed of black velvet. The reverence with which each piece had been prepared and put away in order of size reminded her of a family mortuary. There was merit in the assembly. You could tell at a glance if anything was missing. All the same, anyone else would have just flung them in in a bundle with egg between the prongs.

Her first instinct was to rip down the lists and sully a good glass with whisky to celebrate. She found it was not possible. The lists were useful. It seemed wanton to destroy them unless she had something better to contribute. She hadn't. She was still considering her situation when her own untidiness caught up with her. Webs and dust and little heaps of articles of daily usage sprang up around her. She swept and wiped and sorted in a panic. Matthew was not critical. He kissed her and helped with the housework in a useless, endearing manner. He reminded her that Margaret had been keeping house for a dozen years, that Rome wasn't built in a day. He was endlessly tactful and patient. She underdid his egg and overdid his beef and he said nothing for months. When he was driven to instruct her on his preferences he added: 'It was years before Margaret got that right.'

Already she was learning that marriages are not, as the law so optimistically offers, dissolved. Men are hoarders. First wives have to be accommodated in some attic of the marriage like an embarrassing Mrs Rochester. With Margaret it was different. There was no reason to think of her as a malign presence. It was her goodness that held them. She remained central, like a piece of mahogany that had to be displayed because it was too good to throw away.

Vanessa was overwhelmed by the uselessness of competing with Margaret but she scrubbed the house so thoroughly it looked sore and converted her misgivings to understanding. Now and again there were things that surpassed her understanding. Why on earth should Margaret want to come and see her? She had never met Margaret but she knew about her. Matthew had talked of her while they were having their affair. She was thirty-seven which was twelve years more than Vanessa and she had given him the best years of her life. The divorce would kill her. In the harrowing months of legal severance Vanessa had wanted to talk to her. Matthew would not allow it. It was no use trying to be friends with her, he reasoned. She was entitled to her hostility. She frowned over the trampled field of Matthew's hair. 'Why now?' she wondered. He pushed his head between her breasts and joggled them therapeutically. 'Because that's the sort of person she is,' he said. 'She has survived the worst of it and she wants us to know she's all right – so we won't feel guilty.'

As always she knew he was right. She still didn't like the idea. She wanted her guilt. It had come in a parcel with her new life and she felt that she must hold it all or lose it all.

When the day came she opened tender Charentais melons and bathed strawberries in liqueur. She sliced tomatoes and buried them in a flurry of chopped parsley. Matthew popped in to say he was on his way. The divorce had left Margaret without a car and he had to collect her. He stole a slice of tomato and reminisced. In his first marriage there had been a small pot on the kitchen window with a basil plant. It was like a child's drawing of a plant and it grew abundantly although it was constantly snipped and shredded over tomatoes. He had not actually realised that fresh tomatoes had the taste and texture of a handkerchief soaked in sweat until . . . 'Must be off. I'll give Margaret a drink on the way home so you'll have time to look beautiful.' 'Oh,' Vanessa called out in distress. 'What does she look like?' 'Battered,' he sighed, lowering his eyebrows as if offended. He kissed her and left her trembling amid the vegetables. She pulled a salad limb from limb. She would make Matthew proud of her. Margaret was coming home. Her pink fingernails shook like the blossoms of hydrangea in a storm and were deluged by a storm of her tears.

When she had cried for half an hour she began to feel better. She could see herself back at work, eating sandwiches in pubs, carrying large paper bags with dresses inside, sitting on the edge of a single bed pulled close to a gas fire, sharing a half bottle of gin with a girlfriend. She felt calmer. She put the potatoes on to boil and made a plain salad – nothing that her shaking hand could mangle or her jealous heart curdle. She bronzed pieces of pork and mushrooms in butter and put them growling in cream.

A girl walked into the kitchen wearing men's boots and a fragile white blouse. She had a cigarette in her mouth. 'Hello, flower,' she said in a small voice. Vanessa stared hard at her in surprise. There were women's lines around her eyes. She wasn't a girl at all. She swung her long hair and stamped over to the cooker in her everyday jeans, the curious effect of girlhood and womanhood superimposed. The girl or woman grinned into the pan, dripping ash on the food. 'Aren't you good?' she said. 'All this stuff.'

Matthew crept up on them and dropped a whiskey kiss on Vanessa's ear. 'Margaret – Vanessa,' he presented. The two of them studied each other without reserve. In silence, scarcely disturbed by the hiss of the food in the pan, they made their adjustments. It required great concentration and was necessary for each to become the other, to wind their transposed limbs around the husband and absorb his words of love, to think: she knows he gets dandruff. She knows he can't eat oysters. She knows he whimpers when he comes.

Matthew stood winter limbed, a peripheral hedge to their whirling seasons, until he could stand it no longer and bellowed, 'Sherry, darling?' at Vanessa. 'Yes,' Vanessa said and Margaret said: 'Have a whiskey, dear, or you'll never catch up. We're as pissed as newts.'

They went into the drawing room like visitors and sat in its special tidiness. Matthew poured spirits for himself and Margaret and hovered the bottle over a third glass. 'Sure?' He gave Vanessa a last chance. She nodded her head and boldly asked for ice.

She wanted Margaret to know that she had authority with her husband and to understand that she was not irresponsible in the matter of household management. The lavatory gleamed.

The icebox was crammed with long white rocks like Americans' teeth.

'He's a very hard man,' Margaret said when Matthew had left the room. 'He's very sure of himself.' The woman was an imposter, Vanessa decided. 'You don't understand him,' she said carefully. 'Oh, I do,' Margaret said. 'I spent twelve years understanding him. It's what wives do. It's like bloody housework, dear. You break your back crawling under the bed to scrape away heaps of dust that nobody else even knows are there. D'you know the worst of it? It's not really understanding at all. You're weaving the loose threads back into the fabric, trying to make him into the man you promised yourself. It's only when he's gone that you see him quite clearly – quite a different person, quite independent of all your effort. All that work, and for nothing.' She rocked her whisky lovingly. 'Not that I ever did the other.'

'The *other*?' Vanessa gave the word a sinister emphasis.

'Under the bed.'

Matthew returned from the kitchen and hovered in the doorway with the ice bucket, his big ambling body made fragile by uncertainty, his eyes innocent and anxious to please. Vanessa's heart mushroomed with love. He came to sit beside her and plunked two cubes into her drink. He watched her while she tasted it. 'All right, darling?' 'Perfect,' she said, transferring the adjective to his person with her eyes. His expression sharpened for an instant when Margaret threw back her head and dropped the entire measure of whiskey down her throat like a frog swallowing a fly. 'I think we ought to eat now,' he said, and Vanessa thought he was right so she left her drink and led them through to the dining room.

The table looked like a holy grotto. The melons were shallow rock pools in the light of two purple candles and a tuft of pious little purple flowers nested in a brandy glass. Each fresh venue imposed its own inhibitions and they became strangers again to scoop their fruit. When Vanessa brought the meat and vegetables from the kitchen Matthew gave her a private lover's smile and brought the purple flowers to his nose. They were hybrids – 'Natureless as a model's armpits', as Margaret predicted. He put them back and gave his attention to the food.

The pork had been transferred to a Provençal casserole and the tomatoes rested on a china dish that was painted with green flowers. Buttered potatoes rose in a glossy mound like a Croque-en-bouche from a platter of thick wood. Matthew was leaning forward. His hands hung between his knees. His eyes were round with longing. 'Poor lamb,' Margaret whispered. It was a tiny sound but it almost caused Vanessa to drop a dish. Matthew had not heard at all. He was hungry. He wanted his dinner. 'Look at him.' Margaret smiled into Vanessa's shocked face. 'They're all our children, men. Small fry. You have to get used to that. It can be a bother when you're young and have been brought up to expect that power and wisdom is a little bulge in a person's trousers. It's an unreliable thing on which to found an empire. Most men would rather have something really useful under their belt, like a torch or a penknife. It's women who have the power. Nobody expects them to do anything and look how much they do. They can never be wrong, only wronged.'

Vanessa was concerned that the food might be cold. She began to spoon it on to plates while Matthew splashed purple wine into glasses. She need not have worried. Matthew was too hungry to notice and Margaret was definitely tight. When Vanessa passed the dish of tomatoes she extinguished her ciga-rette on it and handed it back. She herself was unable to eat. She felt ill with shame at something Margaret had said about wronged women. 'Have you been wronged?' she pleaded. 'Oh, yes,' Margaret agreed eagerly. Vanessa shook her head in anguished query. 'And so have you, my dear,' Margaret went on, eating a potato from her fingers. 'Oh, not by the divorce, flower. Oh, no. It's a great freedom to be released from the responsibility of a man. I've got myself a job.' She looked at Matthew. He was twirling a glass of wine in the candlelight, assessing its clarity. 'And a fella.' She went on watching him. He pursed his mouth and fished with the end of his fork for a speck of something in his glass. 'He fancies me. He doesn't look at me with sympathy and tell me I'm tired.' Matthew cornered the foreign body and withdrew it with triumph. He grounded it on a napkin. Margaret's forehead puckered in irritation. She looked away from him and became vague, seeming to forget the route of her thoughts.

'It's this . . .' She made a theatrical gesture with her hands over the dinner. 'We ought never to have met. Don't you see, my dear, we've both lost our freedom. I'll feel responsible for you because you're so young and you for me, because I'm not. It was kind of you to insist on my coming here but it was wrong.'

'But I . . .' Across the table Matthew was nodding at her like a priest. She assembled the dirty dishes cautiously and carried them to the kitchen. Matthew followed jauntily carrying a pepper pot. 'Let's have some of your marvellous coffee,' he cried out. 'For Christ's sake make it strong,' he hissed when they were alone.

Two bottles of wine had been emptied. They picked the strawberries from intoxicating broth with their fingers while the percolator was burping. Matthew talked to Margaret about money. He wanted to know if she had coped with her tax forms and had she been robbed by the chancer she brought in to do the drains. Margaret answered soberly and smoked cigarettes in rapid succession.

They spoke about children. Vanessa said she wanted a child and Matthew frowned. Margaret said it would make him young again and he smiled. Margaret explained that she had never wanted children but still expected to be stricken by womb panic at thirty-nine when every ball would seem a crystal ball. Matthew frowned. He rose from the table and padded to the corner where he fiddled with some machinery. A flood of music rose from a teak cabinet. He sat with his wives. They raised eyes of shiny emotion to him, blurred in the maudlin glow of the candles and it tore at his heart to think that there was only one of him. The music of Schubert had begun upon a single piano as a skipping stream. It had risen to a flood, swirling above their heads, carrying them in its sweetness. Languid and submissive they curved about the table, heads almost touching in the shivering halo of light. No word was spoken until the music found its end. Matthew sprang lightly to his feet, a faint smile touching the corners of his mouth. He rescued the coffee pot and spouted fragrant blackness into two cups. 'None for me,' he exclaimed cheerily. 'For Christ's sake get some into her,' he whispered too loudly, eyeing Margaret, as though it was a decisive move in an important game of cards.

He left them with their coffee to go to the bathroom. The women watched each other over the rim of their cups. 'You're not what I expected,' Vanessa said. 'No,' Margaret said. 'I'm not the person you would picture as Matthew's wife. I tried to be. When I was young I tried. He kept moving the rung up higher. I'm not a good athlete.'

'He's changed,' Vanessa protested. 'He's so good with me. So gentle. '

'Once he did an inventory of all the items in cupboards,' Margaret said. 'He made out little lists and pasted them on the doors of presses. When things ran out he marked a red tick against the item on the list. I felt those red marks as if they had been put on my body with a stick. Whenever I gave myself a drink he would rearrange the bottles afterwards and polish the glasses.'

'The silver spoons?' Vanessa whispered.

'He placed them on a bed of black velvet, like a jeweller's display. It showed up the shine, he said. What he meant was, it emphasised the tarnish. I polished them to please him. "Look!" I said. "It took all day." He threw a hand over his mouth. "Ruined," he said. "You've scratched them all. They're utterly ruined."'

She looked up abruptly. 'You're not happy, are you dear?' Vanessa thought about it. It had not occurred to her that this sodden feeling was unhappiness. She knew that it was love. She had imagined it was happiness. 'It's all right,' Margaret said. 'You don't get extra points for being happy. Happiness is hell, you know. I've been through that too. You're on a peak, looking into the jaws of hell. It's the ultimate despair. '

He returned from the lavatory looking as if he had been on a fortnight's holiday. His hair was full of vigour and he rubbed his hands together, smiling at the women as if he was going to make a meal of them. 'It's time we got you home,' he beamed at Margaret. 'It's all right,' she said. 'I'll get a taxi.' 'I'll drive you,' he said. 'Vanessa likes me out from under her feet when she's doing the dishes. She insists.' Across the debris of their meal Margaret threw her the ghost of a mischievous glance but she rose from the table quite steadily and went with him like a lamb.

When he got back an hour later the room had gone cold and was wrapped about in its own silence. Vanessa sat on a hard chair nursing the dregs of someone's brandy. He patrolled the room to assess its mood and offered it a chuckle. 'I expect you need that,' he indicated her drink. 'It's been quite an evening.' 'I don't need it,' she said quietly. 'I like it.' 'She's gone to pieces, poor thing,' he said cheerfully. 'But I think the evening did her good.' Vanessa said nothing. He began to be perturbed. 'You're tired,' he diagnosed. 'You've been working hard.'

'Yes,' she said. It had been hard work unpacking all her clothes in an hour and finding homes for them. She had had to dispossess two of his older suits of hangers and put his cashmere sweaters in the linen press. The lists had been stuck up with glue. It needed boiling water and a scrubbing brush to obliterate them. 'All in a good cause,' he said faintly, coming over to put a kiss on her pale forehead. 'Yes,' she said.

He unlaced her fingers from the brandy glass and stepped merrily into the kitchen. He stopped. She counted seconds of silence and predicted exactly the moment when her glass would reach the counter with a tiny note of query.

'It would appear,' he called out, innocently bewildered, 'that the dishes have not been washed.'

As always, he was right.

〜〰〜

Bad-Natured Dog

❧‿◦

The gate was locked and there was a sign saying *bad-natured dog*. There was no bell. She stepped through a gap in the hedge and her large foot mashed a frilly little border of petunias. When she was in the garden she looked up and was momentarily disturbed to see a yellow sponge, squeezed out, moving behind the window, as if someone was washing the glass. The sponge was attached to a blue smocked shirt. It was Levingston, his head waving in bewildered disappointment. He had been spying at the window and thought the person rattling the gate was someone else.

She called out. 'Hi! I'm Nellie Fraser. We talked on the phone.' He stayed where he was, watching her behind the wavy glass. She was tall. She had a mass of brown hair in which there were little sprigs of yellow. She wore pink shorts and a white Indian cotton blouse and even at that distance he could see the brown dots dancing underneath like the bouncing ball that helped you keep time at a sing-along (but that was long ago).

At first the name meant nothing for he was confused by irritation. All the young people who loved the telephone grew accustomed to distant communication and could not be bothered to close even the smallest gap in order to lower their voices. They shouted at you through their noses. He saw that the black shoulder bag she carried was a recording machine. He remembered. She was Nellie Fraser. She was nineteen and she was coming for a scoop.

He made tea while she talked about herself. 'Good thing you don't go into the city,' she shouted from the next room. 'It's a hell of a journey on the train. Five hours, wow. The Orient Express without champagne.' A flurry of innocent laughter came at him like a scarf in the wind. He smiled. She was a pretty thing. 'I know you don't go into the city. *And* I know there isn't a dog. I read it in *The Times*. I've been boning up on you. You haven't given an interview in twenty years. I consider this an honour, you know. I think . . .' she paused to make sure he was listening – 'that you are the greatest writer living today.'

With a spoon in one hand, he cowered: that all of his life's work, the good and the bad, the soaring and the waning, the receding tide that made such beguiling clatter over the shingle of a life's experience, should be delivered over to the unqualified admiration of a big girl of nineteen. He remembered one of the reasons why he had stopped giving interviews.

He had not meant to give this one. When she offered her name on the telephone he thought it was someone else. His hearing was not good any more. He mistook the name. 'Do come up,' he had said with enthusiasm. 'Come as soon as you like.' She told him then about the magazine, the scoop, her big break. He could not put her off without sounding foolish. In the interval between her call and her arrival, he once more foxed himself and put a different name in his diary. Watching her arrival through the window, he had been astonished to note that she was wearing shorts. That was just a moment. It came clear in his head very quickly.

He brought through the tray of tea and saw that she had set up her tape recorder and, as if she trusted the device no more than he did, she had a small notebook balanced on her bare knee.

'Right-o,' he said, turning his back on her to pour the tea. 'Fire away. '

There was a click as she turned on the thing. 'Jasper Levingston,' she said severely. 'You are one of the greatest writers of the century. You are seventy-eight.' She sounded like a policeman about to serve a summons. 'What has been the major influence on your work over three-quarters of a century?'

He resisted an urge to chuckle. 'She thinks I started writing when I was three.' He managed to present her with a solemn face and a cup of weak tea. 'Love!' He said.

'Love?' Her amazed voice meandered over several syllables as if he had said bootlaces or bananas. She snapped off the recording machine.

'Come on, Mr Levingston, that's a load of crap, ' she said. 'That's the sort of thing pop singers say. Just talk the way you write, with plenty of guts. The magazine is punchy, you know.'

He was drinking his tea. He wished he had brought out a nice biscuit to go with it. The girl, so far as he could tell, had brought nothing. 'My father,' he said, 'did a bit of acting. When he grew old he spent all his time showing off his photographs and little cuttings from the newspapers. Once he acted with Harry Turtle. That meant a lot to him. He used to tell everyone about that. I've never told anyone before.'

'God,' Nellie said. 'Fantastic.' She had furtively switched on the machine again. 'Who was Harry Turtle?'

'I don't know,' Levingston said. 'Father married late. He was my age when I was fourteen, and he was ill. Mother was busy and she used to send me in to sit with him. It was very boring; the tiny paragraphs snipped from provincial newspapers, the rust-coloured photographs – and Harry Turtle.'

'Yeah, well,' Nellie said. 'Old people.' And she looked embarrassed. 'I have a list of questions. Martha in *Sheep's Head* and Georgina in *Woodcut* experience difficulty in climaxing with their men. Is this reverberative of your own experience or is it a symbol for the sexual repression of a generation of women?'

'One day an amazing thing happened. A man called. He was from the radio and did a sort of looking-back thing once a week. He wanted to put father on the radio. After he had gone, father went into a kind of trance. He sat up in bed clutching his photographs with such a smile on his face. He still told the same stories, but now he prefaced them with: "As I was saying on the radio . . ." To mother he would say: "Are we on yet, mother?" and she would give him the date once more. When it was time for the broadcast mother brought an enamel basin into the bedroom and put it on the locker by his bed. She set the wireless beside this and put the headphones in the basin. Only one person could listen on the head-phones but if you put them in a basin or a bucket and put your head down, the noise came up at you.

'We were all crouched around the radio and father had my hand in a terrible grip. I was fourteen, an immortal. Father was not content to share his moment. He was sparring with me on my level of dreaming. "Harry Turtle," he said, "acted with me, but he was never on the radio." I turned on him furiously. I could see Harry Turtle forever gesticulating on the path of my life. If I could lay hands on him I would break his bones into sticks and fling them on the fire. "Pox and farts to Harry Turtle," I said. I snatched my hand away and ran from the house.'

He lifted his cup to his mouth but the tea did not go in. It made a pink puddle on the rim of his lip and he sucked several times to blot it away. His eyes were mad with the vividness of remembering.

'I can still recall the feeling I had that day. I felt utterly damned and free. I had no money. I walked into town with my hands in my pockets. There was a motor show-room in the town and I wanted to look at a navy blue open Wolsley that was on display.

'When I got to the street it was filled with the music of a dance band and there were crowds of people about the door of the showroom. A man and a girl danced out into the street in their overcoats. I started to run. It was the most exciting moment of my life. "What is it? What's happening?" I shouted to people who were as full of friendship as if it was New Year's Eve. And a girl, a pretty girl, who was about seventeen and had a fur collar on her coat turned to me with laughing eyes and said: "It's a loudspeaker. It's the first demonstration of the loudspeaker. Isn't it wonderful?" "Wonderful," I shouted. We kept smiling at each other for four or five seconds. She had a very full mouth and I could see the shining pink skin of its inside. I have never responded to anyone so wholly in my life.'

The girl had a petulant look, her jaw stuck out, her bare legs spread, like a child left sitting too long on its pot. 'It just came into my head,' he said. Her notebook was empty. 'You said something about love,' she remembered.

'Yes.'

There was silence until Nellie Fraser could not endure it, and said: 'Love is all shit. It's the universal cop-out. "I lived for love", "I died for love". Balls! I never met a man who didn't have sex on his mind when he talked about love but the pigshit hypocrites won't even admit it. I thought you'd be different, you know.' She shook her pencil at him reproachfully. 'You'd like to go to bed with me, wouldn't you?'

He approximated a wry look of chivalry.

'Aw, come on. Wouldn't you?'

Extraordinary. The notion had not crossed his head. When he had seen the brown dots of her nipples dancing beneath her blouse the thing he thought was that young people never felt the cold. The remembrance of young girls' bodies still nested in his limbs as did the feeling of sitting in the top of a tree when he was a boy of six or seven but he had not, in recent years, entertained either idea in any practical fashion.

What struck him now was the extraordinary notion of an unpredicted thing; a break in the routine of naps and cups of tea, snatches of music, regulated hours of dullness at his type-writer. It was a gift. 'Yes,' he said to Nellie Fraser, 'I would.'

She smiled. It seemed to him the first time she had looked youthful and happy and he grinned back at her. She laughed. 'That's settled then. I won't have to stay in that shitty hotel.'

Instantly he felt depressed. There was the whole day to use up. He ought not to have been so reckless. 'I shall have to work for several hours,' he said cunningly. 'That's all right, Jasper,' she said. His eyebrows curled up in alarm. She had used his first name. He thought it an appalling lack of form. 'I would ask you to dinner, but there are only frozen vegetables,' he said. 'I have become a vegetarian.' She was such a big meaty girl that he thought this must strike a substantial blow.

Instead she seemed enormously pleased and had begun writing in her notebook. 'Now that's really something,' she said. 'I guess you've given up meat for humanitarian reasons.'

'No,' he said, 'no.' But she was busy writing down what she had said and she did not hear him.

He had, in fact, given up meat because of meanness. He was horrified by the price of it in the shops. He remembered when steak was two shillings a pound. When he went out to dinner with friends who were paying he always had a nice fillet of steak or a sole.

She asked him about his work. 'Oh,' he moaned. It was the thing he dreaded. He had read once that women in childbirth had bouts of unconsciousness between pains and that when it was over they slept and awoke happy and he thought it was like being a writer; the boredom, the doubt, the waste of vigour that were forgotten once the book was published; the playfulness with which one began to hash about with a fresh plot.

He was being sent back to retrieve it all. It bore in on him like the aches of old age; the meanness of heart and the poorness of pocket; the clamouring of too many characters across one's clear path of vision; insignificant twerps like Harry Turtle, dancing in one's light, swelling the brain with dull rage so that in desperation one flung aside the clogged imagination and turned to real life.

It became, after all, the dry and childish art of the collector, meticulously pinning down human beings, causing them no damage but preserving forever the damage they had done to themselves so that one's whole life and all the people in it, was pressed out, bloodless on the page, and all the love was betrayed.

'I do very little work nowadays,' he said. 'I can't remember. It was a hard slog. There is no such thing as inspiration, except as a pleasurable form of self-abuse, reputed to lead to insanity and blindness.' He was tickled that she wrote this down. It was from one of his books. He began a game then, answering all her questions with passages from his novels. Although his memory was defective in regard to dates and peoples' names, he

could read his novels from his head with ease. She wrote everything down. She had difficulty keeping up with him. It gave
him a wicked sense of glee. He continued until the veins in her
wrist bulged and then he smiled a kindly old man's smile and
said: 'I must leave you now, my dear. Time for my day's quota
of words.'

'Of course,' she said, exhausted.

He crept into his study and sat rigidly at his desk. He took
a flask from a drawer and drank deeply of its alcoholic content.
Then, when ten minutes had passed and he was certain that she
was not going to burst in on him to administer his treat, he
sank down on to the day bed under a woolly rug and fell fast
asleep.

He woke to the sound of music and a smell of woodsmoke
and spices. She had lit the fire and switched on the radio. She
had done some sort of Mexican thing with his frozen food. He
was disappointed because he liked the look of the separate
mounds of yellow and green, corn and carrots and sprouts and
beans. He brought wine to where she was sitting cross-legged
on the floor by the fire. She gleamed healthily in the firelight.
He sat in a chair and munched the horrible food while she
talked about herself. She seemed to have finished with the
interview, which was a relief. She brought him the treasures of
her little life. It was like examining a collection of sea-shells.
She was very fresh and boring. She drank a lot of wine and
stretched like a cat. His eye narrowed to the eye of the hunter.
He reconnoitred his physical points and was relieved that his
hair, though fluffy, covered his head and that the folds of his
face were not gaunt or peevish. When it was time for bed he
stood up and patted her on the head. She smiled, staring into
the flaky fire. He told her where she could find his bedroom
and then, watching the clean curve of her brow, her peaceful
eyebrows, he said: 'There are three other bedrooms. Feel
free . . .'

He brought a bottle of good wine to his room and two
fresh glasses. He put a silk coverlet on the bed, and arranged
genial lighting from some little lamps. He patted his chops
with some scent stuff from a bottle. He caught sight of his

weary face in a mirror and it made him laugh: 'Ha! Old blighter!' All the same he removed his warm pyjamas from under the pillow and hid them and clambered, instead, into a chilly pair of silk pyjamas which had never been used. He got into bed and lay with his hands clasped behind his head in the pose of a thinker. In a moment or two, this arrangement seized his limbs so he curled himself up into a brioche and his eyelids clamped down like bottle caps.

'Hi! I was doing the dishes.' The room exploded into light and Levingston awoke with a snort. There was someone in his room. An anchor of sleep swept him down. Young whatsit? 'Could you possibly turn off that light?' he begged.

She came and sat on the side of the bed. She reached out her fingers and swept back his hair and then lightly dipped a finger in the cleft of his chin. She smiled at him impishly. Young girls. Young girls. Slowly he put out a hand and, scarcely touching, traced the shadow of her breasts behind her blouse. Young girls.

'Clothes,' she said, 'are such a drag. Long live the zipless fuck.' She stood up abruptly. She pulled off her blouse and dropped it on the floor. Her skin had an impervious sheen, like a modern wipeclean surface. She was tanned all over, even her breasts, to the colour of cornflakes. It was not how he remembered the skin of a girl. He remembered the tremendous discovery of breasts beneath a blouse, the softest most beautiful flower, magnolia pale, silken; the merest touch of a finger must bruise, a careless fingernail, crush like a rose petal. No, not for fingers — only for lips. White dome blushing to the ennobled conqueror. It was how it was. Oh, God, remember, the piety of lust.

He poured out two glasses of wine and tried to remember the things he used to say. 'Oh, God,' was all he could think of. The girl bounced into bed on top of him. She made him spill a bit of the wine. He handed her a trembling glassful and she knocked it back, giggling. 'Here's to greatness,' she said. She put her wine-filled tongue into his mouth. The thrust of it was like a pickle. Her arm went beneath the blankets. The big hand descended heartily.

He put away his wine with regret and rolled on top of her. He desired to trace with his mouth the ignorant shape of her lips, but her jaws were open like a cave. He tried to pretend that she was a woman, that their ages had been divided and shared and they enjoyed the forgiving passions of middle age but she would not stop talking and her sharp little teeth champed on his tongue. 'You're a very attractive man. I've always wanted to go to bed with you as long as I can remember. Don't worry, baby.' Her hands went to his head. They felt beneath his hair the dry skin, the veins knotted by thought and they shrank away. They clawed irritably at his back and then sank with hopeless impatience to his loins.

Her fingers commenced some very efficient routine that reminded him, with a nostalgic pang, of the bursts of energy he used to take out on his typewriter very late at night.

He was passive in her hands, tired, very tired. He was amused by the optimism of her years, her determination to turn him into something else. 'It's all right,' she murmured. 'It's okay. Relax. You're beautiful.'

Ridiculous, really, the young could never accept anything. Ridiculous. He began to laugh. Put it down to tiredness. She tickled and kneaded and pulled patiently. His laugh came out like a slow, repetitive creak.

The big, useful hands froze. 'Stop that,' she said, furious. He withdrew himself gently. He wrapped his pyjamas around him comfortably and then put out a hand to pat her poor brown shoulder. She shrugged him away. 'You don't care,' she accused.

'At my age . . .' he defended mildly.

'Don't bullshit me,' she snapped.

'My dear,' he said. 'It doesn't matter. Not at all.'

Her voice tore out: 'I only went to bed with you because I didn't want to hurt your feelings. But you don't have any feelings. At least I can say I found the real Jasper Levingston. Readers, I slept with him. I think you're a disgusting old man. I shall never be able to read your books again.'

She hurtled to the other side of the bed and sighed long and tragically. After another sigh, less tragic, she was fast asleep.

About a week after her departure (he had to remind her to

take her recording machine) the telephone rang. 'It's Helen,' said the voice from the wire. 'Helen?' he enquired cautiously. 'Do come up,' he said with enthusiasm. 'Come as soon as you like.' He hung up and went to write her name in his diary. He was glad to know that he was not totally befuddled. Helen always came at this time of year. She was a woman of habit.

He was standing by the window, his head bobbing anxiously behind the glass as he waited for his friend. 'Aha!' he cried out with glee. A small, stout woman was beating her way down the track. Her right arm sagged with a basket of things. She came to the gate and rattled.

'I thought you weren't going to come,' he said, when he had brought her into the house and was unwrapping, one by one, the treats she had brought for him to eat.

'I always come,' she said.

'I know,' he said. 'I got confused.'

'It's our anniversary,' she said.

'I'm sorry.'

She took his hand. 'My dear,' she said. 'It doesn't matter.'

He went to hunt for her favourite record and found that it was on the turntable where he had placed it a week ago in anticipation of her call. He devoured her delicious presents while she told him about her year, dripping ash everywhere from the cigarette she kept clenched in the corner of her mouth. She bred little dogs, which he loathed. She had been committed to dogs even before they had fallen in love, thirty years earlier. She took the cigarette from her mouth for a grudging moment to kiss him, then put it back again. 'I'm very fond of you, you know,' she said; 'though I can't bear that face you get when you're thinking, that long face.' He said: 'We should have married. We only see each other once a year, now.'

'No,' she said firmly. 'At my age I need something to look forward to.'

How wise she was, how nice. After she had been with him for a day, he always began to be irritated but then she had to get back to her dogs again and as soon as she was gone he started to miss her, and then to look forward to her return.

He waited patiently for her to finish her cigarettes and her brandy and then led her out of her ash-scattered patch and to bed.

'Ah, Helen,' he said. 'Ah, Helen.' When her arms went around him he did not feel that he was holding another person in his arms, merely that he was comfortably fleshed, that his bones no longer poked out.

Her wry mouth patted his lips repeatedly with a 'tut-tutting' sound, breathing sadness, breathing cigarette smoke, breathing forgiveness for the bastard he was that he had not married her thirty years ago when she loved him so much.

She never read any of his books; just as well, since she was in several of them. She had no interest in his work. It was him she loved. He had challenged her with the smallness of his heart but she considered it quite good enough for her. Lately he found himself thinking about her more and more. When she was in his arms he thought she was the good side of himself that he had been searching for all his life and he was ambitious, for a time, to become a part of her. 'Ah, Helen.'

He made it last as long as possible, barely moving, hoarding the comfort, until he cried out with relief, not that he could still be aroused but that he could still be loved.

'Ha!' Helen said. 'You're a lively old devil.'

He had her held against his chest like a hot water bottle. 'I was thinking,' he said, 'about a thing we used to have when we were boys. It was a bun made of rubber. It looked like a nice bun but when you tried to eat it, it was made of rubber. It was a trick.'

'I thought men were supposed to think of cricket,' she said sleepily. 'That's a bad sign, returning to childhood.'

It wasn't his childhood. It was the girl. He had a sudden picture of her breasts, like big brown buns, as healthy and plain as knees; the determination in her hands, pulling and rubbing like a woman doing her washing on a rock. The approach was so lacking in stealth and sequence that he forgot what he was meant to do.

What did one do with a child who was old beyond illusion?

Laugh to make her angry? Prance like Harry Turtle in her cold light.

'At least,' he thought peevishly, as he fell asleep in Helen's sheltering arms; 'in our day we knew about love.'

Appearances

The widow gave my mother a pair of boots. They were biscuit-coloured with little pointy toes darkened with polish. The heels were shaped like an apple core and gave the feet a rising curve that made me think of the neck of a pony. 'They're kid boots,' my mother said, shocked. The widow nodded. She had clutched them to her breast like infants. She handed them across. They were set in the centre of the table and the two women watched them with sadness. 'You're too good,' my mother said, confused. 'They're too good.' 'Just so they get some use,' the widow said. Her eyes found me under the table and she gave me a long look like Christ crucified, so forgiving that I had to suck my lips in over my teeth. She stood up painfully and skushed away in her black sandals.

'She was very beautiful,' my mother said. The boots still held the centre of the table, a monument to her beauty. We had arranged the tea things around them. 'Like a young Indian girl, ebony hair braided in plaits, skin the colour of honey.'

She met her husband at the post-box. They were posting letters to other people who were forgotten in that instant. Ten years later when she was thirty, he stepped in front of a motor car and turned her into a widow. She buried her beauty with him. She took a lodger in the upstairs room and sold paraffin from a shed at the end of the garden leading to the lane.

A frond of rhubarb jam dangled through a hole in my toast. I sucked it through from underneath. I had heard the story before. Each time the widow brought us an instalment of her past, mother repeated it as though it was her task to tend the memories. All I had to do was listen but I did so with a face bulging with disbelief. The widow was not beautiful. Her skin was grey. She was stooped and seamed with sadness. All women were sad but some had the toughened crusts of good old times built into them. It gave them a sense of privilege. The widow's sadness was a mildew that overgrew and enclosed her.

Her young husband took her to France on a boat. They saw the Eiffel Tower and drank wine at tables in the street. He bought her new boots, kid. Nothing was too good for her.

'Put them on. Put them on, let's see!' Mother chuckled as if she had suggested something wicked. We were both caught up in glee. I tore off my own boots with the laces still tied and flung them anywhere. The soles flapped and gaped like corner boys as they sailed across the floor. 'They're sieves! You poor daisy!' mother lamented. We doubled up with laughter.

I was eleven, nearly twelve. My legs were no longer rigid stalks of sinew. When I stretched them out one by one to pull on the boots my mother peered and frowned on their new curve and sheen. They had become miraculously fleshed and golden as a cake does in the oven. I pulled on the boots and she did the buttons. It took a long time and made us serious again. I was a big child. My feet almost filled out the dainty toes. 'Now walk,' she said. I levered myself down from the chair and took a few blunted steps – a hoofed animal. I began to giggle. Mother sighed. 'It's a shame, but they'll have to do.' I tottered over to her and stopped. 'I'll take them off now.' She did not look at me. 'No. Keep them on. You've got to get used to them.'

She started to clear the table, clattering the dishes as if I had done something to annoy her. She would not look at me. 'Your boots are in tatters,' she accused. 'You have me disgraced among the neighbours.'

Disgrace was a shameful word. To be poor was the greatest disgrace of all. My father had left us when I was four although mother always said he was working abroad. He sent us a little money now and then. Spread very thinly, it was made to do. Close to the top of our meagre shopping list came

Appearances. Mother kept a tablet of Pears soap in a tin in the hot press. I could always tell when visitors were coming because I was sent to the press to bring the soap to the bathroom. I can still remember the exact feel and smell, its tortoise-shell transparency, coming out of a nest of cellophane in a butterscotch tin. Sometimes it was thin and had to be prised off with expertise like a new scab. In the end it became a golden monacle which I was allowed to take to my bath, viewing through a sepia haze the coal fire in front of which the metal tub was placed, before going to bed smelling of visitors' hands.

On the kitchen press, beside the china dog with glass eyes, the soap jar was kept. It was where mother saved up coins for a fresh tablet, knowing it was one of the few things that mattered; knowing, like everyone else, that poor people used cake soap.

She was strong and good. She was also stubborn. There were times, as now, when nothing one might say would make sense. Children had appearances to keep up, too. It was not the sort of thing one could explain to an adult. Insignificance was our aspiration. Conformity was all, the trappings of womanhood taboo. High heels were pantomime farce. They belonged to another world that did not incorporate walking, skipping, running, scuffing, climbing. Those delicate leather points had nothing to do with my own square and practical feet. It was hopeless to imagine that I could prance into school like a centaur and not be made to suffer. I would not wear them, never. I would bring my own boots in a bag and change in the park, hide the kid boots in a bush. I caught my mother's patient glance. She was sitting at the table again, very still, hands folded like flower petals. Her hands were not like flower petals but the evening sun was suddenly a flurry of pink tissue paper which lit up the frizzy gold of her hair and her pale, unhappy mouth, rose-tipped her fingers.

She smiled on my scowling rage with such pure affection and amusement that for a moment she looked lovely and I worshipped her. For a moment. I smiled, regretted it, became confused and clumped out of the room and off to bed like a pig on a pogo stick.

School was two miles from where I lived and I was given twopence each day for the tram. In the morning I walked to school and saved a penny for an Eccles cake for The Owl. Walking was no hardship. Most of the girls walked. We did not stride out with unhappy stoicism as people do today, snorting up the air as if it was a ball of string to be sucked up the nostrils in a single, tortuous breath for the good of their health. We stalked and ambled like cats, sniffing at the air without particularly taking it in, scenting incident on the wind. Girls collected girls as they streeled along. There was no organised pattern but it was not aimless. Navy blue arms intertwined. Heads bowed, profiles blurred. The girls stamped along.

'Got anything to eat?'

'Me lunch. Lay off.'

'Cheese?'

'Jam.'

'Keep them.'

'Spell "miscellaneous."'

'M-i-s-s . . .'

'That's the easy one. Gilhawley'll kill you.'

'She can't kill me.'

'No.'

'She can't kill me. She can't kill me. She can't kill me.'

'What have you got on your cheeks?'

'Nothing. What's the stuff on your eyes?'

'Nothing.'

'Are they there yet?'

'I don't know. I won't look.'

'Neither will I.'

'They're there.'

'Fools.'

'Ignoramusses.'

Two unhappy schoolboys now trotted behind. On no account would they be permitted to walk beside us for we had heard that one could become pregnant that way. We spoke to them only in insults. They did not speak to us at all. Each group of girls had a similar colony of misery bringing up the rear. They were our boyfriends.

In spite of frequent threats to our lives from the homicidal Miss Gilhawley and other unpredictable adults, I can scarcely ever remember waking with anything other than happy anticipation. There were exceptions. The morning I opened my eyes to the hateful little glittering toes of the boots was one. It took me twenty minutes to do the buttons. My fingers shook with ire. I limped downstairs and understood that there was no hope of walking to school. I would have to face The Owl without an offering.

On the tram I felt deformed with misery. The Owl had not spoken to me, had not pulled my hair. When I boarded the bus he had given my legs a shocked look, glanced at my face in angry query, but I would not look at him. I slid into a seat and stared out the window. Several times I could feel his gaze on my stupid boots and on my face as if he felt I owed him an explanation. There was nothing to say. I could not let my mother down by making him understand that we were poor. He would have to believe that I had grown mad and indifferent.

When I stepped from the platform in geriatric fashion at my stop he was still watching me that way. I wanted to race away and hide my shame. I could only mince like a Chinese lady, feeling the critical tawny eyes on my back as the tram clanged off down the street. There was a dead cat flung inside the school gates and I kicked its jammy-looking corpse with one polished toe from Paris.

The Owl was my name for our tram conductor. He was a little dark man in early middle age with strange orangey eyes and a long nose and a small, cheery mouth. In spite of liberal oiling, his black hair sprang into hundreds of small curls that resembled clusters of blackcurrants. His real name was Herbert. He did not know my name. He called me his pigeon, his herring, his little hen. The names caused a queer nervous chill in the pit of my stomach, a contradictory boiling flush on my face. I wanted to be crushed in his arms – and more – a nameless something, not imagined, deeply known. He was my Owl. Oh, how I loved him. My mind raced about miserably while my eye slumped on a page of a history book which impersonally mated myth and fact and celebrated the deaths of millions.

'Napoleonic Wars! You, Miss! You with the boots! Dates?' I had a white shirt, a wine tie and a navy gymslip. I had navy stockings and navy knickers, but boots were what Miss Gilhawley specified.

Boots were what identified me from thirty-four other girls in the class. My feet hurt, my heart hurt. I lifted hurt eyes to the teacher but she saw only the non-absorbent eyes of an idler. 'Vain and idle woman,' she hissed. 'You are the bane of my life.' I hid in the toilets during lunch, ate my brawn and biscuits in the smelly dark. When school ended I fled as fast as my crippled heels allowed, praying that I might be on the tram and on my unhappy journey home before the girls came. At the gate I tripped on the cat's corpse and landed with that peculiar flying sprawl so familiar in childhood. Blood and gravel flourished on my knees and palms. A dump of girls circled over my scattered body. They were not my friends but an opposing group, big and evil. 'She's wearing women's boots! She's wearing women's boots. Find her a husband! Put them to bed! Give her a baby!' they chanted. My two best friends hung back. They were embarrassed by my appearance and afraid of the tough girls. I glared up at their big, unkind faces, their lumpy bosoms under gymslips, their ugly knees. My hands scrabbled for some object of retaliation – and clutched. I got on my feet. I swung out in a wide arc with the dead cat, holding on to its tail, exhilarated at my perfect aim as the little, fanged, matted jaw clouted each girl's face into expressions of dumb horror.

'They're *not* women's boots,' I panted. 'They're *kid* boots!'

The pleasure of victory prepared me to withstand The Owl's indifference on the tram. He had looked at me with some curiosity when I clambered on board, muddy and bloodied in my high heels. He had glanced expectantly at my right hand to see if it guarded the baker's bag which carried his customary afternoon treat. There was no bag, no Eccles cake. He turned away and went down the aisle jingling change in his fist. I limped to a seat and concentrated on cleaning the worst of the gore from my skin with a hankie.

'Here, let me help.' A low voice close to my ear. The tram was almost empty and The Owl had settled himself on the

edge of the seat opposite. He licked a rather crumpled handkerchief and began to dab at my knees. He did it with
tenderness. I could only stare. His face looked different.
Normally his eyes crinkled at the corners. They were wide
open now, peering over my dirty knees and troublesome boots
as though he had mislaid something and expected to find it
concealed amidst the blood and endless buttons. 'I do like your
boots,' he said softly. 'Very dainty they are.' He put his handkerchief in his pocket and scrubbed his hands together,
workmanlike. 'Bloody kids,' he grumbled. 'They grow up that
fast.'

When some people got on the tram he stood up very
straight and moved away so briskly that I was left to wonder if
I had imagined his look. He had liked my boots, though, very
dainty. No one had ever called me dainty. My elongated toes
pointed the way to a breathtaking world of enchantments and
vanities. If I could have danced I would have danced.

Later, when I was swinging on the platform as we drew
near to my stop The Owl materialised once more. 'What age
are you?' he breathed against my hair. 'Thirteen.' 'Good child,'
he said. 'Quite the young lady, very lovely.' He asked me if I
ever took the air in the park. 'I go every Saturday,' I said rapidly.
Having already lied about my age, I saw no advantage in con-
fessing that I passed most Saturday afternoons in the cinema,
spending the money I earned in the morning, lighting fires and
stoves for the Jews. The boys sat in a row behind us and passed
sweets to us over our shoulders.

'I could meet you there, at the pond,' he murmured. 'There's
something I want to show you.' I nodded. The hammering of
my heart made me feel sick. 'Good child,' he said. The pavement was still moving towards me when I jumped. I had to do
a little skitter like a music hall turn to keep my balance.

Mother noticed my cut hands and knees. She made a rueful
little mouth of sympathy. 'Had a good day?' she said. I nodded.
I still could not speak. She looked as if she might say more but
instead she came to me and pressed my head against her breast,
stroking my hair fiercely. 'Good child,' she said.

I was going to have a baby. The thought made me feel

important. I would have to take the belt off my school tunic and bring a pint of milk to the classroom for my lunch. If the girls pasted me I would have a miscarriage. There would be buckets of blood on the school steps. I sat in the pokey grass at the edge of the pond and scraped sugar grains from the top of an Eccles cake with my teeth. In a bag tucked into the lap of my yellow frock was another cake. That was for The Owl. The cakes had been paid for by the Jews. I got twopence for lighting their fire and putting a match to the jets on the gas cooker. Mrs Wolfson and her two daughters, Gilda and Tilly, had forsworn housework on Saturdays. The girls locked their plump fingers under their breasts and sang duets, easing their brown eyes and dimpled faces into mists of love while they smiled at their father who was very small.

Mrs Wolfson accompanied on the piano. She kept a glass of wine on top of the instrument for her refreshment. She wore a long silk dress the colour of wine and a garland of black feathers round her neck. Her dress was cut low at the front to show breasts which rose evenly like successful loaves. The drawing-room was a treasure trove. Each piece of furniture was veiled with lace like a bride. There were glass lamps and silk cushions and little crystal dishes of sweets. After my work I was allowed to choose a sweet from one of the dishes. I had to sit in a marshy velvet sofa to eat it. Gilda sank down beside me, embracing me in ladylike smells. 'Now, who is the lucky fellow?' she said straightaway. I grimaced coyly and squirmed with rage. 'There is no fellow,' I said. 'So!' she clasped her hands and surveyed me efficiently: 'You have waved your hair for no fellow. You have put pink on your cheeks and grease on your lips for no fellow. You have borrowed someone's high-heeled boots for no fellow.' The other members of the family watched me with smiling interest. 'He is not a fellow,' I said coldly. 'He's a grown man. He wants to show me something.' The women glanced at one another darkly. Their chins drew back and their breasts billowed forward until they looked like some very peculiar birds.

'How would your mother feel if you told her some grown-up man wanted to show you his something?' Mrs Wolfson said angrily. 'I bet he's got a wife,' said Gilda. 'I bet his wife has seen enough of his something.' 'You stay away from this man,' Tilly said. 'As sure as black is white you will have a baby.'

He had a wife. I had seen them one Sunday afternoon on the beach at Killiney with about half a dozen little currant-haired children who screamed in ragged delight at the waves. The children all had dirty faces. Even when they ran into the water and the waves broke over their heads they emerged with streaks of dirt glistening under the wet. Mrs Owl was fat. She wore a pink bathing cap and swimming costume although she stayed on the shingle. She lay back on a rug chewing sand-wiches and cuddling a dirty baby. He chased the children into the water and ran back to his wife, proclaiming his pleasure with a grin. For a reply she threw back her head and chortled. I watched his squat brown figure like a modern cartoon of a peanut man, shepherding his family with mirth. His hair bub-bled and gleamed like boiling oil. His amber eyes crinkled. My stomach cringed.

In the park the afternoon heat summoned up its swarm around the pond. Young women pumped the handles of prams to maintain the trussed human contents below explosion point. Courting couples crouched tensely entwined. Elderly gentle-men stepped out briskly with walking sticks and followed feebly with inefficient feet. Two boys of nine or ten blundered by in sullen grey jackets and dusty boots. Their appearance caused such a sensation of outrage among the calm possessors of the pond that they galloped off like spiders into the dank trees. If the adults saw me at all they saw a nice quiet child in a yellow dress. If I saw them, I saw them as aspects of my scenery, of no more individual significance than cows or ducks. Grown-ups were parents and teachers and people behind shop counters. I did not think of them as a part of my future any more than I thought of death. To me it was a children's world. Adults were people who were too old to be children. Deprived of all that they knew and that made them happy they grew mad and dangerous. They ate unpleasant food and emanated pun-gent smells. They were angry and violent and constantly had to be forgiven. Men and women locked themselves behind doors together and moaned and argued with restrained madness. They did curious things together of which children were warned but not told. The Owl was a grown man. This fact had impressed the Wolfsons greatly. Tilly had declared that I would have a baby.

In my mind's eye I could see her glistening carmine lips compressed in envy, her breasts swollen like a bolster in awe; now, in my real eye, my Owl approaching, striding past the ornamental pagoda and the flower borders, coming to show me something adult and undoubtedly curious. I felt important and curiously grown-up.

I finished a last moist and delicious mouthful of fruit and flaky pastry and licked crumbs and sugar from my lips. I brushed the skirt of my frock and spread it over my legs like a fan. A few people looked when I waved with both arms to The Owl. My Owl. He looked wonderful. He was specially dressed up in a pale cotton jacket and a blue shirt open at the throat. He plodded towards me with his head down as if it was an uphill climb. I jumped to my feet and extended my hands to him. He scowled into the grass and hurried past, in the direction of the trees where the boys had vanished. I swung my unwanted arms and stared after him, mouth gaping with hurt. After a few moments I swooped to pick up my paper bag and raced after him.

He was guarded by a circle of elms. He had taken off his jacket and it swung stylishly from a branch. He smiled at me now, his crinkly smile.

'That's right, chicken,' he said when I approached.

'You ran away,' I whined.

'Not from you, pigeon. There. I've got something to show you, something special. It is a secret. We don't want the world and his wife looking on.'

'I've brought you a cake.'

'That's my girl.'

I came to him holding out the bag in both my hands. He did not take the bag but put his hands around my wrists and very slowly brought his mouth down to my forehead. It landed like a scrap of paper. He led me away, still holding my wrists in his

hands. We wandered through dim, luminous, wooded paths.
We came to a rather unpleasant part of the park where there
was a dried river bed and a writhing tangle of tomato weeds.
Ill-tempered walls of briar guarded the pit which had once
been a piece of river. It was a place famed for unpleasantness.
Children were warned not to go there. He picked me up in his
arms. My long legs spilled over his limbs. He surged recklessly
through the thorns, clutching my skirt in a bunch to keep it
from tearing. He put me down on a mossy patch that was olive
green and velvety. He sat opposite to me. Our feet touched on
the ground.

'You've always been special to me,' he said.

'I love you,' I said.

'Oh, well,' he said.

'I'd do anything in the world for you. I'd die for you.'

'Hush now. Let me talk.' He reached out a hand to touch my
face, but did not. His fingers traced my body without touching
it. He dropped his hand to my leg and clutched the oddly
curved ankle of my boot. 'You've always been different from
the other kids – noisy little buggers. I feel you understand me.
There's not many people understand. I'd have spoken before
but I thought of you as just a little girl. Forgive me, miss . . . it
wasn't until you ventured into ladies' boots that I saw you as a
lovely young woman. I'm a married man, of course, and you're
still only a young lass but every dog's entitled to his day.'

I had begun to be afraid. I was not used to being treated as
an equal with adults. It was certain to mean trouble. My mouth
was dry. My limbs went prickly. I looked up at the high walls of
briar, the relentlessly blue sky, praying that someone would
pass or rain descend.

'Do you trust me, miss?' he said. I nodded. 'What I'm going
to show you is something very sacred, something private. You
must promise not to tell a living soul.' I nodded. 'Good child.'

He began to unbutton his shirt. I stared in awful curiosity.
'Don't look yet, pettie,' he urged. 'Close your eyes and don't
look until I say.' I clenched my eyes. 'Look at me now! Look at
me now!' his voice commanded. I opened my eyes and
slammed them shut again. I had been struck blind. Where The

Owl had sat nothing remained but a blaze of light. I looked again, cautiously. The Owl was still there, a frowning blur of face in the shadows. He was dressed in a cotton vest and trousers. The entire surface of his vest was pinned with silver medals. Caught in the low rays of the afternoon sun they flashed and glimmered like unnatural fire. I clapped my hands in delight and gazed in wonder on my beautiful Owl, my wizard.

He moved closer. He caught my hand and pressed it to his metallic chest. It made a musical jangle. He said: 'You can touch them if you like.'

I began to explore the dazzling engraved miniatures. The Owl's chest was populated by a lot of unhappy looking men and women in long dresses. Rays of light came out around them and there were messages written in Latin. 'That one's been blessed by the Holy Father in Rome,' the Owl narrated. 'This is a miraculous medal of the Blessed Virgin. Wear it at all times and it keeps you safe from harm. See the little glass door on this. It's a sacred relic of a saint. It carries a plenary indulgence to save you from hell in case of mortal sin. This is Saint Christopher, patron saint of travellers. That heart is the Sacred Heart of Jesus, burning with love for you and me. Here's Saint Jude, patron saint of hopeless cases.' Together we explored each member of his powerful and passionate family and thrilled at their magical powers. I thought I had never seen anything so wonderful in my life. The Owl said he had been a sodality man all his life. He had other medals and relics at home, hundreds. He could accommodate no more under his clothes. He had to keep them under his clothes because there were those who would snigger at holy things. His wife even smiled a bit sometimes. I was different. He had known from the start that I would understand.

I understood. I burned with understanding. I felt that the Owl and I stood alone in all the world, enclosed in a radiant shape like the Sacred Heart.

There were things I still did not understand, and after we had sat in silent understanding for some minutes I began to wonder about them. Had I now been taken across the threshold of womanhood? 'Are you giving me a baby?' I asked. I put my hands around his bristly neck and kissed him quickly to show that I did not mind. His orange eyes lit on me in astonishment. He seized my hands and pulled them roughly away. 'Bloody kids,' he complained. 'You haven't been listening to a blessed word I've said.' He tore the paper bag which was lying at my side. He took out his cake and began to chew on it, angrily and rather hungrily.

Some Retired Ladies
on a Tour

⟨❧⟩

'There's a man,' Alice said. 'She's with a man.' She scrubbed the bus window with a bunched-up brown stretch glove. May sat down heavily beside her, still probing a blasted peppermint. She leaned forward, her menthol breath ruining all Alice's work on the glass .

They could make him out through the window mist, a tall, pale figure, his garments worried by wind and rain. Mrs Nash was holding his hand. The thing that bothered them speechless was an aspect of his stance that was a confirmation of youth. They couldn't see him properly but he was definitely young. 'She's a nutting,' May said. 'She's nutting but thrash.'

It wasn't the first time they had talked about Mrs Nash. She turned up at the slide-illustrated lecture and told them all she had a stall at Birkenhead Market. It was a tour for retired ladies. She was the only one of them who hadn't retired although she was of an age for it. 'Mention my name and you'll get a cut,' she told them, to get pally.

Doris Moore had a laugh about that. Up to the summer she had been manageress at Imperial Meats. 'Mention my name and you'll get a cut,' she said with a wink that pleated her turquoise eyeshadow like a quilt.

Forty years she had been with Imperial. When she left they gave her a set of cut sherry glasses. She put them out on the kitchen table at home and filled them each to the brim with whisky. Not a drop was spilled when she drank them. She was quite proud of that. Out of the blue she had a vision of her first day at Imperial. She was fourteen when she stepped through the metal doors and began a novice's jiggle against the chill. They were all looking at her bowtied blouse that was the colour of red currants. The men wore aprons covered with blood. The women, their noses blue under powder, wore mountains of jumpers and folded their arms over their wombs to protect any life that might be there: Not that many of them married. There was a habit that came with working in the cold, of not changing underwear every day.

By the time she was thirty, Doris realised that she hadn't bothered to look for a man. She had been too busy looking for jumpers. Her big achievement was learning to knit. She came to look on the cold as a constant; warmth and sunshine were interruptions. At the slide-illustrated lecture, she was the one who asked if the hotels had central heating. 'That's all right, then,' she said, when the man apologised for the fact that they had not.

She was the youngest of the ladies but retired all the same. At fifty she woke moaning with rheumatism. She developed a cough that wouldn't go away. At fifty-four she got pleurisy and the doctor ordered her to leave Imperial. After he had tapped on her chest she put back on her jumpers and sat in front on him crying. She couldn't go and work in an office or a shop, not with the central heating. He helped her to get a disability pension. She managed with that and the home knitting, which wasn't taxed. It was quite nice, really. She began to do up her face and to wear fancy knits.

Alice and May had latched up with Doris from the start. They all took a drink and could enjoy a laugh. Doris was something of a star. She had discovered quite late a talent for making people laugh out loud. It was her appearance of not giving a damn. Few people realised that deep down she really didn't give a damn.

She sat in a seat in front of Alice and May. She had actually seen Mrs Nash and her man before the others but she didn't let on. She didn't want to watch Alice's glove fretting him into sharp relief. She preferred looking at him through the condensation on the window, thinking his beige outline like a young

Alan Ladd; thinking the way he held on to Mrs Nash was more like a blind person than a beau; thinking that of all of them he was most of an age with her. She watched until they started to move towards the bus and then she tossed her head back so that the tassle on her purple knitted hat boxed May playfully on the cheek. 'Mention her name and you'll get a cut,' she said loud enough for the whole bus to hear because she knew that everyone had been looking. When Mrs Nash stepped on to the bus the retired ladies were all laughing. She laughed delightedly with them and then trailed off, uncertain, because they stopped laughing quite abruptly.

They were looking at the man. Unless your taste was in your mouth you'd have to admit he was handsome, Doris said later. He was about forty-five with light curly hair and a boyish, diffident smile. The ones who were most aware of him glared huffily and looked away. The motherly ones smiled to make him at ease. Mrs Nash could see they were admiring him. She grinned proudly under her green Crimplene turban. 'She has a nice smile,' Alice said, easily wooed by a show of good cheer. May clicked on her mint reprovingly. Mrs Nash held up the man's hand as if he was a winner in a boxing match or else an item for auction. 'This is Joe,' she said. 'He's my son.'

The drive was a disappointment. They had expected the driver to be a comedian who would take them all on, call them darling, sing over the microphone so they could join in and jolly up the shy ones. Instead there was a snivelling young pup who got his thrills speeding around corners and wouldn't stop to let them go to the toilet. By the time they got to the first resort the outgoing ones were bored and bad-tempered. The eldest ladies were purple and rigid with misery.

He pushed them out of the bus and disappeared into a pub. They found themselves teetering on the edge of a cliff and stood there shivering, staring down at the sand that curved in a thin ribbon around the base, yellow in the twilight, like custard poured on a pudding. 'Bloody hell, where's our hotel?' carped May. 'Across the road, you daft old toad,' Doris guffawed, her sharp eyes picking out the 'Cliff Palace' as specified in the brochure, although the description they had been given did not tally with the outward appearance of the hotel, which looked fat and pink and putrefied.

The younger ones marched across the road with loud complaints and laughter, purposefully heading for the bar. The older ones shuffled and scuttled and snuffled and grumbled. Mrs Nash looked hopefully at the first batch and guiltily at the second. She and Joe walked to the hotel alone, holding on to each other.

At reception there was a bit of commotion that made them forget all about the dismal journey. Mrs Nash was having a row with the receptionist. There'd been a mistake, she said. Her son had been put in a separate bedroom.

The blotched young woman behind the desk pressed her fingers on the edge of the wood in desperation and clung on with her thumbs. A man in a suit came down the stairs and the girl gave him an imploring look. 'She wants to sleep with her son,' she blurted, making it sound much worse than the young couples that came in the season. The manager looked at the agitated sea of post-sexual female flesh, at the shrivelled face under the potty green hat. Christ. He couldn't have cared less if she wanted to sleep with a Marmoset monkey. He wondered about the bloke, though.

He sidled warily past the grannies and crouched beside the girl at reception, his closeness making fresh blotches on her complexion. 'They can have thirty-seven,' he said, with a glance at the book. He took a key from a hook on the wall and held it out to Mrs Nash on his little finger. She took it with a grateful smile but Doris Moore had noticed his sneer. 'Any notion of rooms for us or are you going to make us sleep on our feet like blasted horses?' she said, loudly and rudely, causing a titter among the ladies. Doris had the knack all right. 'Not until you've had your oats, dear,' said the manager, quick as you like, and those who understood shrieked with delight.

Dinner was very nice. There was a lovely mushroom soup followed by roast turkey and a choice of trifle or bread and butter pudding with cheese as an extra. Alice was finished first and she took her cup of tea into the residents' lounge because she wanted a seat by the fire. As she left she had the impression of something dark scuttling behind her like a spider. She turned to find herself gazing at the green turban. 'A drink! You've got to have a drink,' Mrs Nash said, grinning triumphantly as if it was a forfeit. Joe, behind her, seemed a transparent creature, a daddy-long-legs, but her cordiality was echoed in his smile. Alice knew what May would think but her mouth was watering for a gin and orange. 'All right, then, while I'm waiting for my friend,' she said.

'Friends are very nice,' Mrs Nash said, when she was settled into the fire, sucking her port. 'I haven't got many friends. Account of Joe.' 'Oh, yes?' Alice said with a kindly look at Joe who seemed miles distant from them, smiling at the flames and taking sips from his glass of lager. Alice was having a very nice time. The drink was a large and she was going to be the one who would tell the others about Mrs Nash and her man.

On his way to work, Joe had fallen down with a clot, Mrs Nash told Alice. He was brought home in a bread van and she remembered noting a stack of coconut cream sponges and having a silly urge to buy one for when he came to. A clot, the doctor said, which was working its way to his brain. You couldn't tell when it would strike. Next time he'd be a goner. She ought not to let him out of her sight.

She had watched him asleep on the sofa. His feet were up on the olive green Dralon that she was paying off at nine pounds a month. It was the sofa that reminded her Joe was the only thing that had ever actually belonged to her. She wasn't about to let him go to a clot. The clot wouldn't dare strike while she was around.

Alice fished a slice of orange out of her empty glass and severed the flesh from the rind slickly with her false teeth. She was planning how she would tell May that you could never judge on the face of things. She didn't have long to wait. As she tipped the glass on her tongue to catch the tantalising residual taste of alcoholic boiled sweeties, May stormed in, making demolition noises as she crunched on her peppermints in a rage.

'I hope I'm not interrupting something,' she said savagely. Alice didn't know where to put herself. 'I told Mrs Nash I was waiting for you,' she entreated. 'She's been telling me about her son.' She could only hope the implications would sink in and have a soothing effect. May was too hopping mad to hear. There was malice in the way she munched on her mints. Mrs Nash pawed gently at the sleeve of the fawn woollen cardigan that covered her son. 'Is it time you went to the lav?' she said. Joe returned from his dreams without any perceptible change to his expression. He drained his lager and stood up, holding hands with his mother. 'We're going to the toilet,' he smiled at the ladies.

Doris, who had just come into the lounge with the stragglers, couldn't restrain herself. 'Enjoy yourselves,' she called out. When the two of them were gone Doris went into a fit of indrawn croaks that in a girl would have passed for giggles. 'He winked at me,' she squawked, when the fit had subsided. Alice couldn't tell if he had or not but she was cross with Doris for taking the good out of what she had to say and May's sulk was making her edgy.

'Don't be silly,' she snapped. 'That was just a reflex – like a chicken running about when its head's been cut off.'

Doris was off again, creaking like a wheelbarrow left out in the rain. 'That's right,' she said. 'Cut off his head. Cut off everything while you're at it. Mention her name and you'll get a . . .' And the residents' lounge was filled with exhausted titters.

There was no getting any good out of her when she was in that sort of a mood. Alice went and switched on the television and sat in silence through half of a film about Vikings. Most of the ladies had gone to bed by ten. A few of them fell asleep in soft armchairs, which was a problem for management to deal with. Mrs Nash and Joe did not return at all. When Alice and May had the fire to themselves Alice lashed out on two gins and settled down to trade her latest piece of intelligence for a return to her friend's favour. 'I've got news for you,' she said. 'Concerning what?' May said, moodily. 'Concerning Mrs Nash and her son,' Alice wheedled.

May drained her glass in a gulp, screwing up her face against the sting. She snatched her white PVC handbag, which seemed to be writhing in some private torment on the arm of her chair as the firelight explored its folds. 'Listen to nutting she says,' she hissed, before marching off, leaving Alice alone with the task of forgiving everybody.

For those who could remember or to whom it concerned, the beginning of the holiday was like the first days at boarding school. Things got better with each day that passed. The ladies formed into gaggling groups and saved places at table for their special friends. The bad bits turned into laughing matters. They made jokes about the brat of a bus driver and the three days spent in a boarding house in Cornwall that was run by a widower. At breakfast they came down to plates of cold prunes and custard. After dinging the pristine plastic façade of chilly vanilla sauce with their spoons one or two of the ladies chewed on the fruit, which had not been properly soaked, before sliding a ragged brown mess out under cover of a paper napkin and immersing it as best they could beneath the custard. Next morning the prunes and custard were back again. They could tell it was yesterday's breakfast because of the breaks in the custard.

When the same brown and yellow preparation came up as a proper pudding on day five in a different location, Doris Moore whispered across the tables, 'He sent them on,' and the dining room shivered with mirth. The waitress, who had legs the colour and shape of sausages of salami, couldn't for the life of her see that prunes and custard were a laughing matter.

In the evenings there were concerts. Alice, who used to do a turn in amateur dramatics, recited a monologue entitled *If I was a lady, but then I'm not*. Most of the ladies sang a song, which was a sort of exquisite agony. They knotted their fingers in their laps and became marble-eyed with nostalgia. Their voices sailed up at the light bulb, as fragile and dreary as moths. A Mrs Dunbarr accompanied on the piano. That was the nice thing about seaside hotels, always a piano. For her role as concert pianist, Mrs Dunbarr brought out a black moiré gown with batwing sleeves that flowed and billowed over her brittle mauve fingers as they plundered the keys for Old Favourites.

Mrs Nash had a repertoire of love songs which she sang to

her son, gazing into his face as if he was Nelson blooming
Eddy. The real surprise was Joe. You couldn't get him to speak,
never mind sing. But he responded to his mother's serenade
with a song about a fellow in love with two girls, rocking back
and forth, as earnest as a schoolboy. There was a line that went:
'One is my mother, God bless her, I love her.' He would pause
and purse his nicely-made lips to kiss the crumpled pink sponge
clumsily parcelled in green. Nothing could come up to that.
The ladies clapped until their fingers pained them. Joe, strained
by the excitement, would crown it by announcing to all that
they were going to the toilet. 'Enjoy yourselves,' the ladies
chorused, made bold by Doris Moore and their alcoholic treats,
sluiced with lime or lemon or orange.

Aside from that, nobody took much notice of Mrs Nash.
She didn't seem to fit. She courted Alice at a distance with gin
and orange sent via the waitress. Alice was torn. You couldn't
budge May, though. That blasted, savage gnashing of peppermints when her back was up was not a thing you could ignore.

By the end of the week, just when Alice was beginning to
enjoy herself, she found she was also getting homesick. For two
nights she had slept in a room with a curiously shaped alcove
that prevented the bed from fitting flush with the wall. The
bed-head was missing and her pillows fell off in the middle of
the night, which woke her up. She lay alert in the dawn, heartbroken for the weight of her cats on her feet and the mingled
smells of mould and ivy that were the breath of the house
where she had lived from birth. She found herself worrying
about Doris Moore.

You could go off Doris, she discovered. No longer tired and
frightened, the ladies lacked incentive for communal mirth and
Doris looked for new means of drawing attention to herself.
She went on and on about Joe. He winked at her. He got her
in a corner and told her she was his type. He no longer looked
at his mother when he sang his song, but at her. May thought
it was a joke, a laugh at the lad. Alice found it got her goat,
even though she didn't say as much. She could only consider
the mental betrayal of her friend as a flaw in herself and it
gnawed at her in the small hours, a pain sharp as wind.

It was the second last day of the holiday. Alice was up at seven, tormented by the bed and her nagging conscience. She allowed herself a cardigan under her woolly dressing-gown and shuffled to the window in slippers to watch the sun come up. She didn't find it poetic. She was too old. Alice didn't like the violent orange globe that thrust out of the sea. The ocean ought to be the colour of an army blanket, not pink or blue like paraffin. She dressed as slowly as possible, adding a brooch to the bodice of her frock, some peculiar purplish rouge to her cheeks. Time dawdled along with her. It was only half past seven when she went down to annoy the staff for breakfast.

The first thing to hit her in the eye when she entered the dining-room was the green hat. After the relief at not being first down, there came the pleasurable anticipation of forbidden fruit. She hurried to join the lone diners. 'Joe and me likes an early breakfast,' said Mrs Nash through mouthfuls of fried bread and bacon. 'We're not too gone on all them others,' she confided. 'You're all right though.' She embraced Alice with a loving glance and added affectionately: 'You're looking desperate.' Alice told her about the faulty bed and her lack of sleep, though not about Doris Moore, which was just as well because Doris sashayed through the swing doors just then, togged out to the teeth in maroon angora.

'Enjoying the worms?' she said in a preoccupied fashion, all eyes for Joe. Alice looked at her doubtfully. 'It's rashers,' Mrs Nash said, giving no quarter. She shrugged impatiently and sat down, snatching up the menu in an ill-tempered fashion. Joe glanced at her several times and began to titter. 'I get it,' he whispered. 'The early bird catches the worm.' 'You're soft,' she said in a gently mocking way that was not like her.

Mrs Nash and Alice were deep in conversation. Alice was beginning to think of her as a buddy. At her age she couldn't afford to be class conscious. When she got back home she might give May the bullet. Mrs Nash made much of her, made her feel like somebody. She wanted to give Alice her bed-head and was promising to bring it around in the night. Alice, feeling the holiday needed a climax, said she would have a noggin of gin in the room so they could have a party – a midnight feast. She felt a twinge of guilt at not having included Doris, but she needn't have worried. There was no trace of umbrage in the cracked moon face framed with fluffy wine-coloured wool. The silly thing was in a world of her own, muttering and creaking, making a perfect fool of herself with Joe Nash.

Doris hadn't got anything in particular in mind, though like Alice, she felt the holiday hadn't reached its peak. There was drinking during the day. They could afford to lash out with the holiday almost at an end. She was a bit tiddly that night when she went to bed at eleven. Undressing proved a difficult business so she hung up the maroon angora, patting it with her hand on the hanger, and left it at that. She fell asleep thinking of Joe; his nice hair, his admiring eyes, knowing full well it was the only way to have a man, where you wouldn't have to come face to face with his resentments.

At twelve she was awake again, pitched into alertness by a hellish noise that came from the end of the corridor – a scraping and rattling loud enough to wake the dead. Doris sat up, allowing the freezing air to invade the pinhole ventilations in her wool vest. The first twinge of rheumatism brought her back to earth. She swung out of bed, cursing, groped in the dark for a hairy grey dressing-gown and roped herself into it. In the middle of knotting the cord she was taken with a fit of laughing. It dawned on her; it was Mrs Nash and her blooming bed-head.

She tiptoed to the door and opened it a crack. Mrs Nash was in the corridor, dragging her burden as valiant as an ant. Doris had to stuff a hand over her mouth. She thought she would die. Over a lavishly flower-printed pair of pyjamas, Mrs Nash had on the green hat. A bloody sheikh!

When the shuffling and scraping receded, Doris let herself out into the corridor, shutting the door without a sound. If anyone should see her she was on her way to the toilet. Actually she was going to visit Joe. In fifty-four years she had not been kissed – not properly – by a man. It would make the holiday. She wouldn't tell May and Alice and them. They would say 'be your age!' When she got home she would ask round the girls from the factory, break open a bottle and give them all a laugh.

She knew the room. She tapped at the door and walked straight in. 'Joe,' she called, not able to see in the dark. She felt between two single beds for a locker and switched on the lamp that was there.

Joe was curled up in his blankets like a child, fast asleep, worlds away. She touched his hair with her fingers, a curious, damp, disturbing feel. 'Joe!' He opened his eyes and looked at her in alarm, immediately turning his gaze to the bed that had become his mother's by occupation. 'Your Mam's gone to see Alice,' she explained. 'I thought I'd come and keep you company.'

'I was asleep,' he said. 'Mother gave me a pill.' Doris was disappointed with his reaction and her bare feet were frozen solid. 'Hey, why are you latched on to her all the time?' she said. Her voice came out a bit sharp. 'Are you cold?' he asked her. 'Bloody frozen.' She dabbled her toes on the hurtful, shiny floorcover.

He threw back a portion of bed-covers, showing himself respectably covered in nice striped pyjamas. 'You better get in.' Doris gave him her hard-bitten grin. She didn't want more on her plate than she could handle but there was nothing in his approach to suggest anything underhand. She undid her dressing-gown and laid it on his mother's bed before clambering into the small, warm space beside him.

He was leaning on his elbow, not quite sitting or lying, and smiling at her. She couldn't think of a damn thing to say. His hand rested lightly on her waist, a soft, woolly hump of flesh. She was wary but as far as she could tell there was no harm in it. He took his hand from her hip and touched her lips, pressing them with a finger as if to kill an insect. He kissed her; patted her mouth with lips as warm and soft as bath towels. Doris relaxed. She sighed with relish. Romance was something, by heck it was.

They lay in silence, not speaking, just touching enough to warm one another. From the corner of her eye she saw it coming but alarm was too far from her mind to be summoned.

Something reared up and launched itself at her like a dervish. 'Joe!' she cried, as if calling to him for help.

Joe had her pinned down with his bones. His tongue went into her mouth. He ran his hands over her body, under her vest and bloomers, going to places that weren't allowed. His foraging hands found her breasts, warm round cotton cannonballs.

As soon as his mouth was off hers, Doris dug her fingers into his hair and wrenched back his head. 'Here you! What the hell do you think you're at?' she hissed, not wanting to shout and wake up the whole hotel. He waited until her shuddering lessened and began arranging the peroxide curls on her forehead. 'You mustn't mind me,' he said gently. 'I'm a bad boy. That's why my Mam sticks with me.' He was smiling in that pleasing, diffident way but she was too close to him to be fooled. Even in the dim light she could see that his eyes were cold as lumps of haddock. Doris summoned up her old self and slapped on a smile. 'You're a fast operator, you are,' she said. 'I'm not that sort of girl, you know. I only came in here to get warm.' She could see his face misting over again, that suffusion of sex that made him look like the living dead. Bloody hell! The last thing to do was remind him of herself. She took a deep breath. 'Your Mam seems a good sort,' she said. 'I'd say she's a most unusual woman. You know, the way she stays with you thick and thin.'

'The doctor said she had to,' he said pleasantly.

She rumpled his irresistible curls and began to feel capable again. 'Poor old Joe,' she cooed. 'Not well, are you?'

'Haven't you heard?' he said. 'My mother tells everyone. A clot that's working its way to my brain? I could drop down dead any minute.' His fingers reached for the sympathy of her breasts. Doris didn't care for that but she felt she had an advantage now and could handle him. 'Well you'll have to cut this class of caper for a start,' she said lightly. 'You could wreck your health.'

She attempted to remove his hands but he thrust her away and was kneading her greedily. His breathing had gone funny again and Doris could feel her heart trying to escape from beneath the monstrous hands that were squeezing private parts of her body as if they were lumps of wet washing. He began to laugh. She could feel his pleasure in her fright. 'My Mam's a liar,' he said. 'There was never a clot. There was a body.'

Doris tried to think about her maroon dress, so sad on its hanger like a little woolly beast put outside the door for the night. She drove her mind into the chill closets of Imperial. Nothing could stop the chill that was growing inside her, strangling her guts, and threatening to stop her heart, feeding the pleasure of this strange man perched so incongruously on her stomach.

He kept rubbing himself on her. She felt he was sharpening himself to do her an injury. He was giggling. 'The judge sent me up for five years for treatment. Doctor didn't want to let me out. He didn't think it was safe. My Mam swore she'd never let me out of her sight if they let me go. And the woman was dead. There was no bringing her back.'

Doris began to scream. The scream came from deep inside her, a place that was not obedient to her mind, so that even though her brain knew it was better to die than have the whole hotel gallivanting in to find you in bed with a man, her lungs sent out foghorn signals of fright. The manager was first to arrive. Mrs Nash scuttled past him with her green hat askew in a nest of pins and hair as grey and rusty as an old Brillo. Her little black eyes darted about like insects. Splat! She clapped hands with authority. Doris's mouth slammed shut. The monster glided off her and cringed against his pillows. He looked about anxiously. The green hat was a beacon. He searched beneath it and found what he was looking for. The miniscule mouth, like a rubber band on a bunch of flowers, stretched up and up in a smile. By the light of a boarding house bulb, Joe's returning smile, gluey with tears, was that of a four-year-old.

The whole bus was there to witness the reconciliation, the driver leering like a gorilla as Doris Moore slid out of bed and buried her shameful body in the grey dressing-gown. When Doris had brazened it as far as the door Mrs Nash turned and grinned at the retired ladies in a most menacing fashion. 'Nightie-night, now,' she said cheerily. They fled.

Early in the morning she left with Joe. They went home all the way in a taxi. They got no breakfast. The ladies knew that because those who couldn't sleep for excitement came down breathless and bleary at seven. They were shunted off back to bed like children on Christmas morning. 'Jesus save me from geriatrics,' said one frowsy scullion to another in full hearing of the ladies. 'Leaping from bed to bed in the night, down at six with their daft sons for taxis to Liverpool and banging about for breakfast at seven. Roll on the summer couples with more on their minds than breakfast!'

Doris Moore had more on her mind than breakfast. The coach had been revving a full five minutes and those with bad memories of the outward trip were wanting to go back and spend a penny when she appeared at the hotel entrance. She was wearing her purple, that she had on the first day. She was a big woman. Two heavy suitcases dangled from her hands like balloons.

She set down the cases and spent a long time smoothing her knitted gloves. The leaden day hung on her for colour. The wind whipped her blonde curls about in a flirty manner like scraps of paper in the street. Her woolly fingers retrieved her luggage and she stepped out briskly. When she boarded the bus the ladies jostled for a look, feeling nervous and foolish as if she was the queen. She pretended to be hell-bent on finding a seat. Her cherry-coloured lips drooped. Alice wanted to make a space for her. She attempted to move her heavy coat and her paper carrier bag of gifts and momentoes which were on the seat in front but May's hand shot out to restrain her. 'Don't you lift a hand for that hussy,' she threatened. 'Don't do nutting for the likes of her.'

Doris jerked her chin up and glared at May. Her eyes were glittering. Behind the sullen mask there was a look of triumph to them. She was lording it over them as a woman of experience.

She sat in the place that was saved for Alice's bag in spite of May. After hefting her own cases on to the overhead rack she shoved Alice's things to one side and shimmied her large knitted shape into the seat in an insolent fashion.

The bus was paralysed into quiet. When the vehicle whistled around corners the ladies rattled from side to side, uncomplaining. No one rustled a mag, sucked on their teeth, rendered down a peppermint. 'Well, you never can tell,' was what Doris said when their waiting was over. Everyone looked at their laps in order to ignore her properly. Doris speculated upon her knitted fingers with a rueful sneer. 'He seemed a nice enough lad, I mean.' The ladies looked out of the windows, observing Doris only through cracks in their conscience. 'People like him should be locked up for their own good. Stark, staring, raving . . .' She succeeded in luring a few watery eyes from under fragile shells. She sighed, genuinely perturbed. She could tell what they were thinking; that if such things had to happen it was better that they should happen to little silly seventeen-year-olds who really couldn't be expected to know better. She snorted. 'He killed a woman once. He could've done me in.' Doris's face burrowed into her gloves. She had unwittingly revived the demons of the night. She was fed up. It occurred to her that after all there wasn't much to tell. She wanted things to be like they were at the start, with her as the star and everyone in top form enjoying her jokes and getting in the mood for a drink when they stopped for lunch. All she had done was make them miserable and herself look a prize blooming fool into the bargain.

She started to sing. 'Show me the way to go home –' a stern hymnal beat, voice like a vacuum cleaner. 'I'm tired and I want to go to bed . . .' From nowhere, another voice – a *man's* voice. The ladies' faces twitched toward the driver in unison, eyes wide with astonishment. His virile tones surged through the bus like central heating. He took his eyes off the road to leer round at Doris. 'Come on, darling,' he encouraged, beckoning with a hand. Doris shimmied up the aisle, singing loudly, clapping her hands in time. She sat beside the driver, boldly taking the microphone from its stand and pressing the switch. 'WEEE-WON'T go home 'til morning,' she led off afresh with deafening volume, grinning coarsely into the knowing features of the youth.

Alice's feet began to move. She couldn't help it. They always got a life of their own when there was music. She hadn't realised that she was actually singing until May's white handbag rocketed into her ribs. By then it was too late. The whole busload had been infected. A frail, chalky choir of celebration, hermetically sealed into the luxury bus, pledged that it wouldn't go home 'til morning.

Home. The word died on her lips with such suddenness that it left a picture. It was her little house with its smells of mould and ivy, its two cats which received with democratic indifference her argument or endearment; and rising now like thick brown soup to soak up these familiar images and even the sounds of merriment on the bus, its silence. 'I don't want to go home,' Alice thought in a panic. 'I'm lonely.'

She tried to remind herself of the price people pay for companionship; the dreadful shame of Mrs Nash's secret, Doris Moore's damaged reputation. 'It's a bargain!' was all she could think. But she pulled herself together very quickly and sang out. 'We won't go home 'til morning!'

And so say all of us.

Edna, Back From America

❦

She went up to the water's edge and peered in. It looked cold. *Go on*, she goaded herself. *Can't be much worse than a cold shower.* She lit a cigarette to feel something glowing other than the cabaret sign on the hotel behind her.

She remembered this place when she was ten years of age – a row of boarding houses in different colours fanned out along the prom like biscuits on a plate. When she got off the train with her dad she thought that this was where it stopped at the end of the world. A donkey in a hat waited patiently to take them to the bottom of the pier. And then back. There wasn't anywhere else to go at the end of the world. All week they ate chips and went for donkey rides and made pies out of the sand. He left her on her own at night but she didn't complain. She wanted to seem *soignée*. *Soignée* was a word he used. She couldn't believe it when the week came to an end. She saw the look of pity on his face, the rueful way his lips soothed the stem of his pipe. She was doing what he called a war dance. He took her back to mum and Mr Boothroyd.

It was all changed now, cabaret hotels and karaoke lounges and hamburger palaces. *Everything's different except me*, she thought. *I haven't changed since I was ten. Nobody wanted me then and nobody cares about me now.* She sighed and threw away her cigarette. She began to scale the blue and gold railing. Behind her a crowd started to cheer.

She could hear car doors banging and a lot of excited noise

as the cabaret hotel disgorged its patrons. 'Hell,' June said and she stepped down from the railing.

'Edna!' a woman kept calling out.

What would she do now? She hadn't the price of a hotel room.

'It is! It's Edna! Back from America!'

She turned around to discourage whoever was making the racket. A woman in a fur coat ran right up to her and plucked at her leather jacket with little fidgeting hands. 'Edna!' Her eyes glittered with greed as if she was calling 'housey housey'. She had the kind of face that refuses to accept argument or disappointment and that looks betrayed by a jaw settling into middle age.

'I'm not Edna.' June backed away.

The woman frowned. 'Don't you know me? Muriel!' She put out a hand and took it back again. 'Where's your things?'

'I've got nothing.'

'Your handbag?'

Sullenly June showed her hands in which only a pack of cigarettes was held. She pushed them back in her pockets.

The woman nodded. 'You've come as you went.' She seemed quite pleased. 'Everyone took it as proof when you left your handbag behind. No woman leaves without a handbag, they said. Not unless she's dead. You don't know Edna, I told them.'

'I'm not Edna,' June said. 'You've made a mistake.'

'No I haven't,' the woman said patiently. She wouldn't accept anything.

'Now look here . . . !' June began angrily, but her mind had gone blank. She stared wearily past the woman out to sea. Rain had started and the tide lapped delicately at the little mousey shards. Hell, it looked cold. If she had gone into the water and been fished out the following day there would be nothing to identify her. The woman called Muriel would turn up and swear that she was Edna. She began to laugh.

Muriel watched her warily and then she too started to titter. 'You've not lost your sense of humour, Edna. You always were a tease. Now let's not stand here getting soaked to the skin when we could be home by the fire with a nice drop of Scotch. You still like Scotch, don't you?'

Here was one argument at least that June need not resist.

They were settled around the Tudor style fireplace with glasses of Scotch in Muriel's mock-period house when Ted appeared. 'Ted! Look who's here!' Muriel challenged. A big man, uneasy in his successful suit, studied June seriously but without much hope, as if she was an examination paper.

'It's Edna!' the woman said in triumph.

June liked the man. She felt rested under his lumbering gaze and thought that although he had probably lived with the woman most of his adult life, he understood her even less than she did.

'Back from America!' the woman prompted.

'Edna.' He blew air through his teeth. 'America?' He studied her closely while he refuelled her glass. At last he nodded. 'You'd best stay here until things are sorted out.'

As she fell asleep in a room where everything was in matched shades of lavender, she wondered about Edna, what trick of personality she had to make herself so welcome to Ted and his wife while she, apparently with the same face, had no one. Maybe she and Edna were related. Funny how her dad had picked out this place. Perhaps he had a girlfriend here once and left her pregnant. Men were such bastards. Even Alastair. She'd accepted him without question, she'd loved him and nursed him through his illness. When he died there was only the house and its memories. Then his wife turned up. She never knew he'd been married. Alastair's small wealth had gone to her – a woman he had not seen in fifteen years. She was left with nothing. On the train on her way to this place where she had once been happy, a friendly youth talked to her and after he got off at his station she realised that he had taken her handbag. She was relieved in a way, for there was now no smallest point in carrying on for another day.

'You've gone arty,' Muriel observed over breakfast.

June said that she hadn't gone anything, she still wore the same style she had adopted in her student days. She had meant to leave early in the morning, to complete her mission at dawn on the deserted pier. Absurdly, she had slept it out. 'Look, I'm not your friend,' she said. 'You've been very kind, but I don't know you.'

The woman looked crestfallen. Then she began to cry. 'I'd know you anywhere.'

'I had nowhere to go,' June apologised. 'I hadn't any money.'

'Is that all?' The childish face dried in an instant. 'You always were too proud.' She sat down heavily. 'Look, love, I've got bad news and good. Your mum's passed on. I'm sorry. It's four years ago now. She left a bit of money for you.'

'How much?' June said.

'She didn't have much. Five thousand pounds. And of course there's her cottage.'

Muriel drove her to see the cottage, to show how she had tended the garden. It was a safe and modest little house, guarded by lupins and red hot pokers. June, who was homeless, had an urge to move in right away. It was like a fairy story. She knew she must make known the truth but she could not bear to break the spell.

It was Muriel's suggestion that she should revert to her old hairstyle. She allowed herself to be led to a dangerously homely-looking establishment where a big woman called Beattie greeted her with wonder before holding her down like a sheep to be sheared. As she gripped and snipped, Beattie talked about the old days. The lives of women had not advanced here as they had everywhere else. It was like a dance in which one changed partners for a brief number of years and when the music stopped, when you reached twenty-four or -five, you stayed for the rest of your life with whatever partner happened to be opposite you. Terry had ended up with Renee, Joe and Sarah had a child who was backward, Bill Ferret, who used to look like Elvis, had gone bald and Sid and Sylvie weren't getting on too well.

'Sid and Sylvie,' June echoed distantly, thinking how well their names got on.

'Beattie!' Muriel warned.

They grew silent, watching each other in the mirror as Edna's face was summoned up under the scissors. Had Edna been abandoned by Sid in favour of Sylvie? Was that why she went all the way to America? Perhaps June and Edna had something in common after all. Beattie cut her hair into a mound of uneven bangs that gave her an odd, rakish appearance. What would Alastair make of her now? She realised it didn't matter any more.

'There!' Beattie said at last. 'There's your old self for you. All you need now is your old accent. Fat lot of good that'll do you.' And she laughed with a noise like a flock of sea birds scattered in anxious flight.

As Muriel introduced her to Edna's old haunts, June discovered that the village had not really changed at all. It was the visitors to the pier who had altered, demanding an updating of the town's single attraction, which had been the donkey. Alice Cranmer's fashion shop still had slips and lemon twinsets in the windows. Girls tried on pink lipstick in the chemist shop. A small dairy displayed faded windmills and postcards and sold damp ice-cream cones. June liked it. She knew that she must someday leave but for the moment she hung about Muriel watching for clues. 'You won't mind my saying, but I preferred your old style,' Muriel offered. Meekly she submitted to Mrs Harkins who pinned her into an assortment of close-fitting Doris Day dresses and costumes. She had her hair lightened and learned to walk on high-heeled slingbacks. When Muriel ceremoniously handed over Edna's old handbag with its letters and photographs and shopping lists, June did not receive it as a final clue to the other woman's past, but as the lifting of a cloud of amnesia. Everyone accepted her. The one or two who had glanced at her suspiciously soon embraced her and she thought it was not because they had overcome their doubts but because they needed Edna. She was puzzled by the woman who had fled this simple, rich life. She felt entitled to take what Edna had thrown away.

It was a shock to discover that Edna had thrown away a husband and daughter. She found the snapshot in Edna's handbag, a thin man with a solemn girl of eight or nine. 'Sid and Sylvie,

Clipton Pier, 1983.' She read the pencilled caption on the back.

'You wouldn't recognise your little girl now.' Muriel shook her head. 'Sid hasn't changed much.' She gave an anxious laugh. 'Your husband never changes.'

June's attention was on the little girl, a child like herself who could not hold love. Edna had walked out on her own daughter. The thought of it brought tears to June's eyes.

'Maybe it's time you went home, love,' Muriel said gently. 'Ted and me don't want to rush you, but everyone's been notified. They're only waiting for you.'

On the way to the cottage she counted up the signs by which Sid might recognise her as an imposter. Had Edna a scar or mole? Was she eager or reluctant in bed? *I'll make it work*, she determined. *A month ago I had no one. Now I've got friends, a family, and a home. I'll make them want me even if they find out I'm not Edna.* She felt calm.

It was Muriel who was nervous. 'About Sylvie,' she said at last. 'I should have told you. She's no better.'

'I'll take care of her,' June said quickly. She was used to sick people. She had taken care of Alastair.

Muriel sighed. 'They won't keep her in anywhere. Not even that mental place. Remember the time she set fire to the rabbit? She did it to a boy in the last home.'

June drew on her cigarette. 'Why couldn't Sid take care of Sylvie?'

Muriel looked uncomfortable. 'He's been inside again. Got in a fight with a man and left him in a very bad way. It's the drink, Edna. You know that. But he's promised he'll never lay a hand on you again. There was some around here thought he'd done away with you. I never believed that. Well, you have to believe the best of your own brother. Anyway he'll behave with Mother around. She's still a battle-axe, even though she's daft as a brush.'

'His mother?' June raked at her face and hair with her fingers as if a growth of cobwebs enclosed her.

'They threw her out of that Haven place now she's wetting.'

'Sid's your brother?' June cut her panic with reason. 'Then

we're talking about your mother too. Why can't you look after her?'

'I'm sorry, love. Ted won't have it. I don't mind admitting I was at my wits' end until you turned up.'

'Stop the car, Muriel,' June said. 'I'm not Edna.'

Muriel tittered excitedly. 'You've left that a bit late. They're waiting for you back at the cottage!'

She tried the door. It was secured by a central locking device. 'Please let me out. I'm not Edna. My name's June Pritchard.'

The other woman took her eye off the road to sharply assess her passenger. 'You won't mind my saying, but that new pearly shadow makes your eyes pop.' She returned her attention to the road and her plump foot squeezed the accelerator. 'You should draw your eyeliner out at the edges, like you used to.'

⊘⟋⟋⟋⟋⟍

My Son the Hero

On his way home from the pub my son Ken rescued a kitten up a tree.

'Must have been a big kitten,' I said when I saw the state of his shirt. Bits of it had stuck to his chest where something had clawed through fabric and flesh.

'No,' Ken said solemnly. 'It was only small.' He made a shape with his hands about the size of a rat. His nose was cut and there were great big rusty tracks down his face.

There was something about the shirt – all bloody and chewed, like a hen left by a fox. Already I didn't like that kitten. 'If it was up a tree' – gingerly, I peeled it off and pushed it into a bucket – 'you should have left it. Cats know how to get out of trees.' Ken scoured his head with the insides of his eyes. He had a way of considering the simplest question as if it were complex and profound, of looking back into his head for answers. 'There was a gang of kids standing round the tree. They had a dog – big fat bastard. Cat was afraid.'

'Weren't you afraid?' I touched him and he trembled. 'They give you a hard time?'

'Yeah.' He put his hand to his bloody nose. With his fingers close to his face he gave a start and then drew back to study the purple semicircle behind the thumb, as if his hand had been caught in a gin trap. He put his two hands away carefully between his knees. 'She bit me,' he said indignantly.

'Who bit you?'

'Bloody dog.'

'Mind your language, Ken!'

To tell the truth I didn't care about the language, or the shirt. I was proud of Ken. He's not bright. People think I've wasted my life on him. Even his own father said that. Then he left us. Well, there's worse things to waste your life on. I know there's not much going on but there's courage and there's tenderness. That's worth something. You need some tenderness in the world today. Every day you read terrible things in the papers – babies murdered, old women robbed, their jaws broken and their false teeth smashed. Only the next day there was a story of some poor young girl missing. It gave me a start because it was in our own neighbourhood. I did a wash to take my mind off things, but when I went to get Ken's shirt, it was gone. 'Ken!' I said. 'Did you take that shirt from the soak?'

'N–no!' he said, and he looked as guilty as a dog.

He was watching telly, so I went upstairs and searched his room. Break your heart to go in there – trainers, size 12, and a bed full of teddies – everything in a heap on the floor. Under the mattress a stack of chocolate wrappers, and the wet shirt, seeping into a pile of magazines. It was when I looked at those magazines that my heart went through me. They were men's magazine's – not the girlie ones with women showing what they'd had for breakfast, but dirty, cruel filth. I sat there shaking as I turned the sodden pages. Then I bawled down the stairs. 'Ken!' He lumbered up and peered round the door. 'You mad at me?'

'Why would I be mad?'

'My good shirt – all torn.'

'What about these?' I held out the magazines.

He gave a sort of sneer. 'Where did you get them, Ken?' He shook his head and looked away. 'Can't say. Reg told me not to say.'

Reg Fuller? 'What have you got to do with that scum, boy?'

'I'm not a boy.' His eyes filled with tears. 'I'm a man. Reg called me a man. He said men were mad for magazines like these. He sold me them.'

I swatted him with the bundle of wet filth. 'Did you like them, son? Is that the kind of thing you like?' I was scared. To me Ken's still a child. He began to cry. I put my arms around him. 'Men don't like those magazines, pet,' I told him. 'Reg Fuller was lying. They're just dirty rubbish. Where do we put dirty rubbish?'

'In the stove,' he snivelled.

'That's right, Ken. Put them in the stove.'

Poor Ken doesn't understand much. He put the shirt in the stove along with the magazines. Wet smoke belched out and I thought I could smell blood rising over the stench of burning fabric.

He didn't go out that night, maybe because his face was scratched and bloody or it might have been that gang. We watched the news, but it was all about that poor woman appealing for information about her missing daughter. A picture of the girl was put on the screen – little blonde, face like a flower. She was last seen talking to a man with a raincoat. 'Please don't hurt Denise,' the mother kept saying, but I could tell from the way her voice squeezed on the name that she knew Denise was already dead. Ken's face mimicked the anguish of the mother. 'He knows too,' I thought. People like him often do. 'Come on, love,' I said. 'Let's go down the pub for a drink.

Off we went, him hanging on to my arm – the odd couple. Funny to think how much we share. The instinct to protect, for one. I've passed that on to him. Then there's the other thing, never admitted, the need for sex or love, the need to connect. I've taken magazines to bed too, stupid bare-assed hunks – probably gay. We're outcasts, Ken and me. All we've got is each other. No one will have him because of the way he is and no one will have me because I've got him. Something stuck in my brain like a splinter on that walk, but it couldn't work its way out because Reg Fuller turned up with his mates and started teasing my son.

'Got a girl, have you, Ken? We saw you with a little blonde. What have you done with your girlfriend?'

'You leave him alone,' I said. Ken sank his face in his collar, puffy and bright pink. 'Have you got a girlfriend, Ken?' I said gently. He shook his head.

'Wouldn't know what to do with a girl, would you Ken?' they called after him. He shuffled on for a bit, then turned back jerkily. 'I would!'

'How would you know, Ken?'

I hurried him on. I hadn't much covered that side of life with him. Best not to stir up what's never going to crop up. 'Those magazines,' he mumbled. 'Oh, Ken, no!' I held his face. 'That's not what you do with a girl.' He didn't understand. He didn't understand anything.

Denise Carroll's body was found in a wheelie bin. Terrible things had been done to her. She was 21, an economics student, out for a drink with some friends. The thing that struck me was how she had fought to live. Bits of the man's skin and clothing were under her nails. His hair was in her fists. Extraordinary how people cling to life, even when it is most debased. Extraordinary how human evil can make an ordinary thing like a bin sinister. Ken felt it too. When I asked him to put out the bin he gave a shudder. I watched him standing in the rain, just staring at the bin. 'Where's your raincoat, Ken?' I called out. He peered down at his body as if he expected to see it there.

'Gone,' he said in surprise.

'Where?' You get exasperated, but it's no use.

'I left it somewhere.'

'Weren't you wearing it when you went to the pub the other night?' I said and suddenly I remembered what it was that had stuck in my head. He couldn't have rescued a kitten from a tree on his way home from the pub. There are no trees on that walk.

'Ken,' I said. 'Show me where the kitten was.' I grabbed his hand and dragged him back to the pub. 'It was there!' He stabbed his big blunt hand in several different directions.

'There's no tree there, Ken.' I was trying to be patient but my voice was shaking. 'You have to show me the tree.'

He looked around blankly. 'Gone,' he said with interest.

I forced him to look at me, trying to find a way past that blank expression, trying to imagine how she must have felt when she faced him. 'There was a girl, Ken, wasn't there?'

He looked vague for a minute and then he nodded.

'Why didn't you tell me about the girl?' I seized him and shook him. It was like trying to shake a bear. 'I forgot about her,' he said.

'Jesus, Ken. She must have been scared to death.'

He thought about this inside his head. He gave a sentimental smile and nodded. 'Yeah. She was really scared.'

'How could you do such a thing?'

'Because, because . . .' I sometimes thought his brain must be like an old rubbish skip, where he had to throw out nearly everything before he could find anything that was useful. 'Because she wanted me to.'

That evening the police came. They said it was a routine enquiry, house to house. I had bathed Ken, scrubbed his nails, brushed his hair until it more or less sat down but I saw the way they looked at those gouge marks down his face. 'Where were you on Friday night?' they asked him. Ken peered back into his head. There was nothing I could do. There were witnesses who'd seen him – Reg Fuller, people in the pub. 'I can't remember,' he said. The thing that kept going round my head was the same phrase Denise Carroll's mother had used: 'Please don't hurt him.'

'We found a raincoat,' they said. 'We'd like you to come and take a look at it.'

Ken's face brightened. 'I lost my raincoat.'

After they'd left I gave Ken an early supper in bed – a hamburger with plenty of ketchup and four sleeping pills. I had told the police I'd bring him round the station in the morning. They were decent about that, said they'd send a car for him. Ken was quite excited about getting a ride in a cop car. When he'd eaten I sat by the side of his bed and held his hand. He's no beauty, but my heart caught on the innocent arch of his eyebrows, the mild curve of his mouth, bits of my features woven into his unfinished face. How had evil got into him? Was it evil, or just a man's desire coming through some twisted circuit, like carbon monoxide forced through a car window? Anyway, he was mine. I couldn't let them get him. I settled his pillows, slipping out the one that raised his head too high. I watched him a moment to remember how he looked asleep and then pressed the pillow over his head. I did it carefully, like pressing a cutter over pastry. It was very peaceful. Suddenly Ken's arms shot out. he reached out, wildly clawing at me. I lifted the pillow and saw the look on his face. Oh God, that face. I pressed down with all my might. Ken's strong, but the sleeping pills were against him. His arms fell. The doorbell rang. Bloody cops, back again! Of course they didn't trust me to bring him to the station. When I removed the pillow Ken looked like a squashed doll. I stood there clutching the pillow to my chest while the doorbell shrilled. As I turned to go downstairs there was a shudder from the bed and Ken regained his breathing with a mighty snore. I touched his forehead and he smiled.

At first there seemed to be no one at the door, but when I looked down there was a little girl, eight or nine. 'Is Ken there?' she said.

'Ken's in bed,' I kept my hand to my face to hide the scratches. 'So should you be.'

'I only found out tonight where he lives,' she said. 'I had to come and thank him. He got my kitten, Susie, down a tree.'

'Oh, my God,' I said.

'It was being chased by these big boys with a dog and it ran into someone's garden. They went in after it. I was terrified. Then Ken came along. He's very brave,' she said admiringly. 'Those boys gave him a right going over. They set their dog on him.' She was about to go when she remembered the large carrier bag she was holding. 'Here's Ken's coat. He asked me to mind it when he went up the tree.'

She watched me oddly. 'Don't cry,' she said. 'Susie's all right. Oh, and she says she's very sorry. She gave Ken a terrible scraping, but we all do foolish things when we're frightened.'

A Funny Thing Happened

~~~~~~~~~~

A funny thing happened one night at the Empress. There was a woman that didnae laugh. No, seriously. Sandy was away into his Man with the Limp. He hardly had to open his mouth. He looked down at the guddle of red faces, rotten teeth bared, stink of beer and gash scent, unwashed clothing, orange peel, ammonia. He released his grip on them, allowed the tide of laughter to die back to sighs and titters as he hobbled to the front of the stage to deliver a sentimental monologue on behalf of those with disabilities. He took a step forward, squeezed them in his fist again. It was his bad leg and he fell into the orchestra pit. The laughter became a death rattle. As he clambered back onto the stage he cast around him a bitter look. They went wild. Applause rose like a storm of birds and then it rained down on him like ashes. There was a curious moment when he became aware that his cold glance was coldly met. There was a woman in the fourth row who watched him stonily. You could tell there wasn't a dry pair of drawers in the house, but here was this one face, shining solemnly out of the hellish dark, a square, plain face and black, suspicious eyes and beautiful long chestnut hair, a superior being, the one who would not eat from his mucky paw, and with a little twist of his heart he knew he wanted her.

The girl was waiting for him in his dressing room. There was another surprise – more a shock – and it made him laugh his hoarse, sour laugh for which he was famous. She wasn't a woman at all. She was only a wean – a big lass but no more than twelve or thirteen. It explained her blank look. She hadn't a clue. 'What's your name, hen?'

An older woman with the same black, suspicious eyes put her hands on the girl's shoulders and pushed her forward. 'Ida May Gordon.' There was a man there too, shifty wee shite.

Sandy wrote an autograph on a piece of card and handed it to the girl. She took it silently and put it away as if it was money owed. She watched him while he took off his make-up, the towel snagging on bits of bristle. 'Did you like the show, Ida May?' he said.

'Aye, great,' the father affirmed.

Ida May crept forward. Her body was so close that he could smell her skin and he flinched away, not because of her smell, which was of soap and salt, but in case she would smell the beer sweat on him. 'What did you mean about those girls and the clergyman?' When he had explained the joke, she regarded him sternly. 'Is that a commonly known fact?' she said.

Exhaustion descended as it always did after a show; the emptiness, the post-egotistical gloom, the sense of opportunity botched or genius wasted. He sank his face in the towel. Ages later when he looked up again they were still there. He had forgotten all about them.

'She's stage-struck,' the mother said.

'Stage-struck.' The words came out of his mouth as if he was spitting sawdust. What the hell did it mean? A desire for attention? Hardly ever anything to do with talent. The feeling that one only came into plain focus beneath the spotlight, in the slap of applause. There was the other side that you couldn't explain, not to a wee girl, that when the dreadful thirst had been slaked and the crowd had composed you out of dark, you flew above them and they ceased to be worthy of your effort. 'What can you do, Ida May?'

'She can dance,' her mother said.

'Can you dance?' he asked the child.

'She's got a stoatin' pair of pins,' the father said.

Sandy almost laughed out loud as the little girl launched into her dance, which was somewhere between the Highland fling and the verruca. Her strong arms struck out like a Glasgow washerwoman. She trampled and pirouetted. She kicked. It was when she kicked that he saw her legs – a real hoofer's pair of pins right enough, long, with little dimpled knees and slender ankles. Funny to think that a little girl could be grown up down there and still a wee tiddler up top. It was like a boot in the guts when he realised where his thoughts had wandered.

'What do you think?' the father said.

'She's a bloody awful dancer.'

In the pub he began to feel sorry for himself. He had never had luck with women. It wasn't his fault, it was the kind of women he met. The only girls he knew were in show business. They smelled of booze and tobacco. Their hot bodies under painted faces made him think of dolls that had been in the dog's bed. They were like himself, all smiles and no hope, wave their fanny in your face, forget your name, call you Andy or Sandy or any-bloody-thing. None of them had ever called him Adam McArthur, which was his real name. He had almost given up on the whole thing. What a man wanted from a woman was more than sex. It was baptism. To immerse his blackness in her snow. To be dipped and renewed. Ballocks. Men were like bloody dogs. With a mixture of self-disgust and self-pity he sank the night's beer with a whisky chaser.

The things that had amused him earlier now came together in a different pattern. He recalled her curiosity. It was a long time since a female had asked him a question and then listened. He forgot that her seriousness came from incomprehension and saw it again as a kind of aloofness, a supremacy. The long legs, the long hair, the little black eyes that scorned and ferreted were all about him like a spell. It wasn't anything he thought about her, only that he couldnae think of any other bloody thing.

She was there the following evening. 'I could tell you liked her,' the mother said. Sandy had not slept. What periods of daze he had had, the little girl had pestered them. When he looked at her now he felt only resentment. The lassie looked back at him with the same hostility, thinly mixed with expectation.

'What do you want from me?' he said to the mother.

'Take her with you. She's no' fussy. She'd do anything.'

Something about the way she'd said it, he got a shudder. He glanced at the child but she was absorbed at his dressing table, trying out things, like a wean playing houses.

'Is her father after her?'

'Him!' The mother's prim mouth curled in contempt. Already he had noticed Ida May's comic imitation of her.

'What age is she?' Sandy said.

Like all children, Ida May was interested in her age. 'I'm twelve.' She turned to them, ghoulish under a rim of black kohl she had put on her lids.

'Get out of here.' He made a clucking noise when he saw how the two females watched him. By asking her age he had given himself away. He quickly removed his gaze but his eye swept the mirror and he saw his expression, ridiculous, not how you'd look at a woman but the way a wee girl would look at a doll in a Christmas window.

'Get out,' he said again.

'Out,' the mother said to Ida May.

The child slid past him out the door. Her eyes were on him until her pale face vanished, so that he still saw them after she was gone, two candle burns on a shroud.

'It's no' what you think,' the mother said. 'I have to do my best for her.'

'She's only a child,' he said.

'She's no beauty,' the mother said.

'Aye, and she cannae dance.'

'She's at her very best. She has to have her chance.'

There was a shift of scenery and a musical finale in which villains became heroes and everyone held hands. In a poignant moment Sandy saw that the girl could be his and that she was the only thing in his whole life that he had ever wanted. Maybe he could do something for her. 'We're off to London next week,' he said, 'then Sheerness.' The relief he felt was so strong that he wanted to weep. He couldn't get over the simplicity, the forthrightness.

'How much?' the mother said.

He was gawping again.

'How much? She's not some chorus girl that's been handed round like a peace pipe. She's useful to me at home.'

'Away to hell,' he said. The woman stayed where she was, watching him patiently as if she had something to sell that no one wanted. Somewhere at the back of his head was the daft idea that he would show her Ida May really was worth something. He had to have her because she had come within his reach. He had to place a value on his desire. By the time the two females left, he had parted with two days' takings and he hoped to God he would never see either of them again.

On St Valentine's Day, 1914, Adam McArthur, forty-nine, alias Sandy McNab, set out for London by train with his company and Ida May Gordon, twelve. Now that he had her, what the hell was he to do with her? He told the company that she was there to stitch stockings or make tea or any-bloody-thing.

'Well, don't do any-bloody-thing we wouldn't do,' the dancers said with a wink and Ida's small black eyes bored into them until they had to look away.

'Are you all right, hen?' He tried to court her.

'I want to be like them,' she said.

When he laughed at her she looked like a plain, anxious wee girl. Most of the time he ignored her but at times her presence nagged him like a mouldy tooth. Partly it was her fault, although he knew she didn't understand. She had about her a sacramental air. She followed him about, deferential and possessive. She had made herself his property. Sometimes when she brushed his collar he felt the sweet, humid draught of her breath on his neck and it was like a small door opening at the top of a stairs in a dream. When they got to Sheerness he told her that they were to share a room.

'I'm no' your daughter,' she said to him when they were alone, to set right the account he had given the landlady.

When he kissed her white forehead he got the same choking thrill and disappointment as a boy biting into his first green apple pinched from the orchard wall.

Ida May sat at the dressing table with her broad back to him and her beautiful chestnut hair loose on her shoulders. He came up behind her and put his hands on her shoulders. He looked at her hands on the surface of the wood with its ring-worm scars of old bottles and glasses. They were child's hands, restless and stumpy. The nails were chewed and on one finger was a ring out of a lucky bag. Her shoulders felt like a woman's shoulders. They were solid and full of reproach.

'What's up, hen?' He tried to coax the muscles loose with his fingers.

'There should be things,' she said.

'What things?' He pressed himself against her back and let his hands run down her chest. Her breasts were hard and almost flat, with a suspicion of prickliness, like a pincushion.

'Women's things,' she said querulously.

He closed his eyes until her obstinacy drew him back. 'What do you mean? What are you on about?'

'I don't know. Women are supposed to have things, combs and bottles of stuff. You put them on the dressing table and you put cream on your face and dab something out of a bottle behind your ears.'

'Take your clothes off, Ida May,' he said.

She turned her astonished face around. 'What?'

'Ida May,' he said hoarsely. 'We are to go to bed together as man and wife.'

'What?'

'Do you know what that means, man and wife?'

'Course I do,' she said without any hesitation. 'It means you fight all the time.'

He laughed at her but Ida May's face was blank of any expression except its normal wariness and cunning. Clumsily he began unhooking the back of her dress. She did not try to stop him but clutched at the front to keep him from removing it.

'Ida May, do as I say,' he pleaded.

'How should I?'

'Because I paid your parents,' he said breathlessly. 'They took money off me. They knew what I meant to do.'

She turned around to him again. This time her face registered pure disbelief. She looked at him so long and so intently that he began to burn. When he could not face her any longer he dropped his hands and looked away.

'Say something,' he muttered.

'How much?'

When he told her, her eyes blazed with contempt. 'You must be made of money.'

'Come on,' he said. 'It's not so bad. Lots of girls like it.'

'I'm no' going to bed now,' she said. 'I'd miss my tea.'

'No you won't. We'll get up again. We'll go out and have a feed.'

'If you have so much money, you could buy those things,' she said stubbornly.

He asked her what she wanted. Her stumpy hands moved daintily on the dressing table as she mapped out what she wanted and where. 'Soap and scent and a hairbrush. Lip salve. *Ooh dee toilette*.'

She became excited as they walked by the sea. Something about the smell of salt water always got to dogs and children. She stopped to gaze intently into a cake shop window.

'Would you like a fairy cake or a meringue?' he asked her.

She thought about it solemnly. 'A fairy cake.'

'I knew I wasnae wrang.' He laughed delightedly at the old music hall joke.

She gazed at him suspiciously as she ate the cake, delicately peeling back the paper cup and nibbling all around the burnt serrated edges.

After tea they walked along the pier to the music hall. When they got home she was asleep almost before she got into bed. He thought he'd leave her sleeping until he pulled back the blankets and saw her body. 'Don't make a fuss, Ida May,' he begged. 'For God's sake don't make a fuss.'

She scarcely seemed to wake up, except for a look of mild outrage, but after that she merely sighed.

When he woke in the morning she was standing beside the bed. The sheets were flung back and she looked furious. 'What's this? The good sheets! They're wasted! What will the landlady say?'

'Come here, Ida! Hush!' Her little black eyes watched him

with disdain as he attempted to explain about the blemished linen.

'Is that a commonly known fact?' she said.

Jesus Christ Almighty, blood on the sheet! His head hurt. He had drunk too much. He was never any good in the morning. If he was with one of the girls they would have lit a cigarette for him, poured him a dram, done a dance to make him laugh. 'Dance for me, Ida,' he said.

She went to the wardrobe and got her good dress. She changed behind the wardrobe door, either from modesty or to surprise him. At the dressing table she clawed the morning tangles out of her hair. She measured with her shrewd eye the distance from dressing table to door and then, while a shaft of sea light spotlit her through a gap in the beetroot-coloured curtains, she spun across the floor, her square face rapt, her lovely legs rising gracefully and landing with a thud.

Sandy sat on the edge of the bed in his underwear. His eyes felt rheumy with emotion. She was unlike any female he had ever known. She was completely untouched by him. She was like the cat that you kicked and fed and then it lit off across the rooftops. He longed for some pity or some tenderness. He yearned to touch any part of her, her hair or her little thumping toes.

The dance ended abruptly. She planted her hands on her hips. 'Are you getting me work?'

He shook his head. 'I'm taking you home.'

When she marched over to him he could sense the ghost of a future waddle in her walk. 'I'm no' supposed to be home till Friday. What's my mother going to say? If I don't get a job on the stage I'll be into service. I'm finished wi' school. I cannae be hanging around at home.'

He flapped a hand at her, not wanting to look at the dejected woman's expression he had put on her face. 'It's only a few years, hen. You'll be married then and have weans.'

She watched him so long and so suspiciously that he thought she was going to ask was this a commonly known fact, but instead she came to him and took his hand. He was moved by the feel of her little hand and thought it was a gesture of appeal but she took his hand firmly and placed it on her breast.

'Aw, don't, hen,' he said.

'Do you no' like me?' she said.

He jumped up quickly and a flash of alarm crossed her eyes but he struck a pose in his vest and baggy drawers and launched into his old dance number. He'd been dancing from the age of ten but there wasn't much call for footwork in his new routine. Anyway, at forty-nine he had neither the wind nor the figure for it. After a brief solo he held out his hands and Ida May joined in. They did a bit of tap and a bit of waltz and then they tried a tango. Any other woman would have been creased with laughter, wetting herself, but Ida May was fierce with concentration. Her feet on the wooden floor sounded like horses' hooves sliding on ice.

At first he didn't hear the banging because of the clatter of her feet but then there was the unmistakable shrill of an angry woman from the floor below: 'This is a respectable house.' She poked for attention with the handle of a broom.

Clutching Ida May, Sandy froze in the classic comic 'caught in the act' stance. He almost put his hand over the wee girl's mouth. The child's expression had not changed, but it never did. She was squashed against his body, her little eyes so close to him that they made a single disapproving dot. His own eyes very near crossed as the dot closed in on him.

'Do you no' like me?' she said again, and he felt the petal pressure of her pursed mouth.

This time he tried to bring some tenderness to the act but when he opened his eyes he saw that she was frowning out the window at the sky.

'Sky's turning murky. I wanted to see the sea,' she told him sternly.

Little black needles of rain hung about their heads like clouds of gnats when they walked along the coast. Ida May had put on her overcoat. Her hands were in a muff. She had wound pipe cleaners in her hair while he dressed and put on her *ooh dee toilette*. Although her facial set was grim Sandy told himself she was blossoming in his company. He had gone out of his way to be nice to her, took her to a fortune teller and she damn near smiled when the woman predicted her name would be up in lights. He told her jokes to pass the time. There was the one about the Glasgow man whose house went on fire and he rang the brigade. The fireman said, 'Och, we're awfy busy, can you pit some coal on it and we'll see ye in two oors' time.'

She rounded on him furiously and he smiled in anticipation of her incomprehension. 'You should wear a tie,' she said. 'Only labouring men don't wear a tie.'

'Is that a commonly known fact?' he teased her.

'And you should shave before you go down to breakfast. I was ashamed in front of the other couples.'

Other couples? He stopped in his tracks, astounded. 'You watch your mouth, lass. You should have respect for grown-ups.'

Ida had her arms folded, legs apart, the classic wifie's stance. 'You can't go to bed in your underwear and then wear it all day. I'm no' giving cheek to a grown-up. You said we were together as man and wife.'

Sandy threw back his head and laughed delightedly. 'You're a treasure, Ida May.' He tried to cuddle her but she stiffened in disapproval. The honeymoon was over. Already she was kicking him into shape like a husband.

On the train on the way home she sat on the opposite side of the compartment, not looking at him. Her stubborn face had the weary set of a woman adjusting to a disappointing life.

'Ida May,' he said, 'there's a man I know at the Empress. He might give you a job in the theatre. It'd only be selling ice cream but you'd maybe work your way from there.'

She glanced down at her lap and smiled. It wasn't for him but he had made her smile. Her pale cheeks flushed and her lashes hid her scathing eyes. There was more power in that puny token than in all the applause he had had in his life. By God he had worked for it, but he had made her smile. He felt weak and balmy as if he had just emerged from a deadly fever. And who was he to say that Ida May would not have her name in lights? The stages of the world were full of terrible dancers.

He would go straight to the Empress and sort out a wee job for her. Time enough to catch the train back for the evening performance, pie and a snooze on the train. For the first time in years he was looking forward to the show. A thousand people with miserable bloody lives and he could bring them cheer. The Kent countryside fled modestly past as the man and the girl smiled to themselves, each believing their lives to be transformed.

All the time he was inside he remembered her smile, although he could hardly mind the girl at all. She had been at that age when a lassie changes every time you look at her and he only remembered her in the way a man might recall a visit to the seaside as a child; the clean smell, the biting chill, the pearly light that was somewhere between heaven and a line of grey washing. Through the bars on his window he could see the world, a wee rectangle like a savoury served at a ladies' do. The judge gave him two years hard labour. If he could have given him a heavier punishment, he said, he would have done so. Two years, twenty years, his life was over. He could never go back on the stage again. Music hall was clean. He didn't feel sorry for himself. He regretted the girl, though. The Ida May he had known was gone forever. She'd be a woman now. He doubted if she still danced. When the war came he hoped that maybe she got her chance after all, a job in a factory, good money, a soldier to marry. In the end, he had left her with nothing, but he had her smile.

The smile lasted only a moment and then Ida May had her hard, thinking face on again. 'What would you want me to do?' she asked Sandy.

He leaned forward and touched her hand. 'Ach, nothing, hen. You don't ever have to do anything for anybody again. You remember that. You're good enough the way you are.'

A woman got into the compartment. 'Move over beside your father, child,' she said. 'Make room for me to sit.'

'No,' Ida May said.

'You should put some manners on your little girl,' the woman said to Sandy.

'I'm no' his little girl,' Ida May said crossly. 'I'm going to sell ice cream at the Empress. We have been together as man and wife.'

Sandy watched her face first, the set expressions retreating out of it one by one, like lights going down in a theatre, until at last her face seemed dark, although in fact it had gone pure white. He had a habit of noting people's reactions for use in sketches. He recorded then the noise of her heels, the dry tapping like the sound of applause in an empty house, as she hurried off to fetch the guard.

◈

You Don't Know You're Alive

Annie lived downstairs in the kitchen with the wireless and the Sacred Heart. It was a black sort of kitchen with a high, sooty wall outside the window and a long dark passage leading to the sink. The wooden draining board had developed a spongy texture at its edges, which attracted darting insects called silver fish and slow-moving beetles.

Gerald came home to his dinner at one and to tea at six. At noon, roused by the virginal clamour of two Angelus bells, Annie would put on her grey suit and red high heels and go to the shops for some chops and when she got home she changed back into her jumper and skirt and put on the potatoes and got out the frying pan. When Gerald came in he turned on the wireless for the news. He ate in silence unless perturbed by something on his plate. 'What's this?' He would tap with his fork at some perfectly ordinary thing like liver. He seemed wary of food. He livened up when she put out his sweet and told her how much he dreaded his work. He was not suited to his employment, he said, and did not know how to face each day. She told him she sometimes missed work. It was quiet on her own in the house all day. She wouldn't mind if she had a sweet or a cigarette.

Gerald shook his head. 'You don't know you're alive. There's a war on out there.' He angled his glance towards a muddy scar on the grass outside that was called the birds' patch. Annie used to leave bread there for the birds so that she could watch them feeding but it became a stalking ground for predatory toms. When she found she had given herself a view of mangled sparrows, she threw any leftover bread in the bin.

Gerald drank a cup of tea after dinner, stirring in three spoons of sugar, and went back to work whistling. She left the wireless on for 'Listen with Mother' and 'Woman's Hour' and then she went upstairs and lay down, hurrying past the preserved dining room and drawing room, furnished with wedding gifts and never used. Gerald's complaints and the pitiful gaze of the Sacred Heart with His peeled-back chest wore her out. Sometimes in the afternoons she baked a tray of raspberry buns, using the sour pink jam that was reputed to be made from turnips or apples and tinted with cochineal, or she read a magazine which told her how to scrimp on soap and eggs and remodel a suit to save coupons. The medical pages were full of the secretive importance of mothers and babies and problems of a nature too personal to reply to in these pages and please send s.a.e. Sometimes she looked out the window at the wall and longed for a cigarette.

At four o'clock, when the light was beginning to fade and the smell of other people's fires was homely on the air, she put on her suit again and went out, walking as slowly as possible the quarter mile to the church where she lit a candle for a baby and lingered for a glimpse of Maevie Beatty.

Having nothing very interesting in her own life she pursued the adventures of this younger and more mature girl at an avid distance. Maevie had been coming to the church for more than two years. When she first appeared, bursting upon the dimness like a vision of Our Lady in pastel blue, she was Maevie Leddy from the post office, giving thanks for her diamond engagement ring from Billy Beatty. They were a lovely couple – Maevie round and blonde and pretty and Billy tall and silent and wolfish, a dairy farmer who was good to his widowed mother. Maevie was nineteen then, with the kind of glamour that appeals to both men and women. She wore carmine lipstick and said she stuck to powder blue because it brought up the colour of her eyes. There was no sour edge to her conceit. When she showed Annie her engagement ring, whispering in the painted shadows of the long stained-glass windows of saints, she said she never dreamed that such a thing would happen to her. Annie responded fully to the excitement. It was an event, when there were no longer any in her own life, with the prospect that Maevie would soon be a married woman like herself and then they could be friends. Somehow Maevie outran her. She was quickly pregnant after her wedding and became a gorgeous, overblown rose. She made history in the village, giving birth to triplets and got her picture in the paper, blowing out the candles on her twenty-first birthday with three babies on her knees. She was twenty-two now and pregnant again. She was getting to look worn out. Billy's mother had become an invalid and she had to look after her as well as the three babies. Puffing around in the end of her pregnancy, she had no time to bother about her hair and clothes. All the same, Annie envied her just as she envied Gerald in the office and the men out there getting killed in the war. They were swept along by their lives.

On the way back she stopped at Fox's sweet shop and Argosy Library and selected a paperback and sometimes a comic, which she still liked. The evening air, buff and foggy with the breath of coal, made her long for a cigarette and she tried all the tobacconists, saying she wanted five Woodbine for her husband, but they always said the same thing, that cigarettes were saved for working men and her husband could have them if he asked for them himself. She bought milk and bread at Carew's and a half pound of small tomatoes which she ate from the bag to give herself some sharp taste, arriving home at the last possible minute so that the day would be used up to when Gerald got home from the work that he dreaded.

She lit the fire and changed back into her old clothes, patting thick pink powder over her pale skin and a lipstick in a red that was unrelated to any human tint, that was like a hazard warning. While the rashers were on the pan she fluffed up her hair. You could set your clock by Gerald. The key was in the door as she filled the teapot and she had the plates on the table when he came into the kitchen and gave her her kiss.

He liked her red lips. They were his due. If she wasn't wearing her lipstick, he would have asked her if she was all right. He never kissed her ordinary young lips unless they were in the dark. His look changed when she drew them over with that dry red decor. It added an unnerving edge to the evening as they read books or listened to the wireless.

In bed she lay awake and thought about the girls; Joan and Gladys and Kay and Rose. Before she got married they were at the centre of each other's lives. Things that happened only seemed real when they had picked over them in the office. They ate bags of cakes and altered one another's clothes and plucked each other's eyebrows. Everything had to be done with one hand for the other held a cigarette, smartly drooping. How smart they felt, how hard-bitten, deftly pulling out and jamming in the little black cylinders of the switch with two fingers while ash fell from their cigarettes, telling Mr Hanafin to mind his language, please sir, and reminding Mr Arigho he was a married man. They worked for a lottery company that made its money selling tickets to America by mail order. Five hundred women took in orders and sent out tickets and were ambitiously pursued by the small staff of administrative males. They never minded anything the men did. Men were a separate species, like zebras or flamingoes. There were hunks and lechers and mickie dazzlers and good dancers and d.o.m.s, which stood for dirty old man. Good dancers and hunks were in demand but you had to have some sort of a fella because girls never had any money to go to the pictures by themselves. Annie was shocked when she learned that Kay 'went all the way' with men. It was unimaginable. It belonged in marriage. It was like learning lessons when you did not have to go to school. Kay said she couldn't stop herself. There were days on end when the red-headed country girl mooned around white in the face but then she would come screeching out of the toilet that her aunt had come and Joan would say the whole building could hear her and all the men were gone out to light a candle to St Jude, the patron saint of hopeless cases.

They all knew they would get married. It was an article of faith, a fulfilment of the years of straightening seams and ironing satin dresses and lying in steel curling pins. It was a diploma in their lives. The only time they were ever serious was when a fella asked one of the girls to marry him and then they would spend a whole morning, imagining his mother and what his children would look like, what he wore in bed – even if he was only a mickie dazzler.

Gerald wasn't a mickie dazzler. He was serious and had lovely manners. Annie said it was love at first sight, that she knew the moment she first set eyes on him. As far as the moment was concerned, it was the truth, but afterwards it was never the same.

The months of their courtship seemed endless. He kept her to himself and they were unable to chat in a comfortable way. The house he bought for her was big and already ageing. 'Solid,' was the word he used. She felt intimidated by it, as if she was back home with her mother and father. In spite of her doubts it was she who hastened the date of their marriage. It brought her closer to the girls again. 'Tell us what it's like, won't you?' they teased and she looked forward to meeting them afterwards as a married woman, to brightening her dark kitchen with their company.

She bought a hat for her wedding but Gladys said it was the wrong shape, it didn't suit her, and spent a morning in the office snipping it into pieces and sewing them back in an alternative form. She couldn't afford another hat so she had to wear it. The picture now hung in the hall of Gerald looking proud and Victorian and Annie, her eyes wide beneath the reconstructed hat which soared into a crooked peak like a tiled turret in a fairytale.

She never saw them again. She was a married woman. She hadn't any money to meet them for tea in Clery's or to go to the pictures. She had no telephone. She had taken for granted the luxury of her job on the switchboard. There was always some man making an excuse to ring her up, to call her little sweetheart. No matter what he said, or how sharply she had to answer back, she called him sir.

The first bomb was dropped on London the day Annie got married. Gerald often boasted about that, mentioning it to illustrate the indolent safety of her life. He wasn't criticizing her, but fondly affirming that he had given her a life of luxury.

While she rested in the afternoons there were men in the trenches with their guts wrenched out. London city was a heap of rubble. People ran through the streets in their nightwear as shops and monuments were consumed by flames. They huddled in the railway tunnels singing songs. Annie enjoyed these tales of adventure, although it didn't seem fair that none of it touched Ireland. To her it appeared that the people in the war had had a second chance, a reprieve from the lives they had made. Solid homes vanished in the night. Husbands were nobly dead. The women singing in the tunnels had got married and still they were free.

In bed Gerald sometimes told her of his childhood and how he had suffered at the hands of bullies or from jealousy of his brother. He talked of train journeys and chestnut trees. This astonished her. She had never dreamed there was anything to know about him. When she met him he was a good dancer and told corny jokes. She liked that. Now he was forcing her down some dark corridor that was nothing to do with the life she had agreed to share with him. One day, when she saw the girls, she would tell them, Gerald was a human being. Underneath the oiled hair and neat moustache and pristine suits in Prince of Wales check: a person. She would warn them. They weren't just fellas any more, after you married them.

The village where Annie lived was only three miles from the centre of Dublin but it still clung on to the country. There were two churches, a cinema, four pubs, a laundry and a bakery, but there were also farms close enough for the animals to walk to the abattoir that was in the village and Beatty's dairy farm down a lane behind a terrace of cottages. Children after school vanished into fields on the edge of the village. Faded green hills, neatly seamed, were stretched out on its horizon, like the eau-de-nil cardigans of aunts.

Twice a week Annie saw animals being driven to slaughter. They picked their way along the edges of the road, past trams and cycles. Their look of anxiety made them seem like people. On Tuesdays cattle clattered through the gutters, fogging the air with their frightened breath and on Friday it was flocks of sheep. Annie always had to stand back and watch them. It upset her that although they knew what was going to happen, they did not protest, but only lamented.

One Friday, waiting for the sheep to pass, she made up her mind to step on the next tram and simply walk into the office and say hello. She had been married for two and a half years. Joan and Gladys and Kay and Rose might be married themselves, as they sooner or later must.

The air suddenly smelled sharp. She went into Carew's and bought herself some small tomatoes to eat. When she came out the Friday procession of sheep was still picking past its dainty path, bleating out an unhappiness that nobody minded. Annie wanted to let them know she felt for them. Absurdly she offered a tomato to a sheep. Even more foolish, it took it in its soft, luxurious lips. Annie patted its head and turned away but the sheep broke from its ranks and began to follow her. She tried to shoo it, even wasting another tomato by throwing it on the ground, but it was her the animal wanted. In a panic, because she hated responsibility, she jumped on to a tram, not bothering to check its destination. The sheep clambered after her. An old woman laughed at her; 'Mary had a little lamb,' and the animal shivered trustfully against her leg while a herdsman chased after the vehicle in the street. When the tram halted she had to lead the sheep off and hand it to the man who hit it with his stick. She did not want to go into town after that. She just bought the lamb chops for dinner and went home and waited until it was time to cook them.

The incident broke the final thread in some flimsy fabric that bound her to her past. Afterwards the office did not exist any more. It became a pageant of history with colourful episodes that played in her mind, unconnected to any real thing: the legendary parties with endless free drink that were once a year thrown for the staff by the lottery boss and which were plundered by hordes of gatecrashers.

Everyone came for the drink. 'I'm that thirsty, I could drink out of a po,' Kay used to say, her crooked blue eyes alight. The lottery boss had a mistress called Gerda Scully who was a dancer and he made her a present of a white poodle and a white sports car. It was said that any other man who looked at her was a dead man, even though he himself often tried to fondle Annie behind her switchboard. Once, after the party, Annie was driven home by Joe Finnegan, who was a famous lech but was very popular because he was a terrific dancer. 'Holy Malarkey,' he said, 'what's your mother doing letting you out in a dress like that?' She was indignant he should think her mother would have a say in what she wore. She made the dress because it was grown-up, a low-cut red satin worn with no bra. 'That's a bad girl's dress,' he said, when he stopped the car to kiss her. 'You're not a bad girl, Annie, are you?' The phrase pounded in her ears because when Joe Finnegan kissed her in her bad girl's dress she seemed to melt inside and flow soft and red as her red satin. Of course Joe Finnegan tried to go far and she had to slap him on the face. 'I'd give the sun, moon and stars for a night with you,' he said.

She would give the sun, moon and stars for one moment of excitement, for a cigarette. She could not believe that such an incident had taken place. She was more a woman now and more a child as well. She had a lovely body and had loved being unaware of it.

Now she dressed in women's clothes, making herself presentable for the neighbours. She was unconvinced by her married woman's uniform and it bothered her that others seemed to take it seriously. 'Good morning, missus,' the neighbours said when she went to the shops in her grey suit and gloves. They did not think she was an imposter. Was it the same, she wondered, for the soldiers in the war, taken away from all the important things in their lives – learning the latest dance steps and getting a date with a girl like Kay – plucked from tram stops and Sunday dinners and put in the mud of a foreign country, dressed up to kill?

Gerald had a cousin in the war. He was called Kevin and had signed up because he flew small planes for a hobby and wanted to be an airman. He was demobbed after his plane was shot down and now he was an invalid who had to be taken care of by his mother. He limped and had a scar. Gerald invited him to tea, although he did not usually like visitors. The scar on his face was a dark red with shiny unhealed bumps and looked as if someone had flung jam at him. Annie kept wanting to wipe it away. It was impossible to pretend to ignore it. 'Does it hurt?' she asked him.

'Children don't seem to notice it,' Kevin said, telling her that it hurt when a young woman made remarks.

Underneath the scar he looked like Gerald but Annie felt more at ease with him because he had given up the effort of manliness. All his stiffness had deserted him. She would have liked to talk to him. She wanted to say she was sorry she hurt him, and how he, without knowing it, had drawn attention to her disfigurement. When he spoke of children, it made her feel a failure for having no children who would sit on his knee and absolve his ugliness. She thought Kevin would have listened and understood but Gerald gave her a look and interrupted heartily: 'Drink, old man?' and he poured Kevin a giant whiskey.

Gerald blamed her for spoiling the evening for although he put on gramophone records and in spite of the whiskey, there was nothing more said. Kevin and Annie were marooned.

She had wanted to hear about the events that led up to Kevin's scar, to let him know he was lucky, that his was a scar of honour – not the honour of having fought for a cause because she did not understand about such things and suspected that he didn't either – but the honour of having lived through excitement. She was marked too, but by nothing. She had done nothing. Nothing bound and branded her.

If I had a baby, she used to think, watching Maevie Beatty struggling with a big pram, her stomach like a cabbage beneath a stained velour coat, we'd be a family. When she thought of a family she did not picture Gerald nor even the family she had grown up with, but something childish and carefree with games and picnics and a nice little face to look at while she walked to the shops.

She was not resigned to the intimacy of their double bed. As a child she had to share a bed with her sister and hated the touch of knees, the outflung arms or wandering strands of hair. Gerald startled her with his determination. 'He can't kill me,' she used to say, as when she was a child in school and the nun had found out she had done no homework. Soon there would be a baby and he would leave her alone.

When nothing happened she began to suspect she did not know very much. The girls talked about 'it' in work but they used code words which she only half understood. She knew that after you got married you stopped getting the curse and it meant you were pregnant. Her body went on just the same, indifferent to matronly imperative, a law unto itself. She could not talk to Gerald about such things. She attempted to discuss it with her mother but her mother in her absentminded way said, 'You are not putting your mind to it.' It was true that she removed her mind as far as possible from the claustrophobic act of marriage, but every day she went to the church and lit a candle.

She waited there for Maevie Beatty and followed her out, trying to talk above the squall of three giant boys who pitched in their pram like bears in a fight. 'I'm trying to have a baby,' she told her. 'I've been married nearly three years.' 'I'm due next week,' Maevie said. 'It's twins.' She sighed. She seemed to have lost track of her concentration and even of her physical substance. She appeared as a vast, amoebic shape, in which her eyes were ghostly, enormous. Annie hung around, trying to impress her. 'You don't know how lucky you are.' 'I have to get home,' Maevie said. 'Ma wets the bed these days.' Ma was Billy Beatty's invalid mother. Maevie gave a choking little chuckle. 'I'm twenty-three years of age and in a week's time I'll have six arses to wipe.' Annie was shocked by her coarseness and in awe of the fullness of her life.

A letter came. It was from Kay, to say that she was getting married. It did not bring the relief or excitement Annie would have expected. It had come too late. She put it in her pocket and kept it until Gerald went back to work after dinner. Kay was marrying a mickie dazzler called Bertie Gonagle. He was a little fellow with teeth missing. None of the girls liked him because he drank too much and became violent afterwards. She had to marry him, she explained, because she was twenty-nine. She would be thirty on her next birthday. Of course she did not tell Bertie Gonagle she was twenty-nine. She said she was twenty-four, which is what she told everyone else.

There was news of the other girls. Rose was married to a
dote of a fella called Foley and had a little baby girl, Gladys (of
all people) had got herself pregnant and could not even go to
England on the boat because of The Emergency and Joan was
still painting the town. Annie thought she ought to write to
Kay but she knew she wouldn't. She couldn't congratulate her
for marrying Bertie Gonagle and she couldn't try to stop her
either, if she was twenty-nine.

Maevie Beatty vanished from the church to give birth to two
more boys. Annie thought she was like a woman from the
Wild West with her five sons. Her whole life was justified at the
age of twenty-three. She would be surrounded by strength and
admiration. She could do anything she liked now.

One evening, Kay dropped in on them after tea. They never
had visitors. Annie was so startled she hid in the kitchen, leaving Gerald to cope. Kay swept down to the kitchen, which still
had the dishes from the tea on the table, all glamour and a black
eye. Annie and Gerald stood against the wall while she sat
down beside the dishevelled table and crossed her legs and lit up
a cigarette which she had got from God knows where. 'Go
away, Gerry dear,' Kay blew smoke at him; 'and bring us back
a big, big drink. I'm that thirsty I could drink out of a po.' To
Annie's surprise Gerald did not give her a look but cracked a
corny joke about pos and jerries, making a pun on his name.

Annie said: 'I haven't seen you for years.'

'It's different now.' Kay passed her a cigarette and lit another
for herself and Annie at last felt relief. 'I'm a married woman
now. We're in the same boat. Look at this!' She tapped at her
black eye with a red polished fingernail. 'Gonagle did that to
me. Only three weeks married and only half my size.' She
sounded almost proud of his achievement. 'So, how are things
with you?'

'All right,' Annie said.

Gerald brought them proper cocktails with a cherry on a
stick and then when Kay told him to, he went away again. 'A
real tame husband,' she said after he left the room. 'Aren't you
the lucky one;' but, as when she had boasted of her own husband's violence, her voice now seemed tinged with contempt.

'Kay, I can't understand why I haven't got pregnant,' Annie said. 'It's nearly three years.'

'Count your blessings, kid, I say, but otherwise go and visit a doctor. What are they there for?' She left Annie three cigarettes and said she could get more any time she liked. She wrote down her address and made Annie promise to keep in touch, but when Annie went to see her after she had visited the doctor, Bertie Gonagle told her she was gone, she had run off with Willie Eccles who was a Protestant and played the piano in a band.

She had to tell someone her news, which stifled and startled her as if the doctor had announced that she was not a woman at all, but a mermaid. At first she had been harrowed by his pronouncement and protested that it could not be so. She felt ashamed. Was she always to be ashamed? The doctor said it was not altogether uncommon and a small procedure would put it to rights. In spite of his politeness it was so queer, it made her feel so alien, that she had to say it to some normal down-to-earth person or else she would live with the feeling that air did not touch her lungs like other people's, and her heart beat upon empty veins.

It would have been all right to tell Kay. Kay never minded about anything. It had to be someone who didn't care. Maevie Beatty had begun to return to the church and stood before the Blessed Sacrament shapeless and indifferent, her pram filled with new infants while the older ones worked their way loose from a push chair and prowled like incubi in the aisles.

She sat rehearsing the difficult words while Maevie stood and gazed at God and the children made havoc.

What could she be praying for now? She had a husband. She had a huge family, all of them healthy. What more could anyone want?

Maevie let out a cry and raised up her hands. The babies were cheered by this diversion but Annie wondered if she might be ill or in distress. She did not wish to be involved but forced herself to approach the young mother. 'Are you all right?' she whispered. 'Is there anything the matter?'

Maevie laughed right out loud. She turned around so that

her upraised hand swung against Annie, hitting her on the head. 'She's gone mad,' Annie realized in sudden dread. She sat down quickly and Maevie, in a low voice, proceeded to abuse the tabernacle in a litany of foul language, unspeakable words cupped and flung back by the stone arches. An old priest crept out of the offertory and perched like a wind-swept seabird on the altar and then hopped away. The curtain of a confessional twitched and fell. Old ladies ceased their praying and looked up appalled to witness such foulness and such faith. Annie sat and shivered until in due course people hurried in from the street, strong men, a policeman and then Billy Beatty, and they pulled Maevie away. Some women gathered up the infants and wheeled them off in a different direction.

Maevie didn't notice. Her furious eye was still upon the altar. Her feet put up motiveless resistance as the men heaved at the bulk of her body.

When the church was quiet again Annie slipped into the confession box, where someone as cowardly as herself was hiding. 'I've been married three years,' she told the darkness, 'and I'm still a virgin.'

The doctor tied up her two legs while she went down into tunnels of disgrace as he peered into her body as no one had ever done, not Gerald, not herself. She did not struggle as he tried to probe her and, ridiculous, told her to relax. Decently, he said nothing until she had put on her suspenders and stockings and the grey skirt of her suit.

When he gave her his verdict she gaped at him. 'But Gerald . . . It hurts,' she appealed. She turned her mind away when he spoke immodestly of things related to the inside of her body, of vaginal spasm and penetration and dilation. A little hospital procedure, he said, writing on a pad. She would be as right as rain.

When she had made her confession to the priest she felt ridiculous. She would never say such a thing to Gerald. She should have kept her secret. She got up quickly to leave but then the old man spoke to her.

'A celibate marriage is a very beautiful thing.' His dry voice was elated. She pictured it as dust dancing in a beam of sun.

'There is no greater gift for God. I should not have thought to hear of it in these modern times. God gives us all our chance for sacrifice, but few ever use it. God bless you. Your life is as fresh as the morning dew.'

Out on the street, she could feel it, in the winter dusk, the freshness of her life. It was still unused, still waiting to happen. Maevie Beatty's life was all expended but anything was possible for her, after a simple procedure. She was a bride again. She felt the years falling off, the clutter of nothingness blown away like dead leaves in a breeze. With the widows of the war, she had been given a second chance. She celebrated her happiness by walking home behind two women with prams, warming herself in the backdraught of their dull domestic chatter.

The Picture House

My sister and I moved and circled like little flies in dusty light. Heavenly light came through the high lavatory window where exhausted rags of butterflies dangled in imitation of the stained-glass patterned paper that was peeling from the pane.

For a long time we did not meet any other children. We lived in a silent place. There was nothing to connect us to any species. We were each other.

We moved on instinct. When Lily put the pieces of a broken jam jar into her mouth to suck the jam it was I, a year younger, who crouched beside her and pushed out a long tongue. ''Mon Lily.' She responded to her mirror and I picked out the pieces, my tongue extended all the while. When the glass was gone and blood filled her mouth we both ran screaming to the mammy.

I was Matilda. We were planned as Lily and Tilly. Later, when I knew I had a face of my own and looked at it in a mirror I knew I was more of a Matty anyway.

When we were not moved by instinct, it was by stealth. Steal-th. The earliest wilful act I can remember was stealing snoke. Snoke was glucose powder, sweet and cold, which was kept in a blue and yellow box on the top shelf of the pantry. Snoke was meant for warm water and sickness but we preferred to lick it from a spoon. It became a craving. Sometimes I would wake violently at dawn to find Lily looking mournfully at me from her cot and we would creep downstairs in the foggy light of waking day. We climbed on a chair and wobbled there to reach the box. We dipped in our spoons and felt the cold white powder in our throats and drifting up our noses and soon we were comforted and could go back to bed.

Our thoughts ran together but we had our separate griefs. 'The nidle's on the roof!' Lily would cry when a huge moon, pockmarked and grinning, looked in our window. I was pursued by green and yellow girls who came out of the lavatory wall and laughed at me.

When we were four and five we fell in love. 'Are you my mammy?' Lily pursued the larger entity around whom our physical needs revolved and upon whom we had both become fixated with an unbearable crush. 'I am your mammy,' she agreed and we silently cheered.

Our father went away on business. Business was a terrible thing. Once he knocked on a farmhouse door and was pursued by a creature that was half a man and half a goat. He stayed in commercial hotels and locked the door to his room but was frequently wakened in the night by the dry squeak of its handle in the fingers of exploratory thieves. Sometimes, from these fearful excursions, he brought us back meringues.

When Father went away our mother turned the clocks to the wall and silenced the wireless. We piled into the double bed and curled up in the fleshy eiderdown. At odd hours of the day we would rise and do strange elaborate tasks – scrubbing the red-tiled kitchen floor, washing sheets in a tin bath. Sometimes we went to the cinema or to church and when we were hungry we ate cheese sandwiches or chips. Most of the time we stayed in bed, watching a painting on the wall, which showed a purple mountain against grey skies while Mother told us stories of a life that was lived behind the magic mountain.

Her stories were about the girl who lived in a grey cottage on the far side of that hill, a girl who knew no obstacle, who tamed horses, mined gold, sailed rapids in boats of handmade bark. We did not know it then but it was in our mother's bed that Lily and I became different people. Her eyes lit up to the sound of horses' hooves, the splintering of a sailing craft in the teeth of jagged rocks. It was the stone cottage I loved. It had a log fire and copper pans on the wall. Yellow laburnum draped its poisonous charm over the roof and wild roses stifled the windows. The mountain itself, which protected the concealed cottage, had a fantastic property. It had no substance and the girl could ride through it and out of the picture, into the world. I preferred not to think about that.

One day I saw the house from the picture. Our Father had a car for his business and on Sundays after lunch he took us for a drive. The car had made a snorting ascent of a hill and as it floated silently down in a haze of dust and shimmer, the cottage folded back from the mossy shoulder of the slope. It was a perfect house, alone and empty, yet close to several cottages and a farm. Over another hill a grocery shop called Margaret Tuttle had its name picked out in blue and gold.

Around this time we found out about death. A cat had been discovered in the garden, its stiff paws neatly folded. Our parents patiently and confusingly explained mortality. The cat was dead as all God's creatures must die and no one ever knew when. You went when you were called. You could not hide as you hid when your mother and father called, for God saw all things.

'If we die can we all go to heaven holding hands?' I asked our mother but she smiled and said no, she and Daddy would die long before we did.

I did not trust them after that. They would go when God called them. We would be left behind. I began to prepare for death. When we had money I would not spend it nor let Lily spend hers but hid it beneath the wing of a cloth duck.

It happened when I was almost six and Lily was seven. Mother was sick and went to the doctor. She was sent to the hospital for tests. That was the end. We knew because Father would not let us see her. 'No children allowed!' he said, but that was foolish for sick children live in hospital.

After two weeks we asked one another:

'Where has she really gone?'

'She has gone to death,' I said.

'Dead!' We thought of the hairy coldness of the cat. Lily's face trembled and I patted her cheeks.

Father had to go away on business. 'Now what will I do

with you two?' He looked as if we were an inconvenience, left over from better times. 'I suppose it is time you went to school.' His face had a blue and wobbly look like an egg that is not properly boiled. He would not look at us. I knew that he was going to go away and would never come back, that he would not think of us again unless he passed a baker's window and glimpsed meringues.

Our world was being pulled away from us. We were like the birds that lived in the hedges and then the men cut down the hedges and the birds balanced, quaking on thin air while eggs seeped into the ditches and in the grass the crinkly necks of nestlings rose in lonely answer to their mothers' cries.

We ran away. I packed all the things we would need. We went in the night when Father was in bed, creeping down the stairs as quietly as if we were only coming down for snoke.

Things look different at night. Even our own street was stretched out of shape with shadows. We had never been out this late before. We had hardly been anywhere on our own. The cases were pulling our arms off. 'Let's go back, Matty,' Lily whined. 'We'll run away in the morning.' I told her no, we must learn to stand on our own two feet. Father used to say that when we asked him or Mammy to do little jobs for us, to button our coats or put sugar on our bread. By now I was used to telling Lily what to do. Secretly I thought she was right and hoped that someone might see us and take us back. A man coming out of a public house in the village laughed at us. 'Gremlins! Where do ye think you're going at this hour?' He gave us such a fright that we ran all the way home, bumping the cases off the ground, afraid of his big yellow face, afraid of gremlins.

When we got to the house we were reluctant to knock on the door, fearful of waking Father, but I had forgotten to close the door so we pushed it gently and tiptoed in. Lily turned a yawning face to me and smiled and sighed with gratitude.

'Tomorrow,' I told her severely; 'first thing.'

We went to bed and fell asleep and were woken in the morning by Father who was cross and puzzled to find us beneath the blankets with our overcoats and our shoes and socks on.

During the day, when he was at work, a woman came and looked after us. One day she was late and Father had to leave before she arrived. After we had sat for a while with our breakfast I looked at Lily and nodded and her blue eyes flared up with excitement and fright and we got our coats and our cases.

We went on the bus. The cottage was up a road near a church which was past the village next to ours and we told the bus man to let us off at the church. He lifted us down from the platform and handed us our cases and he said: 'Your mammy should be ashamed.' 'We have no mammy,' Lily said. 'Our mammy is in heaven.' The man was thin and white inside his navy uniform. He had a bump on his neck which rose and fell. He looked at us and got tears in his eyes and forgot to punch the bell.

When we reached the cottage I got a fright. This was the first time I had seen it close. It looked awful. The windows were gone and nettles crowded out, waving their dusty teeth.

'Home,' I said doubtfully to Lily. 'Don't be afraid.'

'I'm not afraid.' She spoke through her nose, which was gripped in her fingers. 'I'm hungry. There's a smell.'

'Farmyard beasts,' I laughed. 'Sheep's heaps.' But I was very nervous. I thought now that we ought to go home or to school or wherever there were windows and beds. I saw then, hidden beneath the weeds and grasses, a path. It was made of tiles in different colours to form a pattern. A lot of the tiles were broken but you could still see how it was meant to be and how it must have pleased the people who had come to the cottage once upon a time, when it was new. 'Look, Lily! It's a real house. Look at the path!'

'It's not a real house!' She too had made a discovery. 'There's no toilet!'

It was my house. I would look after Lily here. We didn't have to trust anyone else, grown-ups who would die or go away on business. We had each other and Mammy had said that we would not die for a long, long time.

'Now, Lily,' I took my sister by the arm. 'We must pretend this is a doll's house and that we are the dolls. I will tidy our house and you will make our dinner.'

'There's no food!'

'Well, of course there is food.' I sounded like our mammy now and Lily heaved a sigh.

'In here, look!' I opened the case I had been carrying. At home, over several days, I had taken from the pantry all the things we liked; cornflakes and cream crackers and Marmite, packets of jelly and Mandeville cheese, apples and sugar and drinking chocolate and snoke. 'We won't know ourselves.'

'What's in the other case?' She pointed like a policeman.

'Everything,' I said proudly. 'Bowls and cups and spoons, a knife, a candle, matches, our quilt, socks, my cloth duck.' I had given a great deal of thought to our packing.

Lily stood like a princess, imperious, unwilling to be pleased. 'What about soap and a facecloth and comb? What about my nightie and my teddy?'

'We have put all that behind us now.' I did not want to admit that I had forgotten such important things. 'We must learn to make do with little, like the savages.'

'I don't want to be a savage,' Lily cried savagely. Her knees shook as they always did when she was excited and about to cry.

'Din-din,' I wheedled. 'We can have cornflakes.'

I went into the cottage, pulling my sleeves down over my hands, to cut the nettles. 'There's no milk!' I heard Lily's mournful discovery but I took no notice for, as I cut away the weeds with the steel bread knife I had brought, I saw that there was a part of a stone floor remaining and a fireplace which must still work because there were ashes and bits of burnt stuff in it. I was entranced to think that real people had been in the cottage and that they had used it, not for play, but for real life. It was like seeing Santa Claus.

When I had cut down the nettles I got the quilt and folded it on the stone floor. Then we sat outside and ate dry cornflakes and cream crackers and sucked on some jelly cubes.

We made daisy chains and counted distant cows. We dared each other to climb the hill behind the cottage to see if you could walk through it but we were too tired and uncertain of ourselves. We played 'I spy', watching the village below the fields and then we lay on our backs to look at birds in the sky and soon we fell asleep.

We woke to hot afternoon sun and thirst. We had to have milk. 'What will we do?' Lily moaned. I had money. I was very proud of this. 'We'll go to the shops like our mammy used to do,' I said.

'And whose little girls are ye?' Margaret Tuttle said when we asked her for milk and bread and a quarter pound of corned beef.

I touched Lily's hand and whispered. 'Don't say anything. Our mother told us to hurry,' I said to the woman whose teeth clanked in her smiling mouth.

'Are ye new here?' She put a bottle of milk on the counter.

'We're on our holidays,' I lied.

'Where so?' With a big knife she cut slabs from the block of pressed meat.

'In an old, mouldy, falling-down cottage!' Lily said suddenly, as if woken from sleep. 'Filthy, horrible!' she cried with vehemence.

'The cut of you!' The woman suddenly observed, her knife raised in the air in alarm. 'Where's your mammy?'

'We have no mammy,' Lily said.

'We have to go now.' I reached for Lily's hand. 'Our father's waiting for us. In a car.'

Margaret Tuttle's head reared like a horse's, out the window and around each visible twist in the valley. I grabbed the milk from the counter and we ran.

'Why did you do it?' I pushed and pinched Lily.

'Because I want to go *home*!'

'There's no one there. They've all gone. If you don't let me look after you, no one will.'

'I don't care, I hate you. You're a liar and a thief!' Her voice was high and thin and hopeless.

It was all because she had to go to the toilet. She always hated having to go in strange places, having to say. When I said that she must go behind a tree, must use leaves and grass, her bottom lip folded down and her eyes bulged at me as if I was a boogie man.

I brought daisies from the field into the cottage and put them in a cup. I got sticks and twigs and laid them in the grate to make a fire. I had matches. I had watched our mother light the fire.

It would not catch flame. At first when I held the match to the sticks a little grey thread of smoke appeared. I put a pile of matches in the fire and held a lighted one to them. There was a big flash and a lot of smoke.

I had sometimes seen our mammy hold a sheet of newspaper across the grate when the fire was slow. There was no newspaper. When Lily came back I made her take off her slip and hold it up. A golden light bloomed behind this gauzy screen. We watched, mesmerized as the flames pranced and then very slowly a bright yellow frill of it escaped out of the grate and clung to the bottom of the slip; then waves of it climbing, climbing, eating up the white cloth, leaving a crisp, black smelly wafer dangling below.

Lily danced out into the room.

'Let it go. Let it go. 'Mon, Lily,' I said in a quiet voice.

A burst of orange leaped up and took the froth of hair at her forehead, turning golden curls into blackened cuphooks. Lily clamped her hands to her head and screamed. The slip writhed up towards the ceiling, waving and trembling like a magic carpet. In a while black snow came down, black as the sticks in the grate where the fire had once more gone out.

I made a party to cheer us up, cubes of jelly and apples and a paste from drinking chocolate and milk to spread on cream crackers. Lily cried as she ate and chocolatey spit ran out of her mouth, down her chin and over her dress. It didn't matter for we were both black from the smoke of the fire.

I put her to bed. 'Wait here,' I said. I went and got the glucose powder and a spoon. 'Eat as much as you like.'

'How long will we stay?' Her breath was still shaky from tears and it blew a storm of white grains around her mouth.

'For ever,' I said.

'What about our daddy?'

'He's gone away. Gone to business. He's never coming back.'

'What about my husband? When I grow up I have to have a husband.'

'We'll see.' I took the snoke away and wrapped the quilt around her. Poor Lily looked an awful mess. I thought she would not last very long, that she would start to die like our mother in a little while. I was as strong as a horse. I got the candle and lit it and walked around the cottage. 'This is my house and I am its owner,' I said. Then I went to bed with the cloth duck. Before I lay down I prised beneath its wing. A shower of silver came out, like water from a duck's wing; three pounds and ten shillings.

In the night the real owners of the cottage came; spiders big as spools of thread and slugs that oozed out between the stones. I listened to mice or rats scratching at our case for food. It was a careful sound like tearing or sweeping. I heard a cry and put an arm out to comfort Lily but Lily was sleeping. The cry had been mine.

Lily woke first in the morning. Her eyes and her skin looked red and terrible. 'Milk,' she said in a scratchy voice.

We had none left from yesterday. We could not go back to Margaret Tuttle. By now she would have told on us. Someone might be searching for us.

'There are houses over the hill,' I said. 'I will ask there.'

'Don't leave me alone,' Lily wearily pleaded.

'All right then. You can come.' I would have preferred to go alone for if anyone was looking for us it was two girls they sought, two girls with long hair. 'But we'll have to make a little change.' I took the knife I had used for cutting the nettles and seized Lily's hair. 'Nooo!' She put her hands over her ears, although the noise the knife made was just a small, dry sound, quieter than mice or rats. It only took a minute. I held in my hand a big bunch of her cloudy hair. The hair that was left on her head looked like a drawing filled in by numbers.

I was glad Lily could not see herself and hoped my hair looked better when I had forced my sobbing sister to saw round its edges. We went out, carrying our cups. We were both shivering for it had been damp in the cottage all night. We headed for the nearest house and beat upon its door.

A man answered. We looked hopefully around his bulk, thinking there must be a woman deep inside the house but there was only a girl, not much bigger than ourselves, who hid behind her father. We were both unsure of men and this one wore his underwear.

'Milk, please.' I held out my cup.

'Ragamuffins,' the man commented without interest. 'Would you like to see my rabbits?'

I nodded, deeply ashamed that he had called us untidy.

He gave us cups of milk and showed us wooden cages in his garden, from which white rabbits peered out with their pink eyes. All the time he was followed by the girl who had white hair and pink eyes and who peeped at us from behind him. He said he had bantam hens too but we were both afraid of the rabbit girl and we quickly left when the milk was finished.

The cottage looked safe as we came back to it. I thought it seemed more homely this morning. It looked different but I could not think why until Lily pointed. 'Smoke!'

It came from the chimney, a fat brown curl. Someone had lit a fire. Someone was in our cottage. I broke into a run.

'Oh, no, Matty!' Lily begged, but she ran after me.

It was a dirty tramp. He had lit a huge fire and for a moment this held us and we stood in the doorway and stared at it for it had begun to rain and we were very cold. 'This is our house,' I said then. 'You go away or I'm telling on you.'

He turned angrily but when he saw us he gave a stupid sort of laugh. 'You tell on me and I'll tell on you.'

He turned again to the fire. He was gulping a bottle of sherry wine.

'You should go now,' I said. 'Our father is coming.'

He stood and gazed beyond us to the drizzly field. He looked wild. When he saw that there was no one he gave another laugh, turned once more to the fire and fell with a thump like an apple from a tree. The dregs of the wine trickled into the mud.

For a while we stayed where we were with streams of wet running inside our collars.

'Is he dead?' Lily said.

Oh, no. He was not dead. A torrent of snores sputtered out of his growling face. Soon he would wake and he would tell on us. I went into the cottage and stood by the fire watching him. Steam puffed out of my clothes. He looked awfully hard, the man, but all the same I got the knife and held it up as high as I could and then closed tight my eyes and drove it down and pushed and pushed. I did not look at him but when I opened my eyes again Lily was looking, her eyes huge, her face growing longer and whiter. She came forward with mincing steps, as in a ballet, then moved slowly sideways and lowered her head like a swan and was sick all over the quilt.

We went home after that. We did not know what to do with the man and we could not sleep on a quilt full of sick.

'My God! My God!' our father said, when we walked into the house. He bent to hold us but his face was full of fear and it frightened us and made us cry. 'We thought you were dead,' he said. 'There were dogs out looking for you.'

We were washed and given soup and put to bed – our own bed with our teddies – and then Father asked if there was anything else we wanted. 'Mammy!' Lily sobbed sleepily.

'Yes,' our father said; 'yes. She is getting better. She has been so worried about you that I think we can bend the rules. You will both see her tomorrow.'

We slept all day. In a little while Mother came home from hospital but nothing was ever the same again. Lily had changed. She was no longer mine, no longer beautiful. She kept her hair short and her face stayed long and white as in the moment when the knife fell. Afterwards I asked and asked: What did the man look like? Where did the knife hit him? Was he bleeding? Was he dead? 'I can't remember,' Lily would say in a daze.

I was different too. Perhaps I had the power of death and although I would never know I thought I would never forget. Always, I thought, I would see him, blood growing like an ornament on his head or on his chest, a look of terror in his open eyes like the look on the face of God who sees all things, who is all-powerful, except in His powerlessness not to look.

After all, it was not the man I remembered. Sometimes I even found it hard to remember the pattern of tiles outside the cottage. Mother no longer told us stories of the magic mountain.

She was often tired and liked to rest alone. 'You are big girls now,' she would say with relief. Lily went away to school but I stayed home another year. I was left with time on my hands. I ate a lot, for I had been hungry in the cottage, and waited to see what would come into my mind.

It was the dogs. It was that one moment when our father held us close to him and then gave us the astonishing news that they had sent out dogs to look for us.

Why had they not come themselves?

When I asked him he said that these were very special dogs. They were called tracker dogs and they were trained to follow your scent.

We had no scent. Our mother had a scent called *French Fern*. She hardly ever wore it but sometimes took out the stopper and let us sniff its deep green smell.

I saw the dogs, bounding over fields and hills, past the farm with the white rabbits and the rabbit girl, past Margaret Tuttle, her big clanky mouth full of secrets unreceived. They would come to the cottage and take great alarmed breaths of its past life, of smoke and sick and maybe some old skeleton smell. Soon they would raise their noses to fresher and more appealing scents, wild rabbits and sheep and squirrels. Who would set out to search for them when they grew thin and wild?

I saw them drooping in summer heat; searching old tins and drains for water, or huddled together in the snows of winter, moaning softly in their sleep as starvation came closer, scratching slow as a rat. I saw them rise in the grey and hungry morning, blink softly at some distant memory of home, then shake themselves wearily and totter off, sniffing the ground and the air, searching, searching, searching, for two girls who would never come back.

Affairs in Order

⚜

'Jocelyn's dying,' Rose said to Angela when they met for tea.

The effect on the other middle-aged woman was as if the pink cake she was sectioning had suddenly shown beads of blood on its sawed edges. She did not seem surprised nor saddened but utterly run through with horror.

'Jocelyn?' Her face went white and her eyes were helpless and dreadful

Rose had been through all this the week before and was able to eat her cake. 'He's been given a month – five weeks at the most.'

'Jocelyn . . . oh!' Angela moaned. She dropped her gaze, and found no comfort in a view of her caged bust. 'Is he in hospital?'

'No,' Rose admitted with regret. 'Martha seemed determined to keep him at home.'

Jocelyn Fowler had known many women in his youth. He had a profound effect on all of them. One later went mad and another entered a convent. Those who afterwards married, or who remained married, stayed in love with him all their lives. Their husbands had something to thank him for, for they never looked at another man.

He was a poet, and with the hair for it. In the plain stretches of life, women particularly remembered the buttery feel of his heavy gold hair.

He wasn't especially a sexual man. He was full of conversation and fun, watching his women with blue, interested eyes, waving his long arms and folding long legs. Sex was an interlude or an accompaniment. He made love to his girls as a man at dinner eats from the fruit bowl during intent debate, but afterwards he always wrote so tenderly about their private parts.

His marriage to Martha was a surprise – Jocelyn, tall and graceful, with the golden (now silver) flow of his curls; Martha, squat as a letter box, with her cottage-loaf bosom and brown and grey crewcut. Some said she had money. Others assumed that he had grown serious and that she was to be the custodian of some epic work. In the first year he produced with great flourish (and success) a small volume of verse about housewives in Sainsbury's and cats watching *Coronation Street*. After that there was nothing but an introduction to a book of photographs and an endorsement for a wristwatch. People blamed Martha. She had dulled him. She had swallowed his soul.

When Martha answered the door to Angela, her wholesome face was scarcely altered by grief. She seemed distrait, but not swollen by weeping. She had an air of irritation.

'Oh, Martha! Oh, my dear!' said Angela, who looked a wreck.

'Hello, Angela.'

'It's been so long,' Angela said; 'and now this awful news. How is he?'

'Jocelyn's dying.' There was something strange about her, standing there with her dull blue dress and her bristly hair. She seemed like a child, ill-mannered and feckless, unable to take in the stretch of death. She wasn't even looking at Angela.

It was the shoes. Her gaze had been distracted by the extraordinary height of the other woman's heels. The older women all wore high heels. They took great pains to effect youth in their faces but age crept back in the discomfort of their footwear. The young girls wore any old thing – runners or wellingtons or mountaineering boots. Legs did not seem a feature of the whole business any more. Martha could never think of anything to say to women like Angela. She knew that they discounted her. She had been plain when they had been beautiful. They attached great potency to the past and seemed not to have noticed that they were all getting on anyway when Jocelyn married her and none of them looked all that much better or worse than the other: except Joss.

'Come in, Angela,' she frowned. 'Say hello to him. I'll put the kettle on. He's very weak. Try not to stay longer than it takes the kettle to boil.'

Inside, Angela peered around briefly, surprised by how comfortable the house was, the attention that had been given to flowers and lace and polish. Martha pointedly filled the kettle and Angela fled quite nimbly up the stairs. She found Jocelyn in a bright room in a feathery bed by a window. Most of the flesh was gone from his face and there were lines of suffering on his delicate skin. His hair had been saved and had taken on the quality of rolling clouds. His blue eyes were huge and full of vision. He looked magnificent.

'It's me,' she said shyly. 'How are you dear?'

The look he gave her was kind and full of suffering. Love bubbled to her lips and her eyes dissolved. He stretched out his hand. 'I've been summoned,' he wryly smiled.

'Oh no.' She took his fingers and pressed them to her mouth. 'You're running out on us. You're escaping, leaving the rest of us to grow old and lonely alone.'

'Don't cry, sweetie.' He brushed her cheek with a leaf-dry thumb. 'I've had a good life.' His use of past tense refreshed her sense of terror. 'I've never stopped loving you,' she said.

'Come here, girl.' He put out his two arms and drew her frailly to his chest. She allowed herself to go with him until she was lying against him on the bed, her mouth on his hair, her flesh on his flesh, just as it used to be, apart from the blankets and corsetry that now divided them.

She did not rest her weight against him, for it was more substantial than it used to be, and his was less, but allowed her body to learn again the geography of his bones. In a while, mad memory was awaiting his mouth, which used to turn from energetic talk to find her lips, and kiss. Then he would swing her body underneath his to admire it and then kiss it here and there and then he would make it his home.

He seemed so relaxed against her, so peaceful. Nothing changes, she told herself, except the circumstances of happiness.

After a short duration of this relative bliss Angela heard, in her mind's ear, the furious boiling of a kettle. She sat up guiltily, disturbing Jocelyn, who was almost asleep. When she went into the bathroom to mop her eyes, she was surprised by her wild, tousled look.

At the bottom of the stairs, as she descended, there stood a strange woman. 'Where's Martha?' Angela said. The woman gave her an angry look and swept past her in the direction of Jocelyn. Some sort of aria was going on on the front step – the sound of a young person thwarted and Martha's responses, soft, but not in the least yielding: 'No, I'm afraid not – he's very ill. You can leave a message if you like.'

'An old friend of Jocelyn's,' she explained to Angela, when she had managed to lock her out.

'Not old, by the sound of it,' Angela said.

'No, actually.'

'Poor you,' Angela sympathized. 'So many people to tell.'

'I told no one,' Martha said. 'It was Joss.'

Martha's behind, as she wandered back to the kitchen, resembled one of those family joints of meat that are tied about with string. Angela suddenly thought she understood. The past was not past at all. Jocelyn's life awaited resolution. He had to put his affairs in order. She followed Martha, stalking like a mud-dwelling bird on her aerial heels.

'Let me help you!'

'Yes, get the milk jug.'

'With Jocelyn! You must be worn out. I could come and sit with him. I could sit nights if you like. I'm a widow now.'

'Jocelyn doesn't need anyone to sit with him. He needs sleep. I like to read a little to him in the evenings, but by the time all the visitors have left, he's too worn out.' She looked forlorn, suddenly, like an old tree on a blasted heath. 'Did you know Baba Maxwell?'

'Who?'

'I think she's Mrs Something now. The woman in the hall! He was in love with her once. He told me. He wrote that very peculiar series of poems about her – "Flowers in the Night".'

They were about me! Angela thought with a pang of jealous fury. Jocelyn had read the poems aloud to her in bed. She was young then, and almost innocent. It was a seduction like none other, to be teased with your own body: well, to all intents, your own body. He had employed, as poets do, poetic licence. He depicted a flower, 'with peeping scarlet stamen, winning as a kitten's tongue'. She herself had a very reclusive physiognomy.

The thought of that woman with her scarlet stamen sitting up there with Jocelyn – possibly even lying on his chest – agitated Angela beyond endurance. She could not stay in his house.

'Aren't you going to have your tea?' Martha pondered. Angela said no. A new grief slopped about in her chest. Martha too seemed to have lost heart and stood nursing the teapot with its inch of warming water.

When the visitors first began to arrive she assumed that it had to do with publishing. No publishers came. There wasn't any new work and the old had already been recycled. Had the literary world mourned the death of the poet years and years ago? Had she yielded her life to a gorgeous man? Who was she, in any case, to quibble? Other women seemed to think the latter more than good enough for her.

They came in cars, on buses, by motorbike. Their perfumes fled about the house, their grapes and freesias proliferated and went mouldy. They were used and unused women, successful and failed ones, young and old. There were women with glorious hair, with hairs on their chin, with gold in their teeth, with emeralds sunk into beds of metal, biting plump, waxy fingers.

There was even a nun. She was unique. At first she seemed incredibly old. She was wrinkled and shrunken and had a crone's shambling gait. It was only when she looked up and one saw those vivid eyes that one knew she was woman in her prime. She had merely tipped over from rosiness to an intense withering, like an apple stored in the light.

She, of course, did not wear high heels. Beneath the coarse wool of her robes, her horny toes were splayed in sandals. She carried a large black bag made of imitation leather.

'Soeur Gertrude,' she introduced herself to Martha.

She offered no such relief to Jocelyn but slithered straight up to his bed and stared at him with her bright blue eyes. 'Bonjour Jocelyn.'

He kept his sheets clutched to his chin and scowled at her to deter her. What was Martha thinking of? A terrible notion struck him then, borne on the intense beam of her gaze. He managed to pull himself up a little bit to study her. 'Gertrude?' He gave a gasp of recognition and she a small smile, rather cruel.

'Gertie?' he said. 'Gertie Balfour?'

Soeur Gertrude did not fling herself upon his chest as other women had done. Instead she placed upon it numerous small portions of the corpses of saints, taken with care from her black bag. Then she prayed. He watched the dried fruit of her lips, the rapturous fluttering of her brown lids.

She was the most beautiful of all the girls he had known. For a year he had pursued her, trying to make her say she loved him. When he succeeded, he was frightened by the ferocity of her commitment and he had violently shaken her off. There followed a silence so complete that he imagined she must have died but he found out from friends that she had entered a convent — a contemplative order where the sisters spoke rarely, and only in French.

She finished her prayers and gathered up the relics and put them back in her bag.

'Will I get better now?' Jocelyn jested.

'Si Dieu le veut,' she replied.

He found her more interesting than any of the other women and curiously, less changed. She had the same directness of manner, the same seething air she had had as a girl. Whereas the other women were softly spoiling, she had simply cast off what she no longer needed when she gave herself to God. He was intrigued now, as when he had first met her, by her apparent lack of interest in him. 'Gertie, Gertie,' he said in humblest tones. 'I treated you badly.'

She peered at him rather rudely, as if trying to recollect what he was talking about. 'You were a stage on a journey,' she commented at last. 'Journeys are seldom comfortable.'

'Have you heard the news about Jocelyn?' Rose said to Angela, when they met for more tea.

'Has he croaked?' Angela said brutally.

'No, actually. It's rather the most extraordinary thing. He's begun to get better. They say he's had a remission. It's a miracle, really.'

Angela contemplated her cake. She cut it up and then returned to the pastry any jam and cream that still adhered to the knife. Four quarters of a cream slice were consumed with intent and the debris deftly sifted from her lips with a napkin. When the napkin came away, the lips retained their expert coating of lacquer. There also remained behind a look of disgruntlement which was new, but seemed chiselled in at the edges.

'I wonder,' said Angela, 'if he ever really had cancer at all. I shouldn't be surprised if he made the whole thing up to get attention. He always was a bit of a fraud.'

'I know that,' Rose said sharply. 'I didn't know you knew.'

Now that he was getting better Jocelyn would have welcomed visitors. He would have eaten the fruit and drunk champagne and had a bit of music in the background. Oddly, they seemed all to have vanished. It should have been a festive thing, turning back at death's door, but he was left alone, as if in disgrace.

Now, he needed people. Dying had been an absorbing business but recovery was filled with hindrance and frustration. The absence of pain left an odd hollowness in his life. He could not yet quite do things for himself and Martha was never there when he needed her.

What on earth had happened to Martha? She seemed to have missed the news of his recovery. She trailed about in a grieving daze, eyes bulging with depression. When he summoned her she would come reluctantly and look at him as if he was an interloping stranger.

This morning she had forgotten lunch and he had to ring the little bell she left with him. When she came, she bore no tray of soup and fruit, nor apologized for its absence. He could not ask. He was at her mercy. He smiled his most winning smile.

'I'm going back to work, Joss,' was all she said.

'What can you do?' He spoke rudely out of fright.

'I can do a lot of things.' She faced him quite squarely. 'I was working when we met.'

He stayed quiet a moment, letting the steam go out of his anger. He patted the velvet-covered stool beside his bed and she allowed her bottom to subside on to it. 'This is absurd, Mattie. I'm an old nuisance, I know, but I still need someone.'

'I've arranged for a nurse,' she said. 'I'll be home in the evenings.'

'What am I supposed to do all day?'

The same as me. Go back to work, she thought. She did not say it. She shrugged. He understood that she could not be bothered to discuss it. As soon as she decently could, she got up to leave.

'Is it the old girls?' he called out fretfully. 'Is that it?'

'What?' she turned at the door.

'Something's changed. Aren't you glad I pulled through?'

'Leave it, dear.' She went out quickly. How foolish she would feel if he forced her to tell the truth.

It was his unreliability. Over the years she had put up with him because she understood that they would be together when they were old. Now she felt betrayed. He had shown her that he did not need her. He could turn away without a backward glance and drop out of her life.

She went into the garden and sat sunning herself on a wooden seat over paving stones whose seams were embroidered with alpines. When first married and stricken by joy, she had spent most of her time like a badger, down on all fours, burrowing in the dark earth. She wanted to make a bower for him where he would write his poems. He was delighted with her work. He liked to sit among the scented borders and drink a glass of wine.

Slowly she saw that his work was at an end. She had her own vanity. She meant to make her life a useful thing. She did not have his appetite for squandering. In the end, being practical and in love, she attempted to make her life's work humility.

Oh, love! The loosening force of it. She knew she could have made him work. She had only to pull the pleasantness from under him and he would have taken to verse as a revenge. Instead she hung on, wasting her life, relying on old age to vindicate them. The little retrospective stretch of life must surely acquit its trivia. She imagined them at peace in the garden together, dried out and shimmering like those pearly discs of old growth which are called honesty.

When the doctors told her he was going to get better, she felt no relief. She had done her grieving. Now, some day, she would have to go through it all over again. She had jettisoned trust in favour of the unfriendly skills of survival. Perhaps she was callous. She quite liked the word, with its suggestion of hard skin. She needed her hard skin.

After Martha went back to work Jocelyn felt a peculiar peevishness, which he did not wish to explore. He telephoned a girl he knew, who was lovely and young and round.

'Jocelyn!' she cried joyfully. 'What a relief!'

He kissed the receiver, lapping up her maiden youth.

'I thought you were dead,' she said merrily.

There was a goodish pause on the other end of the line. 'No, no!' he rallied. 'They sent me back. I'm on the mend, but I'm a prisoner. Come and rescue me. Bring a bottle.'

'Darling, I can't,' the girl said. 'Actually, I'm dashing now. Look, it's wonderful that you're better. Do give me a ring sometime.'

Don't be ridiculous, I am ringing you, he thought in an apoplexy of irritation. 'I'll do that,' he said warmly.

He telephoned another of his girls.

He imagined, as he waited, the messenger's silent glide through polished halls, the summoning bells, the harem's pheremone calm. What had they thought when she first came to them with her skin the colour of cider and her unsuitable blue eyes? They must all have been in love with her.

'Oui?' uttered a cracked voice of entrancing indifference.

'Gertie? It's Jocelyn!'

'Bonjour, Jocelyn,' she said with enduring politeness.

'Aren't you surprised to hear from me? I should be dead by now.'

'Perhaps you weren't ready for death,' Soeur Gertrude said.

'What is one supposed to do then, to get ready?'

'Are you really all that keen,' she wondered, 'for death?'

'No, Gert, it isn't that.' He sighed. 'I seem somehow to have offended people. Everyone's gone off me. I've no visitors. Do you know, Martha's gone and left me – gone back to work. It's as if I'd done something unforgivable. I should have gone ahead and died. People were just waiting for the obituary.'

Soeur Gertrude, in her solitary darkness, gave one of her famously economical smiles to think he still saw himself in headlines. 'Maybe Jocelyn Fowler has died,' she suggested.

'Who's left then?' he said fearfully.

'Who knows.'

'I'm bloody lonely, Gert,' he said.

'It is not uncommon,' she assured him. 'Our Saviour on the cross has also mentioned this experience to me.'

'I'm glad someone understands,' he said sourly.

'Yes. Oddly enough, I do. There is a common belief that Our Lord sent His only son on earth to redeem the world, as a supreme sacrifice. In fact, of course, it was envy. By depriving His creatures of paradise, He had given them access to an experience which He had no means to share. He could hardly be God if He was excluded from the privilege of suffering.'

'Damn it to hell,' Jocelyn thought wearily as he put down the phone. 'She's gone nuts.'

He could not shake off his uneasiness in regard to something she had said. In the end he had to crawl out of the bed and drag himself to a mirror to reassure himself with his reflection. The handsome lines of brow and jaw seemed scratched upon the glass. The outline was that of a tree in which strange creatures made their nest and the largest of these was self-pity. 'I'm lonely,' he appealed.

The figure in the mirror mimed mournfully.

'The moping owl does to the moon complain,' he balefully reflected.

About a week after this Soeur Gertrude, unknown to anyone save her silent companions in the cloister, passed away, and Jocelyn Fowler, at the age of fifty-seven and not at all a well man, propped himself up in bed and started, once more, to write.

ᘒᗰᗰᘖ

A Particular Calling

⚙︎*☟☟☟☟*☟

In the window of Dooley's Bar a black Morris Minor slid behind the crusted gold lettering of a misted mirror past an acrobatic display of whiskey bottles filled with something palely whiskey-tinged, some dyed formaldehyde. 'Nice cup of tea,' the driver said kindly and the car sailed into a wide main street which was pressed down by grey sky and lined on either side with grey buildings stubbily imprinted with shops, emporia and licensed premises of a uniform nursery dullness.

The place had the preserved look of a museum. Outflung overalls and silent boots in Carbury's Drapery suggested the remnants of a tribe more than the treat of a new cardigan or a little Communion frock for a child. There was nothing for a young girl to look at – no Ballet Bra, seven and eleven pence, or Bradmola stockings tinted like the skin of Red Indians. In the glass front of the Dainty Bakery the big hard-looking cakes of bread and currant loaves had settled into the sullen permanence of sleeping cats. A cactus plant licked a gilt-framed Our Lady of Perpetual Succour with faded, sawtooth tongues, in among the Milk of Magnesia bottles and tins of sheep dip in Markey's Pharmacy. There was hardly anyone in the street. A few women with empty message bags and a man on a bicycle moved in dislocated isolation, like refugees.

A child ran across the road chewing a stalk of rhubarb and the woman waved, but the girl stepped back and stared as if there was something of which a stranger ought to have been warned. Even the piles of cow dung, heaped up randomly in the road, some flattened by tractor wheels or bleeding thickly into puddles, had a look of old occupation.

'Well, here we are!' The woman brought her Morris Minor to a halt outside the largest of the grey buildings which was Sinnott's Commercial and was a hotel. As she lifted out her cases and stood in the street to refresh herself with the town's odd stout and manure breath, there was a tumult of bells. Hundreds of people were coming towards her. She remained on the dirty pavement, half smiling, her pink face and Toni-waved hair imperturbable as the horde advanced. The bells continued to clang as more people streamed through tall silver gates, the women all in hats and headscarves. 'Oh, it's a Holy Day,' the woman laughed in relief. She had developed a habit of speaking kindly to herself, or bracingly. 'Everyone was at Mass.' She was not a Catholic but had made this difference as discreet as possible and prided herself that she fitted in. She went into the hotel and was shown up to her room with its soiled pink quilt and empty fireplace, the wallpaper patterned with sepia stains. 'Very nice. Thank you,' she said.

While she waited for tea and a Polo biscuit she wrote out two cards.

'Miss Patricia Higgins is in Sinnott's Hotel from Tuesday 14th to Friday 17th for the usual services.' She went out again to pin one of these in the porch of the now-deserted church and she left the second on the noticeboard in the hotel foyer. As she savoured the flesh-coloured cup of tea and biscuit exotically zested with coconut, she laid out her things – her own lamp which counteracted the unsavoury effect of the little plastic shade, a clean white sheet with which to cover the queasy duvet, her black box with its secrets.

Sometimes she was asked if she was lonely. The nature of her work kept her in contact with one sex only and meant she couldn't mix socially with the other. Her clients did not like it known that they visited her, or for what purpose, so she stayed away from the hotel's lounge bar and the cinema and ate alone, mostly in her room but an odd time she came down to the dining room and was shown to one of those peculiar corner tables that are saved for the solitary, imprisoning the diner into a recess in distant view of celebrant groups and couples. On these occasions she forced herself to concentrate on the food in some abstract manner; trying, for instance, to think of words that would rhyme with liver – river, shiver, deliver, giver, quiver.

'Fat chance of lonely,' she laughed at herself. She was a confidante to her clients. When she heard the troubles of married people she could only count her blessings.

Young people with nothing on their minds were even more anxious. When their dreams failed to materialize they themselves grew insubstantial. They needed her, begged her to hurry back. Some of them liked her.

She used to work in Dublin where she lived with her mother. Discretion had no currency in the big city. She did not have to work from a hotel but had a small office close to Camden Street. She had no shortage of callers. One of them came all the way from Mallow in County Cork and had told her that there was a desperate need for her work in the provinces. Such a service was unheard of in rural parts and might be seen as a contravention of nature. People's lives were damaged by its absence. She took her Morris Minor on the road. At first it had been difficult making contact but those who needed her found her. She was overwhelmed with business Sometimes she could not get home to spend the weekend with her mother.

She had her pets, certain young people with whom there was more than a business affinity. She called them her dotes and bucked up their confidence. Country life could be cruel to the young. Parents were strict and there wasn't a lot in the way of social life. They saved up for her the diaries of their hopes and talked of true love and happiness as if it was a harvest that merely had to come ripe and could be plucked off in the hand.

A week from now she would be seeing her best pet who was waiting for her by the sea. She should have been there two months past but was kept at home by her mother's illness. 'Only a week!' she beamed and dragged her mind away from the smug look on her mother's face as the doctor declared her dead.

She liked the seaside. People were friendly and used to strangers. She could walk on the beach and smoke her cigarettes and mingle with the holiday revellers, the children dancing in the waves in their knickers. She did not favour the flat towns of the midland. It was only duty that brought her to this part of the country. Midland was cattle country. The men in the hotels were purple-faced fellows. The rooms were without comfort, designed for men, with bits of lino on the floor and yellow lighting that showed up the sheets an unwholesome colour. She did not sleep well for the hotels were on the main street which at night attracted snorting cars and motorbikes, unseen by day. She had to listen to the sounds of men answering the call of nature against the hotel's facade or hold herself rigid against the violence of men being ill in the street when they had visited the chip shop after the pub was closed. It affected her with nausea. Her own digestion, when she stayed in such places, was made uneasy by menus featuring huge fatty steaks and coarse grills. There was rarely chicken or a ham salad, no sponge cake or dainties.

'Don't you miss having just the one person of your own?' her pet often asked her. 'I have my mother,' she used to say. Her placid eyes filled up but she reminded herself of the success of her business, the satisfaction of her work. Never a minute to herself. She had only time to stand on a chair and pluck from the light cord a strip of sticky paper where flies lay dying and there was a knock on the door.

It was a new client, young and shy with timid eyes and a sparse orange moustache. Patricia Higgins put out a plump hand. 'You're very welcome, indeed you are. Come in and make yourself comfy on the bed.' Still the novice clung to the door and gazed around the challenging decor of the room. 'Does it hurt much?' she said.

When she was first qualified, the travelling electrolysis lady was surprised by the quantity of hair on other women's bodies. She had hardly any body hair. Under her clothes her skin was smooth and cool as marble, as pale as a grey pearl. Her breasts were parchment pale and rather flat but wide in circumference, like saucers of cream. It was not a beautiful body, but it was flawless. In bed she liked to think of those cool unblemished curves beneath her nightie as a temple for the Holy Ghost.

She was an expert at her business. She caused hardly any pain. As she executed unwanted hair roots or cauterized bloody veins she kept up mild conversation. She hardly ever talked about herself.

'You're an intellectual type, aren't you? I said that to myself. I admire a person who can get to grips with books.' She rooted out the orange moustache. She had said that because the girl was plain and would have no romantic secrets to divulge but most likely kept her tufted lip in a book. The girl talked about Karl Marx and Simone de Beauvoir. Miss Higgins said she liked Ngaio Marsh. When the work was finished the girl went and looked at herself in a small piece of mirror that was nailed up over the wash-basin. She ran her fingers over the newly smooth patch above her narrow lips. 'Will it grow again?'

'It does, yes,' Miss Higgins said, 'but you won't have to worry for a long time.'

'Will you come back?' the girl said.

'I keep track of all my clients. I'll be back in time,' she promised. 'Can I have your name for my book?'

'Natasha,' the girl said. 'Natasha Galvin.' She paid Miss Higgins and went to the door where she clung on again, picking at the paint. 'I went to a party,' she said. 'The boys called me Moustasha.' It sounded funny but the poor girl had the look of a cowboy in the pictures when he has just been shot. 'Oh, now love,' Miss Higgins said. 'All that's over. It's just a little thing women sometimes have to cope with.'

She had heard it all before, the cruelty of both sexes towards a woman who failed to meet the standards of grace and beauty. A city woman could be any way, with hair on her face and a baldy head, with warts or no chest and the experts were on hand to remodel her, to curl or straighten, to bleach or paint. Any city girl could be a beauty. A man never knew what he was getting. In the country you were what you were, as God had made you, as they wryly judged. Women whom God had made in vacant mood had to marry an old fellow, half blind, or live at home with the pigs and their father or bury themselves in a convent. 'Sticks and stones,' she tried to remind hurt young women, but the insults were something worse, more akin to boiling oil. Beardy Bridie, Tarzan the Ape Man, Hairy Mary. Just for a small, natural abundance a woman could be shunned like a leper. Only Miss Higgins understood. It was a particular calling.

Her special pet was called Maoliosa Quilligan – known as Maisie – but Miss Higgins thought of her as the doe. She had a doe's eyes, huge and melting brown and softly curling brown hair, although she did not have the nature of a doe. She was bold and full of fun. She had the eye of a fellow called Malachy Boland. He had taken her home several times from dances. The doe said he was a wild bucko, but she was stone crazy about him. 'Oh, Miss Higgins, what must it be like to fall into a fellow's arms and let him go on as long as you'd like? I'd give it a go, only if you make them hang on they marry you to put themselves out of their misery.'

Unknown to Malachy Boland she had a natural disposition to a growth of fuzz along the sides of her face and on her neck. When she was ten years married, she said, she'd let it grow anyway, for either Malachy would be so used to her by then he wouldn't notice, or he'd have grown tired of her and wouldn't care.

'Never fear, pet, he'll be sweet on you,' Miss Higgins said. She often brought a small gift for the doe, a box of turkish delight or black grapes from the city because she knew a fellow like Malachy Boland would only court her with his arms and she wanted her to have the niceties. She criticized herself for having favourites. Everyone was equal in the sight of God. She knew that as she understood that her confidential witness was a privilege which commanded impartiality. All the same her pity was directed to the young. She couldn't see why older women bothered, unless it was a disfigurement of the face such as purple veins or a bunch of coarse hairs on the chin. She disapproved of plain vanity and had been made aware of other more complex motives. The women could say anything to her because she had no business with the men.

She was worn out, that first day in the midlands. Sitting down alone to a high tea of a slice of ham with half a tomato and a scallion she was visited by grief. She felt her mother's shadow passing over her, passing on. There was only one other person in the dining room, a commercial traveller with the grey complexion of habitual hotel eating, but she did not want him to see. She bent her head to pour a pool of salad cream on her plate. She had grown used to unburdening herself to her mother, who was herself bound to secrecy, being house-bound, who never judged but poured the tea and sliced the Fuller's walnut cake. 'Well, it takes all types,' she would soothingly affirm as Patricia bit into the crumbly icing and spoke of the cruelty to the young, or of some middle-aged woman in whom perfection was newly necessitated by a turn her life had taken.

She managed the ham but left the scallion and went outside to her Morris Minor. She wanted to get away from the town. She drove past the tall grey church, past lime-green fields perpetually consumed by dappled cows, past a big concrete cube in a bog of mud that was called The Allanah Ballroom. She parked the car beside a stream. In its dying moments the sun had crept into the grey sky and appeared as a buttery band on the flat horizon. The air felt nice as she walked along the squelchy grass by the water. Her cigarette smoke dangled on the windless yellow dusk.

She understood that it took all types but she was made a party to the types of lives they led. She was once visited by a widow who needed a little beard removed in order to get a job as a waitress. Miss Higgins did her chin free of charge and said she could pay her the next time, when she had wages. 'You are a dear soul,' the widow told her.

Women like Mrs Manning would never think of her as a dear soul. They winked at her. They imagined she envied and admired them – that she conspired with them.

'Your work won't go to waste,' Mrs Manning had boasted, walking about without a screed to admire her thighs which were wide and newly smooth. She had come to Miss Higgins with a flowing surfeit of personal hair. She was more than forty and had been married twenty years. In all probability her husband admired this quality in his wife. Her plucked limbs were for someone new.

The stream went into a field. There were no cars or dogs around so she followed it and felt soothed by its whispering. Someone said hello and she waved and plodded on. 'Hello!' the man said again and she paused, plumply smiling, confusion locked up inside her as she realized she was trespassing and the man was not greeting her but summoning her attention.

'Are you all right, there?' It was a polite way of asking her what she was doing.

'Sorry,' she said. 'I'm on your land. Lost in thought!' she giggled.

'You're all right,' he said. 'Finish your walk and enjoy your thoughts.'

He was loose-limbed with bristling hair and a long thoughtful face. He hadn't the coarseness that came to many men whose business was the death of beasts.

'They weren't really very nice,' Miss Higgins hovered; 'my thoughts.'

'Oh, well then.' He looked around as if seeking something pleasant for her to dwell upon. 'Would you come up to the house for a cup of tea?'

'Oh, no.' She was embarrassed and fell silent.

'No, of course you wouldn't.' Her heart went out to him when she saw that he too was abashed. 'That was an awful thing to say. I'm every way since my mother died.'

Her eyes filled with tears and she smiled. 'Oh, that's too bad,' she said gaily and she hurried back to her car, her heels catching in mud so that she must have looked like a duck.

In bed that night he crowded her mind. Her memory cast about for different angles of him and animated them, putting a cup of tea in his hand, putting his hand on hers. This disturbed her because she had never been foolish. She put it down as a reaction to her mother's death and then was overwhelmed with compassion for his own loss. She wanted to hold his face in her hands.

In the morning she was herself again. She ate toast and drank tea in her room, brightened her lips with her Gala lipstick and spat into her brown mascara, scrubbing a little brush on the muddy patch and then combing colour on her lashes. She could scarcely remember the man's long face. She dabbed Max Factor on her cheeks.

She was glad it was Wednesday. She would be out of the town in two days. Her car would be packed up by the time the men assembled in the hotel dining room to eat a big breakfast before market day. Coaxing her car through the jam of cattle left bellowing in the street, she would be on her way to the sea-side and the doe with a little gift of Lemons' Pure Sweets.

Lips and loins and throats and ears. She applied herself with deft detachment to the parts most usually associated with love, tenderly removing hormonal surfeit while the women faintly groaned and murmured on about the pains of life. Some were long-standing customers and she had years of family history for reference. Some reproached her for her late arrival and had bristly growths arising from the use of razors. She didn't tell them about her mother. She preferred them to think that she was still in the cosy flat in Dublin, waiting with the Fuller's cake.

That evening she drove out again. She stopped by the stream, since it was a place she knew. She walked for an hour until turned back by a starry sky.

In bed she dreamed of the man. He sat beside her on a bench and she offered him a sandwich from a greaseproof parcel. He took the sandwich and called her a dear soul.

She ate her dinner in the dining room next day. Without his mother, he might eat in a hotel. 'Tick or tin?' the waitress demanded. 'Thin, please,' Miss Higgins requested, understanding that the girl referred to a choice of soups in varying textures. The waitress ignored her preference and brought her a thick pink fluid and white sliced pan. Some farmers came in and ate noisily, drinking beer and pots of tea. Miss Higgins tried not to glance at the door but concentrated on her soup (tomato – mulatto, staccato, gateau, plateau, chateau). When her mutton and mashed turnip came she could not eat it, but asked for the jelly and custard and a cup of tea, scolding herself for waste.

She stood by the stream in the lime-green field and gazed all around her. She could not even see a farm that might be his. She wanted to cry out – help me! Oh, imagine if she did and he appeared. She would smile and say she'd caught her heel but she was all right now, and off she'd scuttle.

On Friday morning she was packed by half past nine The relief was enormous. She knew now how other women felt when they talked of love, the woolly bondage that pricked and nagged and soured sleep; the craving for something which, when you looked at it closely, was nothing at all.

She longed for the bracing air of the sea, the bold, harmless intimacies and laughter of the doe. Opening the door of the Morris Minor, she glanced around in pity at the poor cattle, already helplessly besmirching the street.

'Hello,' he said

'Oh, hello.' She beamed at him mildly, her heart clanging. Of course he was a farmer. Because he looked gentle she had not associated him with the brutal commerce of the market. Now she could feast her eyes, could see to her immense satisfaction that she had not made him up. His eyes were green. He had a weathered bit of tan. His shoes were clean. 'You're not leaving?' he said.

'Oh, no,' she laughed. 'Not till tomorrow.'

'Have a bit of dinner with me,' he said. 'Don't be offended now. You will, won't you?'

'Thank you very much,' she said. 'Well, I must be going for now. About one o'clock, then.' She went back into the hotel to book her room again. She had finished her business in the town. She could go to the pictures with him in the evening, if he liked.

They ate a dreadful meal of boiled fish, its warped bones poking through a clout of sauce. It had to be fish because it was Friday.

The smell of cattle came in from the street and the cheap dining-room furniture was imperilled by the restless bulk and noise of farmers. 'I can't hear my ears,' Miss Higgins smiled. 'I'd take you away from here only I have business,' said the man who was called Tommy Kearney.

'Come up to my room,' she said, her eyes blinking in calm horror as it was said. She couldn't say anything about them not getting up to anything – not without sounding cheap. She couldn't say such things anyway. The stairs were in view of the dining room and her ears burned as they ascended together, imagining the eyes of farmers on her plump navy blue behind.

He sat on the pink quilt. 'You should have nicer than this,' he looked around. 'My mother's bedroom was very finicky, very refined.'

'I like nice things.' She did not want to sit beside him on the bed but was happy to stand by the fireplace watching him.

'Do you know I love a little garden.' He leaned forward. 'Most of the farmers haven't much use for flowers but all living things are beautiful.'

There was no awkwardness, no threat of assault. He talked about his farm and his mother and how he had once wanted to go to Canada but did not like to leave his mother and now it was too late.

She told him of her own parent's slow departure, and how she still referred everything to her, even though she was dead. Although they remained on opposite sides of the room, a pleasant glow encased them and she understood now how poor people managed to survive if they had someone they were fond of, for one could be contented anywhere, bathed in this glow. It was the other side of love, the safety side, the harbour.

At three o'clock he had to leave for bidding. At the door he took her hand. She would have liked to have a go at kissing him but she did not wish to seem practised. She sat on the bed where he had warmed the quilt and watched the market through her window until the poor beasts had been led away in vans squelching through the muck, except those who remained moaning in the street while their owners got drunk in the hotel's bar. She supposed he had to get drunk in order to kiss her. She did not like men who had taken drink but the kissing was something they needed to get over before they could be a couple. She put on her pink dressing gown and tried to read an Agatha Christie, waiting for the last of the vehicles to pull out of town and the long-faced man to have drunk his courage.

The knock came after ten. She heard a sniggery little laugh and something inside her contracted. 'Yes?' she said brightly.

The door opened and they came in. Five drunk farmers descended on her, their eyes veined with pink and glazed over like frightened horses.

'Oh,' she said softly, her insides squealing.

'You first, boyo!' They jostled, exploding into little soprano laughs as they pushed each other forward. One of them stumbled and touched her breast and the others made a hissing sound as if he might have burnt himself.

They were what the young girls would call bowsies, leftover bachelors reeking in neglected clothes, their bodies bloated and mottled from beer. Decent women had long ceased to consider them a prospect. They moved in a pack, seeking incitement, still retaining a wistful faith in the filth against which the church had warned them.

Miss Higgins crawled back against the bed-post and held a pillow to her chest. 'What do you want?'

'The usual services.' A bull-faced man reached for her. As he pulled the pillow from her grasp, his hand caught the front of her night-gown and ripped it off like a sheet of lavatory paper. Five men stared at her bare breasts. They gasped aspirations to Jesus, to the Blessed Virgin.

'It's a service for women.' She turned her head away. She could not close her dressing gown. The bull-faced man held on.

'What service could women want? She's a hoor!' A squat man with shiny lips turned inside out from some defect spat on the lino and took off his belt 'A city hoor. What way do ye do it in the city?' The others, excited by this talk, laughed and beat their fists on their hands.

'Go away,' she begged.

'You think we aren't good enough,' he flicked his belt at her, grazing her cheek. 'You think we haven't money.' He took out a wad of notes and flung it on the bed. 'Tommy Kearney was good enough.'

Miss Higgins burned. They had seen her going up the stairs with the bristle-haired man. They had wondered about her notice on the wall. Maybe Tommy Kearney had boasted to them of imaginary feats. She knew nothing about him. A good ride. That was the term. She knew how the men talked from the things women said to her. She had thrown away her reputation. She was anything they called her. She remained passive as two men seized her arms and dragged her on to the floor. They were pulling at her clothing, pulling at themselves, a blunt inhuman mass smelling of beer and sweat. She had turned them into this. However bad they were, she had made them worse. 'Oh, Mother, what am I?' she cried out silently.

'A dear soul.' It was not her mother's voice that spoke in her head.

'I'm Tommy Kearney's girlfriend,' she whispered. 'I'm his fiancée.'

She crouched beneath a petrified tableau, silent save for the men's bewildered panting. 'Oh, Jesus Mary and Joseph, miss, we're very sorry.' They fumbled their clothes together and wrapped the edges of her gown around her. They stuffed their money back in their pockets. 'He's a nice fellow, miss, we wish you happiness.' 'Not a word now, men are very foolish when they've taken drink.'

'That's all right,' she said. They tiptoed out of the room leaving her smiling from the floor.

On the way to the seaside she was overtaken by violent bouts of shivering. 'Bit of a chill,' she told herself. Feeling guilty, she treated herself to one of the doe's Lemons' Pure Sweets. She couldn't wait for a bit of sea air, a paddle in the ocean.

She had a nice clean room in Aherne's Holiday Hotel. She kept a watch out the window. She knew the doe would be waiting for her, even two months late. Any minute now she would come darting down the road, her brown hair flying, her dark eyes full of shining mischief. 'I should have brought her something better than a bag of sweets,' she reproached herself. 'She's probably engaged to Malachy Boland by now – something personal like a leather purse or a signet ring.'

A taciturn woman with long hairs growing out of her nose arrived and Miss Higgins banished her sentimental notions to give her the whole of her attention.

'Maybe she's married already. She could be on her honey-moon.' By the third day she was growing weary of the view from her window. She made it a rule never to discuss clients but when a young girl, about the doe's age, came into her room with towels, it seemed a natural thing to mention her favourite.

'What do you know?' the youngster sat down on the bed. 'She's gone into the convent. She's after getting the call. Now who'd have thought such a thing of Maisie Quilligan that was mad as a March hare?'

'What about Malachy Boland?' Miss Higgins looked out at the sea.

'Ah, him! Gone on the boat from Cobh. He was all out for himself – gave Maisie the push. She was gorgeous too, wasn't she? She used to be gorgeous. Did you know her? Only she suddenly developed this crop of bristles all over her face and neck. Like a warty hog.' The girl gave a snort of laughter.

When the chambermaid left her, Miss Higgins ate the Lemons' Pure Sweets one by one, until the boiled confections bit into her tongue and blistered it. The pain would bring tears to your eyes.

'Nice cup of tea,' she told herself kindly. But she stayed where she was, smiling out the window at the prankish waves.

Technical Difficulties and the Plague

The things women do to their children. I know a woman who called her children Elgar and Mozart. Elge and Moze, they are now. But children can be cruel too.

I called my children Robin and Rosemary, nice names for nice children. It suits their pink cheeks and the light curl of their gold-brown hair. I can say without exaggeration that I gave up everything for them. I gave up the chance of a good career and stayed with my husband, who was never the life and soul of the party. After all that, what do you think they did? They never came.

I don't often brood but I am sitting alone at a cafe in a foreign country and a strange man has just sat down beside me, so you can excuse my mind for running riot. Robin and Rosemary. Their little ghosts do not haunt me but I feel the weight of their ingratitude. I waited so long for them. Everything was ready. I had my insides checked out. They were like a new pin. My husband had his sperm inspected for short measure, but he had been packed to capacity. The little bastards simply couldn't be bothered to turn up.

There is something familiar about the man but I expect that's just my imagination.

You know how it is when you're on your own in a strange place; first there is the giddy freedom. Then you start peering into your handbag. After that you begin imagining things about the people around you.

What annoyed me about Robin and Rosemary was the fact

that they were so much Desmond's children – not really mine
at all. That business of keeping me waiting, they got that
straight from their father. All through our marriage he has been
vanishing on mysterious errands, leaving me sitting at home or
in the car, or God knows where. He says he has to go and buy
a paper or get some money or relieve himself, but he takes so
long one feels he must have negotiated the purchase of Times
Newspapers or held up the bank. Who knows what he does to
relieve himself. Once I accused him of spending time with
other women. His response irritated me so much that I seriously thought of leaving him. 'Who'd have me?' he said, and he
laughed at both of us.

You won't guess where I am now. I am on the Piazza del
Campo in Siena, at that restaurant with the blue and white
awning and tables on the shady side of the square. It is a sunny
spring morning and we came here to have a look at the
Etruscan Museum and then a lunch of asparagus at Guido's.
Suddenly Itchy Britches got up and said he had something to
see to. 'Don't be long,' I begged him, but you might as well ask
Dustin Hoffman not to be short.

This man who has sat down beside me is not unlike Dustin
Hoffman. He is dark with a kind of nervous mouth that
twitches into a smile when he catches me looking at him. He
smokes a lot. In spite of his nervousness he does not look away.

He has a way of holding one's gaze, of drawing you deep
into those Amaretto-coloured eyes. People change but their
eyes never change. At first I didn't recognize him because of his
clothes. He is much richer than he used to be, bits of Gaultier
and Cartier stuck all over him. It was only when I found myself
wandering into those pools of peat-coloured velvet and I suddenly tripped over my own entrails that I realized who had sat
down beside me. 'Jesus Christ,' I muttered. The man laughed.
Giorgio – that's his name – laughed. It gave me a chance to
compose myself. I leaned back, took one of his cigarettes and
held my hand steady to light it. 'Hi!' I said. He beamed at me
(that slightly rueful, vaguely wolfish grin) –: 'Don't I know you
from somewhere?' Two can play at that game. I studied him, as
if my life was an endless queue of Dustin Hoffman lookalikes

awaiting identification. 'Somewhere,' I said remotely. 'Well, you're looking good,' he laughed.

Now that is the truth. In spite of everything I look all right. I'll tell you something. Any woman can look terrific. All you need is a lot of money. I got that from my parents.

I deserved it after what they did – or rather, tried to do – regarding my upbringing. Well, they died young, which shows that there is a God in heaven. Anyway, you have to get your hair done once a month at the most expensive place in town, and tip too much which ensures you are always dealt with by the head honcho. You need four trips to the sun a year. My legs are brown all year long. They never peel. You have to have fantastic clothes. Men say they don't notice clothes and it's true. It's not the clothes they notice but a total effect. Getting the right clothes is my neatest trick. I go into one of those expensive boutiques where the girls are always dressed in tight pants and angora sweaters with silver inserts, and I say: 'Look, I'm having an affair with this amazing guy and I need something really special to wear.' Young girls are very creative in the arena of sex. They take on the part and pick out something for you as if they were the ones having the affair. They're used to the clothes. They know how they sit. Depend upon it, you'll walk out with something good. There is a drawback to this sort of transaction. Quite often the girls are very forward and will ask you questions of an intimate nature. I find it's best to just invent a whole scenario, because otherwise they lose heart and will dump you with something in apricot pleated chiffon which makes your bottom look like a pyjama case.

Today I am wearing black linen with big bone buttons, open almost to the thigh. There is a clunk of gold jewellery on one shoulder and my hair partially hides this from view.

My hair comes down in very pretty strings of mouse and yellow colour with threads of silver and gold. On top it looks as if it was caught in the wind, but only in the right direction. My face is doing well for its age. I have a slight squint, but men seem to find this attractive, and small neat white teeth and a plump sort of mouth.

I wish my husband could see me now. The way this hand-some foreigner – my ex-lover in case you hadn't guessed – is looking at me, would drive even the most yellow-blooded hus-band to a frenzy of fury. He has ordered coffee and brandy for us and is talking about Siena, but his eyes are saying that some-where under that thatch of rumpled-looking brown hair there is a hand reaching out to undo the next button on my skirt and slide in to feel the skin of palest primrose silk which is all there is between me and decency.

Do lovers know when seduction begins? He is telling me about the Palio, but every word he uses is passion, frenzy, sweat, climax. His brown hand beats the table as he talks of rolling drums and clanging bells, of plot and prayer and pantagruelian feasts.

Swirling through the ancient streets come mace bearers, flag bearers, trumpeters, palace musicians; captain, centurians, dis-trict representatives, drummers, flag bearers, pages. There are the knights of the Lion, Bear, Strong Sword, Viper and, of course, the Cock. By the time the riders enter, the surging crowd is delirious with excitement. 'But it only lasts a minute,' I say, 'the Palio. What do all those people do afterwards?'

'They get drunk,' he says. 'They go home and make love.'

'All those poor tourists,' I shake my head; 'having to go home to Stockholm and Texas and Hong Kong and Canberra to make love.'

He laughs. 'They should come to live in Siena like me.'

'Oh, you live here now?' I am all coyness and politeness. Who writes the lousy scripts?

He is lucky enough, he tells me, to live right inside the walls on the Via della Galluzza, a preserved medieval street spanned by eight arches draped with authentic washing. His little house is dark, so he has chosen three small pieces of art – a terra cotta urn from the Roman period, a fifteenth-century manuscript and a small religious painting attributed to Sodoma – and illuminated only these.

'The effect,' he says, 'is . . . intimate. I think you would like it.'

'Are you saying you'd like to show me your etchings?'

'No,' (How can so bad a man manage to look so ingenuous?); 'I'd like to make love to you.'

Strolling beside him across the square which is not a square but the shell of a scallop, I remember what it was about him that delighted and enraged me. Giorgio was never in a hurry. Having made me ready for love he seems to have forgotten he ever mentioned it. He has separated himself from me. He is showing off. He asks how well I know Siena. Siena is a convent, he says, Florence a salon, Venice a whorehouse. Do I know Lorenzetti's 'Madonna of Milk' in the Archbishop's Palace? Have I ever used that slot machine in the cathedral that gives you an English commentary when you put in a coin? He has treats in store for me. Treats. His teeth flash on the word. I could kill him.

Time is not as important now as it used to be. I seem to have put in half a lifetime of waiting. When I was young it was everything. Opportunities came like comets, burning themselves out in a blazing trail. Even memory turns to ash. I can scarcely remember my time with Giorgio, except as a little ache of regret and some even tinier twinge of irritation.

What went wrong? We could have been married. Think what our children would look like.

All the same, I can see why he would earn his place in the Good Lovers' Guide. He is clever. He is a tease. When I ask a question he pretends he cannot hear and leans so close my mouth is on the hair that curls softly around his ear. When he guides me across the street, his hand is on the base of my spine, almost on my backside. He may have forgotten that he invited me to be seduced, but he makes it impossible for me to forget.

By now you must be wondering what happens when my husband gets back. Believe me, I would be grateful for a small fit of jealous rage. He'll have a drink, look at his watch, order something to eat. If I haven't returned by the time he's eaten, he'll have another drink, start falling asleep and then go back to the hotel for a siesta. When I get back he'll ask me if I had a nice day.

To hell with husbands. We step out of the sunshine and into the chill of the Duomo. It takes a moment of getting used to,

like when you first slide into bed and the cool sheets electrify
your skin. The sweat beneath my arms goes cold, my slippery
feet begin to reassert their grip on sandals.

Then comes a rush of heat as Giorgio turns to kiss me.
Right there in the blazing gloom of the cathedral, with crepe-
soled tourists and evil-eyed old black-clad women, his lips are
on mine and it is like the first taste of a fresh fig. I am crippled
by want. I cannot move. He strides off between the black and
white striped marble pillars which make a perfect designer
backdrop for his soft wool clothes. I run to catch him. The
feeble clap of my sandals proclaims the weakness of my sex. He
is making a phone call, no, putting money in something. I
touch his arm. Instead of the embrace I need, he is clamping
earphones on my head.

The device is ordinary enough. A selection of slides appears
on a screen and a commentary gives you all the most boring
details – which century, what pope, how valuable. But the voice!
This is the English commentary and the voice is that of the
young queen at her coronation – a butterfly packed in ice. I am
mesmerized, I am outraged. Is this his idea of a joke, to invade
me with virgin purity so that I will feel like the sordid sweaty
tourist I am? I glare at him. He is smiling, the bastard. The
young queen is telling me about the construction of the New
Duomo. It was a fantastic project, intended to cover the whole
area of the Campo. Heaven was to be pierced by the spire, tall
and blinding with its stripes of black marble and layers of squinting windows.

Great slabs of black marble flew on their high scaffolding like
fragile compact discs. Wafers of glass quivered and snapped in
the breath of a capricious God.

Why do people always want the impossible? You might as
well ask why love never lasts. But that is not the problem.
When a love affair ends, there is no more to be said. The real
question is, why do love affairs fail to end? Look back on any
you've been lucky enough to suffer, and you'll never be able to
remember what went wrong. You can waste a whole lifetime
in retrospective rehearsals, trying to locate some tiny draught
that snuffed out the inferno, convinced that but for that dress

or this word, you could have had happiness as long as you lived.

I look at Giorgio with his amused grin and his brown self full of essential maleness as a truffle is full of its fragrance. My perfect twin. He even knows how to take the starch out of me, how to make me female and vulnerable. I am wistful and quivering, in need of making love as much as sex. How did it end?

'Unfortunately it never reached completion,' the young queen is telling me, although of course she is talking about the Duomo. 'This was due to technical difficulties . . . and the plague.'

I have an unfortunate laugh. I holler. Giorgio still has his wry smile but I holler.

One hundred and seventy-two popes and thirty-six emperors gaze down at me furiously from the walls.

Afterwards we plod up the steep streets through the Jewish quarter, past the church of San Girolamo, and the Via dei Servi to the church of St Mary of the Servants and the Piazza Allesandro Manzoni. From here, the whole city is laid out like a delicate antipasto, the little pink roof tiles as dainty as overlapped slices of carpaccio. The spire of the Duomo is a pencil sketch by Ruskin beneath a stockinged lens of a sky.

As you get older you need a lover to aid long-distance vision, the same way you need glasses. Your sight gets clouded by specks of disaster. You see a child walking on a wall, trying to kill itself. You notice some woman, who has been wrenched and wrung by sorrow until even her feet won't set themselves down straight, and you think 'My God, she's younger than me.' The protection of an admirer makes all these things irrelevant and therefore invisible. I suppose there is violence and discontent and poverty and jealousy in the narrow streets that lead down to the Campo, but all I can see is a vision of heaven. There is a faint nagging irritation behind the bridge of my nose, but you get that from wearing spectacles too.

The celestial effects department have also been at work in Giorgio's little house. The lighting is lovely. Imagine a cathedral that was warm instead of cool, that had soft furniture to sink into, that led on to a flowery courtyard behind. It's like a painting – a Turner – where nothing quite exists but is defined by light. I suppose it might seem gloomy in different circumstances.

He tells me to take off my dress and leaves me on a black sofa while he goes to open some wine. Brown skin and primrose silk panties look lovely in this light.

He brings wine that glows like candlelight. We kiss until I reach a slow rolling boil and then he takes off his clothes and what remain of mine. Unencumbered by worldly goods and hand in hand and toe to toe, we are about to fly into heaven.

'You know,' Giorgio smiles, 'this doesn't feel quite right.'

'It feels right to me,' I say as nicely as possible. 'What's the matter?'

He removes the top half of his torso from mine and bends to the floor for his glass of wine. 'I don't know your name.'

The nagging in my nose spreads upwards and becomes a pulsing band across my forehead. 'Call me Mrs Henebry, Giorgio,' I say. 'That's my married name, if that's what you wanted to know.'

'All right, Mrs Henebry,' he says slowly: 'but my name's not Giorgio. It's Leonardo.'

Giorgio has commenced a feathery, circular massage but the magic has gone. I can't concentrate. I can't stand a mean-spirited man.

'Listen!' I sit up so rapidly that his chin hits my forehead. 'You don't have to protect yourself from me. You don't have to change your identity in case I have you traced or something. I'm not after you – not this time.'

'It's all right, dear Mrs Henebry,' Giorgio strokes my hair. He kisses my eyes. 'I only want to make you happy.'

He's a complex sort of person. I suppose I should enjoy myself, since I don't often get the chance. I'm not young and vulnerable any more. Why the hell should I care about his games so long as I have the company of his pleasure? All the same, I feel I owe it to my younger and more fragile self not to let him get away with it. He hasn't even bothered to change his lines. 'I only want to make you happy.' That's exactly what he said to me the first time.

'Why didn't you marry me, Giorgio?' I say. 'When we were young?'

He gives me an odd, assessing sort of look. 'It is a pity, but alas I did not know you then.'

'How much does it take to know me? You took away my innocence. I gave you my trust.'

He sits up. He shrugs. Naked, he lopes off to look for cigarettes. 'I don't know what you are playing at, but I have never met you in my life before.' When he returns he perches on an edge of the furniture and lights a cigarette. He is back in his leisurely mood. He seems to have forgotten there is a naked woman waiting for him on the sofa. 'You know, Mrs Henebry,' he says; 'you worry me a little. Perhaps you are the kind of woman who makes love to a man and afterwards says she was raped. I think maybe you take your fantasies a little too seriously.'

'What do you mean fantasies, Giorgio?' By now I am furious. 'You think it's some sort of fantasy that we met in Florence as students and you made me your lover and promised to marry me?'

'My name is Leonardo.' He leaves his cigarette poised in his mouth while he bends to retrieve his trousers from the floor and puts them on with a carefulness that indicates an appreciation of his own body. The fall of brown hair over his forehead still tugs at my heart. 'I am thinking,' he says, 'perhaps you are a little confused.'

'Confused?' I reach out and smack him smartly across the face. It isn't the word. It's the awful sliding sense of déjà vu.

All day he has been undermining me but now he has taken me right back. Suddenly I remember everything. Naturally I was confused. I was nineteen and an orphan and had given him all my confidence. I kept nothing from him. 'It was Aunt Lilian, wasn't it? That's why you left me. It was after I told you about our family skeleton – poor loony Aunt Lil. You thought our children might turn out to be nut cases. You thought I might have caught the weird streak.'

He gets up quickly and walks across the room, shrugging into his shirt, buttoning up, protecting himself. 'You're crazy,' he mutters.

There comes a point in life (I believe this happens to most women) where you simply are not prepared to put up with one more single piece of insulting behaviour from any man whatsoever. Feeling perfectly calm, I climb off the sofa and silently cross the floor, pluck the terra cotta urn from the Roman period out of its illuminated niche and break it over the back of his head. It is heavy. I didn't think it would break. 'Sorry,' I say to the figure on the floor, 'about the urn.'

Later on, back at the cafe on the Campo, I wonder if he was alive or dead. There was an oddly permanent look to his expression of surprise. Thinking about that *maschera*, I begin to wonder if it really was Giorgio. The eyes were definitely the same, but now I seem to recall that Giorgio had a deep cleft in his chin.

However, there are other things to preoccupy me. I see Desmond lumbering across the square in the afternoon heat. I am almost glad to see him. I will overlook his awful jacket like an ice-cream salesman's, his squeaky shoes and the thinning patch on top of his head. To look at me nobody would believe that I was waiting for such a second-rate specimen of the male sex but we have been through a lot together. We are veterans of the fertility clinic.

'Where the hell have you been?' I say quite amiably when he slumps opposite me at the table.

Do you know what he does? He doesn't even answer me. He gets up and moves to the next table.

I stand over him like a spider and thump the table until the little wrapped sugars jump in their bowl. 'Desmond?' I say; 'speak to me.'

He looks embarrassed and unhappy, the miserable coward. 'Look,' he whispers, 'you're making a mistake. My name isn't Desmond.'

'Go on,' I yell, commanding an audience as I intend to. 'Tell me now you're not my husband.'

I'm reminded of a figure in a painting by Munch as he flees across the square, his cream jacket flapping, his hands raised in dismay. I feel no remorse. Why would he not have the guts to just say straight out he is not my husband when that is the truth? Actually, for a minute I thought it was Desmond. The light has gone round and the sun is in my eyes.

When I was very young I used to think you could make things happen. I know better now. I was sixteen and entombed in wealthy suburbia by two parents so dull that it is distasteful to think of their part in my existence. I wanted to try my wings, to experiment with life. My parents thought I was crazy. They observed me like a specimen under glass. They wanted me to *see* someone, they said.

What they really wanted was to have me put away. Sadly, they perished in a fire which also took all traces of the ugly house.

After that I thought it was just a matter of getting on with life but I never met anyone to match my pace. I was just passed from one set of fatally indecisive hands to the next, like a bucket in a fire line, destined never to reach the blaze. I waited for my life, for my lover, for my children.

Most of all I waited for my husband whose absences are of such duration and assortment that sometimes, sitting in this hotel lobby or that square, watching the cast change or the weather run through its repertoire, I find myself wondering if he really exists at all.

ᘓᗰᗰᘐ

The Little Madonna

Look at this. I found it in *The Sun*. It's about a sixteen-year-old called Dolores and her three-month-old daughter, Marigold. 'The Little Madonna', they called her. She has a perfect heart-shaped face and rosebud lips that curve up into a sweet smile. The baby's face was a miniature heart with the same rosebud. Dolores had no job and no one to support her. She was given a council flat. People brought her money and food. Everybody looked forward to seeing her out with the baby, her hair neatly tied in a bunch on top of her head, the baby's scraps of fluff tied up in imitation. Dolores wore a long Indian caftan and the baby had a little Indian smock over her pram suit. People agreed it made you think the world wasn't so bad when you saw them out together. A Mr Cecil Dodd, who owned the shop across the road, said it changed your mind about the female sex.

One day the Little Madonna put the baby out in the play-ground in her pram because she wanted to take a rest. It was Mr Dodd, rubbing a clear patch on his shop window, wondering if the papers would be delivered on such a day, who saw a ghostly hump beyond the railings of the flats. The pram was completely covered in snow and although his heart hit off his rib cage when he sprinted out to see, he told himself it was only foolishness, no one would put a child out on such a day.

'There!' he reassured himself when he reached the pram for there was only a toy – a little white woolly bear. It looked so cold he had to touch it and his finger traced beneath the rasping surface, a small, cold slab of forehead, a heart-shaped face, milky blue. His first thought was to wonder who had done it and what they had done to Dolores. He banged on her door, but it was open. She was lying on the floor, near a radiator. He knelt beside her and stroked her face. She opened her lovely gentle eyes: 'I was having a sleep. It was cold so I lay down by the radiator.'

'The baby . . . !' he said.

'It's all right,' Dolores smiled. 'She didn't suffer. I read that people who freeze to death just get very sleepy and then drift off with no pain. I was very careful about that.'

Mr Dodd told this story in court, in support of Dolores's character, even though the inquest had revealed a dappling of long, plum-coloured bruises underneath the little Indian shirt.

The report in *The Sun* is more economical. You have to read between the lines. 'Baby Freezes while Mum Snoozes,' it says. Had the baby failed to freeze to death, she would have been a Miracle Baby, but that is beside the point.

I have this propped up against the milk jug while I'm eating my breakfast. I'm trying to work it out. Who would leave a sixteen-year-old to look after a baby? I remember Rory, who was a good child and sensible, relatively, cut her wrists very neatly with a razor blade when she was sixteen. Being an intelligent girl she read up some books first to make sure the slits would not go through, but it was a very bad moment for me and she meant it to be.

I am not young. I'm a has-been. I'm on the heap and let me tell you this, it's quite a comfortable place to be. When my womb packed up I went through a sort of widowhood although my husband was not yet dead. I went around sighing, drinking cups of tea to wash down the nerve-stunning pills I bought from a doctor. For a mother to learn that she can have no more children is for a surgeon to have his hands cut off. What can she do? You can't make the children you have last indefinitely. After a long time it came to me that the void was not in my stomach at all. It was in my head. The womb does not have a brain, but that is like saying that the rat is not an intelligent creature. It comes programmed with the cunning of survival. When a young girl presents herself and her head full of dreams to her lover it is natural for the womb to say, 'Let me do the thinking, dear. You just use your pretty head for painting your pretty face.' That's how it is. No, excuse me. That's how it was.

This emptiness I located in my head was not new. It had been there since I was a young woman, Rory's age. My hands were full and my lap. I used my intelligence as a rat does, to plot a path through the maze. Now that the high walls of the maze had crumbled I found myself in open fields. Thoughts rose up into my head. I realized that the period of mourning which succeeds the menopause is not a grieving. It is the weariness that follows upon the removal of a tyranny. Now I was free. I made up my mind never to cook again and became an enthusiastic collector of complete meals in plastic bags with added vitamins. I began, recklessly, to allow entry to thoughts that were not my immediate concern – none of my business at all, to be perfectly frank.

I gave up *The Guardian* which was still telling me how to raise my children and my political consciousness. I started buying *The Sun* which told me about homicides and sex scandals and the secret vices of the royals and reminded me how bountiful women's breasts were. It was the start of my expanded thinking. Every day I find a new marvel on which to ponder.

Why, I ask myself this morning, would anyone leave a sixteen-year-old in charge of a baby? What about all those people who said they brought gifts of food? Why didn't they sneak inside and offer to change the baby's nappy to see if it was being fed all right or if it was being beaten? Who would leave a baby with a sixteen-year-old?

And it comes to me, quite suddenly, sprouting out of the scrap-heap of my middle-aged head – God did. God the Father! He gave His only son to a girl of fifteen. There, with my cup of tea in one hand and my fag in the other, I am filled with alarm as if there is something I should instantly do. I can see the baby with his nappy on backwards as his mother puts henna in her hair. He's crawling around on his hands and knees in his father's carpentry shop, his little mouth full of nails, waiting with growing hopelessness for his mother to come and make him spit them out. Oh, God.

Now there's a thing just caught my eye. 'Orgy and Bess' is the heading. It's about an heiress, Bess Hichleigh-Harrow, who is alleged to have offered the sum of £10,000 to any man who could make her experience an orgasm. She looks a nice ordinary woman. Her coat is good.

There is a great preoccupation with orgasms in the modern world, their frequency, their intensity, their duration. Why choose a muscular spasm as an obsession and not something full of mystery, like a bat or a bee? Why not blame the orange for failing to make us happy and fulfilled?

Because it comes to us from our lover, our husband, our mate, our enemy, with whom all things become possible – whose fault everything is.

Of all the things that rose up in my mind after my womb folded up, orgasms wasn't one. I thought of Rory's bottom, when she was a baby – that hot, clothy acquiescence, serene as a Rajah on its throne, pissing indifferently over her legs and my arms while her own arms, entirely dignified and intelligent, patted my face.

She came in the morning. I called her Aurora – a rosy dawn. I was flabbergasted. At long last, after all the false promises, the beloved had come and she came from myself who, being young, I also loved. Men marvel at rockets to the moon and are not astounded by the journey of a sperm to the womb, the transformation of liquid into life. Only women are amazed. 'I'm not pregnant, not me, I can't be!' they tell the doctor. 'Why me?' they rail at God, and are further dismayed when the emergent infant shows no gratitude to its host, but shits and spits and screams like the devil.

Rory was not like that. She loved me, not just in the way little girls love their mothers, but with the deep earnest love that some men have for their wives, which also contains a small element of contempt. Unlike other children she respected me as the bearer of her life but she thought of me as a simple, shallow person, out of touch with reality. I tried to get myself in shape. I read Freud and Kate Millet and Carl Jung and *The Guardian*. It wasn't easy keeping up. Rory grew up in the 'seventies when everything happened.

I was full of curiosity about the new woman; to be free of priests, to see the penis as a toy, to open one's body to men and lock the door of the womb. 'Tell me,' I coaxed her. Do you know what she told me?

'You were lovely,' she said, 'before Daddy died. Why did you have to change?' My generation were the essential women. We were structured to our role and submitted without grievance. That's what she said. We gave birth in our season without ever giving it a thought. That's what she thinks.

She remembered me in a flowered apron and high-heeled shoes, dabbing on my powder – slap, slap, slap – so that it sat on my nose in a comfortable, dusty way, like icing on a bun. A bright, dry, crimson lip was put on, like a felt cut-out, and then blotted on to the lower lip and then the glorious gold compact with its wavy edges was snapped shut with a sophisticated clack, and slipped into a little black bag.

'Remember?' she said. There were tears in her eyes.

Rory comes to visit me once a week although she is not comfortable in the heartless flat I bought after her father died. I hide *The Sun* under a cushion, but she finds it. 'What can you be thinking of?' she asks in exasperation.

She is thirty-two. There are lines around the edges of her eyes and her jaw is starting to set, which is an unnerving thing to see on your own child. So I tell her: 'I was thinking of the Virgin Mary!' I light a cigarette but I have to hold it away at an angle because she doesn't like the smoke.

I suppose the point of it all was that she was only fifteen. Who else could an angel of the Lord have declared unto? I wonder now, why people make such a fuss about the virgin birth? As if making love had anything to do with having babies. What do you suppose she said to her mother and father afterwards? 'I'm going to be the mother of God!'? 'I'm pregnant!'?

'I saw an angel'. I'll bet that's what she said. Afterwards, when she remembered, she told them what the angel said, that like any old mother everywhere, she had conceived of the Lord.

What on earth did her mother say, her good Jewish mother from the house of David who had gone to such trouble to make a nice match for the child? Don't tell me she took it on the chin. An easy lay and a liar, yet! She was too old to have her daughter's faith, but if she had, she would have asked: 'What was its wing span?'

'Look at this!' Now that Rory has pulled my *Sun* out from under its cushion the gloves are off. '"Bag Baby Found in Bin"!'

This is my favourite story today. It's about Norman who was found in a bag which was then stuffed down into a bin. It is a large denim shoulder bag, well enough worn to be prudently discarded. Baby Norman seemed to accept this as his world, or hiding place, and was angry only when disturbed. He has a very red face with rough patches like a butcher's hands. He is not winsome. The item is an appeal for his mother to come back and claim him but his mother has ditched dour Norman, she has sacrificed her battered denim shoulder bag which she probably quite liked, and callously pinned the name 'Norman' on his little vest. She has put the tin lid on him and she is never coming back.

Now I've made my daughter miserable. She says I am growing morbid. As you grow older you see things differently. Cause, you realize, is only the kite tail of effect and God is a lateral thinker. I heard a Chinese fable once which said that fate bestows a gift for life on every child at birth. Perhaps Baby Norman's gift was to be left in a bag. Someday, when he is an ugly man being reviled by a woman, he will tell her that his mother left him in a bag in a bin, and her heart will break and she will take him on. He would have been ugly with or without his mother's indifference, but who else would have loved him if his mother had? Rory says you can't believe anything you read in *The Sun*. I suppose she's right, yet she believes absolutely and without a wisp of doubt that Mr Gorbachev is ready to lay down all his arms.

There is only one mystery left in life, or at any rate in the

Western world, where people have opened out the brain and the soul, analysed the body's responses and claimed for themselves in everything from work to love to life or death, the right to choose. Only the child remains the unchosen one. Who knows whether twin soul or tyrant comes dimpling from the neck of the cervix? Cells gather inside us in secret like a pack of dogs or a flock of angels. It could be the Messiah. It could be the man in the moon. Only a child would open Pandora's Box.

Only a Marigold or little Norman's mother would have the nerve to shut it again.

Rory is right. I was lovely before. I made lemon drops and shepherd's pies and fairy cakes. Women play house to preserve a moment that once was almost theirs, the same way they paint their faces to hold youth a little longer. My husband used to tell me – or tried to tell me – over and over, about a trip in a canoe with his father when he was seven. That's all I remember except for official reports issued daily over the tea table. For all I knew about him he might have been a fish in a bowl. I told this to Rory but she thought I was criticizing him. 'You made your choices,' she said. And I have.

I used to think that Rory would be my guide dog when I went over the hill, would lead me into the new generation.

Now I see that she was hanging around waiting for me to give her the vital information she needed to grow up. We have nothing to do with each other except love and guilt. The terms of reference change with the times and experience is wear-dated. She thinks I turned to packet foods and tabloid papers because I lost interest in life. In fact it is my interest in life that impels me to labour-saving food and literature – that and an aversion to eating anything that still looks like an animal, although I am too old now for the full routine of nuts and pulses. I talked to an Indian on the bus one day (you have to pick your company with care if you intend to say anything you mean) and told him how I could no longer bear to pick up a fish or a chicken and take it home and eat it, because I suddenly knew they were my brothers, but now I worried that such thinking might in due course lead to a meatless world in which the pleasant cow would become extinct. 'But the vast, intensified sisterhood of cows is ruining the ozone layer with its communal breaking of methane wind,' the Indian gentleman enlightened me. I found this exchange deeply satisfactory. How fitting for the Almighty to knock us all off with a massive cow fart.

What appeals to me now is the language of the tabloid. People do not fornicate or have carnal knowledge. They have sex romps. They frolic. They do not exceed the permitted number of alcohol units. They guzzle. 'He Guzzled Bubbly while he Peddled Death,' ran the banner headline above the story of a drugs dealer.

It is not, after all, a chapter of adult corruption but a nursery story of miracle babies and naughty children looking for pleasure or treasure, excitement or escape, and reigning over all is the breast goddess – the giver of forgiveness, of guzzling and joy.

Have we all been let down by our mothers who failed to frolic while we guzzled? Was little Marigold lucky, in spite of the bruises and her cold sleep, to have, for a little while, a mother young enough to romp? If only we had the right to choose.

I have a secret. When you get to my age, your fingers go numb and they lose their grip and then you can choose anything you fancy.

There is a photograph in my secret box of a man and a woman. They are not my parents because I was not born then, but I have chosen them. They do not smile. They watch the camera as if it was a test. The girl clasps her flowers like a doll. She has a dress with square buttons and a hat which claps its brim over her alarmed eyes. The man has a suit but he does not wear it, he is worn by it. Such pure people. When this is over, will they be allowed to take off their good clothes and play again?

After the wedding my mother told me they ate rashers and eggs in a hotel and drank champagne and then went to Blackpool on the boat.

In my mind's eye that is where I see them, leaning on the rail looking into the water that floated them away from the world of rules and responsibilities. They might have played 'I spy' or talked about the enormous meal they would eat when they got to their hotel – chicken and salad and soufflé and wine – for they were thin and were probably always hungry. Now and again the boy might have looked at the square buttons on the pale blue dress and thought: she's underneath there and she's my woman now. It is certain that they did not think about me for I did not exist then, just as they do not exist now, and did not exist after I was born and made them grow up. It is almost certain that they did not think about orgasms although they might have kissed and kissed until they were in an ecstacy of deprivation. They might have thought that ecstacy was just a tiny little moment away – a romp, a frolic, away – like the jam at the bottom of the pudding dish when you had eaten most of your rice.

Most likely they just thought that they had all the time in the world now; that they never, ever had to please anyone for the rest of their lives but themselves and one another, which were one and the same; that for tonight they might just hold each other close on the narrow bunk and rock to slumber on the waves and tomorrow, in private, in another country, start off their lives.

L'Amour

The trouble began because I was an animal lover. I mean to say, that was the source of all our troubles. I was taken from my role of son at the age of eight by the death of my mother. 'Angels lead our sister into paradise,' said the minister but I was left behind on earth with my father and my mother's cat which was blind in one eye and had a fungal infection of the fur, but we hadn't the heart to put it down.

My father and I did not know what to do with each other. We had never taken much notice of one another, being content with the attention of my mother. After her death we abided. At mealtimes we met at table and waited until it became evident that her ghost would not flutter down with meat and pots of mashed potato and then we would rise silently and separately and arm ourselves with jam and cheese and biscuits and things in tins. We did not panic when the food ran out. We recognized my mother as the source of nourishment and comfort and accepted that these had died along with her. After a time my father said to himself: 'The boy is growing. I must see to the business of food.'

He made a jelly. It was constructed in layers of different colours. Each shade had to be allowed to set before another layer was applied. It took several days to complete and was displayed on a plate on the draining board. In some way or other it did not live up to our expectations and we left it there until it slid down into a pool of its own rust-coloured water.

'What would you like?' my father said.

'I'd like . . . a kitten.'

He bought me two. By the time they were finished leaving puddles under the kitchen table, they were leaving their own kittens in the linen press. I got a donkey from a man in the street by giving him my bicycle. A dog followed me home from school. Boys gave me the things their parents would not allow them to keep – a snake, a pet rat, a poisonous spider. I had a thrush too, that the cats had knocked about a bit and I rescued it. It grew so tame it would sit on my hand and we would whistle at each other. Other birds and less friendly animals lived in secret places in the garden and I climbed trees to look at robins' eggs and lay on my stomach over a muddy pool to watch the sluggish sorcery of frog spawn. I was very keen on them all, even snails with their outer space aerials and their pearly trails. Some of them liked me too and in this way, in due course, I learned to do without my mother.

It was different for my father. He could not adapt. Although it was obvious to both of us that no one could ever take the place of Mother, he began, quite soon after her death, to look for someone who would stand in her place. I don't think he cared what she was like. The ladies he brought home to tea were of such varying quality that he might have chosen them from a bus queue. One of them had cheeks like raw liver dipped in flour and I had to kiss her. 'This is Miss Dawlish,' he introduced, (or on other occasions, Miss Reddy or Miss Frostbite or Miss Havanagila, I think); and his eyes would say: 'Be nice to her.' I was nice to them all. I showed them my snake and my poisonous spider. In spite of this they never came back.

'I believe it is because of the boy's animals,' my father confided to an aunt when he thought I was not listening.

'Of course it is,' the aunt said sharply. 'What free agent would wish to take on a zoo as well as another woman's child?' He never said anything to me. He would no more interfere in my life than I would in his. The stream of ladies ceased and he grew very silent.

One spring, two years after my mother's death, I noticed that he was happy again. He had come back from a business visit to Paris and when he fetched me from my aunt, he was full of energy and jokes, the way he used to be when Mother was alive and they were going to a dance. Shortly after this he paid some more brief visits to Paris and then he asked me if I would like to have a holiday there. I said that I would. I was very interested in Paris. My parents had once had a postcard from Paris and on the back was written: 'Watching the world go by in gay Paree!' (which is how Paris is pronounced there). I thought at the time that it would be phenomenal to be in a place where one could watch the whole world go by.

When Father told me that he had a friend there – a Mlle Duclos – whom he wished me to meet, I took no more notice than I had of the Dawlishes and Frostbites. I was too interested in Paris. A lot of my concentration went on persuading Mrs Crutch, who did our housework, to feed my pet animals and insects. I got over these difficulties, Father bought me an astonishing suit of clothes which made me look like a man of twenty, and we were on our way.

I was not able to form an immediate impression of Paris for we were taken first to our hotel which was a chateau some distance from the city, where we were to stay and to meet Mlle Duclos. It was a smashing place, full of towers like wizards' hats. A long drive hid its curves under trees and in between the splashes of leaves, the starker branches of a deer's horns made patterns on the sky. I had to press myself against the window of the car to make out that the grey bumps, crouched behind swarms of bluebells, were not stones but baby rabbits. We came to the castle entrance. A conference of important-looking little dogs with ears like wigs ranged about the steps and in the doorway was a princess.

She was the most beautiful lady I have ever seen. A long yellow soft dress with sleeves like butterflies reached almost to her ankles. She was tall but delicate-looking and had a cloud of brown hair. I glanced at my father and could see that he too was under the spell of the castle and its princess. He drove the car with his eyes, very bright, fixed on the lady.

'What do you think, Nicholas?'

'Brillo!' I whispered.

'Precisely,' he laughed.

He stopped the car and got out, seeming to forget about me, which I did not mind. He hurried up the steps and the little dogs stiffened and shouted angrily.

'Darling!' he called.

The princess turned to him and smiled. She held out her arms and he went into them, humbly, like someone receiving a blessing. After they had kissed he turned and summoned me with an excited wave. I scrambled out of the car and ran to her.

'Say hello to Mlle Duclos,' he said.

Nothing had prepared me for this. She bore no more resemblance to the Dawlishes than did the castle to a dog kennel. With an effort I stuck out my hand. 'How do you do, Mlle Duclos?'

She bent to study me and her hair fell down, framing her face. 'You must call me Marie,' she said. 'I think we are going to be friends.' She kept hold of my hand when she straightened and turned to my father. 'He is exactly like you. What a nice surprise!'

I could see immediately why my father looked at her in such a dazed way. In that moment all I wanted was to have her smile on me, her hand in my hand. We went in to lunch and sat at a table, all of us smiling. 'No one here knows that my mother is dead,' I thought. 'No one knows we are not a proper family.'

Father and Marie ordered escargots and langoustes. 'What would you like, little picture of your papa?' she whispered to me.

'Chips,' I whispered back.

She pushed my hair from my forehead. 'In France, the children are not treated like little animals, fed with the scraps from the plates of adults. Here, you will learn to dine properly, even with a taste of wine. Have you ever eaten escargots?'

I shook my head. I could see my father looking at me hopefully.

'Have them to please me,' Marie said.

'All right,' I nodded.

'What a nice boy.' She rubbed my hair. 'I don't think I am going to let you go.'

How happy my father looked then, no longer lonely, reaching out to touch her arm while her hand still rested on my head so that we were all joined together like daisies in a chain. Later I wished we could have all died in that moment so that none of us would ever know loneliness again, or fear.

The escargots came; little curls of something on a dish with holes. I ate one and decided that if I thought about something else I could probably finish them. I had got about half way around the holes when Marie leaned towards me and said, in that confidential way that made one dizzy: 'What do you think?'

I smiled and shrugged, my mouth full of buttery rubber.

'Escargots! Do you know what they are?'

I saw that my father looked alarmed when she said this and his anxiety flew to me. 'What are they?' I demanded.

'Ha! Ha!' Her giggle was now like a girl's. An older girl's. 'They are snails, my pet.'

I spat it out. The snail. I felt she had played a terrible trick, not only on me but on my father.

'Nicholas!' my father was horrified but I would not look at either of them. Father kept on chewing until he had eaten all the snails on his dish.

I might have forgotten the incident. Marie looked as upset and bewildered as I did. Then the waiter came carrying three poor creatures that were trying to escape.

'Voilà! Our lobsters!' said Marie in excitement.

'They're alive!' I was horrified.

'Not for long!' Her delicate, teasing laugh rang out as their slow pincers struggled with the air.

I ran out of the restaurant and stayed there, kicking a bed of flowers to pieces until Father came to look for me. 'Dirty foreigners! Filthy foreign savages!' I aimed at the heads of quivering daffodils.

'Marie said I should come.' Father looked miserable. 'She thought she ought to leave us alone. She will join us again later.'

I said nothing.

'Don't you like her?'

I shook my head.

'I thought you seemed happy. I was so pleased,' he said.

'She's a sneak,' I shouted. 'She made me eat a snail.'

'No, no! It is the custom of the country. The animals do not suffer. You must learn to adapt.'

He looked as lost as I did. Neither of us was adaptable. I wondered if, like me, he was remembering my mother's meals, shepherd's pies and rice puddings, food that had long lost its connection with any living source. I thought of her apron and her body beneath it, a fathomless cushion, where one could lie when one was confused, and love came out but she never looked for anything as demanding, in return, as friendship.

In the afternoon Father showed me Paris. He told me about the buildings, places of art and war and opera, dulling the sunny streets with clouds of history. I preferred the cafes and markets, the little batto boats on the river. 'What do you think, Nicholas?' Father said. It was a city of the dead; statues of dead generals by dead sculptors. It reminded me of the place where I had stood in the most inestimable fear with, overhead, the foreign storm of adult weeping and down below, in the ground and powerless to take control, my mother. I said none of this to my father. Instead, I said: 'I'd like to go to the place where you can watch the world go by.'

He brought me to a wide, pretty street with trees and heavy traffic and we sat at a tin table outside a cafe. We ate ice-creams. A lot of people passed, some who hurried and some who seemed to regard the boulevard as a drawing room in their own home but although I looked and looked, there was no change of scenery, no yellow hills of Montana nor snow-capped Swiss mountains. 'It's only a street,' I said indignantly. 'You cannot watch the world from here.' Father seemed not to hear. 'Nicholas!' He leaned forward suddenly, his face as serious as if I was another adult. 'You must make an effort with Marie. In due course I know you will come to love her as I do.'

I was confused by this word, 'love'. 'She's not my mother,' I said.

'She will be a sister – a friend.'

'I have my animals.'

For a moment he was silent. 'I haven't told her,' he said.

We were both desperate. 'Don't let her hurt them,' I said.

'She will accept them but first you must accept her.'

The anxiety in his voice made me nervous. 'What if she does not accept them? What if she had a boy and he had a lot of animals, Father? Would you accept them?'

'I would accept anything that was a part of Marie. I know it is not fair to speak to you like this, Nicholas, but I cannot lose her. I would be lost without her. I know she likes you but if she thought you did not like her she would not wish to intrude. She is a woman of sensibility.'

I thought of her laughing at the lobsters.

'Promise me, Nicholas' – my father spoke urgently – 'that you will be friendly and behave.'

I felt sorry for him. I was going to say yes, I would behave, but he did not wait for my answer. He saw Marie approaching then and he stood and waved to her. He looked like a blind man, blinded by her bright smile and I thought that he was lost with her or without her.

In another moment my resolve became unnecessary for her hand was on my head and her kiss on my cheek and a rush of complicit whispers in my ear and I laughed with happiness.

We were all holding hands again when we moved off. We went to see the Cathedral of Notre Dame, huge and black inside with a big window of many colours 'Like a firework in the night,' Marie said, leaning down, close to my ear.

Later, Father and Marie went into a bookshop called Shakespeare and Company and I stayed outside in the sun and read messages from a glass-covered noticeboard. *Widower, formerly married to woman with loose dentures, with whom conversation was like water dripping from a stalagtite to stalagmite, seeks quiet girl like Amelia in* Vanity Fair. It made me wonder if the whole world was full of widowers in search of ladies to replace their wives? If he saw Marie would he think she looked like Amelia in *Vanity Fair*? In my mind, the defect of the widower's wife transferred to himself, and I saw him with his rainy teeth, approaching the bookshop in search of his reply. I looked around quickly. There was no one who resembled the squishy-toothed widower but all the same I went and stood guard in the doorway in case he should come along and see Marie and try to claim her.

That night we ate in a restaurant where each dish was covered in a silver dome. Marie was like a fairy princess with her hair done up on top of her head and a dress of something blue and filmy. She and Father drank champagne, giving me a little in a glass, so that by the time we went in to dinner I was a bit foolish.

The menu was brought – like a huge birthday card with a picture of wildlife on its cover and each inscription inside an exercise in calligraphy.

'Something light,' Marie suggested. 'A little pâté or some cuisses de grenouilles.'

'Kweess . . .?' I giggled.

'Cuisses de grenouilles – frogs' legs!' said Marie with her lovely smile.

'I'll have the pâté,' I said quickly, hiding my horror. 'I have tasted pâté.'

'Not this pâté, little one,' she said. 'This is a speciality – very good. Pâté de grives – thrush pâté.'

'No!' I cried out. I thought of the family of thrushes in our garden, sunbathing on heaps of mown grass, their wings spread like fans. They swooped into our peach tree and called to one another when the fruit was ripe.

'The boy is . . . fond of animals.' Father looked embarrassed. He shot me a yearning glance.

'Of course he is.' Marie was relieved. 'But these are not pets. These are garden pests – frogs and thrushes.'

'I have a pet thrush,' I told her.

'Aah!' She made a face, considering. 'You must tell me about yourself. Everything!'

'I have a dog and a donkey and six cats.'

Father looked as if he was in pain.

'. . . a pet rat and a snake and a spider.'

Marie was nonplussed. She grinned first and then, seeing that I was serious, she shuddered. 'My God, what a ménagerie!' She spoke rapidly to my father in French while I strained to understand but he, seeing my anxiety, gave a little hopeless smile and said for both of us in English:

'I am afraid, my dear, that they are all indispensable. They are his family.'

She sipped her wine and swirled the content of her glass. 'I am afraid of spiders,' she said to herself. 'A donkey! A rat! Mon Dieu!'

When a very long time had passed she turned to me with that bright smile of hers. 'May I join your family, Nicholas?' Father and I laughed with relief and we raised our glasses. 'What a ménagerie!' she said again.

Marie ordered for us all. 'Do you have pet prawns?' she said. I had had a few sips of wine diluted with water by now and I laughed like a drunk old man.

We ate our prawns and made our plans. Marie was going to come and live with us. When she had got the house in order she would work with my father in his antiques business. Sometimes she spoke to Father alone and ignored me as if I was a child, which made me jealous. Sometimes she pretended that Father was an old man and that she and I were the same age. 'Have you ever had a pony? Your papa is too decrepit to ride a horse but you and I, Niccy, will have ponies and will go riding in the fields.'

The argentine domes of our main courses arrived. Marie lifted one and closed her eyes to sniff. 'Now I think I have chosen well,' she said. 'A little crispy duck for your papa and I and for Niccy, a more delicate fowl.'

'Kentucky Fried Chicken,' I cried cheekily, executing a mock drum roll upon the dome of my dish with my knife and fork and making the adults laugh but I retained enough sense to know that I must not actually allow the cutlery to touch the silver. I swept up the cover from my dish. A tiny bird, no bigger than a robin, it seemed, lay dead and bleeding on to a piece of toast. The shock was such that I glanced up quickly to see if the others had noticed but they had lost interest in me and were busy with their plans. 'No!' I said, but silently. I covered it up in its silver coffin. Some chips had come with the main course, and I ate those.

'Have some cheese,' Marie said, when our dishes had been taken away; 'or would you prefer dessert?'

'No thank you. I'm a bit tired,' I said. 'May I go to bed now, please?' I had seen a table of delicious sweet things near the entrance to the restaurant but they might be hedgehogs covered in whipped cream or chocolate-coated mice. I slid down from my chair and left the room quickly before they could argue. In the doorway I turned and looked back. Their hands were joined across the table, their faces lit with happiness. I had not failed my father. He would not lose her. But as I stood there, feeling brave, straining to see them through the teasing filter of candle flames, past the wealthy diners eagerly dissecting small birds and fishes and waiters scurrying with mirrored prisons of more slaughtered wildlife, I suffered another shock. It was the realization that I had not allowed myself that last look to assure myself of Father's salvation but for another glimpse, for myself, of Marie.

In bed that night I had a dream.

I was walking up the path to the chateau. I came across a mass of creatures seeking shelter beneath a large tree from the breeze; furry rabbits, baby deer, lobsters, pheasants and smaller birds, shuddering dreadfully. I went to look for the gamekeeper. 'Look at these creatures,' I rebuked. 'They are so cold! See how they shiver. Why are they not properly housed?' The old keeper pointed to the sunny sky. 'Cold? No, my little man. They are watching the approach of the gourmet. They are terrified.'

In the morning I ran to find Marie. She was on the terrace, having breakfast with my father. She put out her arms and I laid my head on her white angora sweater. 'Marie,' I whispered. 'This is a secret. Don't tell my father. Why do French people eat so many little animals? I don't mind the big ones, but the little ones!'

She dipped her roll into coffee and held it out for me to bite the hot, soggy, buttery mass. 'A secret,' she said; 'yes. God put the little creatures on the earth for our pleasure. They know this. They are happy to die for me.'

I believed her. I would have died for her too.

For some reason Father seemed discontented this morning. He remained silent through most of the breakfast and then he said to me: 'We are going out to lunch. Marie's maman will be joining us.' He said it like a challenge, as if he expected me to object. I did not mind. I knew that it was customary for a lady to introduce a prospective husband to her mother and I was surprised my father did not know this.

'If you marry Father,' I said to Marie, 'your mother will be a part of our family too. She will be our gran.'

Marie stroked my hair. 'You are an exceptionally nice and clever boy,' she said; and Father frowned.

Meeting Marie's mother was as much of a surprise as Marie herself had been. She was dressed in black and she was old, old – the sort of old that seems never to have been young, like a parsnip. I could see that Father did not like to think that this ancient root was a source of Marie. Normally when speaking to old people, he made himself seem older to put them at their ease. Now he seemed very young and offhand, a lout. She did not appear to like him either but gave a very insincere little laugh when Marie presented him with breathless pride.

She was put into the back of the car with me and we drove away. For a while she did not say anything but looked out the window. Then she said to nobody in particular, 'He thinks he is on trial but it is I who am on trial.' She gave me a bitter little smile and after that she did not speak until we got to the restaurant.

It was a very pretty place with plates on the walls and thick lace curtains on the windows and in the centre, a long table, covered with tarts. I was put sitting opposite the old woman. My father sat across from Marie, his eyes smiling and his stubborn look gone.

The menu was scrawled in pen on a piece of card. I read it several times over but could find nothing that was not cruel; the oysters eaten live (I once heard that they flinch when you put on the lemon juice), the foie gras of force-fed geese, the veal of imprisoned calves, lobsters boiled alive. 'I'll have melon,' I said miserably and . . . 'steak'; for at least the cow was large and fed a lot of people.

'No, no, dear little peasant,' Marie said. 'Have some oysters. Have them for me.'

'Melon. Melon and fish and chips.' The old woman spoke out, 'I have no teeth to chew and my stomach prefers plain food. Keep me company.'

'All right,' I said and gave a silent sigh of relief that I would not have to eat anything cooked alive.

My father ordered the food and a bottle of wine and some water. He poured wine for himself and Marie while she half filled her mother's glass and mine with water. She took the wine from Father then and used it to top up our glasses. 'Talk to my maman and I will talk to your papa,' she whispered into my ear.

The old woman was looking around the restaurant, tearing pieces of bread from the slices in a basket and chewing on them rapidly.

'I have to talk to you,' I said after a while.

'Well I hope you have something interesting to say.' She lifted up her glass. 'Santé'. She tasted her drink and then puckered her mouth into an old, savage grin. 'Elle a baptisé le vin,' she said with a look of contempt for Marie.

I told her about my animals but I did not think she was very interested. She kept looking around at other guests and seemed most concerned with old ladies of her own age. 'Watch her!' she would jab a finger at a very dainty old woman, dining on her own. 'See her!' She pointed out an ancient creature presiding over a Sunday lunch of several generations. The woman had whiskers and grey hair cut short like a man's and looked almost identical to her old husband who sat beside her.

When the food was brought Marie's mother ate it as a bird eats, her head on one side, considering the tastes. Every so often a jerk of the head towards me and my glass indicated that I should drink the watered wine.

'I'm not very fond . . .' I tried to say. She made a rapid

movement with her hand to dispose of my argument. 'Good for the stomach!' she said.

Father and Marie leaned across the table so that their faces were close and they talked together in low voices. They seemed indifferent to the food. They ate very little although they drank the wine.

In a strange way, I felt quite comfortable with the old woman. She spoke to herself, sometimes. When her fish was put before her she stared at it sadly. 'Pusspusspusspuss,' she called out hopefully, looking under the table. She pushed the plate aside. 'Des hot dogs,' she said. 'Et des glaces. Avec des noix.' She was dreaming. 'Et des cerises!' Her eyes filled with tears. She looked up then and gave me her sour little grin. I ate a great many chips and drank the Ribena-coloured wine and after a while I got a feeling of exceptional power and peace.

The old woman drained her glass very quickly although each time she drank from it she made a face which suggested she did not like its content. When her glass was empty, Marie would absent-mindedly attend to the mixing of liquids. Granny kept an eye on Marie and on the bottle. She did not look at her the way my mother used to look at me. It was hard to think of her as Marie's maman. She seemed quite removed from her – quite removed from everything, in fact, except the mixture in her glass. When she spoke again it was with a sharp tug at Marie's sleeve. 'The wine is finished!'

Marie gave Father an apologetic smile but he looked understanding and signalled at once for more wine. To my astonishment, the old woman winked at me.

Wine was poured. Father filled glasses for himself and Marie and then they raised them and touched them gently and their eyes had a soft burning look with a gentle light like candles. They moved the glasses, still touching, away from their faces and very slowly their faces touched; their lips.

'They haven't . . .' I was about to protest that they hadn't put water and wine into our glasses but the old woman placed a bony finger on her lips and eyed me severely. I hung my head and sighed in confusion. A touch made me look up. That same finger was on my head. The old woman was smiling at me the way that adults look at each other when they know something that you do not. She lifted her finger from my head in such slow motion that my eyes were forced to follow it. A corner of her eye watched our kissing relatives. The finger swivelled clockwards and stopped upon the wine. With astonishing speed she seized the bottle and filled both our glasses. She made a motion to me that I should drink it up quickly. I did as I was told, too amazed by her boldness to notice the bitter taste. When I had drained my glass I gave a laugh, a hoarse laugh that sounded strange to me and she nodded and gave an ordinary old woman's laugh.

She raised her eyebrows now, with a little smile for her foolish daughter and my entranced father. Father held Marie's face with the tips of his fingers. Once more the old woman's hand moved slowly over the table and made a catlike pounce on the bottle. As she was refilling our glasses Marie gave a funny little grunt – the sort of noise you would make if cream from an éclair spilled on your chin – and her arm groped sideways and took the bottle from her mother. She held it up to Father and gestured sideways with her eyes to let him know what had happened. Father looked quite shocked but he looked dazed too and when Marie laughed he smiled on us all. The old woman gave him a poisonous smile. Father and Marie returned to their courtship but they kept the bottle on their own side of the table.

'Merde!' said the granny.

'That's a curseword!' I said.

She looked at me scornfully. 'I don't suppose you know any cursewords?'

'I do.'

'Go ahead!'

'It's not allowed.'

'Cul!' she said provocatively.

'That's a terrible word!' I looked around in case anyone might have heard it. I lowered my voice; 'It means your bum!'

'Bum!' the old woman cackled with delighted wickedness. 'You said a bad word. Bum! Bum!'

'That's not a bad word. I know much worse than that.'

'I don't believe you.'

'Shitehawk!' I shouted out.

Father looked around in alarm and confusion, as one woken from a dream. 'Nicholas!'

'Sorry, Father.'

'It's the wine,' Marie giggled.

'Don't worry,' the granny said. 'I can handle him. Pphhh!' – she made a noise to suggest that she was already worn out with handling; 'but not without my medicine!' She held out her glass.

'I don't know!' Marie shook her head; 'two delinquents!' She dealt the glass its watery mixture and left the bottle in the centre of the table.

'That spider of yours,' the old woman said; 'is it poisonous?'

'Of course.'

'How do you know? Has it ever bitten anyone?'

'No!'

'Is it . . . deadly?'

'I think a doctor could save you,' I hazarded.

'Then we must try it out sometime.' She raised her glass to her lips but instead of drinking she merely gestured with it and muttered with a grin, 'du pipi d'âne!'; and then with a conjurer's flick she emptied the mixture into a plant which was on the edge of our table, in a pot wrapped in red crepe paper.

She filled our glasses deftly with unadulterated wine and raised hers once more but instead of the usual phrase she said in a ladylike and barely audible murmur, 'Salaud!' I drew in my breath with excitement and admiration. She managed to make it sound like a harmless salute but this was a really strong curse. A boy in school had told me. It meant . . . bastard!

I gulped from my glass. 'Arseholes!' I hissed.

'Salope!'

'Horsepiss!'

'Zizi!'

'Balls!'

'Trou de balle!'

I drank more wine. It had the colour of cherries, the taste of fruit and fire. It filled my head with wildness and I dared say anything. 'Fff . . .' I drew out the worst word of all, pressing my teeth down into my lower lip.

'Non!' The old lady looked alarmed.

'That's a really bad word, isn't it?' My eyes were sparkling and my head swam. 'I don't care how bad it is, I'm going to say it.'

'I know your word,' she said. 'It is not so bad. It is a very sad word.'

'Sad?' I said with a coarse laugh. 'Do you understand it?'

'Do *you* understand it?'

I understood and I did not. 'It's awfully rude. It has to do with men and women.'

'Ah, yes,' she said. 'L'amour.'

'Love.'

'Love? Non. I prefer l'amour. Your English love is too noble – too full of expectation and disappointment. Too full of duty to parents and country. L'amour is touching and foolish and human.'

She leaned across the table until she was as close to me as Father was to Marie. 'It is –'; she tapped the table for emphasis; '– the miracle of creation in the magic of enchantment. Only a sad man would so curse his frustration.'

The moment passed. It was as if it had never happened. The old woman called out for strawberry tart. She dug her spoon into the glistening humps of fruit and made sounds of appreciation.

She had forgotten me. Worse, Marie had forgotten me. I turned to her in appeal but she was lost to me, far away on some voyage of the heart, safe in the magic of enchantment.

'What are you thinking?' The old woman had finished her tart.

I pretended not to hear. Her foolishness had cost me Marie's attention.

'You are thinking about l'amour. You are thinking you know it all and you are a disillusioned fellow.'

I shook my head crossly.

'You are jealous of my daughter and your father because

they have found happiness in each other; because they need no one else.'

'It's true!' I said. 'They're all right. They don't want us.'

'Poor fellow. Have some tart. Already you are a victim.'

I ate the tart. It was glorious.

'There will come a moment in your life,' the woman who looked like a parsnip was saying; 'when you will look at a person the way *they* look at one another and from that moment you will never be free.'

'Then it's a spell! It's a trap!'

'How quickly you are growing up,' she said. 'It is not the spell that is the trap. It is the vanishing of l'amour that imprisons us. Where did it go? How can we live without it?'

'Well . . . how?'

'There is no answer. Whole lives are spent searching for it, trying to entice it back. Look!' She pointed out a beautifully dressed old lady who was dining on her own. 'Do you know who that lady is? That is the dognapper of Paris. Once she was a respectable woman but she fell in love with a man who was married. Love made her disreputable. When he left her she was so lonely she took to stealing little dogs. She has dozens of them in her apartment. Watch her closely! See her now!' She turned to point out the whiskery old peasant at whom she had earlier been staring. 'That is the richest woman in France. Her husband still loves her.'

Almost as she spoke the old man at her side turned and said something to her and then he kissed her whiskery, horrible mouth and smiled into her eyes.

'Then Marie and my father must be very rich,' I said.

The old woman shrugged. 'They are gamblers. Their fortune depends on the turn of a card. Marie is very young. When she looks at him she sees in his eyes a mirror of her own perfection. Wait until they each discover that the other is not perfect! Quelle barbe!'

'But Marie is kind! She is willing to put up with all my animals.'

'She is a clever girl. She has thought to herself: "He is growing up. Soon he will be tired of all these rats and spiders. It is not long to wait." Or else she believes she can charm you away from your leggy friends.'

'But my father!' I said. 'What about him? He would do anything for Marie.'

She gave her sour old chuckle. 'We shall see.'

We were all distracted then by a piercing cry. A woman was standing up, shouting for the management, the police. 'Someone has stolen my little dog!' she wailed in French.

I looked quickly for the old lady in furs but she had vanished. Madame Duclos was smiling at her empty plate.

In the morning Father was alone and in a fury. 'That woman,' he said, rattling the grey printed wastes of a French newspaper. 'I have been deceived.'

I knew he was not really speaking to me so I spooned jam on to my bread and drank my milky coffee.

'She intended to bring her mother to live with us. That foul-mouthed old drunkard! Good God! That would be nice company for you, Nicholas.'

'I don't mind,' I said, but he did not hear.

'If there is one thing I cannot and will not tolerate it is deceit. She waited until the very last minute, until all our arrangements had been made, before springing that pleasant surprise. What an idea!'

'What else could she do?' I said, but he was not listening.

I did not see Marie again. We left quite soon afterwards, on our own.

I thought, later on, that the old woman had been both wrong and right. Father did not appear to be in a trap. In fact, he was freer than before. For a while he was in a rage and then he brooded and after that he resumed life with the energy that had seemed to die with my mother. After several years he married a plump Miss Windhouse and he often whistled with contentment.

The animals were gone by then. I thought it best to face up to the fact that it was not normal to spend so much time with stupid creatures. Their dumb faces began to annoy me.

'How would you like to be cooked?' I shouted one day when my thrush was making a racket for food.

All of that is in the past now and I am free to think of other things. In a little while I shall be teenage and soon after that I will be a man. Then I can start to properly plan for my return to Paris. I know Marie is waiting for me. We had a promise; to be friends, to ride ponies over the fields. We will drink champagne together and I will eat lobster. For Marie.

☙〰❧

Ears

'Father's ears have been at him,' Hilda said.

It was lunch time with lamb chops in the season of lamb chops. George and Hilda sat by a bay window which showed a day of bluebells and daffodils, blue and yellow like the sky and the sun. Out of doors people wore old hats and scratched at the soil for its pleasure and theirs. Compared to George's garden with its polished lawns, disciplined borders and black velvet islands of voluptuous shrubs, their gardens were mere sandpits but all he could see as he looked through the window was a sky growing black with bats.

'Beg pardon, dear?' he said.

'Me Dad,' she said. 'It's his ears.'

By and large George was a happy man. He had a strict mind; he had his garden. He had, as a sort of levy on his good fortune, Dad, the most loudly decomposing old man in history.

With a ready sigh he laid down his knife and fork and rinsed his teeth with a reasonable Beaujolais to free them from particles of meat. 'What seems to be the matter?' he articulated, baring his teeth on the "ees" in a hope of frightening her to death.

'He says they've gone kind of soft and wet.'

In the shed, Sid Millar edged the tip of his finger under a lip of rubber in a genital shade of pink. Excitement knocked the breath out of his body in noisy jets upon which the brown and grey twigs of his moustache danced up and down. A piece of pink flipped back revealing one perfect white paw. 'Exceptional,' he wheezed. 'Exceptional.'

The second paw was simple. Working with the loose piece of rubber he folded back a second edge. Thlok! Two paws. He rolled away the rest of the rubber deftly, lovingly, like silk hose from a hooker. That was the easy bit; a fat rump with a powder puff tail and a face he recognised with affection, returning its grotesque grin as he sighted the perfect, pointy nose and wide-set eyes.

Containing his smile in the edges of his moustache he closed his eyes and placed his fingers on the two projections that remained sheathed in rubber. He held the tips firm to avoid stress and teased the rubber upward with the fingers of his free hand. 'Phwsh, phwsh, phwsh,' went his breath and the tobacco-stained dancers rose and fell. There was a tricky bit at the end that was like taking off socks without turning them inside out. The rubber came away and Sid stood, eyes shut tight, clutching his hand to his heart for strength.

He looked. 'Oh, my God,' he said. It was a Rodin among plaster rabbits. There wasn't an air hole, a distortion, a chip in sight. The ears were like sails, tall, straight, contoured. 'I've done it!' He let out a cackle, wicked in its conceit and did a dance of worship around his perfect rabbit. The rabbit looked so real you could almost see its ears twitching. They *did* twitch; first a sort of outward jerk and then a slow downward droop until they resembled boomerangs. 'Oh, my God,' Sid said. The ears curved a fraction more and dropped off on to the table. The old man touched the fractured pieces and emitted a 'phwsh' that did not move his moustache at all.

'It's no good,' he said. 'I can't do that there ear.'

'You're not to say "that there 'ere". Father doesn't like it.' The voice came from another face which rested on the table. Unlike the rabbit, this face was perfect in every detail and had lasted ten years. 'Not "ere", Edith. "Ear."' Sid pulled at his lobes for the benefit of his granddaughter. 'Rabbits don't have to have ears,' she said. 'Venus de Milo had no arms.'

'Arms,' Sid said. 'They'd be tricky right enough.' He lifted the rabbit gently from the table and laid it to rest on a shelf along with twenty or so others which ranged in quality from a small ghost foetus at the edge to some really splendid fat fellows. None of them had ears.

'Van Gogh had only one ear,' Edith's voice sailed up at him like a gnat. Sid Millar was eighty. It was a time in life when everything in his body seemed to be enjoying final bouts of independent activity which collectively brought his movements down to a totter.

His arteries were hardening, his ulcers bleeding, his toes weeping, his bones going brittle. Oh, and much more. Hilda could tell you. He was turning into a tenement. The result of watching his organs racing each other to an undignified finish gave Sid an overwhelming desire to possess, before it was all over, something of his own that was perfect. There was Hilda, of course. Sid gave a malicious snort of mirth. Hilda had no whatsits. George, damn the misbegotten Mobeydick, hadn't even got a chin.

Edith, from behind, saw her grandfather's shoulders shaking. She thought he was crying. It was a terrible thing, she had once heard, for a man to cry.

On the following morning, which was Monday, it was still spring, a fact which had not penetrated the newsroom of *The Reflection*. Tuohy and Hughes were conspiring over a copy of *The Moon*, in particular a picture of Miss Topsie Thompson, who was wearing a watch. 'What do you make of her?' Tuohy's little marble eyes rolled and his Kerry accent raked the fug of the newsroom air.

'She's a little bit skimpy,' Hughes said. His face was the colour of boiled tripe and he had a straw hat with a dog daisy in the band.

'Ja-a-aysus!' Tuohy yawned and beat his little fists on the air. 'If she was on fire I wouldn't piss on her to put her out.' Tuohy huddled over his big, black typewriter, resembling a wet cloth thrown on top of a stove, where someone had meant to wipe it and had forgotten. Everything about Tuohy, except his typewriter, was small: His malevolence, however, was magnificent. It extended not only to rival newsmen but to women and children, pet cats and stray dogs. He was the best human interest man in the business.

Little Freddie came out of the editor's office looking for tea bags and waving a memo. It was from Mr Pottle, the editor, and appeared to be a matter concerning rabbits' ears.

In his office Mr Pottle, an enormous man with a florid face and fearsome eyes, was simpering at another piece of paper, pink and grubby and written upon in a pencilled print. He launched it across the desk so that it drifted into Tuohy's grey claws. 'Is it clear?' he bellowed. Tuohy read the letter through twice. Frowning so that his features became a tiny pile of dried fruit in the centre of his face, he wrestled for understanding. It was about as clear as a pint of Guinness.

'*Dear Sir,*' read the note; '*my grandfather is eighty years old and has a rubber mould of a rabbit. He tried to make one with casting plaster and found it set very quick but as the days went by it got kind of soft and wet, especially the ears which then fell off. Could you please tell him what to use as he wants rabbits to put in the garden.*'

It was signed, faithfully, by a Miss Edith Parker. Tuohy couldn't believe his . . . 'Ears?'

'The plight of the elderly!' sang Mr Pottle. 'How do we lighten their twilight years, those worthy citizens who have expended their energies in the interest of making Britain great? How do we pay back the pals of our cradle days? How do we make our senior citizens smile? Who cares?'

'If the answer is "nobody" then why the hell are you going on about it?' Tuohy said nastily.

'Pensions are going up?' Mr Pottle said. 'We've got a potential readership among the over-eighties, particularly with our "no sex" policy. This is going to be gold from the oldies. The entire story will be in fourteen point for the short-sighted,' he dreamed. '*The Moon* is going to be sorry it ever bared a breast.'

Edith was swinging on the gate when she saw the two men struggling down the street; the nasty-looking little one with the notebook and the stooping, sad-faced one who was weighted down with cameras. For the purpose of the Campaign, Tuohy had been mated with Mitchell, an elderly, taciturn photographer with a modest cavity of a mouth from which nothing ever issued but a pipe. With the perception of small girls on spring days, Edith knew they were coming to her house.

George sprang through the front door at the precise moment they reached the gate, as though he had been watching from a ground-floor window which, indeed, he had. With enormous effort Tuohy extended his mouth from ear to ear in a hideous grin and extended a claw. 'Sir,' he said. 'We require your assistance in a matter of national importance. We are representatives of *The Reflection*.'

'Gentlemen?' George said in a manner calculated to assure them that they were not. Tuohy pursed his eyes in an atrocious fashion to convey human interest. 'It concerns your garden,' he said.

George had always secretly dreamed of seeing his lawn featured on the cover of *Gnomes and Gardens*. Now it had come to this. His floral displays were to be flaunted in the centre pages of *The Reflection*. He would have none of it. 'I have nothing to say,' he said sternly.

'Rabbits' ears!' Tuohy thrust. 'Do they have a place in your garden?' Lambs' Ears the fool meant, George despaired. He allowed himself a moment's yearning for that most submissive of all his shrubs, its infinitely tactile leaves yielding season after season the softness that men grew up believing to be the rewards of love. 'A pride of place,' he said, before turning on his heel and striding away indoors.

As soon as she was certain her father was out of sight, Edith came forward. 'I know what you want,' she said. 'It's me.'

On the Wednesday following, *The Reflection* dropped the bombing of the British Library to page three and spiked the latest postmortem developments in John Kennedy's sex life.

Instead they led on '*The Broken Rabbits that Almost Broke an Old Man's Heart!*' There was a lovely picture of Sid Millar and his granddaughter Edith standing in a typical English garden at a perfect flower border surrounded by twenty rabbits with no ears. It was a pity they couldn't have had a photograph of the son-in-law who offered the quote: 'They have pride of place in my garden!' Still, it was a smashing story and *The Reflection* with its slogan: 'The Paper that Cares about the Old' was sold out as soon as it hit the stands.

Letters poured in in their thousands. Kind people suggested

alternative hobbies for Sid. Sackloads of rabbits, cloth ducks, pandas, were sent to him for comfort. Parcels of porpoises came in. To highlight the financial plight of pensioners *The Reflection* started up a 'Quid for Sid' fund. Money rolled in at an alarming rate.

The thing that did not arrive was a solution to Sid Millar's problem.

'*The Reflection* will rise to the challenge of rabbits' ears,' Mr Pottle thundered. 'Assemble a research team, Mr Tuohy. Institute a factory if necessary. We're going to show the nation how to make rabbits' ears that Britain can be proud of!'

Tuohy rang the educational hobbies shop that was run by a homosexual scoutmaster. 'We've still got those pictures from the 1965 Summer Camp, Mr Cuthbertson,' he coaxed.

'What do you want?'

'Tell me how to turn a plaster rabbit out of a mould without breaking the ears.'

'Oh, my God, Mr Tuohy, you have me there. An age-old problem, ears. Have you thought of trying gnomes?'

'Try 'em yourself,' Tuohy said and hung up.

At first George thought the small knot of people at the garden gate had come to admire his early showing of flowering cherry. By the time he had tidied himself to meet them the group had assumed crowd proportions. 'There he is!' cried a lady in a headscarf. She was pointing to Hilda's father who stood by his earless rabbits waving to his fans.

George listened to the sound of his own brains boiling. He reached for a garden rake and charged at the crowd. Just before it dispersed, shrieking, an impudent boy held aloft the morning's copy of *The Reflection*. '*The Bunnies that Bug Britain*' ran the banner headline.

When the people had departed George found that he was pointing the rake at his father-in-law. Sid grinned toothlessly. 'They're tort of ditlinctive all the tlame, ' he mused, in regard to his rabbits. 'Either they go or you do,' George hissed. 'If I go you won't get any of my money,' Sid said. 'Money, my eye!' fumed George. 'No,' Sid corrected mildly. 'My ears.'

Hilda and Edith were sorry about Sid's departure. George

combed the whole of his garden meticulously to rid it of paw prints. *The Reflection* was ecstatic. That picture of the bent old figure of Sid Millar leaving home with one small suitcase and twenty plaster rabbits had to be the circulation clincher of the year. Mr Pottle called for Tuohy at home at an early hour to take him to a news stand. 'I want you to witness a sellout, m'boy,' he said, clapping him on the back so that the miserable little figure almost disintegrated. 'I want you to be the first man on the scene at the massacre of *The Moon.*'

The queue at the stand certainly was spectacular. 'Brilliant! Bloody brilliant!' Tuohy cackled as the happy citizens carried off their tabloids. They reached the stand in time to see a pensioner pounce on the last copy of . . . *The Moon.*

At least half the morning's quota of *The Reflection* remained in the racks. Pottle drew himself up to his full height and terrorised the senior citizen. 'Give me that, you ungrateful old garbage,' he bellowed, snatching the newspaper.

The front page of *The Moon* featured a four-column picture of Sid Millar with one arm around an achingly delicious Bunny Girl. With his free hand he was tweaking one of her fuzzy rabbit's ears. The paper, which told Sid's story in full while announcing his engagement to the eighteen-year-old beauty, shamelessly employed the catchline 'Souven-ear Issue'. Inside was a four-page picture supplement featuring pensioner Sid with his bride-to-be in a variety of costumes that ought to have been kept until after the ceremony.

The idea of actually proposing to Bonita Higglesworth had come to Sid when she was perched on his knee with no clothes on. It was a landscape of pink perfection. Her breasts were scoops of peach ice-cream; her knees, apricots. Her ears were like wafers of coral. You couldn't put a woman out in the garden for an ornament, of course, or sit her on the mantle-shelf like a clock.

You could look at her. Sid did, thinking how her cheeks would bulge like pillows when she was eating chocolate, how her amber eyes would melt while counting money, how delicately her lips would dip into a gin and orange: something that might be his; something that was perfect.

'Ummm, ummm, would you marry me?' he said.

Miss Higglesworth giggled. 'What 'ave you got to offer me?'

'I have got,' Sid said, 'twenty plaster rabbits – some of them are very good; fifty thousand pounds from the "Quid for Sid" fund and several terminal diseases.'

'I do,' Miss Higglesworth said, protruding her lips in a manner that caused two young photographers to faint.

'Exceptional,' Sid Millar wheezed.

The Stolen Child

Women steal other people's husbands so why shouldn't they steal other people's babies? Mothers leave babies everywhere. They abandon them to foreign students while they go out gallivanting, hand them over for years on end to strangers who stuff them with dead languages and computer science. I knew a woman who left her baby on the bus. She was halfway down Grafton Street when she got this funny feeling and she said, 'Oh, my God, I've left my handbag,' and then with a surge of relief she felt the strap of her bag cutting into her wrist and remembered the baby.

I never wanted to steal another woman's husband. Whatever you might make of a man if you got him firsthand, there's no doing anything once some other woman's been at him, started scraping off the first layer of paint to see what's underneath, then decided she didn't like it and left him like that, all scratchy and patchy.

Babies come unpainted. They have their own smell, like new wood has. They've got no barriers. Mothers go at their offspring the way a man goes at a virgin, no shame or mercy. A woman once told me she used to bite her baby's bum when she changed its nappy. Other women have to stand back, but nature's nature.

Sometimes I dream of babies. Once there were two in a wooden cradle high up on a shelf. They had very small, dark faces, like Russian icons, and I climbed on a chair to get at them. Then I saw their parents sitting up in bed, watching me.

I have a dream about a little girl, three or four, who runs behind me, trying to catch up. She says nothing but her hand burrows into mine and her fingers stroke my palm. Now and then I have a baby in my sleep, although I don't remember anything about it. It's handed to me, and I know it's mine, and I just gaze into the opaque blueness of the eye that's like the sky, as if everything and nothing lies behind.

It comes over you like a craving. You stand beside a pram and stare the way a woman on a diet might stare at a bar of chocolate in a shop window. You can't say anything. It's taboo, like cannibalism. Your middle goes hollow and you walk away stiff-legged, as if you have to pee.

Or maybe you don't.

It happened just like that. I'd come out of the supermarket. There were three infants left lying out in strollers. I stopped to put on my headscarf and glanced at the babies the way people do. I don't know what did it, but I think it was the texture. There was this chrysalis look. I was wondering what they felt like. To tell the truth my mouth was watering for a touch. Then one of them turned with jerky movements to look at me. 'Hello,' I said. She stirred in her blankets and blew a tiny bubble. She put out a toe to explore the air. She looked so new, so completely new, that I was mad to have her. It's like when you see some dress in a shop window and you have to have it because you think it will definitely change your life. Her skin was rose soft and I had a terrible urge to touch it. *Plenty of time for that*, I thought, as my foot kicked the brake of the pram.

Mothers don't count their blessings. They complain all the time and they resent women without children, as if they've got away with something. They see you as an alien species. Talk about a woman scorned! And it's not men who scorn you. They simply don't notice you at all. It's other women who treat you like the cat daring to look at the king. They don't care for women like me; they don't trust us.

I was at the bus stop one day and this woman came along with a toddler by the hand and a baby in a push-car. 'Terrible day!' I said. She gave me a look as if she was about to ask for a search warrant and then turned away and commenced a

performance of pulling up hoods and shoving on mittens. She
didn't seem to notice the rain. Soaked to the bone she was,
hair stuck to her head like a bag of worms. She had all this
shopping spilling out of plastic bags and she bent down and
began undoing her parcels, arranging them in the tray that's
underneath the baby's seat, as if to say to me, 'This is our
world. We don't need your sort.' It was a relief when the bus
came and I could get out of gloating range but still she had to
make herself the centre of attention. She hoisted the toddler
onto the platform and then got up herself, leaving the baby all
alone in the rain to register its despair in an ear-splitting fashion. 'You've forgotten the baby,' I said, and she gave me a very
dirty look. She lunged outward, seized the handle of the pram
and tried to manhandle it up after her, but it was too heavy.
Sullen as mud, she waded back into the rain. This time the
toddler was abandoned on the bus, its little mouth opened
wide and loud. She unstrapped the baby and sort of flung it up
on the bus. Everyone was looking. Back she clambered,
leaned out again and wrestled the pram on board, as if some
sort of battle to the death was involved. I don't think the
woman was in her right mind. Of course, half the groceries
fell out into the gutter and the baby followed. 'You're going
about that all wrong,' I told her, but she took no notice. The
driver then woke up and said he couldn't take her as he
already had one push-car. Do you think she apologised for
keeping everyone waiting? No! She inflicted a most withering
parting glance on us all, as if we were somehow to blame.

Walking away from the supermarket with someone else's
child, I didn't feel guilty. I was cleansed, absolved of the guilt of
not fitting in. I loved that baby. I felt connected to her by all the
parts that unglamorous single women aren't supposed to have. I
believed we were allies. She seemed to understand that I needed
her more than her mother did and I experienced a great well of
pity for her helplessness. She could do nothing without me and
I would do anything in the world for her. I wheeled the pram
out through the car park, not too quickly. Once I even stopped
to settle her blankets. Oh, she was the sweetest thing. Several
people smiled into the pram. When I gave her a little tickle, she

laughed. I believe I have a natural talent as a mother. I look at other women with their kids and think, *She hasn't a clue, she doesn't deserve her blessings*. I notice things. The worst mothers are the ones with too many kids. Just like my mum. They bash them and yell at them and then they give them sweets. Just like this woman I saw watching me from the doorway of the supermarket. She seemed completely surrounded by children. There must have been seven of them. One kid was being belted by another and a third was scuttling out under a car. And she watched me intently with this pinched little face and I knew she was envying me my natural maternal gift. I knew a widow once, used to leave her baby in the dog's basket with the dog when she went out to work.

And all this time, while I was pushing and plotting, where was her mother? She might have been in the newsagent's flipping the pages of a magazine, or in the coffee shop giving herself a moustache of cappuccino, or in the supermarket gazing at bloated purple figs and dreaming of a lover. Mothers, who swear that they would die in an instant for you, are never there when you need them. Luckily, there is frequently someone on hand, as for instance myself, who was now wheeling the poor little thing out of harm's way, and not, if you ask me, before time.

I can't remember ever being so happy. There was a sense of purpose, the feeling of being needed. And, you'll laugh now, but for the first time in my life, looking into that dear little face, I felt that I was understood.

When my mum died I got depressed and they sent me along to see a psychiatrist. He said to me, 'You're young. You have to make a life of your own.'

I was furious. 'Hardly anyone makes a life of their own,' I told him. 'They get their lives made for them.'

He asked me about my social life and I said I went to the pictures once in a while. 'You could put an advertisement in the personal columns,' he advised.

'Advertisement for what?' I said.

'A companion,' he said.

'Just like that?' I must say I thought that was a good one.

'You put an advertisement in the paper and you get a companion?' I pictured a fattish little girl of about ten with long plaits.

'People do,' he promised me. 'Or you could go to an introduction agency.'

'And what sort of thing would you say in this advertisement?'

'You could say you were an attractive woman, early thirties, seeking kind gentleman friend, view to matrimony.'

I was far from pleased. I lashed out at him with my handbag. 'You said a companion. You never said anything about a gentleman friend.'

Well, I make out all right. I get a bit of part-time work and I took up a hobby. I became a shoplifter. Many people are compelled in these straitened times to do things that are outside their moral strictures, but personally I took to shoplifting like a duck to water. It gave me a lift and enabled me to sample a lot of interesting things. The trick is, you pay for the bulky items and put away the small ones, settle out for the sliced pan, pinch the kiwi fruit, proffer for the potatoes, stow the sun-dried tomatoes, fork out for the firelighters, filch the fillet steaks. In this way I added a lot of variety to my diet – lumpfish roe and anchovies and spiced olives and smoked salmon, although I also accumulated a lot of sliced loaves. 'Use your imagination,' I told myself. 'There are other bulky items besides sliced bread.'

Perhaps it was the pack of nappies in my trolley that did it. I hate waste. It also just happened that the first sympathetic face I saw that day (in years, in point of fact) was that tiny baby left outside in her pram to wave her toe around in the cold air, so I took her too.

I thought I'd call her Vera. It sounded like the name of a person who'd been around for a long time, or as if I'd called her after my mother. When I got home the first thing I did was pick her up. Oh, she felt just lovely, like nothing at all. I went over to the mirror to see what kind of a pair we made. We looked a picture. She took years off my age.

Vera was looking around in a vaguely disgruntled way, as if she could smell burning. *Milk*, I thought. *She wants milk*. I kept her balanced on my arm while I warmed up some milk. It was a nice feeling, although inconvenient, like smoking in the bath. I had to carry her back with the saucepan, and a spoon, and a dishtowel for a bib. Natural mothers don't have to ferret around with saucepans and spoons. They have everything to hand, inside their slip. I tried to feed her off a spoon but she blew at it instead of sucking. There was milk in my hair and on my cardigan and quite a lot of it went on the sofa, which is a king-fisher pattern, blue on cream. After a while she pushed the cup away and her face folded up as if she was going to cry. 'Oh, sorry, sweetheart,' I said. 'Who's a stupid mummy?' She needed her nappy changed.

To tell the truth I had been looking forward to this. Women complain about the plain duties of motherhood but to me she was like a present that was waiting to be unwrapped. I carried her back downstairs and filled a basin with warm water and put a lot of towels over my arm, not forgetting a sponge and all the other bits and pieces. I was proud of myself. I almost wished there was someone to see.

By now Vera was a bit uneasy (perhaps I should have played some music, like women do to babies in the womb, but I don't know much about music). I took off the little pink jacket, the pink romper suit that was like a hot-water bottle cover and then started to unwrap the nappy. A jet of water shot up into my eye. Now that was not nice, Vera! I rubbed my eye and began again, removing all that soggy padding. Then I slammed it shut. The child looked gratified and started to chortle. Incredulous, I peeled the swaddling back once more. My jaw hung off its hinges. Growing out of the bottom of its belly was a wicked little ruddy horn. I found myself looking at balls as big as pomegranates and when I could tear my eyes away from them I had to look into his eye, a man's eye, already calculating and bargaining.

It was a boy. Who the hell wants a boy?

'Hypocrite!' I said to him. 'Going round with that nice little face!'

Imagine the nerve of the mother, dressing him up in pink, palming him off as a girl! Imagine, I could still be taken in by a man.

Now the problem with helping yourself to things, as opposed to coming by them lawfully, is that you have no redress. You have to take what you get. On the other hand, as a general rule, this makes you less particular. I decided to play it cool. 'The thing is, Vera,' (I would change his name later. The shock was too great to adjust all at once) 'I always thought of babies as female. It simply never occurred to me that they came in the potential rapist mode. There are some points in your favour. You do look very nice with all your clothes on. On the other hand, I can't take to your sort as a species.'

I was pleased with that. I thought it moderate and rational.

Vera was looking at me in the strangest way, with a sweet, intent, intelligent look. Clearly he was concentrating. There is something to be said for the intelligent male. Maybe he and I would get along. 'The keynote,' I told him, 'is compromise. We'll have to give each other plenty of space.' Vera smiled. He looked relieved. It was a weight off my mind too. Then I got this smell. It dawned on me with horror the reason for his concentration. 'No!' I moaned. 'My mother's Sanderson!' I swooped on him and swagged him without looking too closely. His blue eyes no longer seemed opaque and new but very old and angry. He opened his mouth and began to bawl. Have you ever known a man who could compromise?

All that afternoon I gazed in wonder on the child who had melted my innards and compelled me to crime. Within the space of half an hour he had been transformed. His face took on the scalded red of a baboon's behind and he bellowed like a bull. His eyes were brilliant chips of ice behind a wall of boiling water. I got the feeling it wasn't even personal. It was just what he did whenever he thought of it. I changed his nappy and bounced him on my knee until his brains must have scrambled. I tried making him a mush of bread and milk and sugar, which he scarcely touched yet still managed to return in great quantity over my shoulder. With rattling hands I strapped him into the stroller and took him for a walk. Out of doors the noise became a metallic booming. People glared at me and crows fell off their perches in the trees. Everything seemed distorted by the sound. I began to feel quite mad. My legs appeared to be melting and when I looked at the sky the clouds had a fizzing, dangerous look. I wanted to lie flat out on the pavement. You can't when you're a mother. Your life's not your own any more. I realised now that the mother and child unit is not the one I imagined but a different kind, in which she exists to keep him alive and he exists to keep her awake.

I hadn't had a cup of tea all day, or a pee. When I got home there was a note on the door. It was from my landlord, asking if I had a child concealed on the premises. I cackled glumly at the concept of concealing Vera and staggered in to turn on the news. By now he would be reported missing. His distraught mother would come on the telly begging whoever had him to please let her have her baby back. It was difficult to hear above the infant shrieks but I could see Bill Clinton's flashing teeth and bodies in the streets in Bosnia and men in suits at EEC summits. I watched until the weatherman had been and gone. Vera and I wept in unison. Was this what they meant by bonding?

Sometime in the night the crying stopped. The crimson faded from my fledgling's cheek and he subsided into rosy sleep. There was a cessation of the hostile shouts and banging on walls from neighbours. I sat over him and stroked his little fluff of hair and his cheek that was like the inside of a flower, and then I must have fallen asleep for I dreamed I was being ripped apart by slash hooks, but I woke up and it was his barking cries slicing through my nerves.

He beamed like a daisy as I wheeled him back to the supermarket. Daylight lapped around me like a great, dangerous, glittering sea. After twenty-four hours I had entered a twilight zone and was both light-headed and depressed so that tears slid down my face as I marvelled at the endurance of the tiny creature in my custody, the dazzling scope of his language of demand, which ranged from heart-rending mews to the kind of frenzied sawing sounds that might have emanated from the corpse stores of Dr Frankenstein. He had broken me. My nerve was gone and even my bones felt loose. I had to concentrate, in the way a drunk does, on setting my feet in front of one another. I parked him carefully outside the supermarket and even did some shopping, snivelling a bit as I tucked away a little tin of white crab meat for comfort. Then I was free. I urged my trembling limbs to haste.

'You've forgotten your baby!' a woman cried out.

My boneless feet tried an ineffectual scarper and the wheels of the push-car squealed in their pursuant haste. Upset by the crisis, the baby began to yell.

There are women who abandon babies in phone booths and lavatories and on the steps of churches but these are stealthy babies, silently complicit in their own desertion. Vera was like a burglar alarm in reverse. Wherever I set him, he went off. I tried cafés, cinemas, police stations. Once, I placed him in a wastepaper basket and he seemed to like that for there wasn't a peep, but when I was scurrying off down the street I remembered that vandals sometimes set fire to refuse bins so I ran back and fished him out. At the end of the day we went home and watched the news in tears. There was no report of a baby missing. Vera's cries seemed to have been slung like paint around the walls so that even in his rare sleeping moments they remained violent and vivid and neighbours still hammered on the walls. Everyone blamed me. It was like being harnessed to a madman. It reminded me of something I had read, how in Victorian almshouses sane paupers were frequently chained to the bed with dangerous lunatics.

By the third day I could think of nothing but rest. Sleep became a fixation. I was weeping and twitching and creeping on hands and knees. I wanted to lie down somewhere dark and peaceful where the glaring cave of my baby's mouth could no more pierce me with its proclamations. Then, with relief, I remembered the river bed. No one would find me there. Feverishly I dressed the child and wheeled him to the bridge. We made our farewells and I was about to hop into oblivion when I noticed a glove left on one of the spikes that ornament the metalwork, so that whoever had lost it would spot it right away. It was an inspiration, a sign from God. I lifted Vera onto the broad ledge of the bridge, hooked his little jumper onto a spike and left him there, peering quite serenely into the water.

At the end of the bridge I turned and looked back. The

baby had gone. Someone had taken him. It seemed eerily quiet without that little soul to puncture the ozone with his lungs. It dawned on me just why it was so quiet. There wasn't a some-one. There hadn't been anyone since I left him.

'Vera!' I raced back. There was no sound, and when I gazed into the water it offered back a crumpled portrait of the sky. The child was drowned. This person of dramatic beauty and argument, who could command such audience, make a strange woman fall in love with him and weave out of his infrequent sleep a whole tent of tranquillity, had vanished off the face of the earth.

'Vera!' I mourned.

After a few seconds he surfaced. At first he bounced into view and bobbed in the water, waiting to get waterlogged and go down again. Then he reached out an arm as if there were an object in the murky tide he wanted. He didn't seem frightened. There was something leisurely about that outstretched hand, the fingers slightly curled, like a woman reaching for a cake. He began to show signs of excitement. His little legs started to kick. Out went another arm towards an unseen goal. 'What are you doing?' I peered down into the filthy water in which no other living thing was. Up came the arm again, grabbed the water and withdrew. His feet kicked in delight. His whole body exulted. I moved along the wall, following his progress, trying to see what he saw that made him rejoice. Then I realised; he was swimming. The day was still and there was very little current. He gained confidence with every stroke. 'Wait!' I kept pace along the wall. He took no notice. He had com-menced his new life as a fish. 'Wait!' For me, I meant. I wanted to tell him he was wonderful, that I would forgive him all his primary impulses for in that well-defended casement was a creature capable of new beginnings. He did not strike out at the water as adults do but used his curled hands as scoops, his rounded body as a floating ball. He was merely walking on the water like Jesus, or crawling since he had not yet learned to walk. As he bobbed past once again I threw off my raincoat and jumped into the water. I stretched a hand to meet the little waving fingers. A puckish gust strained to sweep him off. At last our hands connected. The simple touch of human warmth restored him to the human world. He began to holler.

I would like to report a happy ending, but then, too, I have always hankered after a sighting of a hog upon the wing. It took five more days to locate the mother. She told the police she had had a lovely holiday at the sea and thought their Clint was being safely looked after by a friend who, like everyone else in her life, had let her down. As it transpired, I knew the mother and she knew me, although we did not refresh our acquaintance. It was the pinched little woman with all the kids who had watched me wheel her child away. She said their Clint was a bawler, she hadn't had a wink since the day he was born. She had no money, couldn't even afford new clothes for the baby and had to dress him in their Darryl's cast-offs. She was only human but she was a mother and would take him back if someone gave her a Walkman to shut out the noise.

No one bothered with me, the heroine of the hour – a woman who had risked her life to save a drowning child. It was the mother who drew the limelight. Thousands of women sent sound equipment. She became a sort of cult figure and mothers everywhere could be seen smiling under earphones, just as a year or two ago they used to waddle about in tracksuits. Valium sales slumped as women fondly gazed on infant jaws locked apart in soundless wrath. It was left to us, the childless, to suffer the curdling howls of the nation's unheeded innocents.

Some women don't deserve to have children.

It's Her

'I'm late,' Molly said.

He waited patiently to absorb the clatter of his heart. He lived, nowadays, like someone on a railway line who frequently has to break off conversation while a train passes overhead. Molly watched him guiltily and hopefully. When things got quiet he took her in his arms. *This is hell*, he thought. She nuzzled into him in the way someone does who takes love for granted. He felt for the fleshy parting of her mouth. There was a faint stirring of optimism. They had been given a remission: nine months' worry-free fucking.

The phone rang. Molly struggled free. Women always answer phones. They must be primed to respond to shrill repetition in order to keep babies alive. She tidied her hair back from her face. 'Yes . . . mm . . . yes,' she said to the telephone. Her eyes fixed on him in appeal. She put down the receiver in the careful way a child sets down the pieces of something she has broken. 'It's her,' she said.

Peter took the phone in a rage. It felt like a powerful, useful thing but he knew from experience that it was an old enemy, squaring up to him, reminding him that it was coming to get him. He barked into the machine, 'Yes?'

'You're late,' Joan said.

'While your sense of timing is impeccable.' He kept his voice down, knowing Molly would be stung by his tone.

'I want my money,' Joan said.

'You want my money.'

'Bastard!' Joan's cry flew out into the room where it shook Molly. 'It's not for me. It's for your children. You're breaking the law. I want my money now or you can face my lawyer.'

'Tomorrow. You'll have it tomorrow,' Peter said softly.

'I want it now.'

'I'm posting it now. You have to wait for the post.'

'I don't have to wait for anything. Why do you do this every month? Why don't you make a standing order? You want me at your mercy, don't you? You want to make me beg.'

He took the receiver away from his ear and held it against his chest, as if by hearing his disturbed heart she would know that he was not a monster, he was frail. He had two houses to support. His business, which had always looked on the way up, was getting eroded from the underneath by recession. 'I'll write the cheque now. I'll send it round by taxi.' He restored the piece to his ear. His offer fell off into some empty space. She had hung up.

'What will we do? How can we afford another baby?' Molly was crying.

'It's all right. Lots of people manage.' He was taken aback to think that there might be other men whose lives were dogged by leftovers and webbed with panic.

'I wish she was dead.' Molly crept miserably back into his arms.

'No!' Peter was appalled to hear his thoughts coming out of Molly. He nuzzled at her mouth. It was like trying to burrow back into a dream. 'Let's go to bed,' he said. When they got there he was too exhausted to do anything but lie there waiting for his haunting.

When he married Joan she was unformed, a sketch in outline. Now, she had somehow run beyond herself, become a caricature of whatever she might have been. Increasingly, at odd moments, he found himself preoccupied by the question of when she had actually been herself. If she was nothing to do with him, her straggly blonde hair and sad eyes would have reminded him of a drunk old pantomime dame. But she was his. There was no getting rid of her. She was a leak that becomes a flood, a cut that grows into a gaping wound, a sinister woman who turns into a vampire. She was constantly draining him, siphoning him off, mocking his efforts at recovery. He had no use for her any more. He needed his income for vital, present things. Why couldn't she get a job like other women, or find another man? Was it her life's work to strip him and bring him down? He had never been concerned about money. He was a fairly nice man who cared about emotional things, he liked making love and little children. Now his whole life seemed to be money or the need of it or the demand for it. As Molly's breathing deepened into sleep he found himself propelled once more down a familiar corridor in pursuit of a shadowy image. He tried to recall an ordinary woman, Joan. There must have been a time when he knew why he married her and was happy with his choice. Perhaps it happened in a single hour and he had been out at the time, or maybe she was pregnant and the clear line had been blurred. He had a new little family now. A clean page. He was surrounded by worship and trust. He felt like a man who in a moment of hope and madness agrees to lead a group of refugees through some war-torn country. He had promised them safety when, at his age, he knew that at the end there is only death. Every new thing squeezed at his heart – a late period, a child's fall, a large bill, a telephone call that might be from his ex-wife. He lived with the terror and the relief that his heart would give out and the tender gaping mouths would be left behind.

There came a day when he arrived home to find two men hanging around the house. There was something familiar about them. They waved stiffly and he scowled as he steered the car into the drive. What were they? Bill collectors, bailiffs?

'Dad!' one of them said.

He didn't see much of his sons. Joan accused him of not caring about the boys and it was true that when removed from the pity and the irritation that their teenage presence inspired he had not felt much, although he was still touched by memories of them when they were little boys. They were men now. The thought occurred to him that they would be someone to talk to, someone to drink beer with. In a few years they might marry and have children who would be close in age to his. He felt not exactly a lightening of his burden, but a fractional shift-ing so that it seemed better balanced, less likely to bring him down.

'Martin! Stephen!' He said their names loudly to show he had not forgotten them.

'We have to talk to you.' They followed him into the house and peered out the window at the recent garden and some unsteady flowers Molly had patted into the border. Filled with grown-ups, his new, scaled-down accommodation looked like a doll's house. Martin said, 'It's about Mum.'

'She sent you!' He was foolishly disappointed.

'Chill out,' Stephen sighed. 'She doesn't know we're here. It's bad news.'

Peter felt like a tree struck by lightning. He was being split down the middle. Neither half would be any use to anybody. 'What do you want?'

'We don't want anything.' Martin lit a cigarette and hissed smoke at his father. 'Just as well since you never had anything to give us.' He sat down and spread his legs. His genitals in their too-tight casing of denim were annoying. One could just tell that when he had finished whining at his father he would be off poking some woman. And without a moment's anxiety. Peter was still paying for him. Hostilities had now broken out between the two men with the jostling coldness of a ship's hulk against an ice floe.

'Cool it, Martin,' Stephen said sadly. 'Dad, shut the fuck up and listen. This has nothing to do with us. It's about Mum.'

'Wait a minute there.' Peter ignored Stephen. His heart had commenced a slow percussion like a sound effect in a horror movie. 'Martin, you said back there you didn't want anything? Correct me if I'm wrong, but it seems to me that I'm still paying to keep a school bag on your back. If you don't want my money I could use it myself. You're nearly twenty. Why don't you go out and get yourself a job?'

'Fuck you!' Martin said. 'Everything comes back to you.'

'It certainly feels that way.' Underneath his anger, elation was beginning to rise. Whatever awful thing was happening in his old family – crime or drug addiction or madness – he did not have to know. The money he was paying was to buy him his freedom. His anger had inadvertently created a diversion. It had steered him out of the dangerous swamp of his ex-wife's unknown disaster and brought him safely back, as Martin pointed out, to himself.

Molly came in then with the two little girls by the hand. 'I bought a dress,' she said. She was flustered. He knew she meant she had bought an expensive dress, one he could not afford.

'Put it on.' He smiled at her. 'Let me see.' The little girls gazed up at the two huge young men in awe and admiration. When Molly had gone up the stairs Stephen was flexing his great big hands in a way that clearly said to Peter, 'I could kill you if I wanted.'

They couldn't talk now Molly was back. They sat in silence until she came running down the stairs to show off her dress. It was white with little blue and yellow flowers. It was cut like a child's dress, loose and high-waisted, so that her small bump seemed like a natural part of her figure. She twirled around on her long legs. With each turn she seemed to change from a child to a woman and back again. This dazzling display upset the boys. Martin stood up and tugged at Stephen's shoulder. He managed a smile and a wave for Molly and then turned to Peter. 'Goodbye, dickhead.' Catching these sights and sounds, the little girls' eyes rotated slowly, absorbing light and darkness like planets rolling round the sun.

Peter was full of triumph. *She's mine*, he thought. *They'll never get anything even remotely like her.* It sometimes made him morose to think that Martin and Stephen had grown up in a generation confident that women were turned on by men's cocks whereas in his time male arousal was something that had to be camouflaged by force of personality and the dark, but even though he was modest and possibly repressed, he had Molly, he had got her, and the bump in her front was proof that he fucked her. 'You look lovely,' he congratulated her. 'The dress is lovely.'

'Don't you want to know how much it cost?' She was anxious to get this out of the way while his mood was cheerful. When she told him he suffered a soaring expanse of panic. He had not imagined anything could cost so much. Joan always bought cheap clothes, rummaged around in sales and tried to surprise him with the smallness of their price. In fact he had ceased to be surprised and taken it for granted that female drapery was an inconsequential thing, practically given away. Like his sons, Molly belonged to a different generation in which women no longer took it on themselves to efface and economise.

'I'm sorry,' she said.

'No,' he said. 'You should have beautiful things.'

When he had first looked on Molly he had seen her as a fresh start. Where do people get the notion that they can start again? He knew now (he must always have known) that every stone you turn, every box you open, you have to carry for the rest of your life. Increasingly he felt an envy of celibate priests, who had been slipped this information at an early age, who could drift weightless through whatever there was of life, until it had to be returned to wherever it came from. All he could see when he woke each morning was the range of his burdens and the knowledge that he must pick them up and carry them, and that he himself had chosen them. What right had he imagined he had to Molly? Early on, when she returned his interest, the pulsing of blood, the restitution of self-esteem had made him feel that he was being brought back to life after a very long period in cold storage. He had plucked a Renoir from the museum wall. How the hell was he to pay for it?

He deliberately let Joan's payment run late next month to show that she could not control him through the boys, that blackmail should be a clean thing, without emotion. He let a week pass, then ten days, and then he wrote out her cheque. The extra time allowed him to adjust to the financial shock of Molly's spending. When he finally posted the allowance he felt an unpleasant potency. Joan could hurt him but he had the power. The telephone remained mutely uncomplaining. It meant she was afraid. He was sorry for her, but he was glad.

Three days later she phoned. 'Hasn't your money arrived?' he said.

'Yes,' she said. 'Thanks.'

'I'm sorry it was late.'

'That's all right. It's always late. I wanted to talk about something else. I want to see you.'

'Can't you say whatever it is on the phone?'

'Can't we be friends? I wanted to say that.'

'Why?' he said. (Dickhead.)

'Because we're the only ones who know each other.'

'I don't know you any more.'

'We grew up together. We're the key to each other.'

He hated it when women talked like that.

Joan's face was gaunt and her hair was matted. He felt sure she had been drinking. 'What is it?' he said. 'What do you want?'

'I need money.' Her voice was hoarse. 'I have to fix things up.'

'What things?'

'That's none of your business.'

'I have no more money,' he said.

'Borrow some.' Her mouth was turned down at the edges and something was crusted in one corner. There were black rings underneath her eyes.

She's like something awful you'd find when you clean out the shed, he thought, to distance himself. *Some beetle.* 'Molly's pregnant,' he said.

Joan seemed to be in actual physical pain. He had no idea what to do with her. After a minute she shrugged but the shrug became a shudder that went on down through her body as if she was burrowing into herself. The effort left a kind of vapour on the air and when she spoke her voice seemed distant, almost disinterested. 'I'm a judgement on you. I wonder if all this was planned before we were even born; our lives, our deaths. I think that's probably true. If there was any possibility, Peter, that you could do as I ask and still forgive me, you might be all right.'

'I am all right.' He spoke stiffly because he was frightened. 'Molly and I . . .'

'You're just a passenger in Molly's life.' Her dispassionate croak sounded mocking. 'She's less than half your age. She'll be

living a different life with someone else after you're dead and
gone.'

He could hardly speak for anger. His voice came out as if
two hands were tightly clasped around his throat. 'And what are
you going to do when I'm dead, because you'll have to make a
life for yourself too?' When he left, Joan waved goodbye as if
she was still sending him off to earn money every day of her
life. 'I'm an interloper on the honeymoon,' her hoarse voice
called out after him, 'and you know and I know, old pal, that
honeymoons don't last.'

She knew nothing. Peter could not decide if he preferred
nights or mornings with Molly. Some of the happiest moments
of his life were spent talking to her over breakfast in bed. Her
questions were thrown in from some naive, wise, uninformed
angle that opened new pages in his yellowing opinions. On
Sundays they always had sex and toast and coffee and talk in the
accommodating duvet. Afterwards they took the little girls for
a walk in the park and let them use the swings and then they
had lunch in a place where the children could have hamburg-
ers. His children, the children of an older father, did not have
the scratchy restlessness of young people's offspring. He liked
showing off his new family, his beautiful wife who was sullenly
eyed by younger men. The piping voices of the children made
intelligent comments on trees and plants. The pleasure he took
in this picturesque group was occasionally dulled by an overwhelming boredom, a longing to sit in the car and read the
Sunday papers without interruption, but he made the time go
more quickly by playing games, pretending that Molly was
someone else's wife with whom he was plotting an adulterous
affair. He always found it exciting and was able to flirt with her
through the children who had an instinct for this game.

Since his conversation with Joan, he saw things differently.
He could not but watch from a distance. In a way Molly was
nothing to do with him. The trio of beautiful women his wife
and little daughters would become would go on after him.
They would live a life he would never know. He became fascinated by this idea and in odd moments found himself wanting
to discuss it with Joan. Sometimes he felt that he had already

died, that he was a ghost ogling the beautiful world from some weightless sphere.

When Martin phoned to tell him Joan was dead, the shock was terrible. He felt he had been poisoned. He was choking on it. Anguish infected every part of his existence. Why had no one told him she had cancer? How could she just walk out and leave no note? Molly, anchored by her seven-month tenant, tiptoed lumberingly around him, aching for his guilt. But his guilt was for Molly. There was no one now for her to lean on. In regard to Joan he felt a kind of admiration and a profound sense of betrayal. She had stolen a march on him, had thrown away his key.

One night he dreamed of her. She was a young woman with a baby on her hip. Her hair was tied back and she was wearing a dress he remembered she'd had for years, thin cotton the colour of strawberry juice. Her body was strong and had a swing to it. *Full of life*, he thought. He stood very close to her, watching her curved lids and broad, knowing smile. When she lifted her eyes to him she was saying something. Their glance met and the surprise was so great that he woke at once. He lay awake with his heart beating too loud. *It's her*, he thought.

For a long time afterwards he tried to have the dream again, to hear what she had been saying and to catch her expression because he knew that if he could look into her eyes he would see himself. He couldn't even remember what her face was like, but he was convinced that she had remembered him. She had taken the picture with her. Once he had been a hero to his sons. He had no image of the giant that had filled their gaze. Now his new children regarded him in the same way but sometimes there was another look, a look of watchfulness. It was as if they saw that he was a foreigner homesick for a country he had forgotten and bewildered by the new world, but they knew what he could not know, that they would see him through.

ⱸⱮⱮⱭ

Life on Mars

⊘◢◢◢◢⊘

Midway through dying, Tom grew unfaithful to Anna. He accepted her necessary ministrations with cold politeness, his impatient eye resenting the time until he could go back to his new mistress, his pain. He had no word for her when he went. She couldn't recognise the gaunt figure on the pillow. She could not even call him love. All she could think was that whoever he was, he had been hers and now she had nothing.

A little while after his death he came back to her. She had got into the habit of saying his name as she walked in the door just to hear some familiar sound. One day there was a response – not a voice or anything like that. She came into the house and found that he was there. The diplomacy of privacy, which is agreed in every marriage, was gone. He was there as he had never been, except in part or at odd moments. His closeness made her weak, almost complacent. She did not bother to dress or eat or make any contact with the world outside. People tried to prise her from her mourning and she put down the phone on them or shut the door. There wasn't any room for them.

While she was sleeping he went away. She woke to find the house empty. 'Tom?' she whispered. 'Oh, Tom, *please.*' She couldn't forgive him. He had not, after all, been taken away from her by death. That was just a poor sick body where he had been held as prisoner. He had come back in all his strength to break her to his will and then he had left her. She could not even think of him now. She took down his photographs and put them away.

She found widowhood to be an exclusive and alien colony. Nobody liked her much the way she was. Friends wanted to take her out of herself. Where on earth did they think she would go, dragged forth from her last hiding place?

Just as individuals frequently decide to fall in love or to fall ill as their needs demand, there is a moment when people decide to go mad, and as Anna didn't want anybody or anything else, she thought that madness would do quite nicely. She developed a strange, swift gait, like a woman who knows she is being followed. At home, and even in the street, she talked to herself. *You're mad, you know that*, she reproached herself, but without dismay. She felt quite successful when she started to see flying saucers.

She had come into the kitchen to make herself some tea but instead she poured a glass of gin. She drank it standing at the sink, looking out the window over the garden wall at a sunset which seemed to cling around a naked apple tree like a bright scarf. In the distance, where it was still blue, her vision was spotted by a little cell cluster. She blinked to get rid of this distortion and the dots parted and began to sail towards her. She watched intently until they were no longer dots but discs, shimmering and transparent. When they got to tea plate size she could see that they were not flat but perhaps lenticular, and that they had legs or tripods or some sort of landing device. As they passed over the horizon, violent colours exploded off their surface from the burning sun. When the larger planet subsided and the sky grew dark they could no longer be seen although they must still be there, if they had ever been there. 'UFOs!' She spoke to herself, as had become habitual. 'Unidentifieds fuck off!' She rinsed her glass with the economical housekeeping of the solo dweller and gave her mad laugh. 'Lucky me, I suppose, that I've got no one to tell.'

They were there again the following day. She hadn't even had any gin. She watched until the dots turned into discs and screwed up her eyes when they passed the sun so that she could see them as they drifted into dusk. It seemed now that the rims of the saucers had no actual substance but were a shimmering aura surrounding some central body. There was definitely an extension, legs or antennae or something.

After a few days she found that she was waiting for them. At a certain time in the day she interrupted whatever pointless thing she was doing and moved to her post by the sink. As the sun ripened and cooled, the weighty dullness shifted a fraction in her chest. She never particularly wondered who they were or what they wanted but they made her think of a line from an old movie: 'We are not alone.' She was glad of that. When it got dark she thought she could still see them, skimming and hovering playfully around one another in the dusty purple shadows, but maybe she just imagined she did.

One day they landed in her garden. She stood in utter silence, feeling the shimmer of their approach and then a soft 'whoosh' as they touched down in the grass. She was almost glad there was no one in the house. She had learnt how to hold herself still, how to breathe without disturbing the air. When she finally went to investigate she laughed out loud. There were only four children in the garden. They must have climbed over the wall to get at the few knobs of blighted apples that still clung to her tree.

'What are you doing here?' She attempted severity.

The children looked at one another. 'We're not really doing anything, if that's all right.' They disentangled themselves and stood up, shaking out their wings. In the light from the kitchen window she could see them clearly. The shimmering discs were not saucers but an atmosphere, a thick aureole of light that surrounded them.

'Who are you?' she breathed.

'You are a who,' they corrected. 'We are not a who.'

'Fairies?' she said. 'Or are you angels? I've been watching you from a distance. I thought you were those funny things that crazy people see – unidentified flying objects.'

They nodded and seemed pleased with this, although their expression did not change. They had no expression. Whatever they were, they were reliable. She could count off the seconds on her watch until they made their landing in the grass each night and then, for some measureless time, she was distracted from her loneliness. Mostly, she talked about Tom. They were only children but their solemn faces made them good listeners.

They never spoke about themselves. She came to realise that this was because they had no ego, but when she questioned them they answered politely.

'Where are you from?'

'We come from Mars.'

'But there is no life on Mars!'

'Where there is no other life,' they told her, 'that is where we are.'

'How can I see you when no one else can?' She followed them as they ventured into the house, inspecting things as children do.

'Anyone can see us,' they shrugged. 'People don't look. Hardly anyone looks at the world. They only see what's in their own life.'

'Except where there is no life . . .' she mused, and they nodded earnestly.

It explained, anyway, why it was always weirdos who saw flying saucers, but she wondered why they told other people. She never wanted to. She wanted to keep them to herself, and she wanted to please them. She wanted to give them a treat, like ordinary children. 'Is there anything you like?' she asked them.

'Yes!' they said. 'Everything.'

'Have whatever you want,' she said. 'Choose something.'

They explored her kitchen earnestly, each selecting a treasure – a china cup printed with blue flowers, a photograph of Anna as a child, a magnifying glass.

'That's just a glass, there's nothing special about that,' Anna said.

'It was special the day it was invented,' the child said. 'We do not know time as a dimension. Because we are no age and every age, all things are both old and new.'

'What beautiful creatures you are,' Anna marvelled. 'Are there any creatures in the universe more beautiful than you?'

'Grasshoppers!' they cried. 'Water beetles!'

One day she saw Tom again. It was nine months after his death and she had gone into the city to hear a reading by a novelist. While she was there she ran into a woman she knew and they decided to stay in town for supper. They talked about the writer's last novel, her awful clothes, her predilection for younger men. They drank a nice bottle of wine. Anna was enjoying herself. For the first time since Tom's death she was aware of other people. She turned to look at the rest of the diners and her eye hovered on a handsome man who looked a bit familiar. For a moment he looked like Tom. Something about his chin reminded her of Tom's chin and while she pondered this the man's face turned into Tom's face. *I want to touch his face*, she thought. *I can't bear this.* She glanced again but the man had turned back into himself, back into someone else's man. She waited for the agony to loosen its grip. It wouldn't let go. *Maybe if I could get home and cry,* she thought. She got away from the restaurant and into her car. All the way home the pain tore at her like something that urgently needed to be delivered. She stumbled into the house, putting on the heat, pouring a drink so that everything would be in readiness for her grief. Nothing came. She crouched on the floor, drinking, absently aware of an ache that had settled into her and was violent and impersonal. It did not even evoke Tom. It had turned into some stranger who ground his boot into her chest until she submitted and accepted its imprint of ridges and studs. It went on for weeks, fading into something dull and dirty. Tom was nowhere to be found. First he had gone and then his love had gone. He was wedded now, to something else. It wasn't polite, any more, to hanker.

  She looked at her reflection. *I am turning into another person,* she thought. *When I married Tom I agreed to leave behind the girl I was, to be whatever he wanted. After he died I was waiting to go back, but that was impossible because then the only logical thing would be to start all over again.* She had always done what her husband wanted, not out of weakness but because of a sense of rightness. There wasn't any threat of distortion, only the promise of ripening. Now it was time to let go. In her mind she agreed to this, but the spirit is more accepting than the flesh. Her metabolism rebelled, shot grey through her hair, pulled down the edges of her mouth, put a warning look in her eye. The things she used to apply to make herself pretty – the juicy glints for lip and cheek, the alluring eye tints – sat on her bleak face like rocks of quartz in a desert. She would not give in. She put on what Tom used to call bonking music and hurled herself around to keep her figure in shape but she only achieved the thinness of a beaten dog. After a prolonged hostility she decided to make friends with the monster in the mirror. 'Hello, hag,' she said. The beast grinned back eagerly.

That evening as she was washing her dish she looked up and saw spots around the sun. 'Oh,' she said, and tears of longing filled her eyes.

'I've missed you so much,' she told them. 'Why didn't you come?'

'We were there!' They sounded exactly like ordinary children, high-pitched and self-righteous. 'You didn't look for us.'

For the first time they allowed her to touch them. They had a substance, their cheeks, the hollows of their shoulders. They had a texture, they were completely real. *They trust me*, she thought. *They are as soft as nothing and yet they trust me.* She felt them smile, although they could not smile. They leaned into her. One by one they slept. When she woke they were gone but she had rested without the glare of greyness behind her eyes.

As she waited for their next visit something of tremendous importance occurred to her. She could not wait to question them and the minute they appeared she demanded to know. 'If your time is without dimension, then what about my husband? In another time he was alive. Is he now in some other dimension?'

They watched her guardedly. 'This is your dimension.'

'He was my husband,' she said angrily. They flinched from her but she couldn't help it. She felt certain they knew. 'You don't understand what it's like to love someone and then lose them and never know where they went. I have to know. It's important.'

'It's not important.' They moved away from her. They crouched down in the night-frosted grass and began to pick daisies. 'It's none of your business.'

'That's so cruel!' Anna said.

'We cannot be cruel.' They looked up at her blankly. 'We can't be kind. We do not have imagination.'

She slammed back into the house. She could sense the shock vibrating in their wings and her own resentment coarsely beating in her chest. For a long time she felt them waiting for her in the dark and then the night emptied and there were only tomcats and owls and ordinary things out there.

In the morning she phoned a hairdresser and had the grey taken out of her hair. She bought a bag of clothes and had lunch in a wine bar and then, slightly tipsy, went into a travel agent and ordered up a week in the sun. In Barcelona she met a nice man called Sam Maguire. He made her interested in food again and they talked. She told him about Tom but she did not say anything about her visitors. They were nothing to do with him. Tom was her link with this world and they connected her to another world.

'You've had a hard time,' Sam Maguire said kindly.

'I've had a good life,' she said, surprising herself. Nothing else happened but she was pleased that he asked for her telephone number.

When she got home she was taken aback by the abandoned look of the place. She cleaned it vigorously, enjoying the vacuum cleaner's appetite, the astringent reek of bleach. Then she went to the shops and bought food and flowers. The house looked fresh and clean but it looked like someone else's house. She retrieved Tom's photographs and put them around the rooms. After that she went to bed and slept until noon.

The following evening she took up her place at the window. The sun went down and stars climbed into a muted sky. She began to be afraid. 'I'm here,' she whispered. 'Can't you see me? I know you're there.' Inside her house the phone started to ring. *Sam*, she thought. She let it ring a long time but she wanted to hear his voice so she went to answer it, switching on the light so that the sky outside became an inky plate crumbed with unknown worlds.

⊙⧟⧟⧟◌

The Secret Diary
of Mrs Rochester

There was no possibility of taking a walk that day. The sky was flooded grey and the wind was aroused to a malignant frenzy. Fainting branches clawed at my window and birds held their breath as the forest giants wrestled with invisible foe. Yet it was not the storm that hampered me. I was at the mercy of an element less rational than tempest.

A year ago, I had returned to Thornfield Hall, an heiress, an independent woman with a set of new cousins to my credit, and from one of these a proposal of marriage which I had to decline for its want of warmth. I found my master as reduced as I was advantaged – one eye gone and the other destroyed, missing an arm, burnt out of his manor house and widowed by the most tragical circumstance. At first my pity warred with anger to see a proud giant stumble like a fledgling raw to flight. But compassion was the greater since I too had once been helpless and dependent. This, then, was God's leavening – to catch the falling sparrow; to lay the lion down with the lamb. Reader, I married him.

It is not commonplace to give an unrelieved account of married life so I have set down what is agreeable and reserve the factual report for my private diary, in the hope that it may one day find that true reader who requires not to be assured that all ended happily, but remains curious to learn the point of resolution between human aspiration and human nature.

I will not pretend that ours was an ordinary marriage for of necessity it reached into the realm of the fantastic. I was compelled to be my master's eyes but my vision of life is a plain one whereas his divination dwelt within his head and was whatever capricious fancy served up to him. On woodlands walks I strove to illuminate his dark path by describing the trail which Providence had laid in that sombre place as intimations of Paradise, a posy of wild flowers, a dainty tracery of ferns, a family of fair-skinned mushrooms. But my master prefers a beauty of the man-made kind and would disturb my narration with a kiss. 'There is but one enchantment in this forest. My Jane. My provoking beauty. My little angel.'

What did he see then? 'No beauty,' I reminded him. 'Nor angel as I live. I am as I have always been – puny and insignificant.'

'Ah, Jane – if you could see yourself as I see you.'

I touched his wounded lion's face. 'Oh, Edward. If you could only see again.'

Yet vision is more than the eye can see, agility more than ably directed limbs. We knew the swiftness of sympathy and our days were radiant with affection's transforming light. At times I prided myself that I could be better eyes than those brooding torches that had once lit his world, for my gaze was not clouded by past regret nor my joy in beholding compromised by dissipation. I ought to have been wary of exultation for experience has taught me that pride may precipitate a calamitous descent. We had been married six months when two small incidents set in motion a leviathan of change. The first was a letter from my cousin St John Rivers. It was touching in its plainness and showed a new humility born of the breadth of stern experience. I was relieved that he had forgiven my rejection. I wrote back and found a curious balm in plain speaking, without any need to adorn. I told him of the practicalities of my married life but not of its peculiarities, and especially not of a remarkable proposal that I had just received from Mr Rochester which was to mark the second change. He declared that we were to commence the travels planned for our honeymoon in that ghastly time when he still had a poor fiend of a wife hidden in the house. 'You shall sojourn at Paris, Rome and Vienna,' he avowed anew. 'All the ground I have wandered over shall be retrodden by you: where I stamped my foot, your sylph's foot shall step also.'

What had once been esteemed a grand plan was now mere parody. To think of that same proudly stamping foot stumbling on crowded foreign pavements was beyond pity. I at once declined and declared that I was too well occupied for such frivolity. When he saw that I was in earnest he was sullen a day or two but then resorted to cajolery. 'Ah, Miss Pinprick! I am restless and discouraged. If you will not let me feel the sun upon my blind brow, indulge me with a ramble in my rambling mind. Let me share with you the travels I have already enjoyed.'

To this I consented. We became fireside travellers. In picturesque memory he was my guide through majestic mountain passes, along fashionable promenades. I began to look forward to our nightly adventures, though I deemed them best consigned to history and narrative for their self-indulgent nature. Once or twice he strayed into places I should not suffer my foot to trespass even in fancy and I smartly rebuked him. I had anticipated that as a husband he might grow difficult to please but was unprepared for a conflict that struck not merely at the heart of our union but at its very soul. I yearned to be joined with him upon a path to virtue and he required my presence at those worldly sites that had most profoundly jolted his sensibilities. Perhaps because of his ruined sight his will was stronger than mine, for ere long I had trepidation for company on each of our journeys, and regret for supper in some bawdy inn at which we sojourned. I urged him to restrain his chronicle to nature's attributes but we must have exhausted all of Europe's scenery, for one night (when I was ill attired for it and had a piece of sewing in my hand) he goaded me into society. 'Did I ever tell you,' said he, 'about my first meeting with Céline Varens?'

I was so provoked my needlework fell to the ground. 'Must I remind you that lady set you on the path to ruin?'

He bent to retrieve my sewing and, in restoring it to me, rested a weary hand upon my knee. 'If that was ruin, then what am I come to now?'

'Acceptance, I hope – and virtue – an element not foremost

in the female society enjoyed on your travels.' I kept my voice calm but could feel my heart challenge the sturdy seams of my grey house dress.

'You are right, Jane, they were not virtuous.' He uttered a sigh such as might issue from a captive lion, from the depths of his thwarted animal nature, and then fell to a silence that neither teasing nor intellectual discourse could repair. Then in a voice barely discernible he murmured, 'Ah, but they were beautiful.' There was another void which I was helpless to repair until at last, in a tone of grievous wistfulness, he enquired, 'How are you attired?'

I often had told him that I could be nothing other than I was. Yet something warned me that this need for feminine appeasement was a wound that must be stanched. I took a deep breath and begged heaven's understanding. 'It is a muslin tea gown, sir, with puffs and rosettes. I made it myself.' By this he seemed genuinely assuaged. 'Beguiling elf! So you are as other women after all.'

Yet it was hard to be the eyes of another, and more still of a man, for they do not see as women see, and sometimes, for all my efforts to please, I caught his old scowling look and felt he wished to be alone to do some manly valeting on his head. A part of the difficulty lay in our location. Densely wrapped in forest, Ferndean was not a cheerful place. Edward had once declared that he could not put his mad wife there for fear its climate would end her wretched life. If he could see I felt sure he would have released us from the forest's clammy hold. Sunlight never entered our house and our garden supported no growth save weeping lichens. At times I felt their ranks o'ergrew my very self for, so far from the bedizened beauty I had invented of myself, I had grown paler and was prey to a persistent cough. I often thought of St John in India, and the fact that he too was struggling against an inclement climate. At such times a longing for his plain sincerity made me sit down and unburden myself to him in candid letters.

It was a foul winter. Indoors we lived at a high pitch of coquetry which both flattered and disquieted me (for I believe all deception to be folly). My husband was chivalrous but rarely serious and I accepted this as a necessary antidote to his sightless world, but my own spirits were lowered by a communication from St John, who informed me without the least self-pity that his health was failing. In great humility he wondered if we had each committed an error of pride in undertaking a mission that might be beyond our courage to execute.

When the weather improved I led Mr Rochester for a walk in the woods. His mood was gallant as we entered our familiar charade. 'What are you wearing, Jane?' I indulged him with description of some fashionable frippery. 'What, with brown leather boots?' he laughed. 'I have to say it, Jane, you have no taste in these matters.'

I was stung by his teasing, but far more by his perception. 'How do you know what I am wearing on my feet?'

He turned on me a most devilish look of amusement. 'Why, because it is quite enough for you to spend your evenings stitching away at complicated gowns without having to turn cobbler for my sightless admiration. We have not left Ferndean since we got married. You had no opportunity to buy new shoes.'

'How could you know what I was wearing when I came to Ferndean?' said I. 'You had not seen me for fully a year.'

Something about the wry manner in which he regarded me informed me so shockingly that I was almost robbed of one faculty just as he, apparently, had another restored. When I could speak again I uttered but a single phrase: 'You can see!'

'It's true, Jane.' He caught me up in his arms. 'I wanted to surprise you. I have regained a little sight.'

'When?' I was in too much turmoil to be glad.

'A little while ago – a week. I did not dare to speak until I was sure it was not some temporary reprieve or a trick of the light.'

'Two months ago you picked my sewing from the floor with as much adroitness as a healthy child. Was it then? Could you see then?'

'Why, yes,' said he. 'I believe that I could perceive a little then. Is the particular date significant?'

My cry burst like shot upon the dead air of the forest. I

could hear the wing beats of startled creatures in the trees as I fled, sobbing, back to the house. All the while I had described myself in feminine trickery he had seen me as I was – a fool, and a plain fool. When I achieved the relative sanctuary of our dwelling I managed to compose myself sufficiently to summon Mary and John and informed them that they need make no more special preparations as, by God's grace, the master had regained his sight. I cannot express the dismay I encountered when the servants met my gaze. Humble people have no artifice of expression. 'You knew! You have all been party to my deception.' And then with a sudden running chill like the trickle that pre-empts the flood, a wretched thought crept up on me. 'How long has he had sight?'

'Pardon us, Miss,' said John. 'We are in his paid service and bound to his confidence.'

'And I am mistress of this house,' said I very shakily. 'It is your duty to inform me of the truth.'

In great discomfort they did so. 'He was fully blind when he came to Ferndean. The dark of this place, which ails us all to our bones, served to rest his eyes. His sight was already back before you found him here. He swore us not to say.'

I withdrew to a small room at the top of the house that is kept for visitors, although none ever comes. I remained alone until the following day when I consented to see my husband. 'I know all,' I said at once. I must confess that my strongest instinct upon beholding his rueful countenance, now so expressive of his apprehension, was to forgive him and hope that we could commence a normal marriage such as other people have, but he required more than absolution. He was intent upon my understanding. 'You will say now that I tricked you into marrying me, and it is true, but only because I loved you so much that I could run no risk of losing you.'

'It is a queer sort of love,' said I, 'that so lacks trust in its object. It is a corruption of the very soul of that emotion. Commonsense tells me that I should abandon the charade of loving a man who perverts affection's very nature. Yet I persist in believing that beneath your faithless heart is a spirit still hungry for love's redemption. It was that spirit I heard calling to me on that dark night in Morton.'

'Jane, Jane, Jane!' He shook his head and to my annoyance and astonishment I saw that he was close to laughter. 'You adorable idiot. You do not half appreciate the trouble I have taken to woo you. That was not my spirit you heard, but my poor self, travelled three days by carriage and crouched beneath the window on the sodden grass. I learned in the village that Mr Rivers was courting you and deemed it best to win you back by the most dramatic methods. I called to you in a voice so low that only your elf's ears could detect it. When you came to look for me in the garden, I was concealed beneath some shrubbery. There! I have made a clean breast of it. Come and make up to me.'

I do not quite know what was in my mind but when I came close to that erratic giant who had earned my utmost devotion, I felt the whole extent of my humiliation and struck him a violent blow. 'You never loved me,' I cried, 'for love is kind. You only played games with me. At first you pretended that you were to marry Miss Ingrams in order to excite my jealousy. You then dressed up as a fortune-teller, making jackanapes of both Miss Ingrams and myself in order to trick us into revealing our motives while keeping yours well concealed. You disguised from me that you had a wife still living and proposed unlawful marriage to me to trap me into becoming your mistress. Was poor Bertha always mad or did you drive her out of her mind with similar deceptions?'

'Pray do not be hysterical, Jane,' said he very gravely. 'I know that your nerves have been weakened by many trials and that you were subject to fits as a little child, but I warn you to compose yourself.'

'How many more unfortunate women have you thus deceived?' I was beside myself and could not contain my vehemence. 'Was Céline Varens truly the devil you depicted or another poor girl tricked into bigamous marriage?'

His face was aghast as I accused him and I read in his look the unspeakable truth to which my passion had inadvertently given voice. He did not attempt to defend himself but waited until my tirade was at an end and then withdrew with a single utterance: 'You are mad!' A small scratching signified the turning of a key.

There followed the most wretched interlude. The sky grew dark and I was abandoned in that miserable room without a candle, as when I was ten years of age and locked in the red room by Mrs Reed. I do not know how much time passed, whether weeks or months. In that infernal place my one small window showed no light but only the dun talons of an army of trees. I merely know I had much opportunity for introspection and passed the featureless time in contemplation of all that had been wrought upon me and all I had wrought by my own design. Mr Rochester resumed his old bohemian existence and was abroad for some time. When he returned the house remained quiet until that turbulent evening when I was startled by a clatter of hoof beats. I strained at the tiny pane to see if the visitor would be a lady I recognised, or some fresh sacrifice to his vanity to whom he would have to explain the embarrassment of his unstable wife. I could see nothing and was forced to endure the most hideous speculations. To my great surprise I heard footsteps on the stair and when that same personage applied itself to the door it was with a force unknown to any female. The door burst open and there stood my dear cousin, St John Rivers.

After a heartfelt reunion he explained that he had been much perturbed by the content of my letters and had prayed for guidance. God had instructed him where his true calling lay and he was now intent on finding out if Mr Rochester had yet another wife alive through bigamous contraction, after which I would be free to go away with him.

Now that the door was open I must make up my mind quickly. In the time of my seclusion I had given much thought to St John and even more to Mr Rochester and arrived at the conclusion that dissolute men, while unreliable and unworthy, have about them an air of tumult that is stimulating to the female sex, and that a woman of virtue has no need of a moral partner, since by her own rectitude is her salvation ensured. Reader, I missed the dear flesh that housed the dark soul. I thanked Mr Rivers for his great kindness but insisted on remaining where I was. After this episode Mr Rochester was very remorseful. He begged my forgiveness and even endeavoured to earn my understanding, insisting that he had never meant to keep me contained, but only assigned me to the attic because my shrewd evaluation of his nature made him fearful of losing me. I disposed of this debate by rendering him senseless with a copper pan.

Since then we have pursued a life of ideal domesticity. I will not pretend that his temperament has altered but I have concluded that human nature is as much God's craft as are all nature's marvels and have curtailed my master's excesses by the simple expedient of keeping his allowance very small, whereby he has learnt the valuable lesson that sin and spending are closely allied. St John, alas, went back to India and died there and Mr Rochester became as useful around the house as any one-armed husband, and as blindly devoted as any tamed beast who comes to accord with the source of all his sustenance.

That Bad Woman

Commo

'Are there any shirts?' Henry said.

'I don't know.' Jude felt vaguely guilty. 'Nora did some ironing this morning.'

He watched her searchingly.

'You could look in the wardrobe as easily as I could,' she said. She did not add that if she looked she would see dozens of shirts whereas he might observe the same view and say that there were none at all. He went away without looking in the wardrobe. She stayed where she was, feeling exhausted. She knew that the purpose of the engagement had been to exhaust her but at the same time that he didn't consciously mean her any harm. She wondered if the thought of shirts had passed his mind before or after the notion of unsettling her. *Perhaps we are just a part of the mad animal kingdom*, she thought, *one in which the male is compelled by instinct to aggravate its mate.*

Lately Jude had found a shift in her life. The little clusters of trivia that formed the obstacles to her daily existence now became instead long tree-lined avenues. Each event opened up a vista of contemplation and she would sit for hours before a cooling cup of tea, not brooding, as Henry said, but thinking. For most of her life she had never thought about anything, just put up and got on with, but now the small domestic comedy had become a great drama by deconstruction. There was nothing special about her marriage. They got married, had children and those grew up. Because so little happened to her, she was like a grate that has never been properly cleaned, and over the years the flame burned lower and now there was only a dull glow. Henry every so often flung on a coal, but increasingly heavy-handed so that it only damped down the embers a little more. Quite soon, she thought, there might be the final shovel of wet slack that would put her out. She didn't blame him. She just thought of herself as a heap of grey ash.

The moment this idea occurred to her she ran to a mirror and was excited to see that she *looked* like a heap of grey ash. Her hair was straggled with threads of grey, her skin and eyes were dim and she wore a pile of woolly things that she had put on for comfort. Articles in the magazines would have said that this decline was caused by the menopause or by grief at losing her children, but there was as much relief as grief in the safe passing of the young, and her hours of thinking at the kitchen table had led her to believe that the change of life was a chimera, an excision only of the placation hormone which was necessary to keep the home together for the safety of children, and that she herself was much the same as she had been at seven. 'The point of the change,' she told the mirror, 'is that it does not *happen*. It is merely provoked. One must make the change oneself.'

I need another man, she thought, and then immediately corrected herself. The last thing she needed was another man. What was wanted was a partner for sexual intercourse. She did not think of taking a lover, for she did not want to take him but only to have congress with him, and she did not consider him in terms of love, for love, like religion, involved endless searching and a great deal of wasted time. It pleased her best to think of him as the man who would come and clean out the grate.

She went to gaze out the window at men passing by, interested to see them in the new light of prospective poker. How grim and solitary they looked; hard to imagine any of them lying down and rolling about like cats. One of the men was pierced by her stare and turned around in a haunted way and she laughed out loud, thinking of herself as a strange man might see her, knowing her contemplative face was a bleak and horrible spectacle. Imagine *that* with no clothes.

When Henry came home he was annoyed to find Jude sitting

reading. 'When's dinner?' he said. 'I'm starving.' Dinner had been at exactly the same time every evening for the past twenty years and there was a plentiful supply of cheese and fruit and biscuits to keep famine at bay.

'Dinner is at seven,' she said, 'but have some cheese or fruit if you're hungry.'

He prowled around, teasing the dog and lifting lids off pots. She went back to reading Mary Wesley to find out about the kind of women who took it for granted that they would have sexual assortment in their lives.

Begin: the hardest part is the getting out of doors.

Like all old sayings it was rubbish but she did actually make several false starts. She realised, for instance, that the brushed-felt hat in a rusty shade of red, which she had worn for several years, looked like a placenta. And she had picked it and paid money for it. Did older men, she wondered now, adopt a walking stick before it became necessary as an aid, in order to wave something erect around? When she started thinking about this, it was so interesting that she almost did not go out at all. Besides, she had absolutely no idea where to go. In the end, she decided to sit in a hotel lounge where she could continue to think her thoughts and where men were reputed to pursue adventure. She sat quietly in a corner and was delighted to witness a very obvious pick-up. When she got home she cooked a lamb stew with almonds and apricots and coriander. Henry hated it, as she had known he would, and she was surprised by the pleasure she got from unsettling him. He didn't say anything, but sat before his untouched plate, looking exhausted.

Jude noticed that her hair had developed a mild sheen. She took a bag of old jumpers to Oxfam and bought a blue jacket in washed silk and wore it when she went back to the hotel. This time she sat at the bar beside a man. After about ten minutes he looked her way and after another ten he told her she was a nice-looking woman. She felt a strange sense of power, as if she had learnt to Speak a Foreign Language TODAY!

'Can I buy you a drink?' she said and was interested when he reacted in the over-pleased way that women do when men buy them a drink. Phrases drifted past her ear like sea breezes – in town on business . . . lonely existence . . . charming company. She said to him, 'I've never taken my clothes off in front of anyone with the light on. Not even in front of another woman.'

The man looked as if he had seen a vision of God in a burning bush. 'Are you married?' he said.

Afterwards, at home, she could not help smiling. The smile kept winging across her face in the way a plane slices out from under a cloud. Henry watched her in dismay. 'What's the matter?' he said.

She thought how nice it would be to live with somebody she could talk to. When she tried to tell him anything he was always urging her to get to the point. 'I went into town today,' she told him.

'I have to watch the news,' he said.

The man at the bar said he was called Bernard. He did not reveal his second name, for, presumably, he was married too. He told her she had a very frank way of speaking. He liked frankness in a woman. She said she had run out of small talk, she had used it all up on her children, and the conversational fashion for tact and dissimulation seemed to invest every transaction with disappointment. It was like ordering the cheapest thing on the menu in the hope that someone would urge you to have lobster, but they never did.

'Are you suggesting,' he proceeded with caution, 'that you would actually undress for a strange man – and so on and so forth?'

'On and forth,' she agreed.

Bernard had gone on a rampage of celebration, had ordered champagne and told funny stories, mostly concerning bodily parts and ridiculous women, but she did not mind. Jude thought she didn't really mind anything. It was like going on holidays and not caring where one went so long as it was away. She noted the way he masked his eye to make it harmless, how he caressed, with thumb and forefinger, the little scalloped mat that mopped up seepage under his glass.

'Are you very unhappily married?' he asked her.

'No,' she said.

'But not happy, not really happy?'

'No,' she agreed.

He remained silent for a while. 'I don't understand you,' he revealed then.

'Understanding takes a long time,' Jude pointed out. 'I should scarcely have thought we had time for that.'

'It's not natural,' he said.

'What isn't?' She waited hopefully to see if he might have a fetish.

'Respectable married women don't pick up strange men in hotels. It isn't natural, you know.'

'It feels quite natural,' she said. 'Much more so than sitting alone in the house all afternoon and worrying about whether I should make a sauce for the fish or grill it, but of course I do have my reasons. I wanted my body and my mind to keep pace. It seems to me that the relationship is between them now, rather than with another person. They have been on different paths all my life, bickering miserably with each other. I want them to make it up, and then to get on with things.'

Bernard looked appalled, uncomfortable, *uninterested*. 'I'm not really sure I want to hear all this,' he said. 'It sounds to me as if you're making use of me.'

'I shan't forget you,' she promised him. 'I shall think of you fondly. Much more than you will think of me.'

He stood up from the bar rather stiffly. 'I think you should see someone,' he said.

The encounter pleased her enormously. She could scarcely believe the rate at which learning could be advanced – and without undoing a single button. What an abyss of ignorance the whole subject of the opposite sex was to women – necessarily so, since they mostly had limited experience and no yardstick for comparison. Her own age group rarely even encountered men in a business setting. It was unfair, since women were genuinely curious about men, whereas men only desired women. *If I were younger*, she thought, *I would make it my business to establish a catalogue of men, to cross-index their physical attributes and mental attitudes. Think of all the trouble women would*

*be saved, how swiftly they could make their choices, how much pain
they would be spared.*

When women accept the physical deterioration of middle
age, they are said to be letting themselves go. Jude came to the
conclusion that the opposite was true; they were hanging on,
believing they had outlived their usefulness and must eat up
their pauper's stew of plainness, depression and fear. She
thought about this at the hairdresser's after she had told the
girl that her hair used to be a nice reddish brown and the girl
nodded and nibbled her chewing gum and without any argument gave her back the vivid, sexy head of hair she had had in
her twenties.

Men sometimes followed her in the street now, although
they had difficulty getting her attention for she was lost in
thought. To think that the front door had never been locked!
She could have walked out at any time. What had held her?
The children? She saw again the avid, unfocused infant eye that
had pursued her everywhere in her twenties. The unfocused 'I'.
One could do nothing with small children. Then the narrow
scrutiny of teenagers, watching like a hawk to make sure she
didn't get a bigger slice of life than they did. She and Henry
hadn't even been grown up when the babies were born and
after that any changes in themselves would have unsettled the
young. Children fed on unripe fruit and threw the husk away.
It must be a natural order since children always displayed resentment of successful parents. Poor Henry, too, might have been
dazed and stunted by parenthood.

'Henry,' she said one day. 'Do you ever wonder who you are?'

He watched her warily. 'I have been acquainted with myself
for half a century.'

'Think, though! You are unique. Even your fingerprints are
unique in the world. When you die, that set will be gone forever.'

He looked around the room, which showed the neglect of
her new introspective life. 'I doubt it,' he sighed.

Afterwards, she heard him on the phone, talking to Margaret,
their daughter. 'I'm worried about your mother,' he said.

She braced herself for Margaret's bustling visit, the vague

irritation in her tone: 'Well, *you're* looking well.' She loved her
children but did not much enjoy spending time with them.
Their exasperation made her feel less of a person than Henry's
silences, and afterwards she was left worrying that she had
wasted their valuable time.

It disturbed Jude to think that when first she had
contemplated a change of life, the thing that came to mind was
a man. What a tyrant the womb was, always complaining if it
wasn't served first. She now considered that it might be just as
nice to please the eye. She had developed a new way of looking
at things in her mind but knew that her visual perspective was
lopsided. She used to take photographs but her pictures came
out so cramped and sinister that she gave it up years ago. She
signed up for a course and became so engrossed in the study of
camera that she almost forgot about everything else. But one
day when she was pointing her lens at an arrangement of twigs
and blossoms on an illuminated sheet of paper, she was suddenly
smacked by a feeling of contentment and, without looking up,
she knew it was because of someone standing close to her. For
once, she wasn't thinking anything at all. Going for a drink with
Alec, going to his flat and going to bed with him just seemed a
natural thing, like putting up an umbrella in the rain.

A little while after this, she began to wonder if her husband
was having an affair. His whistle, as he dug the garden or read
the newspapers, was throaty as a thrush's call. When he came
home in the evening he poured her a glass of wine and talked
about events of the day. He even paid attention when he made
love to her. He even made love to her.

She was glad for him, and glad not to have to worry about
him, because she herself was devilishly happy. She was only
mildly disconcerted that her discovery of sexual delight had no
scientific application. Well, there was one interesting discovery.
The treasure she had chanced upon was not a miser's hoard.
Those around her prospered. The plants in the garden
bloomed. The surly cat lolloped and purred. People smiled at
her in the street. Even the children now regarded her as an
adult like themselves, instead of a backward child or a dodder-
ing geriatric. At first she had been fearful of discovery and then

astonished by the immunity lovers enjoy, the fact that no one asked her where she went or searched her pockets for clues. She saw now that they were all living on her luck and unconsciously conspired to sustain the holy fire. *One could go on like this*, she thought, *forever*.

She was admiring Alec's long feet one day when he said, 'Have you told Henry?'

'Of course not,' she promised.

There followed a longish silence in which she withdrew her gaze from his elegant arch and met an oddly peevish eye. 'Do you think that's fair?'

She thought about it. 'Strictly speaking, no, but then it is not fair either that I should have been given this happiness by accident. Henry, too, is happier than he has been in years.'

Alec frowned and she cherished the furred caterpillar curved over his smooth brow. 'Do you think it's fair to me?' he said.

'What do you mean?' she pondered.

'It's all very well for you.' A new note had entered his voice. It smacked of woe. 'You have a family to go home to. You can't have everything, you know. You have to make up your mind.'

'I'm not leaving Henry,' Jude said. 'That wouldn't be right.'

'What we're doing is not right,' Alec said very promptly.

'Well, I'm not sure about that,' she said. 'When a cup of happiness is offered, it seems downright impolite to seal one's lips, but that doesn't mean you have to knock over everyone else's cup at the same time.'

'Why not?' said Alec.

'It would be selfish,' Jude reasoned.

'I think you are the most selfish person I have ever met in my life.'

Parting with Alec was painful. She had known their affair might some day end but she imagined it would be upon the threat of discovery rather than any mutual conflict. She was amazed by how much she missed him. It was as if one of her children had died. Diplomatically, she removed her grief from the range of her family and went on long expeditions with her camera, photographing homeless children, high-rise wives, oil-sodden birds. Her pictures still came out cramped and sinister but now she saw that this was not so much a distortion as a point of view and might even be a talent. She began to plan an exhibition.

She came home one day to find the whole family waiting for her. She was delighted to see them, intensely glad she had not done anything that would throw into chaos the greater part of her life's work. But then she saw how silence had settled upon them. She caught Henry's eye and she was shocked by his look, like an old dog tied up outside the supermarket and then abandoned.

'Jude, what's up?' he said.

'What do you mean?'

He shook his head in angry confusion. It was like asking a small, displaced child for its address. 'What are you doing to us all? You've no time for us any more. The children can't talk to you. You've shut us out.'

'It's the change of life,' she said kindly. 'I'll be all right.'

'Of course you'll be all right,' Henry said coldly. 'What about the rest of us?'

And she understood that, without knowing it, Henry was enquiring for Alec too. When a poor mother puts chicken soup upon the table, does the family ask where the hen has come from? What right had she to turn her back on nourishment when they were all of them hungry and only she was privy to the larder? A part of her mind began to hanker after her darkroom, where a group of adolescent substance addicts awaited her inspection in the reddish gloom. Another part of her accepted that she had left a mess and she must first of all sweep it up. She took Henry's hands. 'Nothing's up,' she said. 'But if there's anything you want to ask me, I'll tell you.'

Henry shook her off. He knew something was up. Her whole appearance had changed. Her figure was better defined and her step had grown jaunty. He yearned to ask about his shirts but he just gave her a bitter look and walked away.

෴

Poor Old Sod

A shower of blossom fell on the girl's hair. As she looked up he saw her blue eyes diluted by the light. An arc of satisfaction was laid across her face. Her mouth was open as if to accept a drink.

He prepared a small portion of conversation as carefully as one might set a tray for an invalid. '*Wahlenbergia hederacia!*' His voice trembled slightly. 'Forgive me, an old man's excitement. It's quite rare.' He was a neat old man defended against the spring in a suit and overcoat. At first she saw nothing where he pointed, but when he poked among the sinking cherry blossoms with his stick she crouched down in the grass and the earth was starred with blue just as the sky was blurred with pink. She smiled at him and he congratulated himself. He had made time and had lured her into this nest.

The next time she saw him she tried to avoid him. He had talked a great deal on their first meeting, of music and letters and the despoliation of the countryside, while she stiffened in the tree's shadowy roots. When she tried to stand up his face fell. 'I'm boring you,' he challenged. She denied this politely but a corner of his mouth curled ruefully to accept an insult. 'Tell me to shut my trap. It's not often I have the luxury of female company. Since my wife died . . .' He fell silent and spanked the earth with his stick.

She was a young married woman with no ambition. Every day she walked alone in the park. It wasn't really a park. The land behind a derelict house had a garden run wild and some woodland. Not many people used it and she thought of it as her own place. Occasionally one crossed paths with silent joggers or doggy women clad in sheepskins or bands of small boys scuttling like wood lice.

She saw him beating down one of the pathways with his stiff, jointless walk and his puzzled face pulled about by the air, like an old blind dog, and swiftly aimed her gaze at some other view, but she couldn't help looking back. He was askew with disappointment. He had no cover for this treacherous exposure and he had to suffer her discovery of him more than ever like an old dog, his jaw dropped and his features a map of anguish. She waved and waited for him and he bounded up the hilly walk like a crabbed boy.

'I've ruined your walk,' he beamed breathlessly.

'He's an intelligent old man,' she told her husband. 'Sometimes he's quite interesting.' Although they did not meet every day she got the feeling when they happened upon one another that he had been waiting for her. She told Ben how he rehearsed his speeches in order to have some new piece of information to interest her.

'Sounds harmless enough,' her husband said.

She said nothing. Beneath the inoffensive guise of his old man's body she could feel the iron strength of his will and a force of pride for which modesty was a mask. It was mad, of course, but she felt under siege. In some way, he wanted to dominate her.

Her husband thought she was definitely mad. 'If you don't want to talk to him, tell him you prefer being on your own, or walk at a different time every day.'

'He's lonely,' she told him. 'His wife is dead.'

'Poor old sod,' he said with indifference.

'What is your name?' he asked her. 'I don't know your name.'

'Angie.'

'Angie, Angie, Angie,' he said.

She had heard the term 'a new lease of life' but until now had not known its meaning. It wasn't that her old gentleman had shed a decade, but the quotient of life in his ancient bones soared. His diffidence was gone. He pranced. 'Angel! I shall call you Angel. My good angel!' He reached for her hand. 'My angel of mercy!' She let her hand stay there, and bore down upon a sigh. 'I must tell you an interesting tale . . .' he began.

One day when she reached the park he was standing outside. He was looking at the ground and his face was bitter with frustration. She thought of a child put standing in the playground. Poor old man. Someone had hurt his feelings. 'You're late,' he said coldly. She was so surprised that she laughed.

'I know that I am an old man and of no importance to anyone but I am not used to being kept waiting an hour,' he rebuked.

'I'm sorry,' she said. 'I had no idea you waited for me.'

He forgave her at once, before she had time to say that she would prefer him not to imagine such an arrangement. His arm linked hers like a clamp. 'There is something else I have to say to you.' His voice was playful but harsh. 'You did not tell me you were married.'

'How do you know now?' She vowed she would alter her walk. It was a pity, because she liked walking in the same place, made different by the weather or the seasons.

'I found out from someone else. Your name came up and then someone mentioned your husband. They said you were a devoted couple.'

'I don't like talking about myself,' Angie said.

'No.' He let go of her to turn around and look at her. 'That is your appeal.' He smiled his bitter smile. 'I'm just an old man. When a man's wife dies he knows what it is to be unwanted. Go home to your husband.'

'I haven't had my walk yet.' Resignedly, she curbed her stride to match his pace. He picked a wild rose, blushing lividly at its centre and creamy at its hem, with little glossy, fanged leaves. He hectored her with Latin terms before forcing it into her buttonhole. 'A rose for a rose,' he said, and she felt his sharp old fingers touching her breast.

'You look pale,' her husband said. 'You ought to get out more.' A month had passed and she had not returned to the park.

'It gets a bit crowded in the summer,' she told him.

'Go in the evening,' he said.

She smiled at him gratefully. She loved the way Ben didn't make a fuss. They liked one another exactly as they were and trusted each other completely. 'I won't be long.' She put on a light jacket and went out into the dusk.

The park was different at night. The light went off and the scents came on. She leaned against a tree and felt the damp air, drenched in musk and herb and the heavy fruitiness of rose. She knew every inch of path and had no trouble finding her way and she could see each shrub and tree in her head as their essence greeted her in the blackness.

'You shouldn't be out on your own at night.' A voice rose above the creak of branches. Something hit her on the leg and she gasped. Two small chips like icicles had materialised in a denser stick of darkness. 'It's dangerous,' the old man said. With each statement, he spanked her, not too lightly, on the legs with his stick. 'You young women have no sense.' His walking aid seemed to have an eye of its own and rapped out a spiteful, unerring Braille as she tried to step out of its way, snapping at branches and tripping on hillocks. The anger she felt was dissipated when she heard the grief in his voice. He couldn't control his disappointment.

'I'm fine,' she soothed. 'You gave me a fright. I think I'll go home.'

He was right, she thought as she lay in bed. She could still feel the affront in her shins. Young women had no sense. Why else had she run like mad as soon as he was out of sight? Why else did her heart still pound when she was safe at home?

After that she went to the pictures in the afternoon. It wasn't as nice as walking but there was the same pleasant sense of solitude. Occasionally she had to move as someone tried to be familiar with her but she was relieved to see how easily other men were discouraged.

One Sunday in autumn her husband bundled her up in scarves and led her out to see the trees changing colour. He was concerned about her. She hadn't told him about her visits to the cinema and he worried that she was growing solitary. He was glad to see her hair blown about, her complexion buffed by wind and air, to hear her laughter as he walked fast with an arm around her, making her run to keep up.

'Ah, the happy couple!' The stick described a rainbow in the air as the old man emerged from a scribble of trees. 'I've heard a great deal about you.' He thrust a complicated hand at Ben. 'Not from her of course!' A wry grimace for Angie.

'I've heard about you,' Ben grinned at the old man.

'No need to tell me. Boring old fart! I dare say she enlisted your aid on ways to get rid of me.'

'Oh, now,' Ben protested. 'She said you were very interesting.'

The old man grinned at Angie. 'You've got a nice husband. I can see why you might be devoted.'

Angie touched Ben's hand. 'I am.'

'I said you *might* be!' He waggled his stick at her playfully. 'I'm not so sure.'

'She's quiet but she's deep.' Ben was amused by the game.

'She's deep all right,' the old man said, and he fell silent.

Ben saw that Angie looked uneasy. He put an arm around her. 'We shouldn't tease her,' he said. 'She's a sensitive soul.'

The old man whacked the earth so violently that it caused an explosion of dirt and pebbles. 'I have never teased anyone in my life.' The stick reared up at Angie. 'You've been keeping secrets from me.'

'She doesn't have to tell you anything,' Ben said mildly.

'Who was that man I saw you with?'

'What man?' Angie said.

'I scarcely have to describe him to you.' He turned aside and his jaw worked fastidiously as if he did not like the taste of the words in his mouth. 'Tall young man with a hat. Good-looking fellow.'

'That's ridiculous,' Angie said.

Ben looked at her in calm, good-humoured enquiry.

'They came out of a cinema, wrapped around each other. She was eating him with her eyes,' he said to Ben. 'So much so that when I passed her by, she would not give me the time of day.'

'I never saw you there,' Angie said to the old man.

'Where?' Ben asked her.

'The truth, now,' the old man said. 'Out with it!' He spanked her once again with his stick, lightly this time.

'The Adelphi,' Angie said faintly.

The old man smiled sourly at them. He lifted his hat. 'I bid you good day,' he said. He thought the join of their hands, which had made them look like a single unit as he spied on their approach, now gave the impression of something broken and then poorly mended.

'You don't go walking any more.'

'That business,' he said, 'is over and done with.'

'It's good for you,' she coaxed.

The old man gave her a hostile look. 'Good for you, you mean. I bore you.'

His wife ignored this. She was used to him. 'What about that girl you were so kind to – that young widow?'

'I suited her purpose for a time,' he said stiffly. 'She has no further use of me.' He turned away to hide his smile but his wife only saw the stubborn curve of his back, like the carapace of a beetle.

Poor old sod, she thought with compassion.

Villa Marta

The sun rose gently over Villa Marta like a little half-baked madeleine but by nine o'clock it was a giant lobster, squeezing the pretty pension in its red claws. Honeysuckle and rose tumbled over the walls of the Villa. The petals fattened and were forced apart. Dismembered blossom dangled in the probing heat. Sally and Rose stumbled down to the patio and ate their hard rolls called bocadillos, and drank bowls of scummy coffee, feeling faintly sick because of the heat and the coffee. The tables on the terrace had been arranged under a filigree of vine and splashes of sun came through, burning them in patches. Behind a cascade of leaves which made a dividing curtain, a group of Swedish boys watched them with pale, intelligent eyes. 'You come out with us,' they hissed solemnly through the vines; 'you come fucky-fuckies.'

They stretched out beside the pool and talked about food and records and sex appeal and sex. Already they had learned a thing or two. Sally had discovered, from a survey in *Time* magazine, that smoking added fifty per cent more sex appeal to a girl. They wondered if you were hopelessly, truly in love, would you know because you would even think a man's thing was nice looking. This was a mystery and also a risk because if such a love did not exist and you spent your life waiting for it, you would be on the shelf, an old maid and hairy.

Built into their contempt for old maids was the knowledge that marriage meant an end to office life and it was so pleasant to lie by the pool, barely disturbed by the prowling vigil of the Swedish boys and the sun rolling over them in bales of heat, that both were intent on a domestic resolution.

It was merely a question of finding the right man or finding the right feelings for some sort of man. When they spoke of their married lives, Sally detailed a red sofa and Japanese paper lanterns. Rose was going to have a television in the bedroom.

Sometimes they fetched a guitar and went and sat among the cacti and sang; 'Sally free and easy, that should be her name – took a sailor's loving for a nursery game.'

In the afternoons, they went for a walk around the streets of Palma. Sally wore a dress of turquoise frills. Rose's frock was white linen. It was the era of the minis but they turned up the hems several times over so that the twitch of their buttocks showed a glimpse of flower-patterned panty. Men followed them up and down the hot, narrow lanes. 'See how they look at you!' Sally shuddered. 'Their eyes go down and up as if they can look right inside you.'

'Why would they want to do that?' Rose said.

In fact she was very aware of their pursuers, of the tense silence in the street behind them as if the air itself was choked with excitement – the stalking whisper of plimsolled feet on cobbles – the hot, shocked breath on the back of the neck. One day one of them captured her as she rounded a corner, caught her by the waist with a hand as brown as a glove and gazed into her face with puzzled eyes and then he kissed her. She slapped his face and ran on giggling to catch up with her friend but all day little fingers of excitement crept up and twisted inside her.

In the evenings they grew despondent for the heat of the day made them lethargic and they did not enjoy the foreign food. 'Drunk-man's-vomit-on-a-Saturday-night,' Sally would sigh, spooning through a thick yellow bean soup.

After dinner there began a long ritual of preparation, of painting eyes and nails, of pinning little flowers and jewelled clips in their hair before going out dancing. They did not bother much with washing because they had dipped in the pool during the day and the showers at the Villa Marta were violent and boiling, but they sprayed recklessly with *L'Air du Temps*.

The dances were not, actually, fun. The boys were young and eager but their desire was not skilfully mounted. They yapped and scrabbled like puppies. They did not know how to make sex without touching so that it hung in heavy droplets on the air. They did not know how to make fire from sticks.

One day on the beach they met a group of Americans, schoolgirls from a convent in Valencia, tall and beautiful although they were only fifteen. They had come to the island for a holiday and the girls pitied them because they still seemed bound by school regulations, crunching the white-hot sand in leather shoes that were the colour of dried blood. The shoes were only taken off when they went into the water and tried to drown one of their companions. The girls joined in splashing the victim who was blonde and tanned and identical in appearance to the others, until they realised that she was terrified and in genuine danger of drowning. 'Stop!' Sally commanded nervously. 'She's afraid!'

'She's a creep,' one of the pretty girls said.

'Why?' Rose pulled the sodden beauty from the floor of the ocean.

'*She* hasn't got oxblood loafers.'

A few days later the Americans came running along the beach, their heavy golden hair bouncing, their feet like aubergines in the shiny purple shoes. 'Hey!' they called out to Rose and Sally who were bathing grittily in the sand. 'There's sailors.'

An American ship had docked in Palma. The girls watched silently as the sailors were strewn along the quay, wonderful in uniforms that were crisp as money. They whistled at the girls and the girls ran after them, their knees shivering on the sweet seductive note. 'Come on, honey,' one boy called to them. 'Where d'you wanna go? You wanna go to a bullfight?' 'Sure!' the American girls agreed, and their leather shoes squeaked and their rumps muscled prettily under little shorts as they ran to catch up.

Sally and Rose had been hoping for something more attractive than a bullfight. Given the opportunity they might have pressed for lunch in one of the glass-fronted restaurants in Palma, where lobsters and pineapples were displayed in the window; but the Americans moved in a tide, scrambling for a bus, juggling with coins and they had to run or get left behind.

Following the example of the giant schoolgirls they pressed themselves down beside the loose forms of two of the young men. 'I'm Will,' the boy beside Sally said, showing wonderful teeth and something small and grey and lumpy like a tiny sheep, which was endlessly ground between them. 'I'm Bob,' Rose's sailor said and laughed to show that names were not to be taken seriously.

The bullring smelled like a cardboard box that had got damp and been left to dry in the sun. It was constructed as a circus with benches arranged in circles on different levels and all of those spaces were crammed with human beings who were waiting for a death. They were pungent with heat and the tension of expectation. This dire harmony wrought a huge hot communal breath which had a little echo in the men who had followed the girls through the lanes of Palma, but here the fear was not exciting and pleasant. Sally and Rose did not believe in death. They sat clammy with dismay, waiting for the animals to be saved.

No matter that it was an honourable sport, that the dead bulls' meat fed the island's orphans; they were unimpressed by the series of little fancy men who pranced around the bewildered animals which lurched and pawed at bubbles of their own blood that bulged brilliantly and then shrank back shabbily into the sand.

How many orphans could so small an island support Rose wondered, as one animal died and then two? She saw the orphans as the left luggage of tourists who had stayed too long in the lanes. She sympathized with this; she too had wanted, in an awful way, to go back alone, without Sally. Her only dismay was for the huge animals crumbling down one by one with hot dribbles and their sides all lacquered red by a pile of little sticks jammed in like knitting needles stuck in a ball of wool.

'He's dead!' Sally accused Will. A third animal folded up its slender legs and rolled in the sticky sawdust.

'Sure is honey,' Will said eagerly and squeezed her fingers. He seemed radiantly happy. 'Say, can I come on back to your hotel?'

Sally gave Rose a careful look. Rose's sailor, Bob, was watching Will for a clue.

Rose thought it wouldn't matter much what happened to Sally since Sally's period was late following some home-based encounter. She calculated some basis on which to make it worthwhile for herself. 'We're late for our dinner,' she said. 'We'd have to have a hamburger.'

'Sure thing,' Bob said amiably.

The girls ate with the speed and concentration of thieving dogs. Their pocket money did not run to delicacies. The sailors treated them to banana splits and the girls thought they should have ordered prawn cocktails and steaks since these men were so rich and so foolish with their money.

On their way back to the hotel after supper they were wreathed in virtue. It was thick around them, like scent over the honeysuckle. Both of them felt like sacrificial virgins although they were not, actually, virgins. In the terms of the understanding, they were going to lie down beside Will and Bob and let them do, within reason, what they wanted. They walked together, no longer feeling a need to be sociable. The sailors were playful in their wake.

When they got to the hotel they let the men into their room and sat with cold invitation on either bed. The sailors took cigarettes from their pockets and asked if there was anything to drink. Rose grudgingly brought a bottle of Bacardi from the wardrobe. 'I gotta girl like you at home,' Bob said. He rubbed her hand and drew up a linty patch on her burnt skin.

He kissed her then and she could feel his dry lips stretched in a smile even as they sought her mouth. He was the most amiable man she had ever met. She had no notion how to treat or be treated by a man as an equal. Sexual excitement grew out of fear or power. She could only regard him with contempt. 'You like to see my girl?' he said. He brought out his wallet and withdrew some coloured snapshots of a girl with a rounded face and baby curls.

Will had pictures too. Chapters of American life were spread out on the woven bedspreads and soon the girls were lulled into yawns by the multitude of brothers and sisters, moms and dads, *dawgs* and faithful girlfriends. The sailors spoke of the lives they would have, the houses and children. They had joined the navy to see the world but it seemed that their ship was in a bottle. Soon they would settle down, have families, mow the grass at weekends. The lives ahead of them were as familiar and wholesome as family serials on the television.

Catching Sally's eye, which was hard under the watering of boredom, Rose suddenly suffered an enlightenment. It was herself that she saw in the balding Polaroids – at the barbecue, at the bake sale – squinting into the faded glare of the sky. She was looking at her future.

She gathered in her mind from the assorted periods of films she had seen, a white convertible with a rug and a radio on the back seat, a beach house with a verandah, an orchestra playing round the pool in the moonlight. All Americans had television in the bedroom.

'Bob, put your arms around me,' she said. She swept the photographs into a neat pile and put them prissily face down. Bob's arms fell on her languidly. She drew them back and arranged them with efficiency, one on a breast and one on a hard, brown leg. He gave her a swift look of query but she closed her eyes to avoid it and offered him her open mouth. 'You're as ripe as a little berry. You sure are,' Bob sighed, and for once his smile faded and languor forsook him. He began kissing her in a heavy rhythmic way and his hands pursued the same rhythm on her spine, on her breasts, on her thighs. Rose had a moment of pure panic. She could not think. Her good shrewd plotting mind had deserted her. Clothes, body, common sense seemed to be slipping away and she was fading into his grasp, the touch of his tongue and fingertips.

She opened her eyes to gaze at him and saw his goodness in

the chestnut sweep of his eyebrows and his hair. 'I love you,' was the first thought to return to her head. She reached out to touch his hair.

Bob felt her stillness. He opened his eyes. He found himself staring into blue eyes that were huge with something he saw as fear. He pushed her away harshly. 'Now don't you go around doing that sort of thing with all the guys,' he said. 'You're a nice girl.'

Rose did not know what to do. Bob shook his head and stood up. He fetched his cigarettes from the dressing table. He tapped the pack on his palm to release one, but he hit it with such violence that all the cigarettes were bent. He lit one anyway and went to the window, opening the shutters and leaning out to sigh long and deeply. Rose, watching the indifferently entwined bodies on the other bed, felt very close to tears.

'Jesus Christmas!' Bob let out a whoop. 'Would you look at that pool!'

In a second, Will had leaped from the disarrayed Sally and joined his friend, his buddy, at the window.

'Holy shit!' Will said with reverence.

'Mind your mouth.' Bob cuffed him good-humouredly. 'Last man in is a holy shit.'

The Villa Marta was constructed on a single storey so the young men were able to let themselves out the window with a soft thump on the cactussy lawn. They breathed muffled swear-words as the cacti grazed their ankles and then ran to the pool, tearing off their beautiful uniforms as they went.

The girls stood at the window watching them playing like small boys in the water. They splashed each other and pulled at one another's shorts. Will jumped from the water, waving his friend's underpants. 'Hey, come back here,' Bob yelled. 'I got a bare ass.'

'Don't worry,' his friend hollered back. 'It's a small thing.'

Bob scrambled from the pool and they tussled on the edge of the prickly lawn. With a cold pang Rose noted that his body was beautiful, every part of it, golden and beautiful. She beat on the shutters savagely with her knuckles. 'You out there! You better go now,' she said.

'Sure thing!' the sailors laughed with soft amusement as they pulled on their clothes.

They came to the window to kiss the girls goodnight and then leaped at the flower-covered wall to scramble on to the street.

'Bob,' Rose howled out softly. Bob dropped back lightly to the ground. He came back to where she was huddled at the window. 'What's up honey?'

'Don't you have a pool at home?' she said. She was troubled by the way he had reacted to the pool at the Villa Marta. All Americans had swimming pools.

'What kind of a question is that?' Bob said. 'We don't have no pool. We live in the hills. We gotta few cows and hens and sheep. We gotta few acres but we ain't got no pool.'

He ran off again but before making his effortless jump at the wall he paused and cried out, 'Wait for me!' and she thought of his chestnut hair and the wild sweetness of his touch and said yes, she would wait, but then she saw the bleak snowfall of blossoms from the wall and she realized that he had been calling out to his buddy. He was gone.

She ran from the room and out into the dark, polish-smelling hall of the Villa. As she stood trying to compose herself, the front door opened and two of the Swedish boys entered. They were immaculately attired in evening dress and carried half-filled bottles of whiskey but both seemed as sober as Mormons.

'Good evening,' one said.

'You like to fuck sailors?' the other enquired respectfully. He had watched the visitors emerging from the wall.

Rose hurled herself at him, slapping his face with both hands in a fury. He delivered his bottle for safekeeping to his friend and calmly trapped her hands with his. 'You act like the little wolf' – he spoke with detachment– 'but you are really the grandmother in disguise.'

He let her go and she fled through the carved entrance, tearing along the street, down one alley, through the next. She emerged into a long, tree-lined street and there were the sailors. She stood and watched them until the young men had disappeared and only the hipswing of their little buttocks was picked out by the moon like, ghostly butterflies in their tight white pants.

'Creeps,' she cried after them.

The Miracle of Life

I grew up on a street that was skilled in competitive sameness. All the houses boasted a radiant darkness. Pine green or wood-stain doors opened to admit or dispatch men in suits, women in costumes, children with long socks and cumbersome frocks and hairy cardigans. The women were constantly afraid that their children would disgrace them in front of the neighbours, the men feared that their wives would let them down by speaking out or earning money and the children worried that no one would know they were unique.

We knew our street had its share of scandals which were much discussed and used as an innoculation against any serious threat of independence. There was Mrs Galvin who ran off with a man and afterwards her small daughter fell out a window. I always pictured the child arched out the frame for a last disbelieving glance, finally toppling as the sinful couple sprinted around the comer. There was Mrs Beech whose husband died and she had to go to work and this so confused her son that he dressed up as a nun. There was Miss Milne-Evans who was a Protestant and a spinster and went mad behind the cobwebby growths that enclosed her big house. Always it was the women. Men's only flaw was failure – failure to make their name or to combat death or keep their hands off the bottle or the women.

I worried about our mother. For instance, although she never went out without her cherry-coloured high heels and her grey two-piece, there was a line of clothes across the kitchen to air and we often ate eccentric meals, tinned sardines with creamed potatoes or curried eggs.

She was respectful to my father but she said heretical things. While she savagely tackled housework in our gloomy kitchen, where light never entered but remained a wistful onlooker at the one small window; she declared that girls were as good as boys, that sex was no picnic, that the key to a woman's happiness was her own income.

One day she told me the facts of life. She drew sperms on a paper grocery bag and concocted a tale so improbable, so far removed from suits and costumes and fathers and mothers that I knew I could no longer trust her. The telling gave her a hectic energy and she went off to scrub the floor, leaving me to look at the bag of human commas. When the red had receded from her face she made tea and grew sentimental. She said the baby that got born was one of millions of sperms that ran in a race until it reached the safety of the womb. She called it the miracle of life.

Awful, I called it. I believed that I had come from somewhere special; I imagined I had been spirited to my mother's body as a sort of fairy doll.

Afterwards I took a bus into D'Olier Street and stood for a long time at the window of the Gas Company Showrooms looking at the model refrigerator. Food was displayed on its shelves, sausages and ham, a roast chicken, a trifle, a bunch of bananas, a whole cheese. It was not real food. It was made of papier mâché and had a dry and itchy look. I liked it because it was both orderly and exotic. It was part of a new world which ought to be my inheritance. In 1960, apart from Elvis Presley singing 'Old Shep', it was my favourite thing in the world.

It was close to Christmas and ropes of fairy lights swooped over O'Connell Street and the shawlies of Moore Street shouted: 'Penny the sparklers.' I no longer cared for all that. The glitter gave me an uneasy memory of Reenee as she had been. Besides, I was not, any more, a child.

Children grow up in secret. They choose their models from the random assortment of people in their path. We did not have a television, which provides the ideals of fantasy for today's children, nor any modern appliance except a vacuum cleaner the size of a St Bernard dog which sometimes spat fire from its hoses. Parents were used only as models for avoidance. I loved my mother and I stuck close to her, drinking tea and eating Hovis in the kitchen after school, but it seemed vital to turn into a different person. I had flung out a schizophrenic net to cover, at the calm end of the pond, our nun, Sister Sophie, and at its deepest and most dangerous extreme, my best friend Katie's older sister, Reenee.

Katie and I had been Reenee's handmaidens. We ran her bath (one keeping a hand in the water until the temperature was exactly right), backcombed her hair, painted her nails. At least once a week we were party to dramatic scenes such as the following:

Reenee was getting ready for a dance. From her bedroom she sent out a thin shriek, summoning Katie and me. 'For God's sake, I've got a spot!'

She was in her half slip and orangey-tan nylons, her sweater flung on the bed, her breasts overflowing the rigid cones of her bra. Her blue satin dress with the tulip skirt and cut-out back was hanging on a chair. We ran about like blind mice, trying to appease her, trying to discern the flaw.

'On my back, for Christ's sake,' Reenee snapped and we found it and it was quite a big spot too.

Katie boiled a kettle and fetched cotton wool and disinfectant and Reenee's Pan-Stik make-up. I got a darning needle and poised it over a jet of flame on the gas cooker. When the needle was red hot I poked it at the centre of the spot and Katie dabbed at its erupting substance. '*Don't* squeeze!' Reenee warned. She began to calm down as we patted in the orangey emulsion that matched her stockings better than her skin. At this stage her eyes narrowed with satisfaction at her reflection in the winged dressing-table mirror and she told us the things she knew. S.A. was what made a woman irresistible. You got it by putting pads of cotton wool, soaked in perfume, in your bra. No girl should go all the way but it was all right above the waist if you were going steady. A married woman must always keep her lipstick and mascara beneath the pillow and put them on before her husband awoke so that he would never have to look on her naked face. She spoke of French kissing, of lurching, of *shifting*.

We knew about French kissing, for it was the fate of all women who were brought to the pictures by their boyfriends. Reenee said it was lousy unless you were crazy about the guy and then it was fab. Lurching was close dancing and an occasion of sin. We never quite found out what shifting was but it concerned couples who rolled about the floor at parties.

We watched Reenee like a hawk. She knew all the rules of life and was confident in their execution. When she spoke on the telephone to her boyfriend, Tom, she leaned back in the chair and stretched out a leg and dangled her shoe. She smiled and made sheep's eyes into the telephone.

We both thought that it was the oddest thing, to smile into that handle of black Bakelite, but we made a mental note of it.

Sister Sophie was entirely different, a pious little stick of a woman who told us of a girl who had dressed up in her brother's clothes on Hallowe'en and afterwards she died and her parents saw her ghost, still dressed in men's clothing, flapping about in the moon. She thought I was a good child and prayed constantly for my vocation. I was not drawn to the nuns' way of life, their gliding blackness and the dull certainty of their salvation, but so far she was the only one who had noticed anything about me.

That year two things happened. The first was that Reenee got a crippling disease. In the beginning it crept up slowly like a bad 'flu and she maintained her glamour propped up in bed in fluffy layers of her favourite blue. Then all of a sudden, she was an invalid, yellow and shapeless and sour and stale. The mysterious womanly parts of her that had been such a source of envy and admiration to us now became the necessity for odious tasks which Katie, blazing with hatred, had to perform. I was no longer involved; I did not have to be so I retreated. Neither of us felt sorry for her. We considered that she had let us down and we despised her. Katie had to share a room with her, with all that soft, sad, dying femaleness. Sometimes when I walked to school with her I could smell Reenee's smell from her and I imagined her pale, intense face had a yellowish tinge. I thought that Reenee's illness would spread and spread like St Brigid's cloak until it covered us all, so I took to going into school early on my own to help Sister Sophie with her dahlias and I stayed on late, when lessons were over, to polish the blackboard and the desks.

I told Sister Sophie I had got The Call. The nun smuggled in special treats for me, Taylor Keith lemonade, Mikado biscuits, iced fairy cakes from the Eaton: She talked about God. She made Him sound like a brother, impractical and all-powerful. I liked that because I only had sisters, but the cakes caught in my throat.

The second thing to happen was that Betty Malibu came to live on our street. Her real name was Mrs Cahill but she told Mrs Elliot next door that she had once sung in the Gaiety as Betty Malibu and after that the name stuck. She was tall and thin with a mock ocelot coat and blonde hair in long waves. She had a husband, Barney, never seen except as a cigar pointing at the windscreen of a Mercedes car. She herself had a car – an unheard of thing for a housewife – a blue Ford Zephyr, which sometimes made snorting sorties down the street, almost killing people. Most of the time she preferred to walk, pushing a go-car to show off her little girl who was called Lucille and who struggled within a pyramid of pink nylon frills. Sometimes when she walked her daughter, she sang to her. I thought she was like Grace Kelly. She was the most admirable woman I had ever seen.

The other women did not like her. They said her American accent had come out of a packet of Mary Baker cake mix. They laughed when she said she put pineapple pieces in her ice cubes. They said that she had come from nothing.

When she was new on the street they tried to impress her. One told her how she had done all her curtains that day because there was a good breeze and another said that she had finished her whole batch of Christmas baking. A third one had cleaned out all her presses to make way for her new cauliflower pickle.

Betty Malibu smiled her dreamy smile. 'I did bugger all,' she said.

Nothing could reduce her in my eyes. If she had come from nothing, then what a remarkable journey she had made to bring such glamour to our street. She always seemed dressed for a party. I thought the pineapple pieces in the ice cubes sounded so smart, and they meant she had a refrigerator too.

When I said this to my mother, when I praised her mock ocelot coat and her blue car and her gold hair, Mother turned from her polishing with an angry look and said: 'If you think she's got more to offer than we have, why don't you just take yourself over there?'

I did. I put on my pink coat, handed down by a richer cousin, and went and knocked on our new neighbour's door. She was wearing a nylon housecoat with frills. She apologized for it, calling it a peignoir.

'Can I come in and play?'

She gave a little yawn. I think she had been having a nap. 'Who are you?'

'I live down the road.'

'Sure. Come in, little girl. Would you like to watch some television?'

'I'd like to see your refrigerator,' I said.

There was a pause. 'Sure, honey.' She led me through the house which was full of glittering ornaments and bright pieces of china, like the prizes on a raffle stall. 'Would you like to do a job for me while you're in the kitchen? I'll give you a Bounty Bar.'

The 'fridge was in the kitchenette, where it took up most of the space. It was both tall and squat and every so often it seemed to give a deep chuckle. I drew back its vaulty door. The cold light inside, the white interior, the rows of ribbed shelves like bars on a coat, reminded me of a hospital ward. There was no trifle. No ham or bananas. There was hardly any food there at all, just some plastic boxes and greaseproof bags and a lettuce squashed under a stippled plastic shelf at the bottom. I frowned into the chill emptiness.

'What's the matter, honey? Did you want a sandwich?'

'There's nothing in there.'

'Sure there is. It's in the bags,' she said. 'You have to cover the food in a 'fridge or else you get odour.' She wanted me to clean out a chicken. 'My stomach just turns over,' she sighed.

Disappointment lay like a stone on my heart but I clawed chicken guts out on to newspaper. I would never do this for my mother. 'What about the pineapple ice cubes?' I said very quietly.

'Oh, sweet! – They're just for parties.'

'Don't you make ice-pops or ice-cream in the 'fridge?'

'No,' she agreed amiably. 'But we will someday if you want.'

I forgave her. She made coffee – not Irel, which we drank at home, but proper Nescafé. She gave me a Mars Bar and a Bounty. These were English and we could not buy them.

I came to see her every day. I told my mother I was going to Katie's house and, forsaking the dahlias, led Sister Sophie to believe that my mother wanted me (which was not exactly a lie, but did not merit the specific truth I gave it). Betty Malibu and I sat in her drawing room, which had a red carpet and satinized wallpaper, and watched Armand and Michaela Denis wrestling with blurred black and white lions. When we were not watching television we talked about the stars. She bought all the movie magazines and knew about the personal life of every actor and actress: *Bobby and Sandra's Marriage Crisis! Has Eddie Left Debbie Holding the Baby? Janet and Tony – Together Again?* I learned from these publications that having a bosom was the true secret of S.A. and indeed the root of every female success. At the back of the magazines were advertisements for wigs and false bosoms and even false bottoms so that having savoured the turbulent personal lives of the stars you could send off your cheque (or check, as they called it) and receive in the post a parcel of parts which made you just like the screen goddesses.

I felt at my chest and found that two small softnesses covered the wings of bone. I developed a great longing. 'There's just one thing I want for Christmas,' I confided to Betty Malibu, the only person in the world to whom I could say such a thing. She laughed when I told her. 'Well, that doesn't sound too difficult.'

But it was. Nobody ever bought you the things you wanted and they never liked the things you gave them. If I told the family I wanted a bra for Christmas they would laugh at me and say: 'What are you going to put in it – your scapulars?'

Apart from my new craving I loved books. I knew this addiction to be a dowdy one but still I bought books for everyone at gift-giving times.

I spent hours crawling around the floor under the bargain table in Fred Hannas, where nothing cost more than sixpence. I bought adventure stories for my sisters, an old cookery book for my mother; for Father I found a volume called *Sailing up the Belgian Congo*. As an afterthought I picked up a book of faded photographs about a tame bear for Katie. There was nothing good enough for Betty Malibu. All my usual pleasure at book hunting turned to panic as I flung aside old Protestant Bibles and street directories, tomes of Dickens and Chaucer, smelling of mould.

It was while I was there, under the table with the unwanted Greats, that Reenee, crying out a lament about a hangnail, summoned Katie to her side and died.

The funeral was four days before Christmas. Everyone was there, full of regret and chilled by the nudge of mortality. Katie and her mother cried and cried until they seemed to dry out and I was crying too but my misery had a different source.

At school the day before, Sister Sophie had given me a mission. One of the bold girls in the class – an Audrey or an Alma or Dolores – (good girls were always Josie or Brid or Teresa) had been found with an object of obscenity hidden in her desk. That's what Sister Sophie called it. She held up a bulky grey cardboard folder. Concerning its contents, she said, she would leave our innocence undisturbed. All that remained was to dispose of the dirty work and she would give this task to a good child whom she could trust. I stepped forward without being asked. She put the book in my hands.

'Promise you won't look,' she said.

'I swear.'

I did not look – not really look – but as the folder slipped into the waste bin its pages parted and my eye was drawn to the flickering show of Hollywood stars. It was a home-made film album, not just with magazine cut-outs but proper glossy photographs of the kind that fan clubs supply. Before I could think my hands had plunged into the dank cavern of refuse and the album was safe in my grasp. It had suffered only a little in the bin and a quick peek assured me that Alma or Dolores had not identified ownership with the usual: 'This book belongs to . . .' I could feel my heart juddering like an old motor engine as I ran back into school and hid the album in the cloakroom, underneath my overcoat.

I brought Betty Malibu her present after school, wrapped up in a sheet of shop wrapping paper, which cost twopence. She was as excited as I was. 'Oh, you sweet child, wait till I tell them all that you went to the trouble of getting me a Christmas present.' I was pulling ribbons away from the box she had given me – too big for a bra alone so I knew there must be other things as well and I kept my fingers crossed for a stiff slip and nylons.

It was a dress – pink Vyella with blue and green smocking on its flat, flat chest. It was what my mother would call a good item, with spare buttons on a card and little loops inside the shoulders to keep your slip straps in place. I recognized it from an expensive children's shop called The Gay Child.

'Isn't that the cutest thing, honey?' Betty Malibu was delighted. 'I chose it specially to go with your pink coat. Won't you be the smartest kid on the street?'

I nodded bitterly. That was just what I would be.

She was still smiling as she tore the wrapping from her gift. When the folder was revealed she got a puzzled look. She flipped through it and I saw that her fingers were as stiff as Sister Sophie's when she had held it up in class. 'Hey!' She gave a funny little laugh. 'What is this?'

'It's your present.'

When I looked at her she had withdrawn from the album and sat quite still, tears gathering in her eyes. 'Is this what you call a joke?' She said it very softly. 'It's not even new. It's garbage. It's *dirty*!' Her shining nails brushed a scar of grease which clung to the cover where it had been dipped in the bin. 'I thought you were getting me a book. I thought you were buying me a new book.'

'I didn't think you'd read a book,' I protested. 'You were going to buy me a bra.'

'You shouldn't judge a person by where they come from,' she said with intense feeling. 'I thought you would have something written on the inside and I would show everyone how you had bought me a book and written in it for me. A bra!' She pulled the rags of the wrapping paper around the gift for decency. 'What would your mother say?'

After Reenee's funeral service the mourners seemed drawn by a need for comfort to the Christmas crib, with its real straw and its nice little plaster donkey.

There had been hymns and inspiring passages of scripture and these helped to wipe away the yellowness of Reenee's illness. We all saw her as she had been, blonde and backcombed and full of S.A., but now with the addition of her heavenly crown, like a seaside beauty queen. In the end it seemed that she had simply got bored with us and gone off to look for more exciting company. It made us sad. We thought we would never laugh again. Then Betty Malibu leaned into the crib and looked at the baby Jesus with interest. 'It just goes to show,' she said; 'you should never judge a person by where they start out from.' Everyone gave a little titter.

My mother made me wear the pink dress on Christmas day. She inspected all the seams and fancy stitches and marvelled at the good taste of a person like Betty Malibu. A funny thing had happened. Mother called around to the house to thank her for the gift and after that she couldn't stop saying what a nice person she really was and how clean her house was and in a day or two all the neighbours were flocking around Betty Malibu and they even began calling her plain old Mrs Cahill. I didn't care any more. I was feeling so rotten I didn't even mind putting on the dress. If someone had told me to, I would have dressed up in the back half of a pantomime horse. All the books I had bought and disguised with pads of newspaper underneath the wrapping ended up as more signposts to my oddness. 'We know!' my sisters teased as I arranged the nicely bumpy packages beneath the Christmas tree. 'They're only old books, aren't they?'

I took the dress out of its box and looked in misery on its neat round collar, the tweaking puffs of the sleeves. I pulled it over my head and felt behind my neck to slide the buttons into their perfect holes. After a long time I looked.

What I saw was something remarkable. The dress did not change me. Wearing it did not turn me into a kid. It did not alter me at all. Inside it, I was still me, a girl with thin plaits and a heart-shaped face on which intelligence sat like a blight, like spectacles; with the beginnings of a bust showing determinedly beneath the flattening bands of smocking.

If it was so, if a child's dress could not turn me into a child, then a bra or a false bust or even a false bottom could not turn me into a woman. I was uniquely myself and the only one of my kind. I had swum in a race with millions but I was the one who had won the race. I could learn from the experience of others without having to share the perils of their fate. My life was mine, whether I learned to smile at the telephone or sing to my children like Grace Kelly, with or without S.A.

'Look at her!' my sisters jeered when I sat down to dinner in the dress. 'Who does she think she is?' My father looked up from his carving with that vague dismay that love of daughters meant. His eye registered my new dress, or something that it suggested. 'She needs a bra!' he told my mother crossly and then went back with relief to his virtuoso solo upon the Christmas turkey.

The Spirit of the Tree

Three weeks before Christmas we began counting trees. Crouched in the back of Father's car, forbidden to talk in case we disturbed his concentration as he approached traffic lights, we silently prodded the window, leaving marks that were veined like flies' wings. The flaring V of light in darkened drawing rooms was like a landing strip for the extraordinary event that would descend among us. In that first week there would be only two or three trees, mostly in big houses. The second week there might be eleven or twelve and then on that last Sunday, days before Christmas, they were convened behind windows everywhere – majestic evergreens bedecked like emperors and little crooked shrubs nobbled with lights that were bright and sticky as boiled sweets, a silent community signalling light.

What were they for? Hardly anyone seemed to know. But I knew. The spirit of the tree spoke to Santa Claus, telling him which houses he should visit. The fairy lights were to guide his way. I can't remember where I heard that, but I knew it must be true because it made sense.

We did not understand it then but the atmosphere in those weeks coming up to Christmas, the sense of an unstoppable miracle, was close to the feeling of falling in love. A space was carved in the ordinary world where we were knocked into shape for hard lives ahead, and we could sit in this capsule for a while and be angels or astronauts. We wore a shimmering garment of rapture. Nothing could touch us – not the sharp

December air, smelling of fog and frost, not even the curious humpy mood that sat over our parents as we drove home from our grandparents' house. The strange thing was that the happy tension surrounding us children seemed to strike our parents at a different angle and one could not help noticing that as the fairy-lit forests ran riot in suburbia, they grew more and more withdrawn. They reacted to the approach of Christmas as to the onslaught of a war, Mother grimly setting forth for the city to lay in supplies, muttering about the crowds and the price of things, Father swearing as he tacked up the paper accordion decorations, which frequently broke and teasingly drifted, snake-like, through the sombre living room. The biggest ordeal was putting up the Christmas tree. The huge conifer was dragged into the house like a dead bear, then wrestled into an upright position and dumped in a barrel weighted with bricks. Father would retreat from this engagement, thistled with tiny green needles and looking offended as the tree flooded the house with its pungent green scent.

The small surprise parcels from Santa contained, year after year, the same novelties, the chocolate coins wrapped in foil, an orange. Our parents gave us books, our grandparents biscuits, a tin of sweets and a box of mandarin oranges tricked out like pantomime fairies in tissue and silver paper. Aunt Josie faithfully produced a bottle of Gilbey's Odds-On cocktail for Mother and warm underwear for us girls. Small gifts from far-flung relatives were dangled from the tree or stacked at its base – bath cubes and puzzles and assorted chocolate bars in presentation packs called Selection Boxes. Still, each year, the shock of anticipation was new and when the long (and predictable) day had ended, my last act was always to search the Christmas tree for one unredeemed gift that I might claim for myself and not know its source. As with love, the rapture was always threatened by some small but fatal flaw. There were only two days to Christmas and we still hadn't got our tree.

We never approached any topic directly with our parents. We would either select a crabwise avenue or else open the subject with one parent and allow them to digest it before offering it to the other in a suitable form. Confronted head-on, they reacted like a rabbit caught in a car's headlights. Years later we understood that this was because their responses to everything were so different that it was necessary to find a meeting point before they could offer a united response. Our stark inquisitions were a challenge to their private relationship, the one we would never understand.

'They are selling Christmas trees off in Camden Street,' Celia said.

'That's because they're afraid they won't sell them at all,' Mercy suggested in an offhand way, though you could see the front of her dress twitching over her heart. 'Nearly everyone has one already.'

'When are we getting ours?' I burst out unwisely.

Mother stood up and began clearing away the plates, although we were still toying with our macaroni cheese. Father held on to his plate and slowly finished eating the wormy-looking pile. He glanced out the window, where the early afternoon had already flung up steel-grey shutters, and then, as if making a comment on the weather, he mildly observed, 'There will be no Christmas tree.'

There was a brief, somersaulting pause and Celia and Mercy began to laugh. Father often made jokes and he kept a very serious face when he did. I had not yet got the hang of humour. I started to cry. Mother raced in to rescue me and Father slapped both hands down on the table. 'There will be no Christmas tree! No turkey, no presents, no nonsense!' He said this angrily but immediately he looked sorry and added in a gentler voice, 'We are in a bad way. We owe money. We must all pull together. It is only one other day in the year.'

We all sat perfectly still at the table until at last Father got up and went out. '*We* don't owe money,' Celia said.

'He has to sell the car.' Mother sounded shaken. 'He's going to have to make do with a bicycle.' She didn't mention any privations that might have affected herself. Women didn't. She did not tell us – and it was years before we found out – that he had lost his job six months previously and they had been trying to live in a normal way in the hope that something else would turn up, and nothing had, except bills. All she said was that there was a tin of pineapple in the press and she would make a pineapple cake for tea.

Mercy, at eight, was an elfin little girl with white-blonde hair that made her look unnaturally pale, but now she seemed completely drained of colour. 'They have cancelled Christmas,' she said when we were alone.

'They can't cancel Christmas,' Celia said. 'It happens anyway. Santa comes anyway.'

'But Santa only comes if you have a tree in your window.' My voice rose in dawning horror. 'That's how he knows which houses to visit.'

'We'd better go and say a prayer,' Celia said. 'We'll go to the church and light a candle.'

The senior saints with their long robes and long faces offered no hope. They were greedy for suffering and would tell us, if they could (as grown-ups tended to), that sacrifice was an opportunity to add jewels to our crown in heaven. We knelt in front of the crib. Surely children everywhere wanted the same things.

On the way home it was so dark the Earth seemed to have gone out. Only the bright arrowheads of Christmas trees lit the world. Despairingly, we counted the trees. Everyone had one. Even our own prim street was ablaze with colour. Even the old Misses Parker had one. I had streaked ahead of the older girls and was reaching for their knocker before they had time to stop me. 'What are you doing?' they gasped. But the elderly sisters, who were Quakers and famously charitable, had already opened their door. I told them our father could not afford a Christmas tree and that Santa would not come to our house if he did not see the fairy lights. At once they agreed that we should have their tree and even carried it down the road with its decorations tinkling and light flexes trailing. Mother was confused, but she accepted the tree with thanks and left it propped up in the hall. We spent the afternoon stroking the cold silver strands of tinsel that the Misses Parker had threaded through its branches and that felt like mermaids' hair.

A couple of hours later Father was to be seen striding down the street, the stiffly bedecked tree clasped in his arms like a war missile. We ran behind him, picking up small ornaments as they clopped off onto the frosty pavement and trying furtively to get around him to retrieve those decorations that belonged to us. The Misses Parker eyed him with hateful sympathy as he told them we had no need of charity.

Mercy and I looked to Celia. She was the eldest so she had to do something and she had to do it before that first, fatal leaching of faith, after which Christmas would never seem the same again. 'It's all right,' she said. 'We don't need the grown-ups. We'll get our own Christmas tree.'

'Where, Cee?'

'How?'

She went out alone the following day. We waited for her, watching behind the drawing-room window. When she came home she looked small and cold, her face pinched with anxiety, her hands dug deep in her pockets.

'Have you got it?' we pestered her, although we could see nothing.

She took her hand out of her pocket and showed a small, greenish pine cone. 'I found this,' she said. 'We'll grow our own tree.'

'But that will take years,' I complained.

'Then we'd better do it right now,' she said in her practical way.

There was one apple tree in the garden, a thin forsythia and, in spring, a clump of wallflowers. There was a forgotten region, which had become a compost heap of leaves and trimmings and pruned branches. Celia instructed us to clear away the rubbish so that we could dig a hole for the Christmas tree. Gingerly we dipped in our mittened hands and began to lift the bits of half-burnt refuse and piles of dead leaves and old potted plants, layered up over some more substantial hulk. Whatever this was, you could tell that its personality remained intact, like a man preserved in a bog for a thousand years. Desiccated fingers pointed up at the sky. We pulled away more rubbish to discover a beautiful shape, like the skeleton of a leaf.

It looked like some old fish that had been nibbled dry so that only its bare bones and its scaly spine poked out. It looked like

the rusted hulk of a ship that had sunk many years ago and its
barnacled frame endured. It did not look like – but definitely
was – a Christmas tree. Triumphantly, we hauled it out. Some
of its branches were broken, but it had been a good tree once,
before it was cast out after festive service in some better year.
And it was ours. We had found it.

'It's a bit brown,' Mercy mentioned, reluctant to criticise.

'We'll make it green,' Celia said.

She had learnt a thing in school, to make leaves for bare
branches from crepe paper. We had sixpence between us and
bought two packets of the dark-green, bark-rough stuff, with
its wrinkles and its rustle of theatre. We cut it into long strips
and wound them round the branches, Sellotaping the ends,
until the entire frame was bandaged in green. Then Mercy,
who was the artistic one, made fringed strips and taped these
along the branches to look like needles. Bumping it forward in
little steps, we managed to get the tree into the house and
leaned it inside the window. It looked magnificent.

There was an anxious moment when Father came home and
discovered the mummified horticultural corpse. He was frowning. He seemed to be thinking. When he spoke, his voice
sounded strange, as if he was getting a cold. 'It's all right,' he
said. He bent to stroke our hair in the cautious way that we had
stroked the silver mermaids' hair on the Misses Parker's tree. 'I
think,' he said, 'it will be all right.'

From then on, everything proceeded as normal. Two big
boxes were brought down from the attic, one with lights and
one with ornaments. Father plunged his arms into the entrails of
frayed wiring and the fairy lights clinked in an insouciant way
like china teacups as he tried to unsnarl them. Then for hours he
was up on a ladder, locked into some intimate contest, cajoling
and cursing, beseeching and loathing, muttering strange, enticing, sulphurous words so that Mother had to drag us away, while
the lights twittered and wavered and at last responded to his
male authority. Tinsel ornaments twinkled with magical depths.
Carnival colours bumped off every sober surface in the room
and, in the window, the lights shimmered enticingly. I couldn't
sleep that night and at dawn I crept out onto the landing to see

if Santa had come. I was worried about the spirit of the tree. It might have grown faint in its old parcelled trunk. In the back of my mind too I had begun to wonder if any part of Christmas could survive now that our parents had no money, if in some way every single thing that came to us must not begin and end with them. Santa's parcels were there. I couldn't resist it and began tearing mine open right away, crying out with pleasure as the familiar objects came into view. From his bedroom came Father's voice, a weary growl: 'Get back to bed or I'll take the whole blasted lot away from you.'

After a fearful pause, Celia called back bravely, 'They are not your property!'

There was even a turkey. Father had won it in a raffle. It was a dinosaur-like creature, its languidly naked form looking like something that ought to be clothed. While we composed a jigsaw puzzle at the base of our tree, we could hear Mother's anguished voice from the kitchen: 'Get into the oven, you big bastard!'

My sisters have related this incident to their children who think it is a sad story but for the three of us it remains our best Christmas ever. It was the year we made Christmas happen. Perhaps it would have happened anyway. Our grandparents and Auntie Josie came, the monstrous bird was finally cooked and consumed and everyone fell asleep. As usual, last thing, I checked the tree, walking around its mysteriously rustling branches, examining its paper folds to see if anything had been left behind. Nestling in the elbow of a branch was a tiny package wrapped in red and tied with gold tinsel thread. I unlooped it and slowly peeled back the paper. Inside was a little enamel box with a black cat painted on its front, framed in blue flowers. I opened the box and it was filled with doll-sized fruit pastilles coated in sugar. As I slipped it into my pocket my heart dipped in that perfect curve that lovers experience when they know, against all odds, the rewards of reckless faith.

A Little Girl,
Never Out Before

Mrs Deveney had a yellow face and lips like withered lupins. When she smiled her lips went down at the corners but the yellow ridges of her teeth stayed behind. Her eyes were like two tarnished salt spoons. She asked Frankie had she any religion and Frankie, echoing her mother, said that religion was for orphans and spinsters. She wanted to know what Frankie knew and Frankie said she couldn't say until she was asked. After that Mrs Deveney went mad entirely. 'You are an ignorant rip,' she told the little girl, 'who may take herself back home to her heathen of a mother.'

'Yes ma'am,' Frankie said, relieved, but when Mrs Deveney had finished going mad and had spun little ropes of white spit between her teeth she told Frankie to get up the stairs to Lena who would show her where she was to sleep and tell her her duties.

After her husband's death Mrs Deveney had opened a rooming house. It gave her an interest in life, which was an interest in making money. She advertised board and residence, superior; piano: £1 weekly. She mentioned its suitability for honeymooners, its view of the cattle mart, a speciality of home-made brown bread. She made the bread herself. It was not so much brown as a sort of greenish yellow with a sourness which was her particular gift.

The actual work of the house was done by a cook and kitchen maid. She gave these girls time off for their religious duties and warm washing water every Saturday, but her goodness was wasted. A week before she had to get rid of Brid Feeney (with her big backside, like a married woman's) when she found her sitting on the edge of Mr McMahon's bed – a teacher – giving his back a scratch. It was not the suggestiveness of the situation that outraged her so much as the nerve of a serving girl making herself familiar with an educated man. It was the lack of proper deference to the male sex.

Brid Feeney only laughed at her; she said it wasn't the dark ages, it was the turn of the century. Mrs Deveney disliked the phrase. It made her think of milk on the turn. The world was turning bad. The past decades had brought flying machines, motor cars, electric lighting, defying the laws of nature and flying in the face of God. She still believed in the old ways, in sentimental values.

She found the little girl through a notice in *Freeman's Journal*. Up to this she had taken girls sent to her by the nuns but the sisters had a redemptive mission and she had a suspicion that they caught their girls in the act of falling. There was something worldly and sniggering about them. They lacked the humility that was proper to the poor.

When she applied herself to the newspaper columns, therefore, she was looking for something more than a kitchen maid. She was seeking a phrase, a niceness.

'A rabbit trapper – has been brought up to it. Highest references from gentleman.' 'Mrs Harford will teach new beginners the pianoforte.' 'Good cook, thoroughly understands her business.' Lena's hard toast crackled beneath Mrs Deveney's porcelain teeth and she softened it wistfully with a mouthful of tea. Downstairs she could hear that same horse of a one bawling that Jesus Mary and Joseph she only had one pair of hands as some couple from the country complained of having to go hungry on their honeymoon.

'An orphan (16) from school, wishes to go to a lady where she would be taught to be a servant;' and then 'A respectable little girl, never out before.'

She explored the notion of herself as a lady but then she thought, sixteen was very old for an orphan to be looking for work. Already she had probably left a brace of triplets in some other orphanage.

She liked the idea of a little girl, never out before. She pictured something as new and unprinted as the Holy Communion wafer, unspoilt, unknowing, modest, and cheap.

The little girl turned out small for her age. She said she was twelve but looked not more than ten. Her brown pinafore had a lifeless look, which was common to the clothing of the poor and came not, as people imagined, from infrequent washing but from insufficient rinsing as water had to be carried up from a yard and the whole wash was rinsed in a single tub. She folded her hands in front of her but they kept unfolding and grasping at air as if she was used to holding a doll.

Lena showed her the wooden box where she was to keep her underwear and her shoes and a nail on the wall for her coat. There was a wardrobe but it was full of Lena's things – clothes and boxes and romantic novelettes. A basin of cold water was left on top of the wooden box for weekday washing but Lena said she never washed until Saturdays, except her hands which Mrs D inspected twenty times a day.

Lena complained that Mrs D expected them to strip down to their raw bones every night and then undress in the morning again for washing but she herself kept her underwear on day and night as the cold was brutal. She advised Frankie to do the same as she didn't want to have to look at her raw bones. Since Lena looked like a fat white fish with pendulums of flesh adorning her jaws and tiny rows of greasy brown ringlets, Frankie was quite agreeable to this arrangement.

The cook was an immense country girl of twenty-two or three. She moved slowly and had small brown eyes. When she recited the litany of rough work that was to fill Frankie's days, the little girl couldn't help thinking it left hardly anything at all for Lena herself to do. All the same the cook had a secret which Frankie recognized right away. In the disappointing house she would wear it against her chest like a locket.

'Get up at 6.30 winter, six o'clock in summer, open shutters, light range, lay breakfast tables, sweep and dust drawing room and supply all rooms with coal,' Lena recited. 'Clean all the flues, black lead kitchen range, wash out kitchen boiler, clean thoroughly the hall, kitchen stairs, passages and water closets. Take cans of hot water to every room. Empty slops.' Lena showed Frankie the house as she reeled off the kitchen maid's responsibilities. Frankie appraised gaunt curtains in the cheerless colours of dried blood or dried peas, the mismatched furniture and pictures of stags or saints bleeding on the walls.

'Never go into the boarders' rooms without knocking,' Lena warned her. 'There's married couples in some.'

'I know all about that,' Frankie was glad to know something, although it would be hard not to know when you lived in one room with your ma and da and the young ones.

'Maybe you know too much.' Lena folded her arms. 'Maybe you think you're Miss Hokey Fly eighteen ninety-nine. Well let me put this in your pipe. It's me be's in charge round here and if anything is took or stole, it's you'll be blempt.'

The older girl went out into the back yard and leaned against a lavatory shed with a festering smell. She hummed a tune that was popular in Dan Lowry's. 'Have you your women's monthlies yet?' Frankie nodded. 'Mine have went,' Lena remarked, 'but they were a nuisance.' She was disappointed that the new girl was only a child. She seemed too young even for teasing. 'What are you thinking, Hokey Fly?'

'The house,' Frankie said. 'It isn't much, is it?'

'What were you expecting, uniformed butlers and electrical lights?'

She had been expecting a garden with asters and dahlias, an apple tree.

The child gave her the pickle, Lena decided, with her delicate lady's air and her rotten span of attention. 'Have you got any questions, Hokey, or do you know it all by now?'

She plucked back her attention from an upstairs window where a long-faced woman stood fastening the throat of an opossum cape. 'Do we get much to eat?' she said.

The little girl sat on the edge of the bed in the dark, her blanket wrapped around her shoulder, her bare legs dangling over the edge. Unknown to sun or sky, it was morning. She had slept a little towards dawn, a dizzy sickly doze, and then woken in a panic because the baby was missing. She always slept with it in her arms and they woke up wet but warm. In the day she carried the infant while she cleaned up or cooked and her hands were formed to its support.

When she opened her eyes she thought she was at home because of the loud, gurgling snores that were like her da's but it was Lena. Lena was who she lived with now. She wondered when she'd ever see her ma again, or cuddle the baby. Ah, she missed her ma. She cried for a few minutes, wiping her eyes and nose with her blanket, but Lena reached out her big knobby foot and gave her a kick so she pulled on her brown pinafore and her stockings and boots and went down to light the range.

Her room was in the attic of the house and she crept down its five storeys in the dark, past the snuffling creaking married couples, past the yearning schoolteacher and the long-faced woman with the opossum cape, past the dark dining room and drawing room which waited in silence to claim life from her fidgeting hands.

The cold possessed her like a drowning. She felt her way to the kitchen and stood there in the dark. Lena had not shown her where to find matches. Who can tell what hides in the dark of old kitchens, scuttling about with mice and mould and skins of dripping? The sounds that live inside total silence are the worst in the world. She crept around, her fingers touching things that felt horrible – soaking porridge, tea leaves in a sieve. Her breath came out in persevering grunts. At last she grasped a match and lit the kitchen lamp. It leaked a little pool of yellow light and monsters swarmed up the wall. She knelt on the floor and began to rake out the ashes.

It was her mother's idea that she should go to work in a big house. They were pals. They comforted each other with sweet tea and the flesh of babies. Her da was always after her ma, all the time. They could have stopped him, disabled him with a knife or a chair, but they had a weakness. They both loved infants, newborn. No matter that there wasn't even enough for the existing ones to eat, Frankie and her ma saw

infants as the marvel of the world. It was worth all the hurting and the hunger to have another, brand new, every other
year.

They were a hopeless pair, she and her ma. When her father
had gone out for the day and the middle ones were in school
Frankie would climb back into bed beside her. They kept
themselves warm with the two little ones. They dreamed of the
feasts they might eat if there was ever any money, but they
didn't bother all that much. Hunger was just a fact of their life,
and there were rewards.

It was after Frankie got her women's monthlies that the
notion arose of sending her away. She was growing into a lady
now, her ma said. It was time to learn a lady's life.

Her ma said that she would learn the quality of fine silver
and how to stitch linen. She would eat blancmange and cold
beef in the kitchen. She would gather roses in a wicker basket
and arrange them on a polished table by a long window. It
became their new dream, after the dreams of food. In idle
fancy they walked under wedding-cake ceilings, exploring the
rooms, peeking into bureaux to spy on love letters, opening the
lids of golden boxes to admire jewels or bon bons or cigars
inside. They mooned over the young man of the house who
was kind but distant, concealing emotion beneath a brittle
moustache as he played at the piano.

She didn't look any more like a lady than she had the year
before. Her legs were sticks and her chest was flat as a wash
board. All the same she was growing up and her father knew it
too. Sometimes when he came in from his night's drinking
and had performed gravely in the bucket in the corner, he
would reach not for Ma but for Frankie, his dimmed senses
directed by nostalgia to the spring scent of womanhood and
not its spent season.

She stuffed the stove's ugly gob with coke and papers and
stood over it while it lit, shivering and warming her legs as she
tempted it with morsels of twisted paper and a sprinkling of
sugar the way her mother had shown her. By the time it was
lighting the kitchen clock said a quarter past seven and she had
to run to catch up. There was no time to wash her hands when

she finished the fires so that the breakfast plates and saucers were branded by her black prints as she set the tables.

In all their uncertain fantasies of grandeur the one thing Frankie and her ma had been sure of was that there would be enough to eat in a big house. Poor Ma wouldn't believe it if she told her she had nothing since her tea yesterday, which was two slices of the sour brown bread smeared with marge. There would be no more until after the boarders had eaten breakfast, when she could have some of the porridge that remained.

The poor learn to live with hunger by moving slowly and sleeping a lot but she had hardly slept and she had to run all the time to keep up with the work. As she set out the bread and sausages and rings of black pudding for Lena to cook for breakfast, her fingers fell to temptation and stealthily fed her a slice of bread. After that she went upstairs to knock up the married couples.

Mrs Deveney was pleased with the little girl's first day. She wasn't sociable. She did not look at the male boarders nor loiter on the landings with Lena. In spite of her dreamy air, she was thorough. Her fires did not go out. An inspection of the dishes she washed revealed no scabs of oatmeal, no rusty stains of tea. She summoned Frankie after she had finished making the beds and emptying the slops. The child looked dazed. Her face was a panic-stricken white and her hands black as the devil. 'What are you?' Mrs Deveney asked her briskly.

'I'm a girl.' Frankie looked surprised. 'A maid.' She knew nothing. She had answered wrong. She waited patiently while the lupin lips wove themselves into a shape for contumely.

'You are a filthy, thieving little tinker of the common lower orders,' Mrs Deveney said.

Frankie looked at the big black piano, as fat and listless as a funeral horse. She wondered if the boarders ever dared to use it, if one of the silent men at breakfast might serenade his new wife, while she leaned across the lid to show him her breasts.

Oft in the stilly night . . . Her mother used to sing that long ago. She wondered what her ma was doing now. Was the baby fretting for her?

'Look at me!' snapped Mrs Deveney. 'Explain yourself.'

A bag of bones her da used to say, until she began to turn into a lady. A flock of dreams. A waking ghost. A gnaw of hunger.

'You left filthy black fingerprints all over the breakfast china and you stole a slice of bread.'

'I was hungry,' Frankie said, and then, invaded by curiosity; 'how did you know?'

'The nerve of you! Every stim in this house is counted. The bread is cut the night before – two slices for every boarder. It was Lena who informed me of the robbery.'

Mrs Deveney demanded to know why Frankie had not worn gloves while doing the dirty work of the house, the grates and the slops, and declared that she had brought a breath of depravity into a good Catholic household. She believed it too but did not add that it was a matter of routine. All the servants stole. She expected it and kept their rations meagre knowing that thieving was in their nature and that they would steal food whether they needed it or not.

In a matter of weeks Frankie would grow cunning and learn to conceal evidence of her enterprise. Lena was by now an accomplished bandit. Search as she might Mrs Deveney could only find clues to modest pilferage yet the girl grew fatter by the hour.

Was ever a slice of bread so richly mourned? The little salt-spoon eyes seemed to corrode yet further as rebuke buzzed from the withered lips. And still she was hungry. She thought about the newest baby, Doris, whose eyes were not like salt spoons but like measured sips of a morning sky. At first those eyes had been blind and it was her little ruched mouth that pondered but in a little while everything was lit up by their wonder as if they saw the face of God, if you believed in that sort of thing, or a fairy.

Jack was next, named by their father after the boxer Jack Kilraine, the Terror of the Age, but their Jack was only two and had not yet fulfilled his father's hopes, having a preference for sweetened milk and women's bodies. There was Ethel and Mick, aged six and ten. Frankie loved them all and felt grati-fied by their need of her. She was proud to be her mother's protector. She had no desire for an independent life. Her own needed her. They always would. She thought of them all alone, with no one to comfort them or cook for them, and panic gripped at her knees. Who would cheer her ma up in the morning after her da had gone, leaving the trail of his temper, a smell of beer and the dank aftermath of his night-time business?

She always lay on the bed looking cold and sort of grey until Frankie brought her tea and opened the windows and sang a few songs and lit up the ashes in the grate.

Christmas was only six weeks off and the small ones were already counting. Frankie was the one who made the ginger biscuits and scrounged for oranges to put in the children's stockings. It was she who saved up new pennies, one for each child.

'I'm going home now,' she said in her offhand way. 'My ma will be wanting me.'

'Ah, now,' the widow looked alarmed. 'Your mammy is depending on the few shillings. You'd only be letting her down.'

'No I wouldn't,' Frankie said. 'My ma loves me.'

'Of course she does,' Mrs Deveney forced her mouth down into a smile. 'You're only in want of refinement and religion. You should pin your hair up and maybe I'd make you a present of a gown for Sundays. Brid Feeney's grey could be cut down for you. I'm going to give you time off to go to Mass and confession with Lena. What do you say?'

Frankie shook her head. She was too tired. She only wanted to go home.

'And if you were loyal to me, of course, you would get a nice present at Christmas – something you could bring home to benefit your poor little brothers and sisters. Say "yes ma'am".' Her smile vanished when she saw ambition enter Frankie's dreamy eye. 'Say "thank you, ma'am".'

She got used to the wearing of household gloves, the smell of chloride of lime and the racking bouts of grief that she carried carefully to the outside lavatory. She learned to steal things that could not be counted, spoons of starch or custard powder, a fistful of dry oatmeal.

The married couples came and went, their honeymoons accomplished with relief, if not much comfort. McMahon the schoolteacher stayed on. Sometimes he invited Frankie into his room, but she said she wasn't allowed. The boys who came to the back door with fish or groceries tried to grapple with her but she was a good kicker. Anyway, they preferred Lena who developed a kind of glamour in the hands of men, allowing them to feel her giant bosoms or anything they liked.

Once she surprised her in the pantry with a bakery lad. The youth and the massive girl turned to gawp at her. 'Get out! Get away you dirty little scut, you cur,' Lena snarled.

'You'll get a baby if you do that,' Frankie told her.

'Don't you be ridiculous,' Lena said. 'How could I get a baby now?'

Frankie laughed, which earned her a blow on the ear. There was no argument to that.

Within a month she had begun to turn into one of those wiry little workers, who are silent and swift and indispensable. Mrs Deveney kept her word and came up the five flights of stairs, carrying, with caution and difficulty, her Christmas gift.

It was a little house or shed. The roof was thatched like those of the poor cottagers who lived in the hills, and animals wandered around inside. A poor little baby slept in a pigsty or something.

'What is it?' Frankie said. She had been hoping for money or a box of biscuits, something for the children.

'It is the holy crib,' Mrs Deveney stood back to let the child peer inside the house where she saw that there were toy people as well as animals and the baby. Foreigners. 'What's it for?' she said.

'It is to put you in mind of the spirit of Christmas,' the widow mystifyingly declared. 'The figure in the manger is baby Jesus and the lady in blue is His mother, the Virgin Mary.'

'She can't be His mother,' Frankie said; 'not if she's a virgin.'

'These are the three wise kings, led to Bethlehem by a star shining from the East, who came to worship and brought gold, frankincense and myrrh.'

'Who were they?' Frankie wondered.

'They were gifts!' Mrs Deveney tried to hide her impatience of the little girl's stupidity, for it was all as plain to her as right and wrong, but her teeth clenched and she sprayed spit. 'Gifts of inestimable value. Lena will explain.'

But all Lena explained was that Jesus Mary and Joseph they had enough junk in the room already. She picked up the little house just as Frankie was examining a mouse-sized ox. She climbed on to her own bed and heaved the crib up on top of the wardrobe.

One Sunday at Mass the little girl grew bored and slipped out of church and used the halfpenny she had been given for the collection plate to go home on a tram. She didn't have to worry about Lena, who never went to Mass anyway but loitered under a big-brimmed hat talking to corner boys.

It was a shock when she saw their room again, so cluttered, so cold. Had it always been so mingy? She stood in the doorway, looking at these poor people, trying to make them her own.

Her ma was the first to notice her. She sat up in bed, tears filling her eyes, unable to speak but silently mouthing, 'Frankie, Frankie.' She seemed astonished to see her as if she had imagined her dead or gone for ever.

'Hello, Ma,' Frankie said. 'I've come home. I'll stay if you want.'

'Ah, Frankie!' her mother found her voice. 'Aren't you a picture?'

Frankie's bones hurt from wanting to be squeezed. She wanted to run to her ma, but she couldn't, there was a restraint. She decided to make herself useful and bent before the cold fire, shovelling out the ash, putting aside any useful lumps of coke.

'Ah God!' her mother cried, 'your lovely dress! Get up, Ethie,' she nagged the younger child. 'Your sister's used to better now.'

Ethel sidled past Frankie in her greyish petticoat. She was carrying Doris. 'She's wet,' she said, and would not let her go when Frankie tried to take the baby.

'I amn't changed,' Frankie said. 'I never stopped thinking about you – every minute of every day.'

Her ma was out of bed now, pulling on her clothes. She kept having to sniff back tears. She snorted with her head stuck in the neck of her jumper.

'Da?' Frankie appealed.

Her father nodded at her politely and pulled up his blanket to cover his vest.

She wanted to hold them all, even her da. They were trying to do things for her. They cleared clothes off a chair so that she could sit down. Ethel put a cup of tea in her hand and her mother spread a tea towel over her knee. 'To save your lovely dress,' she said.

'It's not mine,' she said. 'I only wear this of a Sunday. Mrs Deveney cut it down from the last girl. Underneath, I'm still the same.'

Her mother shook her head. 'You look the part, so you do.'

Ethel fingered the grey grosgrain bow which Mrs Deveney took from a box each Sunday morning to pin to the back of Frankie's hair. 'Can you get me one of those?' she said.

'You can have this one,' Frankie said, knowing she would be killed when she went back, if she went back.

To the family, her carelessness with ribbons was more evidence of her social success. 'Tell us dotey,' her mother said; 'what's it like, the big house?'

She would tell Mrs Deveney that a boy stole her bow outside the church – a Protestant boy.

What would she say to her mother? 'There's a garden,' she improvised. 'Roses and apples – a strawberry bed.'

'What do you eat?' her ma said. 'Do you eat strawberries?'

'Chicken,' she decided.

'You'd never fit in with us now,' her mother nodded, confirming for herself the worst. 'Not any more.'

'I would so,' Frankie said.

'You'd never fit anyhow,' her father grinned. 'Your mother hasn't told you yet. We've another one on the way.'

Frankie's ma held on to Ethel for comfort.

In the afternoon, back in the big house, the ache in her bones became a squealing. None of them had hugged her. They clutched at her Sunday gloves as she said goodbye. She helped

Lena with the dinner and cleared the tables and then the Sunday afternoon silence descended and she was alone. She went up to the second landing and knocked on the door of McMahon, the schoolteacher. He closed the door behind them. While he felt around under her clothes, she watched herself in the mirrored door of his wardrobe. She could see that they were right. She was different. The dreamy look had gone from her eyes. Her legs were getting a shape of their own. Even her chest, which the schoolteacher smoothed with chalky fingers, had developed a springy feel. With her hair up her face looked strange. They'd never leave her alone now. She was pretty.

She felt no better afterwards, although no worse, and went outside for a cry in the lavatory. When she emerged into the yard a big lumpy cat was sitting on the wall, looking down at her. 'You're in trouble,' she noticed, 'ain't you?' She held out her arms and the animal made a leap that looked suicidal but the child managed to catch it. 'They won't let me keep you,' Frankie told the creature, but the rumbling warmth relieved her aching arms. She carried it upstairs. There was nowhere to hide it so she stood on the bed as Lena had done and hoisted the cat up into the Christmas crib.

That night when she was damping down the fires, a terrible bawling came from her room. Frankie flew up the stairs, her boots barely grazing the steps. Lena must have found the cat. She must be having a fit.

She wasn't having a fit. Frankie grinned when she saw the fat girl stranded on the bed, her ringlets pinned to her wet red forehead and howls flying from her mouth like bats from a cave. She was having her baby.

'I'm poisoned. I'm dyin'' Lena gasped.

'You're all right,' Frankie dabbed at Lena's forehead with the end of her pinafore. 'Your baby's coming.'

Lena stopped bawling to gape at her. 'What are you on about?'

'You can't keep it hid no more,' Frankie said. 'I knew from the first minute I saw you, you was having a baby.'

'You know nothing! You're just pig ignorant,' Lena whimpered. 'How could I be having a baby an' I not even married?'

'Don't you have no brothers and sisters?' Frankie began to tear up her sheet. 'Ain't you never seen your mam havin' a baby?'

'I be's from the orphanage,' Lena said. 'I can't be havin' a baby. I bein't married.'

Frankie sighed. 'Take long breaths and try not to make a racket. I'll tell ma'am you've got a colic.'

Mrs Deveney sat up in bed plucking the beads of her rosary as if tearing leeches from her flesh. 'Lena is poorly, ma'am, but she don't need a doctor,' Frankie said.

'No,' Mrs Deveney said; 'no doctor. She is as strong as a horse.'

After four hours a baby boy came. Puce and mummified the infant gave a thrilling cry and Frankie washed him in the bucket of warm water she had dragged up from the kitchen and laid him on her pillow. When she had him settled she turned to comfort Lena and saw that the girl was in labour again. Close to morning a little girl came and the needling cry was answered by a bird from the dawn roofs.

For a long time Frankie could only stare at them. No humans could be so perfect, so perfectly matched. They even had hair, black and silky thistledown tufts. Although she hadn't slept all night, their creamy sleep restored her. She lay down for a little while beside them on the bed and then she went downstairs to light the range.

She had to make the breakfasts herself that morning and clear up after them so it was ten o'clock before she could get back upstairs with tea for Lena.

Lena was gone. The bloody rags and bucket were gone. The babies were missing.

At lunchtime, when the cook returned, she climbed into bed in all her clothes and sullenly stared at the wall.

'Where are the babies?' Frankie said.

'What babies?' Lena heaved around to face her. 'I was poisoned by a bad sassidge. I been to the doctor and he said to stay in bed.'

'Twins,' Frankie said. 'I washed them myself and put them on my bed.'

'Well there be's no twins now and no bucket neither and you better stop behaving like a demented herrin'.'

'I didn't mention the bucket,' Frankie said.

Lena sat up in bed and screeched at her. 'There was no bucket!'

And suddenly Frankie knew. She knew. She saw the little hands grasping at the bloody water, so familiar from their recent swimming home, the dark fronds of their hair rising to the oily surface to explore the air.

'I know there were babies,' she glanced around the room as if looking for a clue and her eyes came to rest on the cat in the crib, who had maintained her conspiracy of silence throughout the howling night. The cat kneaded the straw and blinked at her. 'Twins.'

'You know nothin', Hokey,' Lena said; 'and there bein't nothin' you can do about it neither.'

Downstairs Mrs Deveney was already up and scrubbing a bucket in the yard. She was giving out about Lena's idleness. She thought she might dispatch her back to the nuns. When she saw the way Frankie was looking at her, the yellow of her skin became tinged with ash. 'Go into the kitchen now and get yourself a little egg,' she said and dragged her lips down towards reluctant mirth.

A week after Lena went back to scrub for the nuns Frankie's cat gave birth to three kittens in the straw. She had never seen new-born kittens before. Their tiny paws, like blackberries, and blunt, bad-tempered snouts enchanted her. Her mother told her that people drown kittens in a bucket, but she didn't believe it. No one would do such a thing.

'Any road,' she told herself, 'I'll keep them hid.' Her employer seemed older since Lena's departure. Maybe she wouldn't bother with the long climb all the way up to the attic.

It was the little girl's first Christmas away from home. She couldn't leave. It wasn't just the kittens. With no other help in the house Mrs Deveney needed her.

She got two shillings from McMahon the schoolteacher and spent it on a basket of oranges with silver paper around the handle, and halfpennies hidden in the fruit. She sent this by messenger to her house, with a bottle of port for her ma and da.

In the morning she cooked the Christmas dinner for Mrs Deveney and McMahon, swathed in a big holland apron which showed off her waist. Afterwards she stole milk for the mother cat and a glass of sherry for herself and went upstairs to play with the kittens.

They kneaded their mother with the tiny thorns of their claws, tumbling on the bed where she had imagined twins to have proceeded from the beguiling fatness of Lena the cook. She was all right now. Mrs Deveney got her violet powder for her nightmares.

She picked up the kittens and held them to her chest. They depended on her. She loved them more than all the world. She still knew nothing, but she was learning. Refinement and religion, you picked them up as you went along.

The three kittens were different colours – yellow, and striped and a black one swirled with white stars like the star that had led the wise men to Bethlehem with their gifts of inestimable value. She named them Gold and Frankincense and Myrrh.

To Tempt a Woman

The two old men entered Moran's Fashion House accompanied, unknown to themselves, by the ghosts of their lives. A rich spoor of dung and straw patterned the shop's royal blue carpet in the wake of their boots and there echoed off their insignificant persons surprising bass and alto notes from beer and whisky, from dreams of women that made random raids on the derelict imagination, from liniment and black tea and blood.

Miss Hartigan sensed the spectres before she sighted their human catalysts. She left off the cutting of a good wool broadcloth and rushed forward to defend her stock. 'Do ye want something?' She still held the long-nosed shears. A measuring tape, snaked around her shoulders, seemed there to lay witness to the girth of her chest.

The two old men gazed around the coats and corsets, the boots and bales of cloth, as if they were in a foreign country and all the tribes spoke among themselves in a foreign language. 'Sure we do,' they said. 'We'd like a fur coat.'

She saw them as a couple of bowsies, too addled to know where they had wandered in to. 'I'd like one too,' she sneered.

'We're not buyin' it for you,' they quickly assured her. 'Are you coddin'?'

She eyed the fabric of their overcoats, tweed that had developed a sheen as if something had chewed it.

'Here!' One of them pulled from his pocket a thick wad of

dirty notes of money, understanding her look. They studied with interest the set of teeth she displayed then, not home grown but hard and white as lime.

'Mink or musquash?' she smiled.

'What squash?'

'That's like a turnip.'

'We wouldn't go for that.'

'How much is mink?'

When she told them they knew they were not in a foreign country but on a strange planet. 'There is opossum,' Miss Hartigan said.

'Quids?' One old man rubbed his thumb and forefinger together, harsh in his fright. 'Name your price.' She named it and he reacted with ire. 'Do you think we're amadans?'

'Was there not another shaggin' creature on Noah's Ark? Lynx, weasel, badger, stoat?' They tried to help her out.

She knew that male irritation could quickly turn to fury. She was familiar with the bilious strength of old men. Suits might be ripped and mirrors kicked to pieces. 'There is rabbit,' she conceded. At first she pronounced it as if she would neither eat nor wear it and then she forced some eagerness into her voice. 'It's very popular. Also known as a coney or a fun fur. Twenty pounds,' she added. She waited, suspending her breath until they relaxed into their normal state of unease.

'We'd have to see it on.'

'Would you like me to try it on?'

This suggestion cheered them up. 'God, no! She's not a heifer.' They pointed to a young girl behind a mysterious woman's counter labelled 'haberdashery'. She wore a white blouse with a fretwork of flowers on the collar. Tod Cuddy imagined such a presence in his kitchen, her round little face pink from the heat of stove or washtub. Would she ever get used, he wondered, to the stream where at one point the butter churns were dipped for cooling and at another spot you had your wash and far down, where no one could see, you used the running water for a toilet? He only had a son. It seemed a big thing thirty years ago when the boy was born. Now they couldn't see eye to eye at all. It had been assumed that when he grew up the lad would get married and take over the farm but he only wanted a TV. Since they got it he had done nothing except sprawl at its screen watching black and white pictures of people blowing each other's brains out or having a go at each other in bed, taking longer over it than you'd take to eat your dinner. They spent their evenings in the cold kitchen in front of the telly. Occasionally Tadgh drove into town for chips or an awful thing called a pissa. Tod was too long widowed to think of starting out with another woman but he did nine Holy Hours and went off the drink for the duration, hoping that someone would fall for the lad, knowing it would take a miracle.

It was after this that he met a man called Ned Flavin who was trying to get rid of his daughter. 'Why doesn't she go out and get herself a guy like any normal girl?' Cuddy cautiously enquired.

'Phena's only seventeen. She hasn't got around to that sort of thing.'

'Is she a swank? Is she used to finery?' Tod interrogated.

'Get away. She hasn't a bean. She's a nice little thing. The nuns taught her to make a lovely brown soda. Mrs Flavin prefers a white sliced from the local Spar. Presents it at table as if she cut the slices with the cheeks of her backside.' Flavin's laugh came out as an unhappy growl. He couldn't tell a stranger why he had to get his daughter married. He couldn't mention the letter from the nuns.

Cuddy approached his son that evening and proposed Phena Flavin to him in marriage. The lad did not remove his gaze from the screen but continued trying to catch with his mouth the Tayto Crisps tossed from their bag by hand. 'Do you have any feelings in the matter?' Tod persevered. Tadgh shrugged. 'She's a nice little thing,' Cuddy coaxed. 'You'd want to shake yourself.'

'What do you mean?' His boy now turned from the entertainment, amazed.

'You'd be expected to have a fresh shirt at the ready and to clean your teeth regular.'

'My teeth are clent regular.' Menacingly he bared at his father his durable but unappealing fangs.

'So you're keen,' the father murmured, noting with relief that the screen had reclaimed the lad's attention.

When Cuddy met Phena Flavin he was taken aback. She wasn't a nice little thing as her father had said. The girl was a beauty. There were plenty of females that you'd look at in the town, grand big ones with their figures bursting out of their ganseys, but this creature was of a different order. Perfection sat upon her the way it did on a primrose in a field. 'She could get any guy,' Tod burst out in fright.

'Of course we'd like to see her settled with a nice bit of land, but we wouldn't ask her to do anything against her will,' Mrs Flavin said. 'She'd have to be tempted.'

Tod shook his head hopelessly at the notion of Tadgh tempting anyone. 'We're not short of a bob,' he offered doubtfully.

Mrs Flavin smiled to put him at his ease and offered him a slice of Brennan's bread spread with Spar strawberry jam. She was only half her husband's age but there was a coarseness about her that seemed to infect everything she touched. He couldn't eat the meal, thinking of what Flavin had said about the slicing of the bread. When he was going, the girl got his greasy coat from the hall.

'Are you at school still?' he asked her quickly.

'I've done my Leaving,' she told him.

'I suppose you have big plans.'

'I'd like to go to the uni,' she said, and she blushed.

'Now, miss,' her father warned.

The old men had no ideas about tempting women. Neither of them respected Mrs Flavin's view in the matter. She would probably speak of gin or kisses. In the end Cuddy had the inspiration of speaking to the priest in confession. 'If a man wanted to tempt a woman, what item, failing himself, would render her helpless to resist?' he pondered. The priest answered without any hesitation that no woman born could resist the provocation of a fur coat.

★

They marched down the main street, grim with excitement, swinging the bag by its waxed string handles. They stopped and laughed out loud as if they had pulled off some daring feat. 'A drink, man!' Flavin proposed. They could hear the fur coat languorously shifting in the bag, inside its undergarment of white tissue.

When several pints had worn the edges off his nerves Cuddy found a question rising in his mind and at last, like a belch, it had to be let out. 'Is it fair on the girl?' He was thinking of having to tell her to bring her square of newspaper down to the stream. Would she remind him that this was 1967, that men had landed on the moon and the Beatles were selling in millions? In his mind the fur coat had already imbued her with a glamour that put her out of reach.

'You know nothing about the case.' Flavin rounded on him in a fury.

'What is it?' Cuddy was suddenly frightened. 'What are you trying to tell me? Is she used goods?'

'I've had a letter,' the other old man said bitterly. 'From a Sister Felicity. Did you ever hear tell of a nun with a name like Felicity?'

Flavin fell into a thunderous silence and Cuddy wagged his head from side to side as if making a comment, although in fact it was embarrassment. Nothing more was said. He was shy in matters relating to women. At first he felt a profound disappointment that Phena was not as he had imagined her but after he had taken two or three whiskies he was glad she had some awful bloody secret. Whenever he felt sorry for her he could think about that and hold it against her.

Phena turned cautiously from her task at the table when she heard her father's voice.

'I have to talk to you, miss.'

She could tell from his tone that he had been drinking and when she met his eye she recognised the livid and bewildered look.

'I know,' she said. 'I know what it is.'

'What do you know?' her father demanded.

'The letter. Sister Felicity told me.'

'It would be better if that matter was not mentioned at all.'

She could not contain her excitement. 'There's a woman in America, a past pupil from the convent, wants a bright girl to look after her children. Sister Felicity said that I was her brightest star. The woman will pay for me to go to college.'

'You want to go?' Flavin said.

'Oh, Daddy, I do.'

'America!' Flavin spat on the ground and she had to jump to save her shoe. 'Have you no shame? Do you think I don't know what you're at, trying to make little of me and all I stand for? What would people say if a daughter of Ned Flavin hightailed it off to the Yanks?'

'What would I do here?' the girl persisted, although she was shaking.

'Come here to me now.' Flavin spoke more gently to his daughter. 'I have something for you.'

She watched cautiously as he produced the bag. 'Oh, it's from Moran's,' she said in surprise.

He shook the container as if it was a sack of potatoes and the coat slid out onto a chair. It looked improper against the bare wood frame and beneath a baleful picture of the Sacred Heart.

The girl ran towards it, her fingers reaching out to touch it, but she held them back because she had been gutting fish. 'Oh,' she said. 'Oh, the Lord save us, that's lovely. Whose is it?'

'It's for you,' the old man said and for an instant, when she smiled at him, there was a bond of love between them. 'Now, lassie, we've got a man for you to marry,' he said quickly. 'Will you take him?' He was afraid of the emotional moment.

She slowly wiped her hands on an apron and put out a finger to the coat. 'Could I see him?'

'No.' He shook his head. 'There'll be no nonsense. You'll meet him at the altar.'

She sat on the chair beside the coat. Her hand went furtively into the pocket and caressed it. 'Where would we live?' she said. 'What would he do to me?'

She knew he would not dream of answering such questions. Already his look had turned to scorn for her foolish talk. She began to cry and the old man laughed delightedly for her hand, still stained with the blood of herrings, had fastened itself into the softness of the fur and would not let go.

Thatcher's Britain

Ten Hail Marys and he'll phone. She said the prayers slowly, trying to put feeling into them. The harder she concentrated the more the words lost their meaning. *Fruit of thy womb.* Imagine, though, if little currants came out down there. Or pink blossoms that would scatter when you ran. The reality was more devious, things running riot everywhere, unseen.

All day she had heard a baby crying from some other part of the house, like a donkey braying in a far meadow. She tried to imagine what colour it was, black or chestnut or the dry, flat brown of winter leaves. Would his mother give him a bit of bread and sugar to comfort him? Her own mother used to give her her vest to suck when she was desolate. It became a craving, after you were weaned, the taste of your mother.

Two hundred drops of rain and he'll ring. She made an effort to keep track but the blobs of water slithered into each other on the window like drunks at a dance. Wouldn't you think now water was clear as crystal? Lepping with organisms, in point of fact. Every drop of London water you drank had passed through nine people. She preferred to think it had passed through a woman than a man. The way her hand went to the phone and began to dial reminded her of a character she had seen in the pictures, strangling a woman. He did it as if his hands were nothing to do with him. There was a kind of magic in it, though. She just poked the dial and there he was.

'I miss you,' she said.

There was a small chastising silence and she listened hard,

not even wishing to miss the sigh as he spoke. 'I told you not to ring here.'

'Will I see you so?'

'Perhaps. Later.'

'Will you want some dinner?' Kathleen coaxed.

'I'll have eaten.' He said it grudgingly, as if she had extracted information under duress.

'It's only that I've been invited to dine with someone else,' she quickly defended herself.

'Ah, well. Some other evening.'

'It's an early dinner. I'll be back. What time will I see you?'

'I'm afraid I have no idea.'

'I'll be back.'

To soften the lie she had told him, as well as to put in the hours until she saw him, she tied on a scarf and went out into the rain. There was a little Italian place not too far away where they treated you nicely if you were on your own and you could get a beautiful lasagne at reasonable cost. Her money was nearly gone, but she would find work now her spirits were improved. On the tube she sat opposite a black woman who clutched a parcel labelled 'Mrs Blessings Okara'. A young rabbi, seated beside her, murmured something to her and she could not quite hear, but it seemed he was advising her that you could buy very good diamonds in Harrods. Her attention was taken by an Indian family who occupied a whole row of seats and she was mesmerised by the glittering painted toes of the doe-like teenage girl. She could not imagine how they saw her. She had no clear picture of herself, having been schooled against the sin of self-absorption, but she was going to see him and she felt her happiness must be plain for all to see, stretched across her like a rainbow.

When she got to the restaurant she looked in the window and there were couples already there, early diners, discussing the menu over a drink. Her elation vanished. By the time she saw him he would be full of a dinner eaten alone or with someone else, consumed in that mannerly way he had, the prongs of the fork vanishing between his lips and then only a vague abstraction of the eye and a faint budging of his chin betrayed that any activity was going on at all. You never saw him swallowing. He had taken her out to dinner once and she knew she loved him because she ate snails to please him. That was how they got around to sex as well. You would do anything for someone if you loved them.

She went instead to a joint with loud music. Her salad was full of hard bits, red cabbage and brown beans and sweet corn and lumps of onion. The entire nation must be consumed with the state of its bowels, the grub they ate. No wonder they looked undernourished. Rubble like this would go through you like a dose of salts. She was suddenly homesick for the salads back home, a few petals of soft green lettuce, a hard boiled egg with buttercup centre, a sliver of home-cured ham and a sprig of scallion. With her mouth full of red cabbage she burst into tears.

What was it she saw in him? At first it was what she thought of as his Englishness, his beautiful manners and the way he spoke, without a trace of harshness. She had lost her way and looked around for a respectable person to give her directions. He offered her the shelter of his umbrella, 'to protect your beautiful hair.'

'Ah, sure 'tis only old wire,' she mocked.

'Gold wire,' he said. When it was time for him to go he left her his umbrella. 'You can return it when the weather changes.' A gentleman like that would never be unkind to you. She hung his umbrella on the mantelpiece where she could watch it from her bed, a piece of England, furled tautly as a new oak leaf. Every so often she would shake out its folds and smell its good fabric smell and know that she had left behind forever the mean little black umbrellas of home, always busted, the spokes sticking out at all angles so that they lay on the step like a mangled crow.

'Call me J,' he said. She thought of him as Jay, like a bird, but the few notes he sent her were tersely signed with an initial. She imagined he must be something very high up and secret in the government and of course, as he was compelled to mention, he had a life before he met her, all the trimmings. He could not speak about his job and was too discreet to discuss his personal life but she was content to hear him talk about things he liked, good wine, the opera, poems, books, ballet, restaurants where whole sides of beef were carved.

'Oh, I'd love all that,' she said.

'You should have it,' he smiled. There was such happiness in the assertion that she would like to have had it bottled and sent back home as a tonic, only they would have laughed at his accent.

He took her to a restaurant with candles on the table and small silver vessels of flowers such as you'd see on the altar. In fact the whole event had about it the air of a religious ceremony. When the waiter poured a sup of wine J raised it up to the light and twirled it round and then stuck his nose in the glass and swilled a drop in his mouth with a mystical look. Kathleen expected to hear a little bell ringing. 'To England!' he toasted. After he had drunk some wine he grew maudlin. He raised his glass again. 'To loved ones left behind.' She thought first of his wife and then of her mother. As always, she pictured her mother in wellingtons and a man's overcoat, her hands mottled mauve like Swede turnips, her face closed off against the danger of emotion.

She had been shocked when she arrived in London to discover the young Irish people living in derelict houses with broken windows and boarded up doors, paying no rent. She took a room in a house in Notting Hill where there was a respectable Irish family, but one night they vanished and she was surrounded by silent people with amber skin and dark-skinned people who played loud music and addressed their neighbours by shouting out the window. All the women had children and because she had no child they had nothing to say to her but she thought that inside they must feel the same as she did. The things you did at home did not apply in this unrelated landscape. There was no one to advise you. She found out that the beautiful buildings and shops in the heart of the city were occupied only by politicians and pilgrims. One day she looked out her window and the entire street was filled with foreigners, and a white man with no legs who was in a wheeled cart pulled along by a giant Alsatian dog. They were singing and cheering as if they had won a great victory and she stayed in her room all day, petrified. In the evening she crept down to the corner shop for something to eat and the Pakistani shopkeeper was giving out about the Notting Hill carnival.

She kept to herself and found work in a nice respectable coffee shop where each customer got their own pot of coffee and little pastries that were eaten with the side of a fork. The girls there were Spanish and Italian, and a Puerto Rican. They did not speak much English and spent their free time going to American films. Their lives were built around these excursions. They brought in bags of sandwiches and spoke gutturally in their own language throughout the performance, occasionally lifting their eyes to make admiring groans when Michelle Pfeiffer or Julia Roberts achieved a passionate understanding with some fellow strangely burnished beneath his clothes, as if he had been sanded and then waxed.

J never asked that of her. 'I have nothing to give you,' he said. 'I want nothing from you except to admire you.' He turned up his hands to show both their emptiness and that they concealed no tricks. She gazed with pleasure on the smoothness of his palms and his short, clean nails. At home, if a man said he didn't want a cup of tea, there was a moral obligation to brew up at once. When she pressed him to kiss her he refused before obliging her with a dry, shy kiss and then he smiled at her sadly and said, 'Oh, I must just have another,' and he began to consume her in small mouthfuls, before falling on her, like a dog on its dinner. She had been shocked by his eagerness, shocked by the whole thing, which gave her a sudden sharp understanding of her mother, but afterwards he was so grateful that she could only feel she had not given him enough. The awful thing was that although she had not enjoyed the event, it made her fall in love with him. Now instead of his umbrella, she carried around the whole baggage of his life, the plays and poems and sides of beef. J had a phone installed so that she would not have to run down to the public phone in the hall which was adorned with notices from women offering to torture men in return for money. After that he rarely called. Sometimes she did not see him for weeks on end.

She could not tell if it was him she missed or the life he lived without her. She was so obsessed with the thought of the things he did apart from her that she could not be happy when they were together. 'You must not sit around like a servant girl waiting for romance,' he rebuked her. She tried to explain that it wasn't just romance she craved, it was the life he had mentioned. He laughed and told her the things he described did not belong to him, she could avail herself of them any time she wished. He made out a list of places for her to visit, but the galleries and concert halls were full of sour Americans disguised in expensive English raincoats, and she thought that culture was a cold thing when you could not laugh with someone at the pictures of naked men and women or touch their hand when the music was soulful. Once he mentioned a club he belonged to, a gentlemen's club. 'It's rather grand,' he said in that way he had, as if apologising.

'Take me there,' she said.

'You'd be bored,' he smiled. But he had spoken of his club with reverence and in her mind it became the equivalent of paradise.

When she was not waiting for the telephone she spent most of her time in a park, walking and sometimes talking to other foreigners who sat on benches. It was to one of these she confided that she was pregnant. 'Go home,' he said, not to dismiss her, but to use his small store of English words usefully. She longed for home but she could not go back even though when the baby arrived everyone would dote on it. She remembered the merriment of the younger women, the careless slide into domesticity and how sometimes when they had had eight or nine kids they would shake themselves off and go to university or enter politics. The women always ridiculed sex, removing the sting with a swipe of sarcasm. She missed their softness that was like the softness of rain, and the knife edge of their humour. She missed them so much it was like a sickness. And then – lunatic – she found herself nostalgic for the men, whose irresponsible ways meant you never had to take them seriously. She stayed in the flat for a week counting whorls and dots on the virulent old wallpaper and then she just stayed there because the coffee shop seemed too decorous a place for her now. She began to look forward to having a child. As soon as the notion of it became a reality she felt stronger. She made up her mind to go and look for J, although she had no idea where to find him. Then she remembered his club and looked it up in the phone book. It amazed her to think she could have gone there at any time but had only got the courage because she was at the end of her tether.

A flunkey took her coat at the door. 'Who are you meeting?'

'J,' she said boldly, because she didn't actually know his name.

Like magic he directed her up the stairs and told her to turn left for the visitors' lounge. And it was kind of like a fairy tale, the big curving staircase and the ceiling dripping with chandeliers. She ventured into a room full of men in suits and roosted on a hard leather sofa. While she waited, a galdy oul' lad with his eye on her bust asked her would she care for a spot of bubbly. She was looking around her all the time to see would J come in and her new friend urged her to relax. But she couldn't. She didn't fit in. She could tell from the look of the club members that dowdiness was *de rigueur*. People were staring at her dress. The champagne arrived but they hadn't the proper glasses and put big silver tankards on the table.

'Are they pure silver?' she asked.

'Not exactly,' the old lad said in his buttered shortbread voice. Not *exactly*. Tin more like. And then she had to jump up and tell him she needed the toilet.

Ah, now, that was beautiful. She had an urge to write home to her mother about that toilet. The long mirrors were like looking into a lake. There were flowers and little bottles of water, like Lourdes water only they were for drinking, and ladies who dabbed their noses in a very discreet way, as if it was an act akin to wiping your bottom. The women had a vegetable look, like something grown underwater or nurtured in a walled garden. There wasn't a mark on them. Their bland bosoms had been sketched in by some artist with averted eye. She went into a cubicle to check and, sure enough, her aunt had arrived. Already there was a mark showing on her brocade skirt. She patched herself up with toilet paper and poked out her head. 'Has anybody here got a sanitary towel – the loan of a sanitary towel – please?' The women said nothing although one of them smiled at her. Possibly they had a different arrangement down there, or had found some long-term method of coping with it. 'Thank you anyway,' she said. She could feel them watching the small scarlet stain shaped like a star when she left. Probably they would think she had been shot in the arse. She couldn't go back into the big room for she felt certain that whatever the ladies might think, the men would know. She was sorry about her gentleman, left alone in all that stuffy grandeur to drink champagne out of tin mugs.

She walked around the city for hours, not caring that she was bleeding, bumping into tourists who were looking for strange women to sleep with, and lonely foreigners with zombie eyes. When the night had consumed all its leftover souls she stood alone in some big gaunt place that was marked by a monumental arch. She leaned against the arch to rest and there, beneath it, was a little bundle rolled up in a pink blanket. 'Oh, a baby!' she cried. Someone had left a baby. As she pulled back the blanket she thanked Saint Anthony for finding a replacement for her own little lost baby. A girl, barely teenage, reared up her head. She was rickety thin, her face as grey as nuns' porridge. Kathleen gazed, first in amazement and then in pity. 'Oh, you creature!' she said.

The girl eyed her sleepily. 'Got any money?'

'What you need is nourishment,' Kathleen said firmly. 'You need a proper place to sleep.'

The girl told her to fuck herself. Her little sparrow's wrist struck out and while Kathleen was nursing her face the girl snatched her handbag and vanished like a skinny demon into the dark.

Once, on the underground, she heard this announcement: 'If passenger Pavelzciek is on this train, would he please proceed to Trafalgar Square, where his mother is waiting.' Everyone laughed except Kathleen who closed her eyes and felt with Pavelzciek's mother the panic of recognising no one, of being left alone with the guzzling pigeons, afraid to move from this seething spot in case you never again laid eyes on the only thing you knew.

The most shaming thing was that he wasn't even married. A few weeks afterwards she spotted him getting into a taxi and she followed in another taxi. She knocked on the door of a house in Marylebone that bore his name beneath a bell and barged in past him, into his flat, and without a word she had poked into everything, into his fridge with its little tinfoil ashtrays of frozen meals for one. 'You haven't even got a wife,' she accused him.

He defended himself, holding up his empty palms in that way he had. 'I never said I was married.' He was watching her with an odd sort of gravity and it took her a minute to realise that she had hurt his feelings. 'I'm very fond of you,' he said. 'Don't think I have been hiding anything from you. Quite the opposite. I have been sparing you. You and I have shared a remarkable happiness in spite of our differences but as far as my life is concerned, darling girl, you would be bored and unhappy.'

She tried to make sense of this but she was confused. She had imagined his flat would be very grand but it was shabby, not with the respectable dowdiness of his club but in a lonely way, as if life was dwindling around him. Kathleen thought that even though she had made it out of the sticks and got herself a man with a very high up job in the government, the subtleties always eluded her and possibly she wasn't really very bright.

She ate a little bit of the red cabbage from her salad and some brown bread and butter. The rain had stopped and black taxis, shiny as eels, hissed on the wet road. A weak sun put a halo of mist on rooftops and a faint tinge in the sky, a delicate lemon yellow like ladies' pee. She walked back, thinking of a dog she once had, a wall-eyed creature called Scrap, which had no idea of its function as sheepdog and stole a lamb and smuggled it into its bed and nurtured it after its pups had been drowned. She bought a bunch of anemones, thinking they would catch the last rays of sun through her window and draw the eye away from the wicked little sink with its pipes exposed, like a spiteful beggar showing off his deformities, but the sun had gone down and the Jamaicans had begun to fight and she had set herself the task of counting stars as they took their places in the sky by the time she heard the doorbell's peevish drone. 'Terrible day.' He kissed her cheek. 'You don't know how I envy you your simple life.' He kissed her lips in a fatherly way and she began to relax. There wasn't anything devouring in his kisses. They weren't even exciting. They made her sleepy. When she was in his arms she couldn't imagine why she suffered so much when they were apart. He lowered her onto the bed and his jacket grazed her face. It smelled of wool and had a hard edge like a rope. His legs grew restless and he grasped and pulled at her as if he was trying to get his footing on a cliff face. Something about her – not her personality, she knew – had tripped a switch, and he was off on his demented quest like a prisoner trying to dig a tunnel with a teaspoon.

To make the time pass she thought about a Russian she had met in the park. He was beautifully dressed but had the look of a refugee. His sad face gave her permission to sit down beside him, and to break the ice she asked him why he had come to London. It was the phrase 'Thatcher's Britain', he said. It made him think of a pleasant place with thatched houses and fields of hay and employment for all. She asked him if he liked the city. He said nothing but stared ahead and she thought that behind that gaze, both blank and intent, he still saw a sun-warmed scene of honest labour and contentment. 'What do you like best?' she persisted. When he told her the rats' kitchen, she thought it was a joke – some dosshouse he was staying at – but she could see he hadn't a sense of humour. Actually, it was interesting. It was an attraction they had at Regent's Park zoo, a cage that had been equipped with chairs and tables and utensils and every manner of home comfort to see how the rats would adapt to domestic life, and they lived like lords, in and out of their kitchen, holding little tea parties. 'It is proof,' said the Russian, 'that any creature, given a chance, will improve itself.'

One of these days she would go to Regent's Park to see for herself the rats' kitchen but in the meantime she got pleasure from taking out the notion of it now and then and turning it over, the finicky little creatures entering this minefield of a

cage, full of obstacles and breakables. She pictured them puz‐
zling over the cups with their dainty little claws, gnawing at the
legs of chairs to get the feel of them. Had someone given them
an inkling, a bit of training, perhaps, in the correct use of
knives and forks, or had they to bash along like everyone else?
She saw them seated around the kitchen table sipping their
cups of tea, arresting the crumbs of cake on their plate with tiny
little silver forks, perhaps making small talk in rat language and
scarcely able to believe their luck.

～

Horrible Luck

The two middle-aged women breakfasted together every day. They had nothing in common except their age. Their relationship was based on Mrs Lemon's familiarity with Mrs Lee's underwear, and Mrs Lee's acquaintance with Mrs Lemon's private life.

'How are you today? said Mrs Lee.

'Horrible,' said Mrs Lemon.

'What's horrible?' Mrs Lee still had an eye on her newspaper.

'Me luck,' said Mrs Lemon.

Camilla Lee generously detached herself from Auberon Waugh to give her fullest sympathy to the less fortunate woman. 'Is it himself?'

Mrs Lemon lit a cigarette and commenced a vigorous bout of scrubbing. 'Haven't seen hide nor hair of himself this past six months.' Turds of ash fell from her gasper and as she cleaned the kitchen counter it was dimmed under a coating of lava. Camilla watched in fascination as the trail of grey ash replaced Frederick's more wholesome trail of brown breadcrumbs. Mrs Lemon began to cry. 'It's this letter.' She rooted in her clothing and handed across a sheet of notepaper. Mrs Lee scanned the childish scrawl. It was about St Jude. It enumerated his miracles and favours and attributed oddly material benefits to his supporters, new cars or houses, a big lottery win. It urged the recipient of the note to pass it on to another. 'If you do not do so,' it unsportingly suggested, 'horrible luck will follow.'

'A chain letter,' Mrs Lee laughed. 'It's just rubbish. Here! We'll throw it in the bin. Have some coffee.'

All Mrs Lemon's luck was horrible. Her husband was violent and her children uncontrollable. The woman was so dazed with sedatives and nicotine that she was a fire hazard as well as a terrible housekeeper. Mrs Lee sometimes wondered why she employed her but Mrs Lemon was both her good deed and her talisman. One needed a good deed to propitiate the gods and she liked having her there for comparison, to think that this was the alternative. She herself had married wisely and kept her looks.

Mrs Lemon lumbered back to the table and sat down, rubbing tears from her withered yellow skin. She leaned forward for the sugar and a bolt of ash detached itself and landed in the butter.

'There!' Mrs Lee said kindly.

For some reason the episode bucked her up. It made her count her blessings. Life, as she always said, was not merely a matter of luck but of management and she had managed hers nicely. She worked well that morning, dined with pleasure, but without wine, for she was going to a party. It rained when she was emerging late that evening and there weren't any taxis, but a boy with whom she was vaguely acquainted offered her a lift.

'It's kind of you,' Camilla said. She didn't think so at all. She supposed he wanted something. Kim Taylor was young and beautifully made. She admired the selfish curve of his mouth with an edge of temper on it. Young women would think it sensitive. He had a reputation with women. He glanced at her with his piercing turquoise eyes. *I'm enjoying this*, she thought. She supposed he was anxious to drop her off and be with some girl. This did not make her uneasy. She had her aura too. Mrs Lee was successful and had plenty of money and all men liked that. They drove through the night in silence and comfort, each thinking their own thoughts and well pleased with themselves. She was looking forward to tomorrow and, before that, to her tremendously comfortable bed with dear old Frederick asleep in it. They had no children and she thought this was

probably a good thing. Children rarely understood how pleasant and absorbing the lives of older people could be. She had
no idea what the boy was thinking. Well, how could she? He
turned slowly and touched her cheek as the rest of the cars
edged forward at the lights like greyhounds at a starting line.
'You're very pretty,' he whispered.

'Don't be ridiculous,' she said, rather pleased.

She was woken in the morning, as usual, by a series of trum-
peting laments like a ship bewildered by fog as Mrs Lemon let
herself in and began to unshroud herself of waterproofs.
Frederick had gone hours ago, departed at dawn, considerately
silent, to make money. The smell of coffee ascended. This was
the signal for Mrs Lee to get out of bed but as she rose up on
an elbow something very peculiar happened. She rolled over,
gave a low chortle and then stretched out her body until all the
nerves and sinews set up a humming. After that she got up and
went downstairs.

Later in the day there was a moment when she studied her
reflection with a new interest. Pretty. It was a long time since
anyone had called her pretty. Actually, when young she had
been striking more than pretty. The word suggested that its
bearer needed no other function than to be. It was a tinkling
word. It was . . . absurd. She went out to lunch and success-
fully snared a year's advertising from a French cosmetic
company.

In the middle of the afternoon the phone rang. 'It's Kim.'

'Kim who?' she said, but her heart, fired by a single glass of
Chablis, did a silly dance.

'Come to the opera with me. I've got tickets for tomorrow.'

'I can't. I have an engagement.' She took a deep breath and
added formally, 'Nice of you to think of me.'

'Cancel your engagement,' he persisted. 'I'll call in the
morning.' He hung up before she had time to put him in his
place.

She could never have guessed how pleasant it would be, sitting
next to his composed beauty and listening to the beautiful

music. There was a starkly sexual quality to his self-assurance. When not attending to the music he had the knack of devoting himself to her completely, ignoring the haunted eyes of younger women.

On the way home he stopped the car. 'What do you want, Kim?' she said and the young man replied, 'I want to go to bed with you.'

'Don't be ridiculous,' she said again.

He stroked her cheek and her mouth with his finger. Then he sighed, turned back to the traffic, drove her home in silence. She passed the night in a frenzy of longing.

Mrs Lemon's husband came back and gave her a black eye. She sat at the kitchen table and wept. He went away again. Her daughter, fifteen, got pregnant. Howls dimmed the hoover's hum and ash gathered in funereal piles. Sharon fell off her boyfriend's motorcycle and she lost the baby. Mrs Lemon grieved amid the alien cornflakes. The house looked terrible. Camilla thought she should give Mrs Lemon a few days off and get one of those cleaning agencies in to do a really good job, but Mrs Lemon shook her head, scattering tears and the dust of tobacco leaves. 'I'm better kept busy. I haven't been myself. It's me nerves. You've no idea what it's like having a threat hanging over you. I can't get on with my life. I keep thinking something bad will happen.'

Considering the normal run of Mrs Lemon's fortune, Camilla could not suppress a smile. 'Whatever can you mean?'

'It's that letter,' said poor Mrs Lemon in a passion. 'That chain.'

'But I threw it out.'

Mrs Lemon excavated the portable black bucket she called her handbag and fished out the crumpled note. 'You have to pass it on. If I don't me luck will be horrible,' Mrs Lemon said stubbornly. 'If I do, there's some other poor soul's misery on my conscience.'

'Now this is plain foolishness and you know it.' Camilla spoke sternly to her domestic. She made a similar speech to Kim Taylor. He had begun sending letters, silly, trivial scraps of flattery better suited to a dizzy blonde of nineteen than to an imposing woman. 'Kim, I do wish you would stop. I'm married, you know.' She listened hard into the line. 'Look,' she added kindly, 'we could talk about it over a drink.' She put down the phone with a shaking hand. Dear God, he had nearly slipped away.

When he drove her back to his apartment there was the briefly unpleasant sensation that she was losing something of value. It was like watching her credit card slide through a grating in the road. She pushed him off feebly. 'I'm not really used to this sort of thing,' she protested.

'You are sweet,' he said.

'Darling Milly,' he wrote (no one had ever called her Milly – it too blatantly rhymed with 'silly'). 'I dreamed all night of my sweet, delicious nymph. How pretty you looked, all dimpled with bliss . . .'

Of course she did not take this seriously. All the same, the succulent little tributes began to assume a sort of integrity. Camilla was changing. She grew softer. She was so happy that she felt able to dispense this benefit. She could be genuinely nice to Mrs Lemon, for instance, and the poor thing grew less abject, for which her employer awarded her a very nice knitted suit, hardly worn, and some advice. 'You have to take control of your life. It is a mistaken belief that you get out of life what you put into it. In fact, you get what you take out of it. Realise your own value. The solution to all your ills lies within your own hands.' So beguiling was her new womanly charm that Mrs Lemon slavishly pursued her prescription. She got a barring order against her husband, though they sometimes met up to go to the pictures or visited a hotel for sex. She gave up Valium and took up yoga. She asked advice about face creams and once Camilla was touched to see her squirting herself as if to extinguish a fire with her new spray of Joy. 'Here!' she said on impulse. 'Take this one for yourself, Mrs Lemon.' And she gave her a half-full bottle of Calèche.

'That one is stale,' Mrs Lemon said. 'And my name is Rosemary.'

Sometimes when she rose from Kim's bed, heavy with gratification and drenched in compliments, she was surprised by her reflection in the mirror, of a tousled middle-aged woman. She expected to see what he described, someone sweet and pretty. And young. In some ways she felt younger than him. She had always been in control of her life but no one had ever taken charge of her. They had not understood the burden a success-ful woman carries, each day having to don her brittle armour of conquest. He had recomposed her, had braved the daunting battlements to rescue the little princess imprisoned within. She was weary of attainment. She wanted to lie down and be praised for the pinkness of her toes. She felt now like a sugar-icing flower on a birthday cake. That is how she *felt*. But what did she think?

'What are your thoughts, Camilla?' a client asked her during an important meeting.

She tried to compose an expression of intelligence on her face, which had lapsed into an aspect of carnal vegetation. *My breasts*, she realised. *I was thinking about my breasts*. She used to look upon these sturdy organs rather as Mrs Thatcher might, like an advance guard which declared her sex and at the same time avowed that it was not to be trifled with. Now they were heavy flowers that sprang from her ribs, narcotic and exotic. She could never have imagined that breasts could have such personality, could crave and declare. Now she understood the French artists and their models and the nature of the great works that occasionally ensued their alliance; that art might be sex and sex might be art. With an effort of will she brought her mind back to the business of the moment and brought the meeting to a conclusion.

'You are a marvel,' her client told her, 'and you get younger all the time.'

Now and again she had the uneasy notion that she was indulging her body too much. It was getting the upper hand. There was the feeling that it sulked if she gave any priority to cerebral issues. The great explosion of happiness that had accompanied the start of her affair was sometimes overtaken by a dreamlike lethargy. The curious idea came to her that Kim had sucked all the steel out of her body and left behind only accessible flesh. Employing his array of compliments he had filleted her. She was becoming like one of those pallid boneless joints that butchers sell for easy carving. She let her hair grow long and her voice became gentler. When they spoke on the phone it was the merest kitten's mew. Now that she had been made meek she discovered a whole new world of women she had not noticed before, young women with eyes of slate and bulletproof shoulder pads, ever watchful of successful older women, not to learn from them but to discern their weakness. After a long lunch with Kim she found that one of these girls had taken over her meeting. When Camilla entered Amy said smoothly, 'I hope you're feeling better, Mrs Lee.' Camilla felt sorry for the girl and the aridness of her ambition. While she worked she was assailed by pangs of emotion. Gusts of erotic longing swept her off her feet. Sometimes she felt euphoric and full of energy. At other times she was morbid and breathless and obsessive, as if she had spent all day searching the attic for something that could not be found.

'You're working too hard,' Frederick said.

'Nonsense,' she said, and tears filled her eyes.

He put an arm around her and kissed her fondly. 'You're worn out. You're working too many nights. You're getting that demented look career women sometimes have.'

She took a few days off and her languid body wilted into fever. She was unable to eat anything but devoured from her precious hoard of Kim's letters the sugared phrases to which she had become addict. All she had for company was Mrs Lemon, who hitched up her skirt to show off her new oestrogen patch. 'You should try one,' she crowed. 'It gives you back your libido.'

The malady left her weak and abstracted. When she returned to work she found herself increasingly reliant on young Amy. She went to the doctor to find out what was wrong with her. He examined all her lovely parts without remark and then confessed he simply did not know. 'Of course you don't!' Camilla cried. How could he know, for she had only just realised herself. She had fallen in love.

She phoned Kim right away. 'I've something to tell you.'

'Me too,' he said. 'Meet me tonight.'

Something had happened during her sickness. She was not as glossily powerful as she had been before. She painted her face with care and it looked back at her anxiously. She had got too thin. She was beginning to look old.

None of this seemed to matter with Kim. 'Darling, I've never felt this way before,' he said at once. Leaving Frederick would be difficult but at least they would not have to live in a garret. Kim was one of the rising young men in his field. They would have a splendid life. First thing, she would get rid of Mrs Lemon and hire a proper housekeeper. Kim was talking about marriage, his turquoise eyes transformed by tenderness. 'Congratulate me, darling,' he said. 'Her name is Heather.'

She would fire Mrs Lemon anyway, get a woman who could do flowers, make decent coffee, launder silk underwear without bringing it to the boil.

Kim thanked Camilla from the bottom of his heart, which was not the bit of his heart she craved. Heather was a pure girl, very young, and *sweet*. He could not have held out without Camilla. 'I picked you with great care,' he exulted. 'It had to be someone whose life was totally fulfilled. Otherwise, I would have felt a shit.'

Mrs Lemon turned up in a coat made up of many small dead animals. Tufts of ash adorned its collar and a musky aroma surrounded her. She was smoking cannabis now. Camilla had ready a small speech of termination. She handed over a cheque first to soften the blow.

'Bless you, Missus,' said Mrs Lemon with an explosion of mirth which scattered ash over everything. 'I don't need your money. In fact, I have a little something for you – a parting present, if you like. You see I've had a bit of luck on the pools so I reckon it's time Rosie gave herself a rest.' She watched with happiness as Mrs Lee unwrapped the package which exploded into a parachute of pink nylon. 'Brighten up your night life, if you get my meaning,' said Mrs Lemon with a wink. 'I wouldn't have the cheek to say this only I'm handing in my notice, but we're of an age and it's meant in friendship. You're giving in to your years.'

Oddly, she missed Mrs Lemon. Two other cleaning women

came and went and the effort of keeping house along with the demands of her career got her down. Frederick was right. She was working too hard. Midway through an appalling day she handed in her notice. Everyone was very understanding.

Except Frederick. She came home needing sympathy but he was absorbed in something he was reading. 'I found this. I knew something was up, Camilla, but how could you have been taken in by such rubbish?' His voice was mild, but he sounded shaken. Her heart gave a dreadful lurch when she saw the slip of notepaper. Camilla had the unpleasant but literal sensation of her world turning upside down. The blood vanished from her head and her legs went weak. She had forgotten to destroy Kim's letters.

'I'm sorry, Frederick!' she said humbly, and sank to her knees.

Her husband watched her in dismay. 'Get up off your knees, old thing. Let me give you a good stiff drink.' Gin was ruinous to the complexion but she drank it anyway. 'We must get to the bottom of this.' Frederick's nice old face searched her gaunt and guilty one benignly. 'Now, who on earth would have sent you a chain letter?'

Confession

The two girls ran between the aisles. They had a penny which they had decided to invest. They would light a candle and pray for Uncle Matt to come and visit, because he always gave them a shilling. They slowed down as they passed a pew which was full of people who shuffled on their knees to fill the gap left when a man stepped off the end and vanished into a box.

'Where did he go?' Betty said to Fanny. Fanny did not know so she told Betty not to speak in church. Betty turned her attention to a kneeling woman whose bowed head was wrapped in a scarf. 'What's in there? Why is everyone going in there?' She clutched the carved end of the pew in case Fanny would drag her away. Her face was level with the kneeling woman's head which rose so slowly that there was a moment when Betty feared that the scarf might not actually contain a face.

'It's the confession box,' she told Betty. 'We go in there for forgiveness.'

'Forgiveness for what?' Betty said.

'For when we have been wicked,' the woman smiled.

'What's wicked?' Betty said as Fanny dragged her away.

'She is. She eats children,' Fanny told her.

'You'd go to jail for that,' Betty said hopefully.

Fanny held her sister's hand. She lit the taper and touched a candle and the wick curled and sizzled and a black straggle of smoke grew out of it and then a bright eye of flame blazed and gazed at them. 'No one ever finds out,' Fanny whispered. 'She eats every bit of them, first the fingers and the eyes and then she nibbles off all the flesh. By then she is too full to stand so she sits down and belches to make some room and then one by one she crunches the bones. Last of all she eats the hair, holding it up and licking the strands off her fingers.'

The moment she had said this Fanny forgot about it, but for years afterwards Betty woke in the night to the muffled eager munching of bones, and then she would see the woman's face and have to watch her eating the hair, which waved and straggled like the black smoke on the candle. The woman had had black hungry eyes that burned into Betty and when she smiled she showed long, bone-crunching teeth, and the red on her lips made a saw pattern in the wrinkles, as if the blood dripped down.

By now Fanny was going to confession. She had to take Betty because she had to take her everywhere, and Betty was made to kneel beside her in the line. When other people emerged they looked subdued but Fanny always came out smiling. She held her joined hands over her face so that people would not see, but Betty saw and once or twice she noticed her licking her lips.

'What happens when you go in there?' Betty said.

'It's a secret,' Fanny told her. 'I'm not allowed to say.'

The younger sister became obsessed with the confession box and pestered Fanny, pulling at her skirt or poking her in bed at night so that Fanny at last had to relent. 'Well, then, I will tell you if you promise never to mention this to another living soul. Behind the door there is a smaller door and beyond that a great big room with a party going on. There is a long table with cake and ice cream and jelly and meringues. Every person who goes in can eat as much of everything as they like. I had three meringues.' Betty was five and it would be two more years before she could go to confession and each week Fanny added more and more enticing details. Once she took a silver-wrapped sweet from her pocket and handed it to her sister. 'I saved you that.' And every Saturday when she left Betty in the pew, shivering with envy, she told the priest, 'I lied.'

When Betty's turn finally came her whole life was dominated

by the ordeal. In school she was prepared for her first confession. It was revealed to her that Christ had died for her sins. 'What sins?' she said in terror, but it was a bottomless pit, an unending menu written by the devil. She supposed that sin would come naturally to her now that she had reached the age of reason, but soon she came to realise that like long division, it would remain forever a puzzle. 'Bless me, Father, but I have no sins,' she said. The priest was full of contempt and wanted to know how every man on earth was a sinner but she alone was above reproach. She was introduced to some invisible and unpleasant part of herself called a conscience and compelled to examine it, employing a litany of the seven deadly sins, from which flowed all iniquity; pride, covetousness, lust, anger. She knew she did not possess the extreme emotions necessary for such passionate-sounding weaknesses. At night she lay awake trying to imagine ways in which her thoughts or actions might be sinful, but when she produced some sins they sounded too evil and the priest's breath was drawn in in revulsion. She often had to tell the same ones because she couldn't think of any others and it seemed that even in the dark she was recognised, for the confessor would demand, 'Am I right in thinking you were in here before asking to be forgiven for the selfsame acts of badness? You are turning out very degenerate.'

In desperation she would come to confession half an hour early and inspect all the boxes. The confessors' names were inscribed in gold on a wine-coloured plaque above the door and she always hoped that there might be a new one. Sometimes in the dark, while the priest was censuring her, she felt with her fingers the grainy wall of the box, hoping to encounter a little latch or catch that would spring open the door to the big room with the party. The confession box was constructed like a moth, with a solid central part where the priest wielded mercy behind dusty curtains and on either side of him were spread out two sections like wings where one sinner waited and one confessed. While she waited Betty could hear the murmured vices of other sinners and the priest's disillusioned drone of pardon but Fanny always came out smiling behind her hands and still Betty imagined that beyond the old priest, waiting like a spider to dissect your rotting soul, the room waited, the long table set with the devil's unending menu – the jellies only half eaten, the meringues bloated with sweetened cream.

The two girls grew up. Fanny was a striking, spiky young woman, around whom jealous feuds broke out among men who had not even known they liked her. Betty was a soft, shy, pretty girl, who blushed and was enraptured by romance. Into the dark, musty confession box they brought the fragrance of young women and the provocation of other men's lust. The dim, coffin-like space grew tropical with the scent of their hair and their breathless whispers of tentative carnal celebration. Gone was the pastor's dolorous drone. He quizzed them eagerly, relentlessly. Fanny enjoyed these sessions.

'*Where did he touch you?*'

'On my breasts. My thighs. On my . . .!' And she stopped and gave a little gasp, as if remembering.

'*Was his mouth open when he kissed you? Did you touch his private parts? Did you? Did he put it between your legs? Did he waste the seed?*'

When Betty entered the box, even before she opened her mouth, the priest appeared half demented with rage. She often let boys go a little bit far because it seemed kind and anyway it was no harm for she had made up her mind that she would not get around to actual sex until she was married. These physical interludes passed in a kind of pleasant blur that stopped her thinking about them too much except when she went to confession and the priest forced her to articulate all the pleasant acts of tenderness in a way that made them appear vulgar and brutal and, in a particularly revolting way, caused her to feel that she was being forced to do them all over again but against her will. There came a time when she knew that she must never, ever do them again. She still dressed invitingly and made little mews when she was kissed and blushed and flapped her eyelids until her suitors were beside themselves and then she seemed to turn to ice. Betty was miserable. She hated being mean to boys and when they called her a tease she felt she was turning out like Fanny, disclosing a feast to which they were not invited. One man told her it was her own fault for driving men crazy and he raped her and then he strangled her. He was haunted by the look upon her face which was a look of recognition and, almost, a look of gratitude. The thing Betty finally understood was that she had known all along that this would happen and now, at last, she need no longer dread it.

Fanny got married and everyone breathed a sigh of relief. She had a routine sort of life except for a restless phase about ten years after that. There was something on her mind and she was tormented by an urge to tell her husband. She knew the kindest thing was to say nothing but it was like a thorn in her system and sooner or later it was going to have to work its way out. 'I've been having an affair,' she said to him one night when he wanted to sleep and she wanted to make love.

'Who with?' he said, and she told him it was his friend, his best friend, the man who had been like a brother to him since childhood, whose company he preferred to anyone else's.

There was a period of unpleasantness with accusations and denials, and in the end the two men never spoke to each other again but that was none of Fanny's business. The only thing that concerned her was to confess properly, before God, who has the power to wipe away all sins. She had not been to confession since Betty's death. The brown box looked small and quaint now, like a music box left over from childhood and stored in the attic, and for a moment she felt foolish, but for all Catholics there comes a time when they need to feel once more the pleasant abrasion of total cleansing so she went inside and bent her bony knees and put her dry red lips up to the little wire grill and told the priest, 'I lied.'

⊘〰〰〰◌

Concerning Virgins

These things no longer matter because the house is gone and the people are dead but ghosts only settle when they have got over their surprise and history shows that concerns last longer than matter.

An old man, Narcissus Fitzgall, lived with his two daughters in a house called Herons' Peep on the edge of the water in County Wicklow. It had been built on a hill above the river but appeared, from the inside, to be suspended in water. Water dappled its ceilings with luminous shadow and moved in spotted motion behind the curtains. It gushed darkly underneath the bedroom windows and vanished in a silver trail miles away, between lacy wands of ash. Where the river ended the sea began. There was a stretch of marsh fed by seawater and wild birds nested in giant reeds. Beyond this was a little shingle beach on which to stand in the wind and listen to the soft crumple of the waves and a tempting chatter like glass-beaded curtains as the tide dragged its dead water back across the stones.

The house and its steeds and its birds and its reeds seemed made for pleasure but Narcissus Fitzgall was not a happy man. 'I need a wife,' he sighed. 'God grant me a wife. Sweet suffering souls!' – he damaged his gouty foot upon the martyred rump of a favourite hound – 'it ain't as if I want a cook or a beauty – only a wife.'

He did not need a wife to care for him. His two daughters, Blanche and Grace, served the old man with silent loyalty.

They were aged somewhere between thirty and forty and looked as if they had been washed too frequently – and he detested them.

Although he insisted absolutely on purity in women his personal preference was for a woman you could whack on the behind, whose breasts grew lax in their moorings after champagne and claret. As he grew older his days were poisoned by the constant filial presence. They had developed a preserved look as they began to dry out as if they would live, rustling and dispirited, for ever.

He did not need a wife to soothe his passions. Fancy these days was an irksome intruder whose name he sometimes could not remember. When the need arose, a young scullery maid made less of a compliment and could be dismissed if she grew argumentative. He needed a wife to give him a son. Time was running out. His body had grown unreliable. It had lost interest in his will and seemed embarked on an excavation for its own skeleton, neglecting to send blood to his extremities or to digest the fat of game or the esters of old alcohol. Unless he could soon put a squalling heir to the breast of a woman who bore his name, he must go to his grave in the horrible knowledge that Herons' Peep would fall to the busy, timorous fingers of his daughters.

For all its beauty, Herons' Peep was not a feminine estate. It was a man's house. Unlike most Irish houses, which look stern on the outside and graceful within, it showed all its gentleness in its face. Inside it was handsome but harsh. The uncovered floors answered the stamp of boots. Grates were vast marble maws where whole trees were splintered and consumed. The sofas had been built big enough for a horse or a hound to sleep on, and they did if they liked. Plumbing, when it came, was a series of thunderous geysers and gullets that caused many a superstitious maid to leap from her seat, believing she would be sucked down to the very floor of the ocean below. There were no flowers, no little lamps nor Venice glass. Gilt-framed shepherdesses and darling little painted dogs did not sentimentalize the walls. The kitchen was the very pit of hell, enlivened only by a bright patter of gore from the dripping corpses of the day's sporting slaughter. The river alone was allowed to indulge in female whim, making her music softly on the ceilings – a solitary clemency for many a stolen maid.

In the early days visitors were shocked by the severity of the house and put it down to the lack of a woman's touch. The little girls heard the whispers and assumed this responsibility. As soon as they were able, they hoarded lengths of fabric in their room, begged from neighbours or bought in parish sales, and sewed up assortments of curtains.

Their father locked them in the nursery and fed them boiled rabbit for a week. When they were released, thin and faintly green, they had turned an old velvet ballgown into a set of frilly cushions for a sofa. In spite of Fitzgall's fury they persisted for it seemed as vital to them as salvation to leave the mark of their gender. As little girls deafened by paternal wrath they would hide and cry for their mother. Now when he raged at them they lay down on their beds or stole his spirits and returned gaunter and more enduring. Their nervous fingers never ceased in dainty toil. Although the old man used their finest work to blow his nose or rub down his dogs, the house was sinking under a creeping infection of embroidered samplers.

One day when he was seventy-five he decided that since God would not trouble to send him a spouse, he must get one for himself. He had exhausted his store of charm, influence and menace with all the women in the county, so he resorted to a wise old woman who lived in the local village of Rathwillow and who did a bit of hairdressing in her spare time.

'I need a wife,' he told her.

'What sort of a wife?' She studied him most acutely, as if measuring him up for a suit or a coffin.

'A drudge, a bag, a bat, a hag – any wife so long as she has in her the makings of a boy.'

She kept looking at him, making no comment but holding his eye as if awaiting some response from himself. At length she turned away and observed: 'I knew a man wanted a ferret an' he put a notice in a periodical.' For this, he had to give her a guinea.

All the same, he did advertise for a wife, withholding his

name and that of his estate, for he was not a popular man –
merely describing himself as handsome, unfettered and rich
and offering a box number for reply. After that he had only to
add his small requirement in the woman who would fulfil him.

He had been married once to a very beautiful girl called
Alice Clements. She was demure and pure as a swan. He went
to great efforts to lay claim to her, thundering about the countryside on hunters, shooting pheasants and peasants, spending
most of his money on Herons' Peep so that his brothers were
left with bare tracts of land to build on. He took her to Paris for
her honeymoon and gave her all her heart's desire, and she had
treated him abominably. She gave birth to two daughters and
showed no repentance. When the younger of the girls was only
two she jumped into the river, leaving him in his prime with a
house of motherless daughters – and no son.

He sought another wife as soon as possible. He had
exhausted his store of sentiment on Alice and formulated more
economical styles of wooing.

Sometimes he simply canvassed the parents of an intended
with his financial statements. Oddly, the response was poor. He
lowered his sights to the landless gentry but even their luckless
female tribes resisted him. He offered his fortune to poor, pure
peasant girls but they fled into convents or painted their faces
with the scars of smallpox. He could not understand it. He was
a man of substance; handsome – the blood a bit too close to the
skin and the brow too beetling, but a good feast for a hungry
virgin.

At first he wondered if he had transgressed the narrow
boundaries of county form by resuming courtship a month
after his bereavement but a crueller truth emerged. His wife's
ghost spoke against him. It was said he had driven her to her
death. Her pallid spirit came back dripping from the deep and
called him callous – he, who had lavished his fortune upon her
and expended his best energies in bringing her to bliss.

When he married chaste Alice, he meant her to become his
amorous masterwork, his private whore. Naturally she had
repulsed the passionate sieges of his courtship. He could not
have married her otherwise. He perceived all virtuous wives as

irresistible hypocrites who enjoyed the joke of public modesty and twinkled for their husbands like the stars by night. He introduced his bride to his symphony of connubial themes, inspired by the most expensive houses of London and in the arms of plump, intuitive girls of fifteen, and she gazed at the water patterned ceiling. Her lips, obediently fastened to where he directed them, moved ticklishly in prayer.

So deep was Alice's resistance that Narcissus Fitzgall could not resist it. Instead of leaving her alone to be a good wife and mother, he persisted over the years in tormenting her with different systems of arousal. Rumour has it (but whoever believes such things?) that at length he brought a serving wench to their bed to demonstrate the true nature of female response. Alice lay mute in muslin cap and shift until, at a point where he was unable to give her his attention, she leaped from the sheets with a small mew, went downstairs with her candle and slipped into the river.

A little bitterness is fitting to the victim of a tragedy. 'How do we look, Father?' said his two young daughters twelve years later as they prepared for their first dance in gowns cut down from the remnants of their mother's wardrobe. 'The woods would be very silent if only the nightingale sang,' their papa sadly smiled. All the same they did well at parties – well enough to make him suspect that some young scoundrels had their minds intent on robbing his female property of their only worthwhile asset. He had no interest in his daughters but he had ambitions for them. He wanted them to marry well. There were good estates within riding distance where advantageous connections might be made for the son he would eventually get. The girls looked fair enough. They had no wens or marks and were growing pretty little figures. All he had to do was keep them safe until they were old enough to marry. He forbade them further dances and banned visitors from the house. He locked up his daughters and had men with dogs patrol his grounds. The girls attempted to smuggle out notes and make secret trysts and gnawed noblemen limped about the county to testify to the fact that they had once been attractive, as Narcissus Fitzgall's dogs had once been vicious.

Fitzgall was getting old. He had forgotten that in order for men and women to marry they have first to meet. Memory had flung out the souvenirs of courtship – the teas and dances and rides and picnics, spread over with lace and perfume and roses and manners, laid under with a thunderous compression of lust.

The girls met no one. Lace flew from their nervous fingers and their lips grew pale. They read and walked and stitched and stitched and took little nips of tonic wine. By the time they were deemed of marriageable age, they already had the look of spinsters. Wicked rumour flourished once more, enclosing them like a wall of brambles. Why had the Fitzgall girls been locked up for years and years? It was said they suffered from the phrensy, that their mother had jumped in the river to quench her candle when the moon was full and had left her orphans a legacy of queerness in the head. When Narcissus Fitzgall put them up with a fair dowry there were no bidders. He was enraged and blamed his daughters for plainness, resenting them more with each sparrow's foot that left its tiny print beneath their downcast eyes.

It was indecent that no man had married them, that he should have to bear the brunt of their unflowered withering. One only put up with older women because of the children they had borne, as an example of virtue to those maturing young. It was insupportable that his lovely, adventurer's house might one day fall to his unclaimed daughters.

Now that he had taken measures to prevent this, he might have grown kinder, but as he awaited a response to his advertisement for a wife, the old man became very odd indeed. Sensing an end to his detestable dependence, he grew spiteful and rash.

He filled the sherry bottle, where he knew the girls helped themselves to secret refreshment, with vinegar, and put hare's blood in the port decanter. He employed a poor thing in the village to make up a series of samplers stitched to his direction and disposed them through the house. He found Grace standing rigidly in front of the one that read: 'If hell is a well of whiskey, oh, death where is thy sting?' Blanche was being timidly sick in the bathroom after an appalling sip from the port decanter.

The poor girls knew nothing of his plans and were alarmed to hear him croaking with cruel laughter in the night. 'Tea, Papa?' Bravely they crept up beside his bed.

'Leave the poor teapot in peace!' he roared at them. 'You have a spinster's preoccupation with little pissing spouts.'

When he had frightened them away he returned to his amusement of imagining the procession of applicants for his marital favours – the lonely, the ugly, the fat. He thought he might choose a very fat one. He enjoyed imagining the hulking brute of a son they would make and what sport he would have with his decrepit siblings. His daughters would flee to some chilly wing of the house where he need never look at them but could, when he remembered, dispatch milquetoast or a little thin soup.

Disappointingly, this pleasure was deferred. When he went to collect his post there was nothing but a begging letter from a widow, pleading for a fragment of his fortune in order to feed her children. After three weeks had passed with no single answer, he consulted the wise woman again.

'Did you maybe set your sights too high?' she wondered.

'I asked for nothing,' he protested, 'not looks, not charm, not money! See!' He handed her a copy of his notice and she read it, her gnarled face slowly unravelling to reveal a blackened pit of mirth. 'You wanted jam on your egg and no mistake,' she cackled, and read aloud: 'Handsome, landed gent of considerable means seeks virgin bride of childbearing age.'

'What proposal could be more modest?' he begged.

'God bless you, sir, and saving your presence, you black-hearted oul' blackguard – with curs like yourself around, where do you expect to find a virgin?'

'Silence, hag! I'll have your head,' Narcissus Fitzgall was infuriated by her impudence.

'Why not, so, since you had my maidenhead more than fifty years ago – not that you'll remember – and that of every other poor girl who had neither man nor money to protect her.

'Forget about virgins now, sir. Look out for a nice widow

lady who'll give you a son without even troubling you to father it.'

'The mother of my son must be a virgin.' The old man remained stubborn.

'Give me another guinea,' she said.

He put the money in her hand and she transferred it to her corset and slowly began to write. 'Old man, solvent, wishes to make contact with maiden lady in desperate circumstances, view to matrimony and mutual advantage.'

There were desperate women then as there are desperate women now and always will be. When next he went to inspect his mail a couple of letters awaited him. Having passed the previous month in disappointment he felt exhilarated, spoilt for choice. He determined that one of the authors would be his bride no matter how dire her circumstance, how horrible her impediment. Bad breath would not stand in his way, nor apoplexy nor skin blackened by mercury poisoning, he vowed as he tore open his post and scanned the spinsterish script of two virgins who pleaded to become 'Yours truly . . .'

When the girls found him he had begun to go brittle and the letters were locked into a mortified grasp. They stooped solicitously to their father's corpse. With barely a glance at one another and only the mildest of sighs, they retrieved their very private correspondence.

꧁

Gods and Slaves

❦

Their mother always said that if any of the girls got pregnant their father would throw her out in the street. This warning acted more effectively than any threat to their own security, keeping them in a state of grace for longer than was necessary or appealing. Modesty flowed around them like a moat and there was no brother who might act as drawbridge. They wondered about men a great deal and sometimes begged their mother, 'What is a man like?' and she replied that if they wanted to know what men were like they had only to look at the picture in the hall. The picture was a framed photograph of Roman statuary, gods or slaves, but the chiselled unmentionables had crumbled into dust long before the camera was invented and they had to ply their fervid imaginations to vague porous whorls, not very large, they suspected, even before air pollution had attacked their finer points.

It is likely that they would have continued gazing vexedly at this faded image until middle age dimmed their eyesight had not Phelim Hartigan appeared. From that moment it became clear that at least one female in the household was going to be seduced and each one was alert to the event. The mother wore high heels and hid her hair net. The girls washed their long blonde hair in camomile flowers and did special exercises that promised bosoms as big as melons. Phelim Hartigan was not a tall man but was of a forceful structure. Other men looked like suits filled with cushions or coat hangers, but he was all muscle, sprung from a root of generation. He had thick black curly hair and green eyes and when he sang in *basso pro-fundo* it sent vibrations right up through the furniture and through the person who was sitting on it too. From the moment he entered the house his prerogative was established. The black cat, Mrs Danvers, flung herself on his knee and picked impatiently at the weave of his trousers. Even the father, when he opened the door, appeared to be handing him a menu.

They got Phelim through an advertisement. The sisters sang in close harmony in the manner of the Andrews Sisters for the entertainment or endurance of visitors at Christmas. As they came into their teens the notion presented itself that this talent might transport them into the larger world, where men were. Their mother was very proud of them and relaxed her normal vigilance to see their gifts admired. They were paid ten shillings a week to sing in variety concerts for which she sewed up an assortment of costumes, depending on her mood. Sometimes they were chaste white frocks in cotton piqué and on other occasions they were scarlet satin shifts through which the unfulfilled peaks of their whirlpool bras pointed like the horns of minor pantomime devils.

The theatres were in the poor suburbs of Dublin and had been first cinemas and then bingo halls. Cinerama was dragooned in as a final bid to save the cinemas. Trains apparently came off their rails and hurtled into the audience or rivers were seen to burst their banks and explode through the screen. Stereophonic systems surrounded the audience with noises of disaster, but neither miracles nor disaster can compensate a loss of faith. With the start of the sixties people had jobs and money. They wanted real life. This fad was short-lived. Later on the picture houses would be pool halls or carpet warehouses but for a few years variety became popular, with clamorous rock groups imitating the Crickets or the Comets and male comedians who dressed as women, stuffing cabbages inside their jumpers.

The girls stood rigid upon the stage, one day perky as the models in Persil ads, the next sleekly gleaming like women in motor oil commercials. They made uniform swipes at the air with their hands, and their voices, tonally perfect, flowed about them like a cloud of summer flies. But they got no further. People in the nearest rows looked bewildered. 'We can't hear you.' When they moved close to the microphone it whistled. 'Get them off ya!' yelled the gurriers from the back. Within a few weeks everyone got used to the silent girl performers, as they had once accepted silent films, and they continued to appear weekly, but neither their careers nor their lives progressed. In the dressing area, with the smell of cold sweat and beer, they were timidly pawed by midget pop performers. A squint-eyed comedian in his forties invited Kay, who was thirteen, to dinner. She asked could her sisters come too and he, gazing soulfully askew, declared, 'There are times when a man likes to be alone with a woman.' They decided that they must look for more sophisticated outlets, nightclubs or television. They auditioned for television, where the volume could be adjusted with knobs, but were turned down on the basis that they were lacking in 'oomph'.

For two shillings you could place a card in the window of a music shop on the quays and it was like purchasing a magic spell. 'All-girl professional singing group seeks male backing,' the notice read. A stream of young men arrived at the house, where once it had seemed that no man would ever come. They travelled on foot, by bicycle, on throbbing motorbikes, with guitars, mouth organs, accordions. Most of them were wan and spotty, no adepts in oomph. The sisters had lived too long on a diet of pure romance to accommodate any imperfection. They entertained a good-looking country boy until a dispute arose about the division of their fee. 'What do ye care about cash?' he had said bitterly. 'Youse birds are sittin' on a fortune.' After a series of disappointments they took to stationing themselves within the folds of the drawing room curtains, and there they lived, quiet as the cat. When a fresh applicant pushed the creaky gate they would signal one another and make a swift appraisal before informing the youth that the position had been filled.

The notice in the music shop must have grown sallow and flyblown by the time Phelim Hartigan found it, for several years had passed and the girls had all but given up singing for more useful pursuits, such as typing and dressmaking. Kay came home from school one day and found him sitting in the dining room strumming his guitar and singing in his beautiful deep voice. He fixed his eye on her and sang on, and she grew very pale and then very red, and fled to the kitchen. Mother was thrashing pastry with a rolling pin. 'That is Mr Hartigan. He is to accompany you girls,' she said and then, surprising her youngest daughter beyond all measure, 'I have invited him to tea.'

They never knew where Phelim came from. He was much older than the other young men, being about twenty-nine. They had no idea why he answered the advertisement, for he was a good musician as well as a good singer. They questioned him but he rarely made conversation. He would strum a few pulsating chords and name a song. He began in a voice that was low and sweet but carried strongly and they, without any direction, followed in, as a woman is led by a skilled dance partner. Their voices, which had been bland and thin, at once improved, for the exciting male presence injected their singing with a tremolo of yearning. They knew every time they opened their mouths that life had begun. That fundamental tremor was akin to a biblical upheaval that could breathe life into dust, roll back the stones from caves, rend their clothing, make them free to do anything. Yet they had been brought up as spinsters. They had no idea how to persuade. 'Rehearsals twice a week,' they told Phelim sharply. (They had always been once a week.) On the days between they silently examined their noses for blackheads and blew on their palms to test their breath.

'Stand up straight,' he commanded Maeve. 'Of the four of us, you are the only one with breasts. Little breasts, but let them be seen.' The girls eyed him suspiciously. No one said breasts. Bosoms were all right, being a joke word, but breasts were a portion of the anatomy not openly acknowledged between the sexes. 'Let down your hair,' he told Cecilia. He unpinned her plaits and raked them loose with his fingers. An electrified cornfield fled over her shoulders. 'You girls cannot hold your breath for the whole of your lives.' He inhaled deeply, allowing the air to go all the way down his body. 'You must sing from . . . here.' And before their very eyes he touched himself. There. They had stopped breathing completely, their eyes riveted to that part of his clothing that had a restless, lumpy look, like a boy's pocket where a mouse was hidden.

Two weeks later the restructured group made its first appearance at the Apollo in Sundrive. The girls had begun to change. Released from the petrifying spell of innocence, they were less gawky, less astonished. Touches of colour appeared in their cheeks. They no longer carried their bodies as the mortifying baggage of looming fecundity, but with a swish, like the net slips, stiffened with sugar, they introduced beneath their skirts accentuated with Waspee belts. Toenails, hitherto the yellow torment of an older generation (hewn into a V when ingrown), became pearly lozenges, winking through peep-toe shoes. The sisters were in white. He wore black – black shirt, black leather jacket and jeans. The audience looked rebellious. They remembered the silent girl trio fondly. Phelim began to mumble something unrecognisable in a little Woody Guthrie voice, making the audience strain to listen. When they were lulled he made a mighty twang on his guitar, gyrated the middle portion of his anatomy and the song became recognisable as 'Jailhouse Rock'. The girls clapped their hands and bent into the microphone for the chorus. Phelim thrust his guitar floorward as if to tango, bent backwards with angled knees, projected his hips at unsuspecting housewives and filled the cold little theatre with his great warm voice. The women in the audience did something that no Dublin audience had ever done before. They screamed. That night their weekly earnings were promoted to thirty shillings a week.

For a moment, poised before the baying housewives, the sisters had felt afraid. Then melodic whistles interposed the soughing dirge and this was pulsed with the crisp percussion of applause. Phelim was laughing as he gathered them forward to share the praise. The wall of discord that swept around them like Cinerama became a jubilee march. The scuffed stage was a triumphal platform. Acid stage lights on twisted wires rained down dazzling splinters that dusted their hair and their white dresses with gold. Oh, they understood they were not fit for worship, they were ordinary women who knew better than to rise above their station, but they were the brides of an idol. Phelim their creature. The sisters exchanged sated glances. They felt fulfilled, accomplished. They had achieved the primary object of mating, which is to make other women jealous.

The idyll that followed this conquest was of short duration. The notion crept in on them that each of the sisters was another woman. A man could not be jointly claimed. Possession was a singular objective. The enchantment of his appearance in their life was soured by the need to clarify his position in it. All their lives they had been fused by curiosity. Now they were sundered by the more powerful force of rivalry. When Phelim gave Cecilia a lift on the pillion of his motor-cycle, Maeve stormed out of the house and came back with a startled boy, whom she called a boyfriend. Kay wore a dress so short that her mother said she would be ashamed to have it hanging on her clothesline, let alone on her daughter.

The brides were stymied. All their efforts to claim his attention appeared only to cultivate his indifference. One day he did not appear for rehearsal. 'And I had bought crinkle chips for tea,' the mother said disconsolately. It was not to be a solo occurrence. He told the girls he had other things on his mind, there was a difficult decision he had to make. Delight deserted them. They grew anxious, inert, waiting for him to make the difficult choice between them. 'Of course,' the mother crushingly mused, 'a man like that would have other women.' Had they not been so uncomfortably tethered by the baffling hex they might have taken pleasure in the success of their singing. The group had been offered a fee of three pounds by a rival theatre. They were invited once again to audition for television.

All week the mother laboured on their new costumes, cream art silk with gold coin spots. All day they steamed their skin, singed their hair and scraped tiny golden strands from their legs, tautly humming choruses and harmonies. They had been stiffly poised in the drawing room for half an hour awaiting

Phelim when the doorbell rang. Their mother went to answer it so that their attention had fled with her to the hall even as they listened to the news on the wireless that President John Kennedy had been assassinated. The mother came back and leaned in the doorway. She seemed shaken, as if she had received the same terrible bulletin at the door. 'That was a boy,' she said. 'He was sent by Phelim. Phelim will not be coming. He will not be coming back at all.'

The girls sang alone at the audition. They were turned down, as they knew they would be. When this was out of the way they found themselves husbands as quickly as possible. Even Kay, shrugging off her school bag, broke her mother's heart by riling a boy with her short skirt and struggling up the aisle as a teenage bride and mother-to-be.

They talked about Phelim only once after his disappearance.

'He is dead,' Maeve decided. 'Mother would not tell us.'

'An accident with his motorbike,' Cecilia agreed.

And Kay proposed that if not dead, then he had certainly been called to the priesthood. Any other possibilities were too painful to contemplate, but even this resolution brought no relief. It only turned them into women. That the Lord should claim two such prizes on a single day! After all, there was no contest, only sport for the gods.

They settled down to marriage with that look of bewilderment and resignation that young wives had before the Beatles. They never again regained the closeness of their childhood for they had been healed of curiosity and naturally, they no longer had recourse to the question, 'What is a man like?'

Perfect Love

When the editor of the *Sunday Chimes* told Miss Churchill she was to do a Christmas special on Arabella Cartwheel, the young lady responded by naming twin attributes of the male anatomy wholly unconsidered in the literature of that venerable lady.

The great man was upset. Something about the festive season always brought out his sentimental side. 'It's time for a return to basic values,' he said, quite pleased with this novel concept. 'I want something edifying for my organ.'

He also wanted to teach Miss Churchill a lesson. Gilly Churchill, ace journalist and literary assassin, enjoyed her work too much, making column mince out of celebrities. Arabella Cartwheel, drifting through her tenth decade in a cloud of wilting tulle, had a reputation for being as tough as old toenails. You could rake through the rotting cuttings and find that she danced with a man who danced on the Prince of Wales but, no matter how provoked or confronted, she would continue to smile through her admirably sturdy yellow teeth and talk of what she always talked of – profound and perfect spiritual love.

Gilly chuckled as she quickly prepared a low-calorie meal of Havana cigars. It would come as a surprise to the editor to learn that she was very good with old people. Every Christmas she visited her Aunt Grizel (the one with the dosh). She always brought a bottle of Bailey's Irish Cream. Old people do not drink alone for fear of being labelled alcoholics and bunged in a home. They love to booze and all their gratitude is given to those who facilitate this with their company.

She had been annoyed when the editor disturbed her for she had been feeling organically challenged, having innocently drunk a bottle of mineral water to clear her head of last evening's revels and then, too late, discovered that it was, in fact, a litre of tequila. All the same, she couldn't resist a challenge. Her opponent would be out before the first round and she would be back at her desk by cocktail time.

She chose a little gift for Miss Cartwheel and dressed with care in a gymslip and stilettos. She knew exactly what she wanted. She wanted to confirm that the doyenne of romantic fiction did not actually write her love stories but had a team of zombies chained up in the cellar. She wanted her to boast that she used to be a rattler in the sack (anyone who lasted that long had to be living on someone else's hormones) and most of all she wanted to climb so far up her nose that the old lady would tell her to ★★★★ off and then she would have the first sentence of her interview: 'I was just a kid looking for a heart-warming Christmas story, but the queen of love told me to ★★★★ off.'

The authoress answered the door in full evening regalia.

'You do look wonderful,' gushed Miss Churchill.

'I know.' Miss Cartwheel gave her a jaundiced beam and blinked through two blackened Christmas trees. She swept down the hall in a lampshade of pink gauze.

In fact she felt like hell. For the first time in her life she was suffering from writer's block. For three days she had been stuck on *Never Mind the Bells*. Normally she was aglow with inspiration. Her stories lived with her. From the moment she reached for her eyelashes and her pen and her first cup of ginseng tea, the words flowed like honey . . . *By the time Sir Florian arrived at his beloved Glenfarlow, it was a crimson inferno on the leaden sky. He did not think of his heritage, but only of Willow, trapped in the dungeons* . . . She had been trapped in the flaming dungeons since Friday. By now she would be kippered.

The girl had taken out a notebook and was asking her what had been the biggest influence on her life.

'Profound and perfect spiritual love,' Miss Cartwheel said at once.

'Balls!' The journalist lit up a cigar.

'Indeed!' Miss Cartwheel's face was alight with radiant recall. 'I remember them well. How divinely the young men danced! It was all so beautiful and we were so much in love. In my long and exquisitely happy life I have been fortunate enough to experience the very pinnacle of bliss, which is to love and be loved with a pure heart, for nothing but one's inner self.'

'Let's not beat about the (if you'll forgive the term) bush, Miss Cartwheel,' Gilly said. 'Your ankle tremblers, bustle rustlers, spinster steamers, or whatever you call them, aren't they really the same as my own phenomenally best-selling novel, *Apathy* – tales of man's eternal quest for a spot of how's-your-father?'

'He's dead, thank you.'

'All that surging and churning! Isn't it a metaphor for bonking?'

'I'm afraid I know very little about modern music,' Miss Cartwheel smiled.

'Horizontal jogging, you daft old bat.' The girl bit the end off another cigar and lit it.

'Fie!' Miss Cartwheel was finally nettled. 'I will not have you speak of such things! The word 'jogging' is anathema to me. I cannot imagine why young women should wish to have muscles of steel. Muscles are a manly attribute; women should be soft as kittens – although not, perhaps, as soft as that bulge of thigh showing above your stockings. Those lumpy bits, my dear, are known as cellulite. It is a massing of toxins in the fatty tissues. I would recommend a course of *drainage minceur*.'

Miss Churchill ate her cigar, including the lighted end. Arabella Cartwheel watched her with concern. The girl swallowed like an anaconda and then, surprisingly, produced a sweet childish smile. 'We have a lot in common,' she wheedled. 'You have written eleven thousand romantic novels. I have had roughly the same number of gentlemen friends and I can say with absolute authority that not one of them was thinking of profound and perfect spiritual love. Go on, old fruit, admit it. It's a load of rubbish.'

Arabella Cartwheel looked uncomfortable.

'I've got you, haven't I?' Miss Churchill crowed.

Miss Cartwheel nodded reluctantly. 'It's true. I can quite see that you would not inspire profound and perfect love.'

For the first time in her life Miss Churchill was almost speechless. 'You what?'

'It's your eyes, dear. They are the windows of the soul. If the eyes look muddy how can a man see the clear light of the spirit shining through? Your bowels are in crisis! It's the first thing anyone would observe – the yellowish white of eye, the dark circles underneath.'

Miss Churchill was about to rip off her opponent's eyelashes and bash her in the teeth but the old lady had risen like a sprite from her pink velvet sofa and was gone from the room in a whisper of tulle. 'I shall make you a nice cup of senna-pod tea.'

While she was absent Miss Churchill busied herself rummaging in drawers and bookshelves. She found nothing – not even a secret stash of Mars bars. She discovered a giant box of the mauve, violet-scented notepaper for which Miss Cartwheel was renowned. There were vats of vitamins, firkins of fish oil, rafts of royal jelly. She opened one of the containers and sniffed hopefully to see if it might contain gin instead of ginseng. When she was putting it back she accidentally knocked the box of notepaper on the floor. She scooped up the sheets and stuffed them back into the container. Then she saw what had been left behind – a small bundle of yellowing slips of notepaper. Oh, merciful providence! Oh, happy, happy Christmas! A lot of it was soppy tripe. At last she came across the section of correspondence which had been signed 'Shag' and which began, 'My dearest Arab . . .' Miss Churchill chortled horribly as she crouched on the floor to read.

When Arabella Cartwheel arrived with a pot of her evacuating brew, she was still engrossed. 'What are you doing?' the *grande dame* of gush expostulated. 'My private correspondence!'

'Not any more,' Miss Churchill exulted. 'I know all about you now. I know all your little secrets.'

Miss Cartwheel emptied the infusion over her visitor's head. 'Now get out of here, you dirty little faggot,' she said.

The girl stayed where she was, picking what looked like a lot of small black insects out of the turbid liquid that streamed down her face. 'Boo-hoo.'

'What was that?'

'Boo-hoo, you silly old cow. Can't you see? I'm crying.'

'It is Too Late for Tears.' Miss Cartwheel recited with dignity the title of one of her novels.

'Timeless is My Grief,' Miss Churchill snivelled with gusto. 'My mother – who, er, died in childbirth – left me Her Tears for My Tiara.' She cunningly recalled another of Miss Cartwheel's titles.

'From Where Springs Sorrow?' Miss Cartwheel could not resist flinging in one of her most memorable headings.

Miss Churchill stole a fleeting glance at her hostess's book shelves where all 11,000 of her published titles were ranked. 'From The Groves of Lovelessness,' she uttered on a sigh.

'All the same you were ferreting in my private effects.' Miss Cartwheel made a graceless return to reality. 'You are a thief.'

'A Thief of the Heart?' Miss Churchill essayed hopefully.

'Give me back my letters and get out.'

'Of course, Miss Cartwheel, but first I must explain.' She still held tight to the correspondence. 'You see, I never really believed in love. When you spoke so movingly about the voyages of the heart I just had to find some proof – to see if you were really telling the truth. And now . . .' – she held out the most nauseatingly sentimental of the notes – 'I know you were.'

'I am glad I convinced you. Goodbye.'

'Wait!' The girl rose shakily to her feet. She took from her handbag a parcel fetchingly done up in an Oddbins bag. 'A small tribute! Even if I failed to understand the sentiment of your work, I have always been a fan and would like to thank you for the many hours of happiness you have given me.'

Miss Cartwheel unwrapped the parcel and found herself looking at a bottle of fluid roughly the colour of methylated spirits. 'What is it?'

'I chose it specially for you. It's a liqueur. It's called Parfait Amour. It means "Perfect Love".'

The authoress peered closely at the label. 'It's alcohol!' she gasped. 'You know I never drink alcohol. All my life I have kept to my motto: "Lips that touch liquor will never touch mine!" '

'Yes, well you could just pour it in through your nose, you contentious old crow.'

'What did you say?'

'I said, that's why you have a complexion like a rose.'

'There is more to it than abstinence,' Arabella Cartwheel preached severely. 'Every morning I apply a mask of avocado and horse chestnuts. Your own skin, if I may say so, might require some more intensive treatment – a Swabian mud scrub, for instance.' She put out a finger and touched the younger woman's cheek. 'Ah! Perhaps you are already wearing one?'

All her life afterwards Gilly Churchill would congratulate herself on her self-control. 'It isn't really alcohol this,' she asserted meekly. 'More a sort of breath freshener. It's a floral tonic – made from violets – the alcohol keeps it from going off. Do try some – just a little swiggy.'

Miss Cartwheel pursed her lips reproachfully.

'Very well then, I'll go.' Gilly held out most of the letters. 'Just answer one more question.'

'If that will send you on your way.'

The hackette batted her opponent playfully with the remaining clump of correspondence. 'Just tell me, who was Shag?'

Arabella Cartwheel looked stricken.

'Why did he want to roll you in the hay? Why did he refer to himself as your stud?'

The queen of hearts cringed. 'Some things are best left alone. That word is not "stud" by the way – it is "steed". The handwriting was always hard to read, but that is understandable.'

Gilly Churchill loomed over her victim. 'Who was he?'

'He was . . . a horse,' Miss Cartwheel said.

'A what?'

'Now you've made me feel silly,' Miss Cartwheel said crossly.

'Shag – otherwise known as Sir Rutland Shag – was my favourite horse. He was a very sensitive animal.'

'A horse that wrote letters?'

'No, of course not, you absurd girl. He merely whinnied his intent. The groom did the actual transcription. His education was frugal and his spelling poor.'

'I don't believe this! It's rubbish!'

'Poor child. You don't believe in anything. You are a cynic. It stems from an unhappiness which is all too evident in your hair.'

'My *hair*?'

'Lank tresses, split ends, ne'er helped true lovers make amends!'

Miss Churchill cracked her knuckles. 'You want to know what I don't believe. I don't believe you write all that tosh yourself. It's not possible. I've worked it out. You'd have to have written a novel every two and a half days for the whole of your life to have achieved your output.'

The great novelist did not bat even her exterior set of lashes. 'Unlike the idle little slovens of today, I perfected my speeds in typing when I was a girl. I type 60 words a minute, which is 3,600 words an hour, or 30,000 words a day. As my novels are inspired, I do not have to pause for thought.'

'Pull the other one! What are they inspired by?'

'Profound and perfect . . .'

But the ace journalist had vanished.

After the girl's departure Miss Cartwheel felt disturbed. She was not much disconcerted by her adversary. She frequently had far more invigorating conflicts with her cook. Something else was unsettling her. She did some exercises to the Zsa Zsa Gabor fitness tape and settled at her typewriter with an infusion. Still she could not compose. Sir Florian remained frozen on the moor. Willow was being subterraneously sautéed. Perhaps if she had a little swiggy of the floral tonic . . .

She poured a thimbleful, dipped a finger in and tasted it. Delicious! It reminded her of those scented cachous that used to be popular when she was a girl.

Now, who on earth had set fire to Glenfarlow? Why was

Willow tied up in the dungeon? She finished off the glass and at once she heard an evil laugh. Of course! It was Sir Rutland Shag. Shag had laughed maniacally when he set Glenfarlow alight. *'Have you ever made love by a roaring fire?'* he guffawed as he tied up the hapless Willow.

She lifted the bottle and swiftly refreshed her throat. A strange energy infused her. The story flowed from enkindled fingers. Never had she written so fluently, so speedily, with such mystical inspiration. She knocked back a half pint of the magic potion and returned to Willow and Sir Rutland in the dungeon. To her surprise, the heroine's bodice had become undone and her bosom was glowing rosily in the light of the flames. *'If I must die, then I must die,'* Willow cried piteously, *'but first I should quite like to find out about bonking . . .'*

By midnight the story was ended. It was a masterpiece. Arabella typed a title page for *Never Mind the Bells*, her fingers never faltering until they reached the final noun, where she inadvertently hit an 'a' instead of an 'e'. Her finest novel was finished. The bottle of Parfait Amour had also, mysteriously, been exhausted and Miss Cartwheel felt a little dizzy. She made her way to the bathroom, singing. Her warbling was disturbed by the peremptory return of the entire bottle of liqueur. She peered at the pool of mauve on her marbled tiles. She thought it looked much prettier coming back than all the muesli and yogurt she had kept down over the years. Re-siting her eye-lashes and splashing her face with *eau de rose*, she went to make a phone call. Extraordinary that she had forgotten . . .

'Sir Rutland Shag's residence,' said an ancient and exhilarating voice.

'It's Arab,' she enlightened. 'Remember? I've just finished a wonderful novel, and it's almost Christmas. Why don't you come over? Bring a bottle and we'll let our hair down.'

'Mine let me down years ago!' Shag boomed gleefully. 'But everything else is in sporting order.'

Gilly Churchill sat at her typewriter with a mashed avocado on her face. Several times she had crept away to peer in the mirror. She looked terrific – well, nothing that a good night's sleep wouldn't cure. But there was something wrong, a hollow feeling which she could not place. Perhaps she was hungry. She went into the kitchen to look for something nourishing. That was when she found the avocado. She thought about eating it but there are limits to what the human spirit can endure. Still, waste not, want not.

She drank a bottle of Southern Comfort, but it failed to cheer her. She could only envisage the mud it would put in her eye. A cup of coffee was what she needed. She decided to go next door and borrow some from her new neighbour.

For several minutes she gazed in silence at the sublime specimen of manhood that responded to her knock, and he gazed back at her. He was the first to break the spell. 'Aargh!' he screamed. 'What do you want?'

She tried to ask for a loan of his Copper Blend but the words kept changing their shape in her mouth. Her bosom heaved and her innards churned. 'I want love,' croaked the creature covered in green slime. 'Profound and perfect, if you know what's good for you.'

❧

A Reproduction

Some people shouldn't be given reproductive equipment, but it's standard issue. Ladies are like window boxes, painted and shallow and open to the elements. Men, like colds, are catching.

'Stop me,' he smiled.

'It's quite safe,' I smiled. 'The seventeenth is the day.'

'I really think you've got it all wrong,' he smiled.

When I found I was pregnant I didn't tell my husband right away; none of his business since it probably wasn't his.

'Stop me,' teased my lover.

'It's all right,' I smiled. 'I'm pregnant.'

One smile too many and they were all gone. My lover turned into a pillar of salt. I myself was more like a little glass dish of salt on a boarding-house table, weeping copiously because I had not been stopped.

He spoke through the sheets like an obscene telephone caller. 'We'll get you an abortion.'

'I want my child,' I sniffed.

'You told me I was all you wanted,' he argued.

'Abortions are dangerous,' I sobbed.

'Less dangerous than childbirth and you've already been spared the hazards of the Pill,' spoke the sheets, reckless now and veering perilously close to logic.

'I know all about those lunch-time abortions with doctors in crimson aprons and screams from the incinerator,' I wept.

'It's twenty-four hours with a full English breakfast.'

I threw up and felt I had had the final throw.

When I told my husband he went off to commit suicide. In the gas oven or the tallest tree, he met Anthea. She came home and started scrubbing his wronged underwear before I had packed my cases. I found her sitting by the fire drinking a tumbler of the whiskey I only got when I had a cold. She put another log in my open brick fireplace and grinned at me through long, white teeth. 'Made a frightful hash of things, haven't you?' she said amiably.

I moved in with my lover, creaking with condemned pride and trying desperately to appear healthy, like a pensioner going to live with the marrieds.

There are manuals filled from cover to cover with excuses for husbands. Every girl knows that husbands suffer from sexual fatigue, go prematurely bald, forget birthdays and prefer their mothers' cooking. Lovers are to be found only in romantic fiction as dark maned, well hung, square jawed, with burning eyes and no relatives, permanently erect and permanently smiling.

He wore nylon socks. He liked warm milk with his cornflakes. His hair was shaped with hairspray and his face was cast with gloom.

'Perhaps it won't be too bad, darling,' I said, running my knitting needles through his hair. A face filled with dread floated into my vision, like a spectre in a nightmare. 'It will be a tiny, blue-eyed intellectual. We'll feed it sieved smoked salmon and red wine in a plastic bottle.'

'It's still there, then?' he said.

Anthea opened the door to me when I arrived with my suitcase. 'Oh, I say!' she greeted. 'How many of you are there?' My husband bounded forward looking scrubbed and mischievous, like a schoolboy in an advertisement. I moaned piteously; 'Take me back.' The three of us trooped into the living room which was transformed with macramé and little fat candles as ugly as toads. 'Have a drink,' Anthea said, waving the whiskey. 'Oh, golly, sorry – I forgot.' She filled herself a quarter pint and sat back, waiting.

I addressed myself to my husband. 'I can't live without you, I'm so miserable I could die. I love you.' My tears volleyed like angry little pellets into the calm silence. I opened one flooded eye and could see a brown-suited swimmer, smiling.

'No you don't,' he said agreeably. 'Not at all.'

He made tea. It was good tea. I hadn't had a good cup of tea in ages. We sat around the fire eating Anthea's awful oatmeal biscuits and talking about her nerves. 'I wouldn't know sleep if it sat on my face,' she said. I congratulated her and said good-bye. I hadn't stood a chance. My nerves were weighted down with hormones.

When I got back my lover was reading a book. A pink puppet reared up above the literature and bowed to me. It was his hand, clothed in one of the tiny pink dresses I had been knitting, absurdly small for a human being. My heart leaped. He was waving to me in greeting. He was reading Dr Spock.

'Girls,' he said, 'are more intelligent than boys up to the age of nine years.'

'I didn't know you cared,' I said.

'You didn't tell me it was going to be a girl.'

I came over and hid my mouth in his hair. He patted my behind with a big hand innocent in pink drag. We put away the knitting and the reading and went to the bedroom holding hands. It was a long time since I had undressed in the middle of the day. 'I'm a whale,' I giggled. 'A meringue,' he contradicted elegantly.

'Stop me,' he said suddenly.

I sat up. 'It's all right . . .'

'Dr Spock disagrees with excessive physical contact.'

'But that's for parents and children,' I argued.

'I know,' he frowned. 'That's what I mean.'

It was a boy. I apologised profusely but there was nothing I could do. The nurse slapped it to cover its screams and then washed it in cold water like a fish and placed it, floundering, on my chest. In many ways it was a better person than I. Its face was a squint of honest malice while I was still trying to smile. It understood its role more than I did mine. While I was trying to pluck the little pink leech from my breast it stopped howling and drew the furious wet cavity of its mouth into an amazed 'o' which it clamped on to the cotton over my flesh.

'He wants to feed,' the nurse said.

I was paralysed by its lack of modesty.

'You specified breastfeeding,' she prompted.

I remained rigid, as in a nightmare where one finds oneself in bed with one's boss. The nurse schluk-schlukked swiftly across the floor in determined canvas shoes. She jerked at the ribbon of my nightie and pulled out a breast which she plugged into the child. I felt as if I had been caught hoarding beneath my clothing something not rightfully mine.

It was a relief, all the same, that the business had begun. Its urgent, predatory kiss was all at odds with the vulnerable, feathery feel of its body and it hurt me, like an inconsiderate man, but it forced me to think of it as a person. There were moments when I felt I could be drawn into the marshy world of motherhood. It made little squeaks of bliss while it fed and I was grateful someone was pleased with me.

'Sorry, ' I said again, catching sight of my lover who had sat there through it all, breathing in and out and bearing down.

His face was appalled, as if it had been stretched on a last, far out of proportion to my perfectly human error in having got the wrong number of chromosomes into the recipe. His eyes pierced my peculiar little pink gentleman; his horror was woven into the child. For the first time I, too, looked directly at my baby, but defensively, to counter the evil eye.

I searched the small, fussy face which was red as a rasher and furrowed as a waffle. It seemed that in his first few minutes he had already been stamped with an identity. He looked . . . like all other babies, for goodness' sake.

'He looks,' said my lover, digging up my thought, solicitous as a dog, 'exactly like your husband.'

I did my best. I defy anyone to say otherwise. I called him Julian although the name sat as awkwardly on his angry florid form as did the crochet bonnet I tied on to disguise his lingering alopecia. When I brought him home I put him in a fashionable wooden cradle, hung about with ethnic mobiles. I dyed the pink dresses purple, which seemed a creative compromise between pink and blue. Yet he was not the best of company. He belched and scowled and bellowed like a scoundrel. Sleep was nowhere among his skills. All night there was the grizzled thread of reproach so full of misery that it drove us grown-ups to opposite edges of our bed lest our comfort deprive him of the full complement of our futility.

His demands for food were a Wagnerian opera and he cunningly adjusted his appetites nightly so that I could not anticipate his needs and leap to his side, bare-breasted, a Wagnerian offering, before the storm broke.

The storm broke after six months. My lover and I sat in the kitchen looking like death, sharing breakfast with the cautious concentration of famine victims. We ate, quickly, furtively, hunched up against the onslaught of the monotonous music of human wrath.

When the singing started, we leaped up and began running in different directions, rescuing bottles from the sterilising unit not inaptly called 'Milton' (for who, more than new parents, understands about paradise lost). We mixed formulas to a consistency of wet cement. It was eight seconds or so before we realised that the sound was the telephone. 'Thought we'd just drop round and say "hi" to the little home-wrecker,' Anthea boomed. Did she mean me or the baby? 'Ten minutes, say. Good-o.' She hung up. I hadn't said a single word. We might have moved house or anything. She could have been speaking to a perfect stranger.

I dropped the speaking set and scurried about the house gathering to myself a small community of colouring agents and camouflages. 'Not for you,' l said ruefully as I collided with my face in a bathroom mirror.

They arrived on the dot and stood bouncing like yo-yos behind the glass door panel and pressing the bell. The noise set the baby howling. Their shining good health and good spirits were an intrusion on our chaos. Anthea savoured the screams, the spilt feeding mixture, our faces as dim and grey as pillow covers in tenements. 'So,' she said; 'this is where the other thing gets you.'

'This,' said my lover, speaking for the first time in months, 'has nothing at all to do with the other thing.'

At the sight of Anthea looming over his crib, the baby stopped crying and assumed a coy expression that made him look, under mountains of lacy knitting, like a bridal gnome. I had covered most of his face with a bonnet and powdered his shiny pink cheeks for a disguise. Anthea was studying him oddly. She deftly polished his cheek with a thumb and it showed russet like a pomegranate.

With a twitch, she deprived him of his pixie. An army of orangey hairs crept up the back of his neck and over his skull to a point quite near his forehead – the point, in fact, to which my husband's orangey hair had retreated.

'I say,' she said.

I went for a long walk after they took him. It wasn't regret, exactly, but just as Anthea settled him into the car for the first time in his life, he smiled. I felt an awful twinge as I recognised that smile. There was surely no mistaking that smile. 'Stop me,' he seemed to say to me, as he betrayed me.

He still has that smile except when he shows those long white teeth that make him look so like Anthea, when he grins with delight and says: 'Tell me, auntie! Tell me about the man with the hairspray.'

When I got back there was no one there. All his clothes were gone, nothing left of him except his note. 'Gone forever,' he wrote. 'I lived for that child.'

ফ্রেমঃ

A Nail on the Head

On several evenings in the year Benjamin Hart brings home people to his wife. They are for dinner. The characters belong to the life he leads between outward and homeward-bound trains. He assembles them with care and selflessly – a good assortment; wit and distinction, pretty faces and ones that have been photographed for the newspapers, the occasional homosexual or journalist. The people are not vital to his situation in life. They have not stretched his talents or contributed to the bulk of his pocket. He chooses them for Mirabel. On these occasions his wife wears a long green dress that she has had for many years and puts upon the table items in aspic and troublesome puddings supported with eggs. It is very nice.

To understand Benjamin's solicitude it is necessary to know about Mirabel. She is thirty but has withstood cellulite (Benjamin is unclear about cellulite but imagines it as a form of breakfast cereal harmful to the intestines).

Her face is free of flaws. She read in a magazine article that crumpling of the eye tissue could be forestalled by smiling with an outward curve rather than an upward one. She practised this in a mirror and now produces a smile so strained and frugal that people imagine it has to do with sex. In fact her passion is invested mainly in the stripping and re-covering of old furniture. Mirabel is a skilled housewife. She renders down the tailbones of beasts into delicious stews and cakes of jellied meat. She does not work in a job. She does not demand children. In spite of the fact that she once went to the university where she read Medieval English, she never complains. Benjamin believes that this is because he has not increased her housekeeping allowance in keeping with the cost of living, nor his own substantial increments. She runs the household wonderfully on a modest budget. It extends her capabilities.

Benjamin once heard a woman complain about being left to rot in the house. It haunted him. There was a suggestion of wastefulness, as if some perfectly good leftover had been neglected in the fridge until disfigured by invading organisms.

He made up his mind that it would never happen with Mirabel. It was a problem. Although he did not wish her to rot in the house, he could not countenance the idea of her gadding about outside, prey to the corruption of the world beyond. Owing to the pressure of his work, he had very little to do with her. He often mentioned her, though, when people complained about the state of things. 'My wife . . .' he would impress, offering a point about her skill with over-ripe tomatoes, her stand against cellulite. They all agreed that she sounded a marvel. They clamoured to meet her. This was how Benjamin hit on the idea. He would bring Mirabel company. She would enjoy the fruit of his social labours, the pick of the crop. He felt he had hit the nail on the head.

The Harts live in a house which is called 137. A new road veers muddily out of the town, found hoarding a plot of ground behind an oldish council estate. Two hundred red-brick houses were crammed into this space. The buildings pursue a series of small zigzagging roads as though fleeing in panic from the bulldozers that rumbled into the ground for a year.

In fact this apparently meaningless pattern was the ingenious design of an architect, facilitating the intrusion of five extra houses. The residents, having a homing instinct, do not notice, but it confounds the logic of the numbers. Visitors and debt-collectors can be seen swerving their cars out of different cul-de-sacs well into the night. A series of false trails leading to 137 is particularly cunning. On previous occasions there have been guests lacking in persistence who failed to locate it, leaving gaps like missing teeth in the evening. One fellow, knocking on a door to refresh his directions, had struck up an acquaintance with a perfect stranger and gone off with him for the night. Since then Benjamin has made a point of fixing a neutral place of assembly, usually the new cabaret lounge, with its myopic red sign blinking over the town. He allows his guests to purchase a round apiece to work themselves up into a party spirit, so that by the time he leads them back to Mirabel they are, so to speak, at room temperature.

All the way to the pub he smiles at this piece of humour which he has just thought up. He would find it hard not to smile. Having just left his kitchen where little French beans gleam waxily like a pile of green crayons in the sink and ox kidneys on the stove succumb their toughness to a splash of Spanish brandy, his joy is large and assertive. He nestles between twin monuments. At home, beauty and thrift are testimony to his successful marriage. Two miles away, a knot of mildly successful people, petrified by strangeness, await his unifying phrase, his warming presence. He seeks nothing in return. Their very adherence to him will testify to his significance in the larger world, even though he hardly knows them.

Mirabel has bought a spray of lilac. It cost forty-five pence. It lies on the kitchen counter, swaddled in white like a baby, while she worries. For the same price she could have had a bunch of tulips, five or six in egg-yolk yellow or chilblain pink. They were not very nice but they had bulk on their side.

She fetches a decanter without a stopper. It was ten pence at a sale of work and she knew it would come in handy. She fills it with water and inserts the lilac. It lolls like a plume in an ink well. She carries this through to the lounge and puts it on a low coffee table which she herself lacquered in black. She sighs with relief. The single pinkish bloom flames like a candle, warming up the pale silky covering of the sofa. The money has not been wasted.

The sofa is old. Its cushions are filled with down. She bought it second-hand for fifty pounds and sewed the covers herself. The curtains are in a similar shade although they do not match. She had to do the best she could with what was in the sales. The walls are painted like the undersides of mushrooms and there is a rug of whitish animal hair on the floor. With a small fire in the grate and a dish of brack olives gleaming on the black table, the room will look like one in a magazine.

From a cabinet in the lounge she fetches a decanter which has a stopper. From a bag advertising a supermarket, she withdraws a bottle of sherry. *Ernesto Sanchez* the label admits. It cost a pound and fifty pence. At the end it swarms like brown sugar in hot whisky.

She admires the components of the dinner, bathed in oil or cream and bursting with nutrition. The entire meal (excluding the wines, which Benjamin will carry home in a brown paper bag, not counting the expense) is costing less than five pounds. In spite of some inauspicious ingredients it will be delicious, even the cold rice pudding, boiled then frozen, then crowned with a plastic basket of strawberries and a French title. Mirabel would like to have the neighbours in, Mrs Stanley and Mrs Winter, to pick over her bargains and consolidate her achievement but she imagines in advance their resentment at not being compelled to take something more than a cerebral pleasure in her work. She contents herself with stealing one of the strawberries – her first of the season – and making a wish. 'I wish –', the thought rises like a wisp of smoke on her neat brain.

She does not wish for a better home or a new dress. She does not even wish for a better sherry. She visits the rooms of her tranquil and economical home. She sighs, flops down into the sofa, rises upon hearing bashes of greeting on the front door, and repairs the small damage inflicted on her cushions by her bottom. She straightens her lips into a smile and hurries to the hall to welcome her guests, berating herself for foolish thoughts. After all the trouble she has gone to, it would be ridiculous to wish they weren't coming.

There stands on the doorstep a tall youth with shorn hair and rosy cheeks and a coarse-looking middle-aged woman in a fur coat. Between them is a child with short blonde hair and a pointy nose and in the background, a tall foxy woman, frozen into fashionable repose. Mirabel, standing on the warm side of the door, keeps her mouth rigid with welcome. She imagines that behind this group she sees a large dog and someone draped like a towel over the fence. She is further confused when the boy with the rosy cheeks extends a big red hand and says: 'Hi, I'm Roxanne.'

There is a moment in which Mirabel thinks that they may be Jehovah's Witnesses or Friends of the Earth but then she sees Benjamin coming up the drive, bow-legged under a clanking brown paper bag, so she murmurs 'Do come in', and shrinks back into the hall.

They crowd into the living room and stand shouting out their names, further identifying themselves with occupations. The woman in the fur coat is called Norma. She writes for a newspaper. Roxanne, in spite of crew-cut and combat clothes, is a girl. Benjamin introduces her as an artist but she has already confided to Mirabel in the hall that she works as a char. The gnome turns out to be the same age as Mirabel. Her name is Flora and she says she is a seer. The tall fashionable woman is Sybil King. She makes dresses which sell for hundreds of pounds. 'And this is Lionel,' she says of the man around whose hips her fingers flutter. 'He does heads.' 'A sculptor!' cried Benjamin. Mirabel cannot give her attention. She is focussed on the man's pink jeans. She could swear she saw them hanging on her fence a few seconds earlier.

'He's a hairdresser,' Sybil says. 'Everyone goes to Lionel. He's divine.' Mirabel looks doubtful. 'He's a bit under the weather tonight,' Sybil explains. 'He's been mixing his drinkies. I'm afraid he had to have a little sicky outside but we made him lean over the fence into your neighbour's garden, didn't we, darling?' Lionel belches threateningly. His knees sag and he collapses into an armchair covered in oyster-coloured Dralon velvet. Mirabel watches his trembling lips in terror. She tries to think what she will say to Mrs Stanley in the morning about her begonias, shrivelled under Lionel's illness. Her concentration is damaged by a commotion in the hall. There is a sequence of gruff yelps and some language. An enormous dog, which she had earlier thought she saw in the garden, drags Benjamin into the living room on a lead. 'Sorry, dear,' Benjamin says as the dog grinds mud into the white rug. 'He's very strong.'

'Come to Mummie?' Sybil pats an arm of the sofa. The

dog bounds over, scrabbling the silk with ferocious paws. 'She's a Borzoi,' Sybil boasts.

'What's her name?' Mirabel says in a high tone of voice.

'Lucrezia.'

After a silence there comes a high-pitched whinny of laughter which floats like a streamer over the room. The woman in the fur coat is pink in the face, gobbling with mirth. 'Lucrezia Borzoi,' she yelps. 'Oh, Jesus God, I'm going to have a heart attack.' Her body shakes as if inhabited by an unreliable engine and tears dribble down her bunched-up jowls.

'Pardon?' Sybil says.

Mirabel feels it is up to her. She grabs Norma by her furry shoulders and rattles her vigorously. 'Let me take your coat, please,' she says. But Norma will not let go her fur. Mirabel tugs at it a few moments more but Norma says no, she is cold, it cost three thousand pounds.

Mirabel offers her a glass of sherry to warm her up. 'Horse's wee-wee,' the woman laughs with contempt, before eagerly accepting.

In the kitchen Mirabel arranges the decanter of sherry on a round wicker tray with seven little matching glasses. The glasses are engraved with flowers. She bought eight of them so that she would not be heartbroken when one got broken. Her matched glasses, her perfect dinner, snoring in pots on the stove, lend her strength. She lifts the lids from saucepans and smiles at the contents as if they are children in prams. Mercifully, the smile stays in place as she seizes the tray and marches back to the lounge.

The guests have all found places to sit. The three women are on the sofa, the gnome is on a cushion on the floor. Lucrezia, the dog, lies in front of the fire, roasting her behind. Benjamin sits on the edge of a brittle Regency chair, studying Lionel for signs of life.

Crammed with people the room has taken heart. Mirabel notices a frill of Sybil's pleated chiffon dress fanning out around an edge of the sofa. She watches Flora's cap of yellow hair, nicely cut by some Lionel or other, and the neat lotus fold of her ankles on the cushion. She sees the bluish shimmer of Norma's fur and Lionel's handsome head flung back in the armchair. She feels a little thrill of pride. It is nice to have one's home filled with friends. She hands round the sherry, passing by Lionel's chair, but his hand shoots out and appropriates a glass with speed. She takes her own glass to the remaining armchair by the fire.

'Well, this is very nice, Harold,' Norma says when they are all settled. Mirabel looks up in surprise scanning the room for a new face, a Harold, but Norma has her eye on Benjamin. 'It's Benjamin,' Mirabel says. 'What's Benjamin?' Norma says eagerly. 'My husband's name is Benjamin,' Mirabel persists.

Norma looks at him with respect. 'Benjamin. I never thought of him as a Benjamin.'

'How did you meet him?' Mirabel says.

'D'you know, we've never actually met. We travel on the same train sometimes. He reads the back of my newspaper. Damned irritating habit.'

'He's a bit of a dark horse, our Benj,' Sybil says crossly. Mirabel is astonished. 'He never told me he had a wife tucked away in the suburbs.' 'Have you known him long?' says Mirabel. Sybil squints back into her memory. 'We met, oh, two, three years back. Your husband came into my shop and asked to see something for less than five pounds. "You can add two noughts to anything in my shop, dear," I told him. Quick as a flash he said: "Give me something with two knots for less than five pounds." I like a man with a sense of humour. I told him straight out. It's what makes a man sexy. I'll bet he's a rattler in the sack.'

'Three years,' says Mirabel faintly.

'That was the last I saw of him,' Sybil goes on; 'until last week when he walked into the shop, out of the blue and asked me to dinner. Mind you, this wasn't quite what I had in mind. You can bet your sweet bippy I wouldn't have worn a five-hundred pound dress if I'd known we were going to wallow in the family trough.'

Mirabel feels dazed by all this talk of prices. She is used to discussing bargains with her neighbours. It is her favourite topic. Her mind cannot accommodate talk of hundreds and thousands. At least Roxanne is giving her no worry in that quarter. The girl, who appears to be falling asleep, is wearing clothes that must have come lately from a rubbish bin. She remembers her manners and is about to tell Sybil that it is a lovely dress but Norma rends the air with a shrill cry of triumph. 'Five hundred pounds? Well, *that's* a figure to impress. The dress is divine, darling. What a pity your ribs stick out more than your tits.'

Sybil frowns at Benjamin. 'You should have told me you were married, dear. It's a bit of luck I had old Lionel tagging along for a drink this evening, that's all I can say.' She stands up and picks cautious steps to where Lionel is sleeping. She falls heavily into his lap. 'I have lovely tits, don't I darling?' she says. She squirms her bottom in his crotch, disturbing the rhythm of his snoring.

Roxanne has been lustily eyeing the space on the sofa vacated by Sybil. 'Far out,' she says. She heaves her boots up on to the cushions. Clumps of mud scar the silk as she shuffles her legs to make herself comfortable. 'Dinner's ready,' Mirabel shouts.

It is a lovely dinner. Everyone says so: pools of green soup in white bowls, little rolls, home-made with milk, and poppy-seed crusted. Benjamin measures yellow wine into their glasses and voices carve the air above the clash of spoons. Mirabel catches his eye. They smile at one another.

Everything has been towards this moment. Their home, the offspring of their endurance, has been kissed to life. They are accomplices, woven together with parental pride, aglow with reflected glamour. Her breasts shimmer beneath candle-light in the old green dress; his red silk handkerchief flares irresistibly in his worn corduroy jacket. The blurred, dancing edges of their smiles are a living, vital language, like the intricate frame of strange phrases that surrounds them and isolates them. The guests are on the outside. Eat, drink and be as merry as they may, they know they will be flung out into the cold before the night is over; and who can be absolutely sure that this scene does not continue forever inside the house, without them.

Mirabel asks Flora if she will always be happy, always have love. Flora, who now that she has a cushion on her chair and no one can see that her feet don't touch the ground, looks more normal than anyone, says: 'Oh, love, yes, that's no problem.' 'What do you mean?' the others clamour peevishly. They are all, except Mirabel and Benjamin, on their own, are they not? And Roxanne's husband, the louse, did he not once try to strangle her?

'Anyone can have love, ' Flora says. 'We've all got love. It's just a matter of making up our mind to the fact that it may never be returned.' Flora's face is pink and round. Her lips are moist. Her hair moves in a piece, shining gold. Although she is much less than five feet in height and probably tells fortunes behind a velvet curtain in a council flat, anyone can see that she is a person of quality, a priestess. They cannot hide their tawdry hearts. They make up for it by being pitifully good, eating all their bread, listening without interrupting.

'Love may not be mutual,' Flora says softly. 'It may not be rewarding. It may not even benefit the person at whom it is directed. But real love is indestructible.'

Mirabel thinks it is beautiful. She cannot imagine where this small, tidy, sensible person has been all her life. She is about to raise this point when she notices that the soup bowls are empty and that Norma has had time to smoke a whole cigarette and grind the stub into a green puddle of soup. She seizes this stinking arrangement and the other bowls and hurries to the kitchen to reinforce supplies.

When the main course is put on the table it appears to present a problem to Lionel. 'What are these?' he says, aiming his fork fuzzily at what look like a lot of very small boxing gloves in cream. 'Kidneys, dear,' Norma booms. 'Glandular organs for the excretion of urine.' 'God,' Lionel groans. He gazes on the kidneys reproachfully for a moment before bolting from the room. On his way through the lounge he leans against the wall and with an expression of surprise, vomits explosively over the white fur rug. Some of it, Mirabel notes, goes on the sofa. 'There, there, old man,' Benjamin cries out in alarm. He hurries into the lounge, closing over the folding doors so as not to offend the guests any more than is necessary, but after that none of them does more than toy with the meal. They eat the strawberries off the Riz à l'Impératrice and at last Mirabel is able to leave them with an excuse about grinding coffee. She does not grind coffee, nor even her teeth. She puts on the kettle to boil for the Nescafé and prepares a solution of bleach and soapy water for the rug.

When she gets back to the dining room no one is there, but the dog, Lucrezia, has mounted the table and is trampling the remains of dinner into the cloth with her paws and splattering sauce from dishes with her great purple tongue. She pushes the animal hopefully but it digs in and she can hear the sound of its claws gouging the surface of the wood. She opens the folding doors and peers cautiously into the lounge. The room is empty. She takes in her bowl of soapy water and begins dabbing at the stain on the rug. She works quickly and has made the mark fade considerably by the time they all burst back in to tell her they have been putting Lionel to bed.

Roxanne wants to dance. 'The rug?' Mirabel whimpers but Roxanne says for Christ's sake, life is for living. She whips the tainted rug from the floor and rolls it up in a corner. Benjamin puts on a rock record and Roxanne begins to gyrate, digging her workman's boots into the polished parquet floor.

Mirabel takes her mind off it by thinking about the neighbours. She imagines she hears a thumping on the wall but cannot make up her mind if it is the music, which is very loud, or Mrs Winter with a shoe, urging its cessation. In her mind she paraphrases the events of the evening for serving up to her neighbours the following day, along with the remains of the kidneys, browned under the grill with crumbs and freshened up with some lettuce leaves, but these thoughts have to be discarded. Her neighbours do not take kindly to noise and are unlikely to be on speaking terms with her for a time.

Dancing, Roxanne exists in a different plane. Her face is washed clean of all its charlady's conflicts and deprivations, her lumpish limbs take flight. She has shaken off her combat jacket and her large breasts pummel wantonly at a greying tee shirt. Mirabel find her eyes drawn to this swift-moving, sensual Roxanne. Benjamin too is mesmerised. His eyes are glazed. He positively drools. When Sybil whines that she wants a piece of the action, he rises like a sleepwalker and falls gratefully into her tense clutches.

Roxanne's hands slice the air like a solitary juggler. Benjamin struggles round the floor with Sybil like a wrestler on the final round but his smile is full of happiness and his palms are filled with her buttocks. When she moves away, snakelike, to change the record, Benjamin collapses into a chair in ecstatic langour. Mirabel takes advantage of his state and sits on his knee and puts her tongue in his mouth, but he pushes her off and tells her not to make an exhibition of herself. She looks around for someone to talk to. Lionel is still in bed and there is only Norma, sitting in her fur coat on the clean end of the sofa, and the dog, trailing dinner all over the floor on its paws. She would like to have a word with Flora to find out what the future holds but Flora seems to have disappeared. 'Where's Flora?' she says to no one in particular. Sybil stops dancing abruptly. She stamps across the room and switches off the music. 'Flora!' she calls out harshly. She glares around the room, then at each of the guests in turn as if they might have hidden the diminutive Flora in a pocket or handbag. 'What's going on?' says Mirabel mildly. Sybil's face has taken on a peculiar, beaky, frozen aspect, like a hen immortalised in stone.

Norma's face, on the other hand, is of a particularly vivid pink from the effort of trying to suppress some giant mirth which escapes in small squeaks and snorts. At length there comes a soft chortle, increasing in volume, on and on, chortle, chortle, chortle, chortle, whee, whee, so that one expects to see a train emerging from the tunnel of her mouth. 'What is it?' Mirabel says in horror. Norma raises distraught eyes at the ceiling. 'She must be a rattler in the sack,' she howls.

Sybil's green eyes narrow. Her lips compress into purple wafers. 'I hardly think you're in a position to pass comments,' she hisses. '*Anyone* who would wear a mink coat to Neasden . . .'

Norma's jaw falls. Her look is helpless in the face of Sybil's marksmanship. Two huge tears shiver in her eyelids and then plop into her blue fur. She looks to each of them in turn, beseechingly, reproachfully. None of them is able to speak.

Now that the music and the loud debate have been killed they are compelled to strain their ears to the faint gibbering of springs above their heads.

Without a word she grabs her handbag and marches from the room, slamming two doors so viciously that a little china bird falls from the wall and explodes upon the wooden floor.

'She was giving me a lift home,' Roxanne says after a time. 'How am I supposed to get home?' 'I shall take you,' Sybil offers. She claims her dog and her overcoat, and eventually, Mirabel's lifeless hand. 'It's been so pleasant,' she says. The two women make a perfectly normal exit, dragging the dog.

'Well, my girl,' says Benjamin when Sybil's little sporty number has ripped through the exterior silence. 'You have to admit I know some interesting types.' 'They're in our bed,' Mirabel says. 'Together.' 'For God's sake,' Benjamin savagely slaps her bottom. 'Men and women do that sort of thing' – he guffaws – 'Don't tell me I married a prude.' A rapid chorus of strange, tormented sighs, quite loud, drifts from the bedroom. Mirabel think of the holy souls in purgatory. Benjamin's face twitches in embarrassment.

'None of this would have happened,' he accuses, 'if you'd had the good grace to offer a drop of hot coffee.' His face lights up quite unexpectedly. 'Coffee!' That's it!' He strides to the stairs and arranges his expression into one of benign joviality. 'Coffee's ready,' he bellows up the steps. He swivels around to his wife, eyes full of cunning. 'That'll flush them out,' he predicts.

The four of them sit around the lounge drinking re-boiled instant. Flora is neat and calm as ever but Lionel unzipped, unbuttoned, unshaven, looks completely beyond repair. Mirabel still wants to ask Flora to tell her fortune even though she is no longer sure she can trust her future to a woman who seeks her satisfactions so unpremeditatedly. 'I'd like you to make a prediction,' she says quickly and nervously, stirring at the thick liquid in her cup. 'Sorry?' Flora says cheerfully. 'You know, tell my stars, ' says Mirabel. Flora stares at her hard for a moment before rudely addressing herself to Benjamin. 'What's she on about?'

'Search me,' Benjamin sniggers.

'I'm sorry,' Mirabel says. 'I ought not to have pursued it but it's the first time I've met a seer and I thought it would be ever so interesting . . .' She trails off. Flora squints in honest bewilderment. 'Blimey dear,' says the priestess. 'Your ears need washing. I'm not a seer, I'm an overseer. At the factory. Overlocking department.'

'Benjamin,' Mirabel pleads.

'It ought to have been Mrs Arnott from Pressing,' Benjamin reasons. 'She's a gifted amateur comedienne. She keeps us all in stitches. Alas, she received offer of a paid engagement.'

A small nerve begins to vibrate in Mirabel's jaw. At last she cries out: 'Who are all these people? I don't know them. You don't know them. We'll never see them again. We never do.' She begins to gather up cups and saucers, heedless of the breakage potential in her trembling fingers. Tears stand out in her eyes.

Benjamin strikes his knee so hard that his own cup of coffee leaps out of his hand and into the sofa. 'Good God, girl,' he says. 'Where is your sense of spontaneity?' Mirabel shakes her head in guilt and perplexity. She does not know. She has been cooking all week for the party. She goes to the kitchen and stays there, running scalding water over her hands to improve their circulation, until she hears Benjamin bundling the last of the guests into the back seat of his car.

When he gets home the dishes have been washed, the sheets on the bed have been changed and Mirabel has swept and mopped the floor. The house, no longer disastrous, wears a rakish expression. Benjamin waltzes about, humming fragments of a tune played earlier on the record machine. 'Wonderful meal, darling,' he reminisces. Mirabel is on her knees, scrubbing vigorously at the rug.

'I say, rather a Bohemian lot,' he establishes. When she has finished with the rug, she will go to work on the sofa. 'God, those women dancing!' He does a thing with his fist to signify sexual arousal. Mirabel grunts with concentration. It is a challenge to her, this carnival of disrupted substances which must be cast out before they have had time to claim tenure. She does not care if it takes all night. Benjamin bends down to plant a kiss on top of her pneumatic head which moves in time with her urgent fists. He notes that on her pale, tired face, a tiny smile is starting and he is gratified to have married a woman who appreciates the good things in life. 'Jolly good evening, actually, dear,' he says fondly.

Mirabel does not hear. As her fingers travel through matted trails of animal hair, her mind charges to a primitive hunting call. She will be up early in the morning to wash out the table-cloth, remove the mud from the carpet in the hall. In the back of her head, there is a foetal thought which shifts and grows and claims its space so assertively as to blot out everything else, even the dancing figure of her husband.

She half hopes the sofa is beyond repair.

There advances on her ear the distant shrill and stampede of the sales; the remnant counter, rich in colour and danger as an Eastern bazaar. Her blood is up, she can feel it. It is almost time she went scouring the sales for newer material for fresher covers. Her hands, already in imagination plundering bales and billows of cloth costing good money, are guiltless. She has to keep the place nice in case of visitors.

Mama

William was in the garden looking at the house, which was square and yellow. Behind it and around, there was scenery; patchwork fields, cosily bumpy like an eiderdown, little hunchback shrubs, cowering in the hollows, a horizon with a tooth-edge of firs. A green vegetable, immense, William thought. He shivered in the watery warmth, feeling guilty. 'I don't think we ought to go in. The house belongs to someone,' he said.

He liked his city flat with its neat pretence of a garden where short-haired city toms stalked between the polluted flowers and a solitary bird (hired by the Tenants' Association, he said: that was his joke) gave a terse recital at eight a.m. He wrote his successful novel there and it had insulated him with the sort of superficial social life that suited him perfectly. There were parties where he could entertain people by saying nothing at all. Good-natured girls admired his writing and his grey eyes, clasped him to their marvellously assorted bodies and disappeared into cigarette smoke. Except Joanne; she married him.

She went up the three granite steps that led to the door and swept back a mass of cobwebs and thorny growths with her hands. It was a wooden door, unpainted, with a good steel knocker and two panels of glass set into the upper half. At first it appeared to be a pattern of flowers but when his eye traced the pools of plum and olive and amber, William found he was looking at a montage of faces. Joanne's fingers went out to the glass. As they did, ugly pink ridges, seeping pinpoints of blood, leaped up on her hands and wrists. 'I've never seen anything like it. It's the most beautiful house,' she said.

'Your hands . . .' William said.

She splayed her long fingers to admire them. She noticed the weals and made a noise of irritation. 'Damn brambles,' she said. William was looking absent-minded. It was a look that meant doubt. Someone seemed to borrow his bones now and then, leaving a tall pile of pale flesh to try and stand up by itself. It was a thing that had to be coped with. She arced a polished arm to hold back the brambles for him and their dappled shadow gave her a fringe.

'What am I and where am I?' she said, her face radiant with schemes. 'I don't know,' William said, which was the truth. 'Do you give up?' she said. 'No!' He bounded up the steps, ducking under rusty coils of thorn to be near her. She put her arms around his neck. 'I'm the wife of a famous writer,' she coaxed. 'I'm in *Vogue* in glorious colour in their "Writers at Home" series.'

It was Joanne who had decided that they ought to live in the country. She said he needed peace and quiet to get through his next book. There was nothing to do but agree, although a part of him niggled that the upheaval of moving house wasn't going to help him meet publishers' deadlines. It was Joanne who had spotted the house, an architectural castaway, as they drove through remote countryside in the rain, looking for tea on the way back from a weekend with friends.

'Try the door,' she said. It was meant as a dare but it sounded to William as if he had forgotten his manners. He hurled his hands at the wood. The door yielded, squealing at the assault. It carried him into the hall. She pursued him through the shadows, closing the door behind her. William wouldn't have done that.

He watched as the placid landscape diminished in the gap of the door and went black. He stood with his eyes closed, still feeling a purple sheen of sun under his eyelids, listening to Joanne's heels tapping the bare wood floor behind him in an uneven rhythm. 'This house,' she said. 'It's a dream.' She began to twirl, her heels making the sound of somebody running around a diminishing circle. 'Shh,' William said. 'Kip, kip?' her heels queried softly. Seconds dropped off into the dust. William became alarmed in case she was in a sulk. He turned abruptly.

She stood like a child, contained in a frugal stalk of sun that got in through a broken skylight. She was holding in each hand the parts of a dismembered toy. 'A doll,' she whispered. 'It's broken,' William said. Her face was a clownish mask of puzzlement! 'It's been pulled apart.' 'We'd better go,' he said. 'Wait! There's a room in there that's full of toys.' She sounded as if she was blaming him. He trotted into the room after her, almost tripping over a roller skate. 'Shit,' he muttered, kicking it. It skittered over the boards on its wheels, thudding into the side of a giant panda which collapsed without complaint.

The room seemed to be the nursery of a spoilt child. Toy soldiers and train sets, cloth toys, a tricycle, had all been touched by dust and destruction. William explored a lump of self-pity that came up in his throat. He had never had toys. He would have cared for them. 'It looks as if the people who lived here just picked up their beds and walked,' Joanne said. 'A lot of these toys are perfectly good.' William was on his knees setting to right a rocking horse. The leather ears had been tugged so hard that they stood askew on lumps of glue. 'There's something . . .' Joanne's probing was emphasised by the rapping of her shoes as she explored. 'All the windows are barred.'

The horse had been carved from a single piece of wood. Curves as smooth as skin delighted William's fingers. The glass eyes were rounded to catch the light and it gave them a nervous life. It had a real leather saddle. When he was small his father had nailed two pieces of wood together for him like a crucifix. He held the longer piece between his legs as he hopped down the lane going 'glop-glop' with his tongue against the roof of his mouth. One day the boys came down the lane and they laughed at him. In an ecstacy of rage that exhausted his whole life's supply of anger, he had raised his horse above his head and hacked about him until they were a red blur in his tears and their blood.

'William.' Joanne's voice crumbled from her lungs like sand from a bank. He gave the horse a reassuring pat to say he would be back and went to look for his wife. She was standing in another doorway, not posed for an entrance but artlessly, feet apart like a middle-aged woman. He heard the other noise. 'Mama.' It sounded like one of those dolls with a mechanical box set into the body that emits a wail when you turn it upside down. Joanne's clenched fingers were empty. A child? William forced his feet to perform a man's heavy step, needing the reassuring sound. On the bare planks his steps sounded villainous so he tiptoed to the door trying not to be put out at the way Joanne's body jerked when the sound came again. 'Mama.'

There was a man in the room. He sat in a little pink wicker chair. He was dressed in a flannel nightshirt and looked like an invalid. His skin had a sticky texture and he was stunted in height, but fat. He billowed over the basketwork. William picked a path through a dusty jumble of toys, looking out for the doll that had given such alarm to his wife, seeing only his own shadow which seemed somehow less substantial than the other shadow that spanned the floor like the legs of a giant spider; the bars on the window. He attempted a smile. The man, watching him, seemed to expect more. His eyes were like withered figs. 'I'm sorry.' William was miserable with embarrassment. 'The front door was open. We'll go.'

Joanne, who had followed him with the teetering steps of a geisha, gave one small jerk when the door slammed. For an instant they watched it mistrustfully, then stepped forward together and exchanged a nervous smile as both their hands shot out for the knob. 'It's stuck,' William said, testing it. He worried it exploratively. He gave an energetic tug. 'Jammed.' The man was watching them with a pleased intentness. 'Warped!' William called out to him. 'Must be damp.' There was no damp in the house. He had checked on that. His hands were damp, his forehead.

He wanted to cope with the situation, to make Joanne proud of him. He stamped across the room, knowing there must be a sensible answer and dinner somewhere in a nice hotel with a fire lit. He crouched in front of the little man. 'Old doors, ' he said, 'do that all the time. It takes a bit of know-how to open them.' The man's dusty eyes conceded nothing. Behind, the nagging of the brass door knob as Joanne persisted, sounded like a criticism.

The noise stopped. 'William!' The titter of Joanne's heels, her voice high with relief. 'William, it's open.' He basked as her cool fingers greeted his hand. Another hand, not cool and familiar but monstrous, flew out and severed their union. The fat man's fingers manacled Joanne's wrist. 'Mama,' he said again. He was pawing at her. 'Don't do that.' William's voice hardened hopefully. 'Mama,' the man whimpered. Joanne shuddered. His hand tightened. A bloodless band on her wrist framed his fingers. She looked to William for help. He couldn't meet her eyes. He dropped his gaze instead to the fingers locked on to her arm.

There was no escape for him. He felt that. The house was not civilised. It wanted to strip him. In the slow, sedated moments of shock the man in the chair became him, holding on to his mother's wrist, his small, tearing nails catching in clunking chains of her bracelet. He had developed an ear for despair on the delicate chatter of the metal links. Each night when her bracelet went on, she went out. Once he had tried to stop her. 'Mama,' he had cried, catching her wrist. She had jerked away, shock and revulsion in her face – Joanne's face. 'Your mama,' Joanne said, taking a deep breath to steady her voice, 'went to the shops.' He looked up quickly but she was speaking to the man. 'She's at the door now. I'm going to let her in.' She attempted to stand. The man would not let her. 'He knows the hall door is open. I told him,' William said uselessly.

'Your mama,' Joanne said, 'went hours ago. It's beginning to get dark outside. She's walking through a forest and she's frightened. Unless we go and find her she's never coming back. You'll be all alone.'

He understood. He sighed and let go her wrist. It was a child's comprehension, understanding the moment but believing it to be eternal. Like most women, Joanne thought it was all right to do anything so long as it was for the best. For a moment she hovered, waiting for the right instinct of disciplined kindness. 'Mama!' the man cried, flinging his arms around her so that her breath came out in choking gulps. He buried his head against her breast. Over the top of his baby skull her face was almost a caricature of horror. Her hands were held outward stiffly as though in supplication, although it was really to keep some part of herself free from contact. William launched himself at the man, slapping his head, tugging on his shoulders. The man's hands went to Joanne's neck. She sobbed in fright. William clawed at the obese paws. They had turned to iron. 'Go!' Joanne whispered at him. He remained where he was, crouched and stiff with shock. 'Get someone,' she begged. He scurried to the door, almost made it. His foot was mocked by another roller skate. He tripped.

He put out a hand to save himself. The toy steered playfully into his fingers. His fist clenched around it. He leaped to his feet without a thought and charged back across the room hearing with mild surprise the noise as the metal bar and wheels struck the bald man's skull. The man rolled back in his chair. The basketwork gave an endless groan.

'You've killed him,' Joanne said. William's voice shuddered: 'Let's get out of here. ' He took his wife's hand and helped her to her feet. Without looking back, they went to the door, walking to pretend it was quite normal. William opened the door. 'There,' he said. When he moved aside to allow his wife to pass, a freak draught caught at the door and swung it shut with a venemous crash. He grasped the knob. It was stuck fast. 'I . . . can't . . .' His voice rose on the edge of panic. He didn't like being locked in a room with a corpse. 'Let me.' Joanne pushed him aside and wrestled with the knob. For five seconds while her small body attacked the jammed door he resisted the temptation. On the sixth, he turned.

The man was grinning at the door. A trickle of blood was allowed to wander unchecked down the side of a nose like a mushroom and over his petulant little mouth. William touched his wife with stiff fingers. She glanced back irritably, then froze. 'We've lost,' she whispered. 'No, darling,' William said, horrified. 'He knows this house and its draughts. He's mocking us. There's nothing he can do to us. We'll find a way out.' He reached for her hand. She swatted it. 'Stay here,' she commanded. 'You don't understand this. You'll have to leave it to me.' Her voice had that tight edge of irritation that he dreaded. 'Oh, Jo,' he pleaded. 'I read about a case like this once,' she said. 'There was a man with one hugely developed area of his brain that gave him . . . powers . . . and crushed his other mental faculties.' 'Where did you read it?' 'Christ, l don't know, what does it matter? Maybe it was a film.' William sighed. 'What does it matter?' 'Don't patronise me,' Joanne said. Her voice was hard. 'If this is left to you and your logical thinking God knows what will happen. We'll be found by someone, someday, covered in dust like the toys.' The things she said frightened William. His anxieties engulfed him.

'Oh, for Christ's sake, don't look like that,' she said contemptuously. 'One ghoul's quite enough for any room.' He gripped the door knob, cool and solid. He could not feel anything except the knob and the ache in his throat. He was an amoeba suspended about the knob, a vapour. 'He probably can't actually move objects or he would certainly have put on a cabaret,' she mused energetically, 'but he can certainly direct natural elements, draughts, say. He must have incredible concentration. Our only hope is to break it. He's got to have a weakness. I'm going to try and find out what it is and hold his attention long enough for you to open the door. Whatever I do, don't move. And keep trying the door.'

He felt an unpleasant admiration for the efficient way in which she went to the little man, wiped at his bleeding face with a handkerchief and then caressed his head and the sides of his face. She was whispering in his ear. He watched her warily for a time and then put out a hand to touch her face. He smiled. His hand dropped to her body and moved over her breast. He grinned.

William commenced a desperate and monotonous dragging on the doorknob. In the background he could hear Joanne's voice like a stream of honey. He tugged at the knob harder, louder, hoping to drown out her voice but the words came at him like figures in a nightmare. The clatter of the brass fitting was the sound of a spectre in chains. William no longer held any hope. He knew that this was his life and he furiously performed his function of joggling the archaic knob, not with the smallest hope of escape but to divide Joanne's attention.

The noise he made was so relentless that he was not aware of the moment when she stopped speaking. She was eyeing the man with that expression of hers, her arms folded as precisely as laundry. 'I give up,' she said quietly. In that instant it became evident that the whole house depended on her. The man scoured her face for some sign of leniency. Shadows lengthened in the room. 'I'm leaving,' she said.

The man, crafty, glued his eyes on the door. 'Don't try your tricks,' she warned. She grabbed him by the shoulders and shook him like a rat. He lowered his eyes. William tried the door surreptitiously. It was stuck fast. 'I can walk out any time I want,' Joanne was saying. 'I would like you to open the door.' The man was confused. He rattled his chair. Joanne smiled and stroked his gashed head. 'There.' She bent and kissed his mouth, allowing his hands to fondle her. 'Like!' the man said. She offered him a coy look of reproach and glanced at the door. The man's face crumpled in angry disappointment. 'Open the door,' Joanne commanded. He glared at her. His jaws trembled with rage. 'Open it?' she said in a voice that played like water on stone. She came and sat on his knee, placed his hands on her breasts. She began to undo the buttons of her blouse.

William, punishing the door in his agitation, found that it was open. He blinked at the dusky hall through his tears, surprised at its provincial ordinariness. Through the glass panels in the hall door he could make out the hump of his own car.

He could leave now – alone – drive until he came to a hotel and have hot whiskey sent to his room. A deep bed, feathering him with oblivion; morning heralded by discreet knuckles on the door and a girl with fat legs bringing the comfortable smells of toast and coffee and her own sweat. He reeled at the homeliness of the fantasy.

'Aah,' said the man. William whirled. He spun the door so that it hopped into its lock. 'Nooo!' he howled.

Joanne and the man, piled up on the wicker seat like children in an absurd nursery game, turned faces surprised and

guilty. Irritation quickly claimed his wife's features. 'I thought
I told you not to move,' she said. 'Get back to the door.' Her
eyes, darting, groped about for some memory hastily flung in
her brain. 'The door!' she exclaimed. 'I heard it slam.' Her
eyes burned with accusation. 'It was open. You slammed the
door.'

'I had to stop you,' his voice gurgled with tears. 'He's a man.
You can't do that.'

Joanne slid from her perch, managing not to look foolish.
'So he's a man,' she sneered. 'Mr Universe.' The man looked
uneasy. He split his face into a boy's smile of ingratiation.
Joanne wheeled on William. 'What would you know about it?'
He backed away. She pursued him. 'You don't look much of a
man to me – more like a grubby child. If I leaned on you, I'd
squash you like an insect. As a man you only exist on the page.
You're the real monster. A paper monster! How white you
are!'

William concentrated on trying to stop the tears. 'You're disgusting,' Joanne said. 'Wipe your dirty nose.'

He had to stop crying. She was terribly cross. He caught his
cuff in his fingers and slid his sleeve under his nose, searching in
his mind for happy things to dam this abysmal waterfall.

The things he found in there were terrible; school reports,
forgotten birthdays, murderous boys. He was tired. It was
wrong to be on one's feet in the dark, people's faces eaten away
by shadows, distorting without warning into nightmare shapes.
He didn't like the dark. A bolt of blue steel attacked the shadows, brave and good like King Arthur's sword. He fixed his eyes
on the glittering shaft. A crossbar! Crikey! It was a bicycle.
Why hadn't he noticed it before? It was a beaut.

He revoked his tears with a snort and scrubbed his face with
the back of his hand. He swam in the shadows, his eyes seeing
everything, holding back the night. At his age they should.
He gripped the cycle in hands. Wow! Five gears and a
Duraluminum frame. He swung a leg over the crossbar and
eased his buttocks on to the saddle. Worship filled his lungs. His
toes bit at the pedals, enjoying their friskiness. 'Giddyup!' He
set them orbiting like chairoplanes.

His suspended foot captured one flying pedal and drove it earthward, his other foot tackling its ascending twin with ease. The wheels surged. Around, around, around he flew, wobbling just a bit as the bike negotiated strewn objects, sometimes not bothering to steer but enjoying the sensation as he squashed some silly toy. The wheels, squeaking from lack of oil, cried 'wheee!'

'Stop it!' Joanne's voice grazed like gunshot. He slowed down, pleased with the new sound the wheels made, like grating laughter. Her voice ranted over his lovely noise: 'This is too much. I'm finished with you. If we get out of here alive, I'm leaving you. Are you listening?' He was not listening. He would not. He cycled faster. Her voice was on a pitch with the hyena shrieks of his wheels. 'As for you –' she rounded on the man who sat quite still in the chair, boneless hands enveloping the wicker arms like pastry – 'no wonder no one likes you. No wonder you're all alone. Dirty, disgusting, untidy . . .'

'Not,' said the man with small defiance. She stormed over and slapped his wrist. He began to snivel. 'I know how to deal with you,' she said. 'I'll make you sorry for your tricks. Stupid boy!' She began picking up the toys with frenzied efficiency, deftly avoiding the bicycle wheels, stacking the toys in a neat heap in the corner, out of harm's way. As she crouched by the door, scooping up pieces of Meccano, she found she was able to identify the colours of the parts; green, yellow, blue. She watched, mesmerised, as it advanced toward her, spilling over her hands, her toes – a pool of light. She looked up. The door was opening. A shaft of moonlight climbed in from the skylight in the hall. The door opened quite wide. She looked back with a start. The man was watching the door, urging it open, wider, wider.

'William!' An excited shout. 'We're free. Oh, honey, I did it. Let's go!' She smiled as the gleaming metal came toward her; with surprise as the machine began to circle around her, closing in, round and round and round.

'Oh, William,' she said gently. 'Don't be silly. Come on.'

Round and round, faster, faster, making her skip a bit to avoid injury. 'William,' she said angrily. In the moonlight his face was terribly intense. His grey eyes stared at the door. 'Wheee!' went the wheels. 'William!' Joanne screamed. Crash! went the door.

He pedalled slowly from her. She ran to the door. She knew, she knew but she tried anyway. She crept into a corner and huddled there.

'Mama.' It sounded quite far away, quite faint. She covered her ears with her hands. 'Ma-ma.' Closer. She could hear the clumsy shuffle across the floor. She tried to back away, pressing into the wall. In the dark he might not find her. A sound of fright tore loose from her throat. Something touched her. 'William!' she screamed.

He felt proud to be there when she needed him. They needed each other. Now she would never go away. Joanne's heart began to pound at the same time as her body started to respond to the familiarity of the hand reaching for her in the dark. 'Mama,' William smiled.

ೞﬄﬆﬄ

The Complete Angler

❦

'I grew up in the city,' Ormond said. 'Everything around me was dirty and dry. I began to dream about water.'

It wasn't as if he lived in the desert. There was rain and secondhand bath-water; taupe dishwater creeping with fried leftovers and puddles emulsified with mud and suspicious objects. He dreamed about oceans and rivers, vast, clean expanses of blue where he would bathe or float. He never knew what it was like to drift and dive, warm and weightless, until . . .

'Didn't you have any hobbies?' Bernadette said.

With his eyes closed he couldn't imagine what she was thinking so he forced himself to look at her and was shocked by the shape of her face, lapsed on the pillow. 'I collected stamps.'

'Stamp collecting, you poor little prick,' she yelped.

He told her all about himself, surprised at the eagerness with which he stripped to the bone, flesh and fantasy, for her inspection.

He didn't think she was listening because after a time she turned to him and asked him if he had ever thought about fishing.

Ormond Sedge was dreadful in bed. He knew he was dreadful because Chrissie had told him: and Chrissie was his wife. Six months after they were married she had begun to tell their friends. She called him 'poor Ormond' because it gave the telling a sympathetic ring; but 'poor' in her own mind because he had failed to endow her with libidinous riches. Their friends minded being told that poor Ormond had reached a new low, as if he was the pound. It divided their loyalties, both between Chrissie and Ormond and with their own partners. If a woman sided with Chrissie it was saying she understood, which came out as a criticism of whatever man bore responsibility for her orgasms. The man who offered Ormond a reassuring wink across the room was seen to be beaconing signals of sexual distress.

The one who minded least was Ormond. He sat in a corner, smiling, and basked in the glow of pink her raspberry-coloured satin shirt threw on her pale skin, making her seem luscious with frustration. When her arms rose in irritation he admired the effect of perfect, ornamental breasts pressed against the thin fabric of her clothes and counted the hours until he could be in bed with her again.

Chrissie lay absolutely flat in the bed, defensively dead like a cat that is being patted by children. 'You'll have to hurry up,' she said crossly. 'I've got to work in the morning.'

'Coming,' he called out with gay insincerity. He knew he had stayed too long. He would come out in a minute. He would come out as soon as the pleasure diminished. He was floating. Tropical waters lapped his mouth. A Pacific whirlpool sucked at his groin. By moving very gently he could make tiny waves but he had to avoid sudden movements or there would be an end. If the end was death he might take a chance. It was a small injury, nothing to speak of. It left one disarmed, diminished, excluded.

Once, when he was very small, he had been taken to the sea and the ocean was all gone. 'Silly boy, the tide has gone out,' people said when he summoned witnesses to the catastrophe. He put on his bathing knickers and squatted like a frog on the coils of parched purple weed, spiked with shells and skeletons, that set apart the portions of the earth where creatures swam or walked. Hours he sat there, clawed by wet winds and terrified by sudden small eruptions in the sand until, like a frog, he went green. The water came back but it was not enough to know that these things happen every day.

'Ormond,' said an oracle. He opened his eyes just wide

enough to look at Chrissie's lips. It was lovely to be called Ormond by a woman with a mouth like a plum. He took a small dive from sheer elation. A little breeze sighed and whispered, stronger than he'd expected because it pushed a shudder right through his body. He took a deep breath and held himself very still. Everything went dead calm. He grinned in relief.

When she saw him smiling she pulled her plummy lips down into a droop and jerked away from him. 'You'll have to get yourself a mistress,' she said.

It was hardly any trouble finding a mistress. The bars were full of single women who paid for some of their drinks and sat with legs shaped for cello practice. The difficulty, Ormond discovered, lay in persuading a girl that she ought not merely to be a mistress in general but a mistress in particular. To a person. To him, actually.

He spent a week tapping girls on the shoulder, hoping their faces wouldn't horrify when they swished their shiny hair to get a look at him. He spent a lot of money on Pimms and Martinis. He was getting nowhere.

'I want to ask your advice,' he said to a girl called Virgin, who had fascinating white eyelashes and small breasts that pointed through her chiffon tabard like ballet slippers. 'Gin and lime,' she advised, handing him her glass.

'If you were a man how would you set about getting a mistress?' Ormond signalled the barman for a fresh glass of fluorescent. 'You're looking for someone to screw,' the girl said helpfully. 'No not exactly. I'm married,' Ormond boasted. 'It's my wife who wants the mistress. In fact she insists on it.'

'Your wife wants a mistress?' Virgin said. 'Gosh.'

In the end he had to settle for Bernadette, whose make-up had a look of boiled butterscotch sauce; whose figure was warm yeast rising under skimpy damp satin; who was a lot older than anybody. If she wasn't exactly what he had in mind, she allowed him no time for consideration. Shortly after he had introduced himself he found that he was standing naked in her bedroom, marooned on an island on his own clothing which her deft, typist's fingers had unleashed to his feet as raddled anchors. She twiddled his genitals as if they were a squeaky toy to make him chuckle and bundled him into bed tucking herself around him like a duvet.

'How was it?' he asked. With his eyes closed he liked Bernadette. She had an affectionate scent and a magnificent foreign tidal swell. It was like going on holidays. 'How was it?' he whispered in her ear. She felt quite limp in his arms and when he touched her face her mouth was open. His heart began to thud in case she was ill or dead but she groaned and turned over and said 'Christ' and he laughed at his foolishness. She had only been asleep. 'My wife thinks I lack technique,' he told her when she was properly awake and she laughed like a dolphin.

He told her about growing up in the city, his visit to the seaside. Then one day in a stranger's house in a dark room at a party he had found himself entering a woman. His whole body seemed engulfed in warm, fluid depths and he could smell the salt. With his eyes closed he could make a picture, a child's painting of a seaside scene. Salt and searing blues met on a scalloped horizon where a grapefruit sun bounced. Three linear gulls were piped on to the sky. On the ocean, quite close to land, a boy floated, as light and as nice and as brown as a biscuit. Ormond knew there was something called a climax. He had no wish in his life for climaxes – only an absence of irritation; but the girl beneath him joggled so fiercely that he had to concentrate just to keep his balance. She vacuumed him relentlessly while he sobbed that he loved her. Just as he was burrowing into sleep she snapped on the light. He had to look at her blotched face and tell her she was lovely. 'Thank you,' he had said. For teaching him a lesson.

It was then that Bernadette asked him about fishing. She lit a cigarette and propped up her breasts in a nest of sheets, considerate of their age. 'I was thinking,' she said. 'Lakes and rivers can be just as pretty as the seaside. Fishermen spend a lot of time in the water.'

He couldn't seem to grasp what she was talking about. He tried to focus on her but her whole appearance seemed to have slid sideways. She clucked her fuzzy mouth in a gesture of impatience and heaved herself out on to the floor, her big, naked backside looking oddly innocent as she ploughed across the carpet, full of purpose. It was most confusing. She was rummaging in a bureau. She turned to him, smiling with success. She had got herself a book. 'If you're bored I'll go,' he said, but she paid no attention, merely crashed back into bed again and began leafing through the pages as if it was a dictionary and she was seeking a phrase in a foreign language. After a time the pages stopped whirling and she began to read. 'For Christ's sake,' she said several times with interest, as her garbled features settled into intelligent repose.

'. . . *And for that I shall tell you, that in ancient times a debate hath risen, and it remains yet unresolved, whether the happiness of man in this world doth consist more in contemplation or action?*' came the words of Izaak Walton through the bruised lips of Bernadette. '*Concerning which, some have endeavoured to maintain their opinion of the first; by saying, that the nearer we mortals come to God by way of imitation, the more happy we are.*

'*And they say, that God enjoys himself only, by a contemplation of his own infiniteness, eternity, power, and goodness, and the like.*

'*And on the contrary, there want not men of equal authority and credit, that prefer action to be the more excellent; as namely, experiments in physick, and the application of it, both for the ease and prolongation of man's life; by which each man is enabled to act and to do good to others, either to serve his country or to do good to particular persons.*

'*Concerning which two opinions I shall forbear to add a third, by declaring my own; and rest contented in telling you, my very worthy friend, that both these meet together, and do most properly belong to the most honest, ingenuous, quiet and harmless art of angling.*'

In the days that followed Ormond contemplated. He contemplated art and virtue and the maintenance of human society. He contemplated doing good to particular persons for the ease and prolongation of life. When the time came, he contemplated his grease-painted mistress, sitting up in bed with no clothes on, reading her book. Her big, aquatic eyes bulged at him affectionately and a tranquil stream of sweat meandered through her breasts. 'Hi there, Pisceator,' she said. When he moved to the bed to kiss her she disappeared beneath the sheets. He dived in after her and rolled on top of her musky bulk. She squirmed away with strength and determination. 'I'm a fish,' she gurgled. 'You've frightened me.'

She taught him how fishes had to be surprised, tricked, teased, baited. '*First let your bait be as big a red worm as you can find,*' she read out, diligent as Mr Chips, '*without a knot.*'

She planted the book on his chest and slid down on him to prepare the bait. It was an action that caused Ormond to re-think his entire philosophy. He wondered if there was something he ought to be doing but he didn't like to interrupt her, so he began to read. '*Note also,*' he read, '*that when the worm is well baited, it will crawl up and down as far as the lead will give, which much enticeth the fish to bite without suspicion.*' His exhilaration was more scientific than sexual when her teeth explored flesh and nipped him daintily. He continued on, find-ing his own instruction. '*Having thus prepared your baits, and fitted your tackling, repair to the river . . .*'

'*And you must fish for him with a strong line and not a little hook,*' Bernadette instructed, reading on over his livid left ear.

'*And let him have time to gorge your hook.*' Her voice began to go funny. '*Then when you have a bite, you shall perceive the top of your float to sink suddenly into the water . . . then strike gently and hold your rod at a bent a little while; but if you both pull together you are sure to lose your game.*' He wasn't going to lose his game. He was winning. Twice she had lost her place in the book, and when she found it her recital came out with sounds like a church organ being tuned. '*. . . then mark where he plays most and stays longest,*' she continued valiantly. '*. . . and there, or thereabouts, at a clear bottom and a convenient landing-place, take one of your angles ready fitted as aforesaid, and sound the bottom which should,*' she finished with a tremendous amount of noise, '*be eight or ten feet deep.*'

Bernadette was a big fish. Landing her left him drenched and exhausted. Weariness pinned him to his pillow. It dragged his hair down and numbed his toes but before the first snores chugged laboriously up his lungs, he was an amazed witness to the spectacle of his spirit dancing like a two-year-old with a fisherman's thrill for the one that didn't get away.

In the weeks that followed Ormond began modestly to

believe that he was acquiring some skill as an angler. It was easy to strike with a singing heart in such a yielding stream. Once, for practice, he pretended he was with Chrissie. His mind sketched her deceptively languid face and round pouting mouth. Her eyes flew open, gentian blue, brimming with spite. 'You call that bait?' she hissed. 'I call it bird food.' He clung to his mistress and babbled his apprehension. Bernadette ruffled his hair and looked for her book. She read him some lines of a poem.

'*The jealous trout, that low did lie,*
Rose at a well-dissembled flie.
There stood my Friend, with patient skill,
Attending of his trembling quill.'

'Sir Henry Wotton wrote that,' she said, adding as a reprimand: 'He was over seventy.'

There were days when Bernadette's whole body looked tousled as she groped in the bed for her handbook. '*Observe, lastly,*' she read in a cracked whisper following a spectacular siege that neglected several suns and moons, '*that after three or four days' fishing together, your game will be very shy and wary, and you shall hardly get above a bite or two at a baiting; then your only way is to desist from your sport, about two or three days.*'

'Couldn't you just say no?' he teased.

'I couldn't say no,' she told him. 'I love you too much.'

She looked at him guiltily, her eyes already receding behind a screen of water; his big, sad, scaly catch. His catch. What did one do with a catch? It had not cropped up anywhere in his tuition. It was a problem, especially as he felt he was near to graduation. Lately he had found himself eyeing Chrissie's hard little hostile bottom and longing to sound it. He would simply explain to Bernadette. She was not after all, a child; nor even a fish.

He told her it was time for him to go back to his wife. The words seemed to make no sense to her. That was the arrangement, he reminded her gently. It had been understood from the beginning. She shook her head until it threatened to disconnect. He couldn't remember, actually, if he had explained to Bernadette or merely told all the other mistresses. He felt there ought to be a way to finish things nicely. It occurred to him that he lacked technique.

'If there's something I've done wrong . . .'. The plea leaped from her and bounced around the walls in ramshackle desperation. When he could no longer stand the raw look of her he dropped his gaze. His eye connected with an open page of the book, thrust into his hands earlier for the initiation of their sport; and there it was. '. . . *which I tell you, that you may the better believe that I am certain, if I catch a Trout in one meadow, he shall be white and faint, and very like to be lousy:*' he recited with feeling. '*And, as certainly, if I catch a Trout in the next meadow, he shall be strong, and red, and lusty, and much better meat.*' His voice rose with emotion, with gratitude, with overwhelming lust for his wife. '*Trust me, scholar, I have caught many a Trout in one particular meadow, that the very shape and enamelled colour of him hath been such as hath joyed me to look on him: and I have then, with much pleasure, concluded with Solomon, 'Everything is beautiful in his season.'*'

For some reason Bernadette seemed to be coming to pieces. It must have been to do with her age. The tears appeared to be melting her face. He was eager to be on his way and forget her. 'I'll never forget you,' he told a palette of running colours. 'You led me through troubled waters, like Moses.'

'Sure,' she sniffed. 'Grandma Moses.' He left her then, rolled up in her ivory satin sheets like Neapolitan ice-cream dripping down a cornet.

It was a week before he was ready. There were library books to be read. They didn't tell you everything. He had to ring Bernadette to clear up one point. She was surprisingly good about it. Chrissie could sense a change. 'Have you got yourself a mistress? Have you?' she demanded repeatedly as he was poised at the washbowl with his toothbrush or standing with one leg in his pyjamas or collapsing over the edge of a dream.

'Yes,' he answered, grinning to himself under the blankets on the seventh day. She was silent while she delicately packaged herself in the bed beside him. 'What's she like?' she asked. Ormond began to laugh. 'She's fat and ugly,' he chortled. 'She's the ugliest woman I've ever seen.'

Chrissie beat him savagely. 'You liar,' she shouted, showering him with knuckles. He faced her, risking blows on the nose. She looked so beautiful. 'Do you love her?' she asked, leaning over him with raised fists. 'I'm . . . grateful to her,' he said. She made a dreary noise, a snort. Her arms fell to her sides and she dropped down in the bed like a stone. He wanted to take her in his arms but he had been too well tutored. 'Surprise, trick, tease, bait,' his mind recited obediently while he waited for his wife to go off her guard. She snorted again. 'Poor little lamb,' he thought full of compassion until an explosion of sound broke loose from her lungs, not sobs but unkind laughter. 'You nearly had me there, toad-face,' she spluttered. 'You really made me jealous. So help me, I married a deceitful weevil. Did you think I'd believe you got yourself a mistress? Virgin brides are ten a penny but with a mistress you've got an entrance examination to pass.'

For an answer, he sat up and started to sing in a solemn, dusty voice.

'*And when the timorous Trout I wait*
To take, and he devours my bait,
How poor a thing, sometimes I find,
Will captivate a greedy mind.'

Chrissie had not shared bed and book with Bernadette. Nor was she much given to the classics. It was understandable that she had never heard of 'The Angler's Song.' She did what anyone would have done in her position, lay there gaping with her mouth open, exactly like a fish. Ormond seized his moment. He swooped and kissed her open mouth, not hungrily but merrily, dartingly, like a fly over the surface of a lake on a summer evening. His lips lighted on her breast, her knee, the sole of her foot, with the idle delight and presumption of a Mayfly who has just a day to live.

His tongue was the feather of a partridge, the feather of a black drake. He lapped her with the harle of a peacock's tail; teased her with the wings of a buzzard and the small feathers of speckled fowl. When all the scorn had fallen from her body and she lay trembling like a leaf waiting to be taken by the wind, he heard the sly voice of Izaak Walton in his ear: '*Thus have a jury of flies, likely to betray and condemn all the Trouts in the river.*'

Having thus prepared his baits, and fitted his tackling, he repaired to the river. '*First let your rod be light, and very gentle*,' he remembered, but later, '*you must fish with a strong line*.' He knew how to tease a fish. He had developed an old fisherman's instinct and understood the exact moment for sounding the bottom. He had a bite! Her breath came in faltering sighs, quite separate from the violence of her body. 'I love you,' she sang. 'Oh, I love you.' It was a violin solo borne up to heaven on the notes of an orgasm, accompanied by orchestral movements from her body. 'My darling,' Ormond said with triumph and, just before he picked her up by the amazed hair and smashed her head very hard against the brass bedpost, 'My catch!'

She was dead. He never meant to hurt her, he explained to her surprised body, telling her he loved her, trying to make her understand. It was simply the thing that one did with a catch when it had been landed and was floundering and gasping, out of its element; a part of the angler's code. Bernadette had told him.

A Model Daughter

'Think!' said my friend Tilly one day when we were deep into a bottle of lunchtime Meursault; 'if we had had children when we ceased to be impervious virgins they would be seventeen by now. Seventeen or thereabouts. Lovely girls!'

For a moment before her words misted into grapey vapours I could see them sitting opposite us with shiny hair and loose frocks of Laura Ashley prints.

In her early youth Tilly had been very fast and a famous mistress. She was slower now and more faithful and our friendship was occasionally shadowed by a creeping sentimentality that made me fear she would one day rush away from me and into the arms of Jesus.

'Do you regret not having had children?' I said briskly.

'I would like a girl.' She was stubborn: 'Seventeen or so.'

'You could have one. You still could.' She was forty-five but friendship entitled her to lay claim to my age, which was not quite forty.

'Have one what, darling?' Her beautiful blue eyes always had the attractive daze of myopia but after lunch and wine they shimmered under a sea haze.

'A baby!'

'A baby?' She recoiled as if someone had just thrust a seeping member of the species on to her silk knee. 'Don't be revolting!'

'Babies are where children come from,' I pointed out; a little shortly, for I had a worry of my own.

'Not necessarily,' Tilly said. 'It seems to me absurd to go to such lengths. There are young girls everywhere. In primitive countries people drown them at birth. Still they outnumber the men.' She seized the bottle and shook the dregs, very fairly, into either glass. 'If I feel the need of a daughter, I daresay I can get one somewhere.'

'But where?'

Her confidence was shaken but only for a moment. 'A model agency!'

I had a daughter. It was my one secret from Tilly. Her name was Hester and she was seventeen. My daughter was born not of love, not even of sex, but of necessity. I married Victor when I was twenty and we were both pretending to be actors, knowing perfectly well that one day we would have to grow up and get ourselves proper jobs. Six months later, to everyone's surprise, he got a break and was summoned to America. He fell in love, to no one's surprise, with his leading lady. The divorce was quick and uncontested. Shamed by my failure I kept my mouth shut and my head down. I got a small settlement and descended into that curious widowhood of the heart which an early broken marriage brings.

I was too lethargic to work and faced a frugal living on my mean allowance. 'If you had a child,' my mother scolded, 'he would have to pay a proper maintenance.' Even in this I had failed. 'Well I can't just manufacture a child!' I cried. Mother made a face, as if tasting some invisible treat inside her mouth. 'Pity,' she said.

'Dear Vic,' I wrote, alone in my little room by the gas fire. He no longer seemed dear to me. I had grown sullen and immune to attachments. 'I did not want to tell you this earlier as I had no desire to destroy your happiness as you have mine, but I am expecting our child. I am letting you know now only because money is short and it will be so difficult to work.'

Vic was generous. He was a successful actor now and relieved by my faint-heartedness. A card arrived, offering congratulations, and a decent-sized cheque which was to be repeated monthly.

I didn't bother Vic much after that except in due course to announce that Hester had been born and from time to time when I badly needed a bit of extra money (for a furry coat in a really dreadful winter; for a Greek cruise because Tilly was urging me to accompany her) and then I would say that Hester had a little illness or needed her teeth straightened or that she was plaguing me for pony lessons. Once, after his second marriage had broken up, he wrote and asked if he could come and meet Hester. After a momentary panic I answered with a very firm 'no'. I had never asked him to come to her side when she was ill, I pointed out. It would be unfair of him to disturb our peaceful lives.

He accepted this, with a sort of written sigh. 'Just send me a picture of her,' he said. I was shaken, but underneath the dismay there grew a kind of excitement. I said earlier that I had grown immune to attachments. In fact it was merely romantic attachments to which I was resistant, and my friend Tilly consumed enough sexual adventure for both of us. I had a deep secret attachment to my Hester. As soon as Vic asked for her picture I realized that I too had longed to know what she looked like.

I began to carry a camera around. I sought Hester in restaurants, outside schools, in bus queues. One day I was seated in the park in the shade when a child came and looked at me; a solemn dark-eyed girl with a pink dress and a little shoulder bag of white crochet work. I snapped the child and smiled at her. She stood, quite still and graceful, fulfilling her role. I closed the shutter on my camera and closed my eyes too, to carry the moment past its limits so that she came right up to me and called me Mama. When I looked again, the girl was gone.

I wonder how often Victor looked at the picture I sent him, if he kept it in his breast pocket close to his heart; if he placed some of his hopes on that unknown child. I know I did. It helped to pass a decade swiftly and quite sweetly. Soon I was heading up to forty, the extremes of my youth gone (but not regretted) and I found myself thinking idly that Hester would be leaving school by now and we might be planning her college years. I liked this fantasy for the placing of Hester in Oxford or

Cambridge would make her actual absence more plausible and allow me to enjoy my dreams with no disturbance from the dull utilities of fact.

'Dear Vic,' I wrote. 'It is some time since I have been in touch but the years have flown and we were so busy, Hester and I, with work and school, that we had no time to consider the world outside our own little one. However, the news now is too big to keep to myself. Our girl has won a First to Oxford. I want you to know that I sustain no bitterness in regard to our marriage for Hester has been a true compensation. I only wish I could indulge her with all the silly clothes students love and a little flat of her own where she could invite her grown-up friends for coffee.'

It would have been a better letter (I would have been a better person) without the embellishment of that final sentence but the truth is I got carried away and there really was a nice little flat which Tilly had been urging me to snap up.

Vic wrote back immediately. 'Wonderful news! Of course my daughter shall have everything she wants but this time I am determined to deliver it (and my congratulations!) in person.' He announced a date when he would arrive and named the restaurant where we would meet for a celebration dinner.

I suffered several moments of deep shock before my brain broke into demented activity. How should I forestall him? My first thought was a death. Hester dead in a tragic horseback accident! But he would want to see her burial place. Besides, I could not bear that loss myself. I could say she had gone abroad with friends for the summer. Vic was rich. He would insist on following her there.

Nothing I could think of was any use. All my little plans fell apart in the face of Victor's strength of purpose and superior cash flow. Besides, I did not entirely want to put him off for there was the bait of Hester's pocket money. I felt it was a point of honour to collect it safely.

On several occasions I was tempted to confide in Tilly but Tilly is like a viper on the subject of superficial friendships and I knew she would find it impossible to forgive my years of concealment. However, I stuck close to her in those worrying weeks, hoping that I might find the courage to blurt it all out or that she might inadvertently produce an anecdote or experience which would prove the solution to my dilemma. It was exactly four days before Vic's arrival that Tilly, in vino, produced her unlikely veritas of maternal regret and provided me with an answer.

A model agency! I had often glanced through fashion magazines when goaded by Tilly into visiting a hairdresser and I knew those purveyors of fantasy by sight. I was not especially interested in clothes so I gave my attention to the girls who showed them. Unlike Tilly, I did not envy them their taut busts and tiny backsides, their perfect skin and carefully arranged clouds of careless hair. It was their determination that made me wistful.

Their qualification, apart from beauty, which can be used or abused in so many ways, was epitomized by an enduring personality which helped them adhere to a diet regime of meagre, proteinous scraps, to drink prickly Perrier instead of easeful gin, to go to bed at ten o'clock rather than allow themselves to be lured on some exciting, promiscuous prowl. It was more or less how I had pictured Hester.

All I needed was a sweet young girl to help me through a single evening. I know Victor. His passions are burning but brief. Once he had met his daughter, he could peacefully forget all about her.

'I want a girl,' I told the telephone of the Modern Beauties Agency and I gave it the date; 'just for an evening.'

'Daywear, beach or evening?' said a voice.

'Just a simple dinner dress.' I was slightly taken aback.

'Own shoes or shoes supplied?'

'One was rather hoping she might have a pair of her own.'

'Size and colouring?'

I could be confident about this, at least. I described Hester as seventeen or thereabouts, tall but slim, with dark hair and a lily-pale skin.

'It's Carmen Miranda you want,' the telephone decided. 'Will you require a hairdresser and make-up artiste?'

'Carmen Miranda? Now wait a minute!'

'Thirty-five pounds an hour and VAT. To whom shall I make out the invoice?'

'Thirty-five pounds? But . . .! Heavens!' I had anticipated that beauty might be remunerable at about twice the rate of skilled professional housework. I had put aside £50 for the evening. At this price it would cost about £200 – an impossible sum.

'Do you want to confirm that booking or make it provisional. Miss Carmen Miranda is our top professional model. She is very much in demand.'

'No! I mean, yes, I'm sure she is. The thing is, I don't think I have made myself quite clear.' I explained that I did not really require the services of their top professional model. What I wanted – *needed*, was an ingénue, an unspoilt young girl with little or no experience. And cheaper.

'The rate is standard,' said the voice, with a new, steely edge. 'Unless, of course, you want one of our new girls who have not yet completed their training.' She mentioned something that sounded like Poisoned Personality Course and added that these incomplete models could be rented hourly at a reduced rate of twelve pounds, for experience.

'Yes, yes,' I said eagerly. 'That's just right. A young girl, barely out of school. That sounds lovely.'

'All our girls are lovely.'

'I'm sure they are. Thank you so very much. You've got the description?'

'Yes, that's no problem.'

'You've been very kind. Can you tell me who to expect?'

'I'll have to see who's free.'

On the evening of our meeting I felt more excited than on my first date with Victor. Acquiring Hester's childhood photograph had been a rewarding experience. Now I was to meet her in the flesh.

I was looking forward to seeing Victor too. I had often watched him on the television and was intrigued that his face, with its strange orange American tan, had not aged at all while his eyes had, so that he looked like a spaniel with a bulldog's gaze. 'Tricky Vicky', Tilly called my ex-husband but his unreliability did not bother me now; I wanted to hear about his exploits and to be praised for my achievement – Hester – and I was looking forward to getting some of his money. The evening had acquired an additional significance. We would meet as a successful family, untouched by the tension, the sacrifice, the quelling of self that normally accompanies family life. We had got off scot free and yet would not be exposed in loneliness.

I checked with the agency to make sure that my surrogate daughter was still available and they, wearily, assured me that Angela or Hazel or Patricia would meet me in the lounge at the appointed hour. Such nice names! Nothing could go wrong. All my little Angela or Hazel had to remember was to answer to Hester. There were no shared memories to rehearse. Vic had no experience of academic life so she would not be quizzed on that. In any case I had taken the precaution of booking the girl half an hour in advance of Vic's arrival time so that I could give her a little briefing.

It was almost that time when I was startled by the arrival in the lounge of a sort of human sunburst. Women started to wriggle and whisper. 'Good Lord,' I said ungraciously. It was Vic, thirty-five minutes early.

He cast his gaze over the women in the lounge, not really looking for me but allowing each female present to melt and open to his boyish charm. Perhaps he would not recognize me. I could slip out and wait at the exit for Hester to prime her on her role. I rose, face half averted – and drew attention to myself.

'Barbara!' His voice had gained boom and timbre. He put a little kiss on the air and flopped down casually beside me, fastidiously raising the knees of his trousers.

'Hello Vic.'

'Sorry I'm so early. First night nerves,' he said, his nose wincing appealingly under his drooping eyes. He had developed an American accent.

'That's all right. Have a drink.'

'You look good,' he said. 'How's life been treating you?

What a time I had, getting here! You would think, since we were shooting in Europe . . .' And he launched, as I had imagined he would, into a story about himself.

When Hester comes, I shall rush to the door to greet her, I thought. I gave Victor my smiling mouth and my nodding head but my attention was elsewhere. I shall see a tall, pale, beautiful girl – probably shy – in the entrance and I shall run to her and put my arms around her and if she doesn't cry out for help I shall just have time to explain before we get back to the table.

Something Victor said brought my mind right back. '. . . Anyway, I'm glad I got here early so we could talk about money before Hester arrives.'

'Money?'

'A sort of financial plan. I thought, twenty thousand dollars now, or five thousand a year until she's twenty-one. If you take the lump sum now you could invest it but there's less risk with an annuity.'

'Twenty thousand dollars?' My head spun as I tried out a string of noughts against the little digit and attempted to perform a dollar conversion.

'Well, I guess that's not a lot these days. What the heck – make it pounds.'

'Oh, Vic. I'm very – she'll be very grateful.'

'Say, what's she like?' Vic leaned forward and touched my knee.

'Quiet. More like me than you, I'm afraid. I hope you won't be disappointed.'

'I've been disappointed since.' The bulldog eyes attempted bashfulness. 'I wasn't disappointed then.'

We were getting along quite nicely when a wretched autograph hunter recognized Vic and hovered at his chair. She just hovered but her presence sapped one.

'Look, dear, if you don't mind . . .!' I said.

The girl glared at me. I flinched in the dull light of those purple-ringed eyes set in a yellowish face and crowned with gluey horns of hair. She wore a cheap Indian cotton anorak and an extraordinary satin dress from which her uncooked-looking breasts popped unpleasingly. Quite suddenly, tears bubbled up in her eyes. 'Aw shit,' she said and she tottered off. She did not leave the room. Her perambulation took her in the opposite direction where she paused, glancing back. Vic and I laughed uneasily and he called a waiter for champagne. He was appraising the label when the girl returned and crouched beside me, breathing wetly and heavily in my ear: 'Look, are you Mrs Marshall?'

'I am.'

'Well I'm Araminta.'

Victor was staring.

'Look here, dear . . .'

'From the agency.'

'What?'

'My real name's Angela. Araminta's my professional name – going to be.'

'No!'

'What's the matter?' Victor said.

'I think she's sick or something,' said Araminta.

'Sick!' I echoed faintly. It was not a lie. I rose and bundled my arms around the repellent Araminta. 'Please excuse us.'

Araminta and I faced each other in the uneasy pinkness of the ladies' washroom. 'You must leave immediately,' I said. 'There has been a dreadful mistake.'

'Who says? Whose mistake?' Her voice was a whine.

'You were brought here tonight to represent my daughter Hester, to celebrate with her famous father – whom she has never met before – her scholarship entrance to Oxford University.'

'That's beautiful. Like an episode from "Dallas".'

'If you think, for one instant, that you are fit to stand in the shoes of my daughter then you are even more deranged than you look. Now go away!'

'Here!' Her wail was like a suffering violin string. 'I want my money.'

'Not a penny!'

Araminta's mouth opened into a grille shape and a loud gurgle of grief issued therefrom. 'It's not my fault. No one told me I was to be your frigging daughter. I borrowed money to have me hair done an' all. What am I going to do?'

I was pondering the same question when the door opened, and Vic came in, looking confused. 'Is everything all right? Who's this?' he said of the screaming, streaming Araminta.

My soothing utterances were lost in the noise that Araminta made, of a train reversing, to sniff back her sobs. Her face was striped with purple but erased of tears. 'Hello Dad,' she said. 'I'm Hester.'

We were all congealed like the victims of Pompeii. After an eternity of seconds Vic showed signs of recovery. 'Hester?' he whispered. 'Barbara . . .?'

I closed my eyes. I could not look at him. 'She is going through . . . a phase.'

I heard a tap running, a tiny strange bark of dismay as, presumably, some woman attempted to enter and found her path blocked by a famous heartthrob. When I could bear to look I saw Hester calmly splashing her face, applying fresh scribbles of purple to her eyes and daubing her lips with mauve gloss that resembled scar tissue. Poor Vic looked badly shaken. On an impulse I seized the girl and ducked her beneath the tap again, washing every trace of colour from her skin. I scrubbed her dry on a roller towel and then patted her complexion with my own powder puff and a smear of my blusher. Her eyes, even without their purple tracing, resembled Mary Pickford's in their worse excesses of unreasoned terror. 'You some kind of frigging maniac?' she hissed. 'Shut up!' I wielded a hairbrush which I used to remove the glue from her head, and some of her hair. When I had finished there stood a tall, pale girl with wild dark hair, a little overweight, quite pretty, although her eyes and her breasts still popped nastily.

Whatever Vic was feeling he used his actor's training to conceal it. 'Come along, girls,' he said. 'It doesn't do for an actor to get himself arrested in the ladies' loo!'

Hester cawed with mirth.

Back in the restaurant there was a period of peace while Hester ate and Victor brooded. The girl appeared to be ravenously hungry. She did not pay any attention to us until a first course and several glasses of wine had scuttled down her throat and her cheeks were nicely padded with roast beef and then, with a coy, sideways look at Vic, she produced a classic line:

'Where have you been all my life?'

Vic eyed her gloomily. 'Hasn't your mother explained?'

'Not bloody much.'

Odd that I had not noticed before that they both had the same pessimistically protruding eye.

'I think your mother has rather a lot of explaining to do,' Vic said.

'Pardon?' I was so startled I could only squeak.

'Barbara, I am disappointed.' He put up a hand to swat a second squeak of protest which was escaping. 'Yes! I have been let down. Over seventeen years I have given unstintingly to the support of my daughter, trusting that you would bring her up as I would wish. You denied me access to her. I did not attempt to use the force of law in my favour. You did not want your lives disturbed, you said. What life? I ask you, what life have you given this girl? It is clear from her speech that she has been allowed to run wild in the streets. She's even hungry. Look how she eats! Have you anything to say?'

Very little, really. It was true the girl was appalling. 'Just be glad you haven't had to put up with her,' I snapped.

'She won't give me my money,' Hester complained. She shoved another roast potato into her mouth and seized Victor's sleeve. 'You'll give me my money, won't you?'

Victor retrieved his garment. 'Young lady, I'll give you something more valuable than money. I will give you advice. Reach for the moon – not its reflection in some puddle in the gutter. Look beyond the superficial values of youth and fashion. Stand up proud – alone if needs be. You'll have self-respect. You'll have *my* respect. What do you say, dear?'

'Vic,' I interjected, lost in our improvised drama; 'it is you who must look beyond the superficial. She has won a First to Oxford.'

'I'm not talking to you, Barbara. I'm speaking to my daughter. You know I don't believe the academic world equips you for real life. Now Hester, what do you say?'

'Why don't you ride off into the sunset on your high horse, you big ballocks?' Hester said, and she importuned a waiter for profiteroles.

Victor looked so stunned, so *dis*armed, I was almost sorry for him. 'She is overwrought,' I said. 'Think what she has achieved! She has been locked up with her books all year and now she is in . . . revolt.'

Underneath I had begun to warm to Hester. Victor was not used to challenge. My once-husband seemed quite broken by her reproach. 'You know I don't expect much,' he sighed. 'It's the simple things I like in women – feminine grace, charm and wit.'

'I'm with you, mate!' Hester spoke up through a mouthful of gunge. 'This university lark was all her idea. Personally I've always thought women would be better off burning their brains than their bras. Could I have a liqueur?'

'You mean you don't want to go to university?' I was quite hurt.

'Too bloody right. I'm really a model, you know,' she confided to Vic. 'Although what I'd like best in all the world . . .' (her eyes glittered greedily) '. . . is to be an actress.'

'You'd like to be an actress?' Vic threw me a tiny look of triumph. His expression began to brighten.

'Dearest Dad. . . . !' She leaned across the table so that her breasts rested on her pudding plate like a second, uncoated helping of dessert and it began to dawn on me that she might be a little bit drunk: 'All my life I have worshipped you from afar. My one dream has been to emul . . . follow in your hallowed footsteps.'

Vic smiled. His bulldog's gaze flickered with warmth and interest. Their eyes, inches apart, wobbled glassily. The child's look grew positively rakish and I had to kick her under the table to remind her of her filial role.

'Chip off the old block!' Vic said in admiration and he patted her pudgy hand.

'Thank you, Daddy.' Hester wrinkled her nose in exactly the way he often does.

'Would you really like to go on the stage?' he said.

'More than anything – except of course, the movies.'

'Then the movies it's going to be. I'm bringing you back with me.'

'No!' I moaned.

'You mean it?' Hester said.

'I can get you a small part in the film I'm working on. Just a walk-on but it will be a start. Come back to America with me and we'll get you into stage school. I'll make Hollywood sit up and take notice of my beautiful daughter.'

Hester glowed so that, in the flattering candlelight, she did look rather beautiful. I felt depressed. Vic was taking my daughter away. There would be no more secret dreams for me; and no more money.

'Of course we'll have to tidy you up a bit!' Victor had advanced to practical planning. 'You're going to have to learn to speak properly and I'm afraid, darling, you'll have to lose some of those curves. First thing tomorrow you're going on a diet. I want you skinny as a stalk of celery before we go back.'

At this Hester's face began to alter shape, the jaw extending, the eyes receding into pink slits, the mouth widening and lengthening. We watched in awe until a horrible howl came out. 'I can't!' she wailed. 'I'm pregnant!'

It was some time before I saw my friend Tilly again. There was such a lot to do with the baby coming and poor Vic in such a state. 'I insist that you tell me everything. Everything!' he had said in the restaurant after Hester dropped her bombshell, and of course the wretched girl did.

She has gone now. I think it's for the best. She ate such a lot and would answer only to Araminta. In any case now that the baby is born it would be confusing to have two Hesters in the house.

In the end Araminta did go back to America with Vic. No longer father and daughter, they had found a new role which seemed to suit both of them much better. And Vic left me really a very generous allowance for the child.

I hope I have explained my story clearly to you for I simply cannot seem to make Tilly understand. 'Good God, darling,' she said, peering with fascinated horror into the pram on the day I introduced her to the infant. 'Did I never tell you about the Pill?'

And there was Hester, so sweet and solemn in her frills, her hands waving like pink sugar stars; her life stretched out before us, its mysterious curves and dazzling prospects, its sunlit patches and shadows, like the carriage drive to some enchanting manor.

I tried once more to tell my friend about my daughter's coming, but Tilly, fearing tales of childbed, waved a dainty hand burdened with costly mineral rocks, and said: 'What matter the source of life so long as it is lived happily ever after.'

She is right of course, for which of us anyway ever truly understands where babies come from.

☙

PUBLICATION SEQUENCE

Stories 1978–1983

Appearances
Housekeeper's Cut
The Wronged Wife
Bad-Natured Dog
Some Retired Ladies on a Tour
Ears
A Reproduction
A Nail on the Head
Mama
The Complete Angler

Stories 1984–1989

A Little Girl, Never Out Before
You Don't Know You're Alive
The Picture House
Affairs in Order
Technical Difficulties and the Plague
The Little Madonna

L'Amour
Villa Marta
The Miracle of Life
A Particular Calling
A Model Daughter
Concerning Virgins

Stories 1990–2000

A Funny Thing Happened
The Stolen Child
It's Her
To Tempt a Woman
Poor Old Sod
My Son the Hero
That Bad Woman
Edna, Back From America
Horrible Luck
Thatcher's Britain
Life on Mars
Gods and Slaves
The Secret Diary of Mrs Rochester
Perfect Love
The Spirit of the Tree
Confession

Clare Boylan's stories have been widely translated and published in three volumes, *A Nail on the Head*, *Concerning Virgins* and *That Bad Woman*, from which these stories are collected. Several of her stories have been filmed. She is also the author of six novels including *Room for a Single Lady*, which won the "Spirit of Life" award and is due to be filmed. *Black Baby* has also been optioned for film. Non-fiction works include *The Agony and the Ego*, essays on the art and strategy of fiction writing, and *The Literary Companion to Cats*.